"If you ever wondered what life ~~...~~ book for you. Here is a man who ~~... ... ...~~ monastic life for sixty-four years in which he was abbot twenty-six of those years. Entering the monastery in 1947 he knew the 'old' intimately. He embraced Vatican II with open arms and was a leader not only in his own community as Abbot but also on the international scene at our General Chapters. He had the ability to take complex questions and break them down to their essentials. Abbot Gérard lived through some of the most important times of monastic and church history and he lived it with grace and integrity. If he lived during the era of the Desert Fathers, he would have been considered an elder whose words would have been passed on from generation to generation."

> —Fr. Brendan Freeman
> New Melleray Abbey, Iowa

"A deeply engaging and delightfully personalized glimpse into genuine monastic life and experience, including his own meaningful path to La Trappe. Much more than a memoir, Dubois's book whets our appetite to taste and see the *conversatio morum* of Trappist community, so personally and profoundly spread before us as though at table with the brothers. The English translation captures the narrative and insight of Dubois beautifully."

> —F. Tyler Sergent
> Associate Professor of History and General Studies
> Berea College, Kentucky

MONASTIC WISDOM SERIES: NUMBER FIFTY-EIGHT

Happiness in God

Memories and Reflections
of the Father Abbot of La Trappe

Dom Marie-Gérard Dubois

Translated by
Georges Hoffmann and Jean Truax

α

Cistercian Publications
www.cistercianpublications.org

LITURGICAL PRESS
Collegeville, Minnesota
www.litpress.org

A Cistercian Publications title published by Liturgical Press

Cistercian Publications
Editorial Offices
161 Grosvenor Street
Athens, Ohio 45701
www.cistercianpublications.org

Translated from *Le Bonheur en Dieu: Souvenirs et réflexions du père abbé de La Trappe* (Paris: Robert Laffont, 1995), with permission from the abbot of La Trappe and Robert Laffont.

1	2	3	4	5	6	7	8	9

Library of Congress Cataloging-in-Publication Data

Names: Dubois, Marie-Gerard, author. | Hoffmann, Georges, translator. | Truax, Jean, 1947– translator.
Title: Happiness in God : memories and reflections of the Father Abbot of La Trappe / Dom Marie-Gerard Dubois ; translated by Georges Hoffmann and Jean Truax.
Other titles: Bonheur en Dieu. English.
Description: Collegeville : Cistercian Publications, 2019. | Series: Monastic wisdom series ; Number fifty-eight | Includes bibliographical references.
Identifiers: LCCN 2019008219 (print) | LCCN 2019009472 (ebook) | ISBN 9780879076580 (eBook) | ISBN 9780879070588 (pbk.)
Subjects: LCSH: Dubois, Marie-Gerard. | Trappists—France—Biography.
Classification: LCC BX4705.D793 (ebook) | LCC BX4705.D793 A3 2019 (print) | DDC 271/.12502 [B] —dc23
LC record available at https://lccn.loc.gov_2019008219

CONTENTS

Preface
to the English Edition of
Le Bonheur en Dieu

In writing *Happiness in God*, Dom Marie-Gérard Dubois has led his readers beyond the monastic cloister and made them enter into the daily life of the Trappists as it has evolved during the last decades. In so doing, he has allowed the public at large to join the human and religious experience of numerous men and women who entered the monastery and who have lived and still live in accordance with the Rule of Saint Benedict and the Constitutions of the Cistercian Order of the Strict Observance.

To a certain extent this book, which is first and foremost a personal testimony, refutes the traditional clichés associated with the monastic life, which turn it into a caricature or distort it, and enables the reader to perceive that life in its effective reality. It is probably this authenticity that made the book successful among French-speaking readers. They then considered monks and nuns not as unusual people, cut off from the world, but as beings totally similar to themselves, who, like them, have faithfully tried to answer a particular call of God to the best of their abilities. These people who had previously seemed so remote from readers have thus become like familiar friends.

Consequently, readers feel personally called, and these monks and nuns make them understand that they too are called to a spiritual life of intimacy with the Lord and of service to their brothers. They perceive that this search for God in a brotherly community is accessible to them. Through this book they too may practice, within their capabilities, liturgical prayer, silent meditation, and *lectio divina*. They learn to "never lose hope in God's mercy" (RB 4.73). A kind of intimate collaboration, a sharing of life, is established between each reader and the brother and sister Trappists portrayed in this book. A bond is created of sympathy, solidarity, and affection in God that enriches and transforms life. *Happiness in God* leads us to live an experience of communion.

We, the brothers of La Trappe who lived with Dom Marie-Gérard as the abbot of our monastery and still have in our memory the sound of his voice when he was teaching us in chapter, telling us the recent history of the Order, and sharing his anecdotes, are delighted that his testimony is becoming accessible to English-speaking readers.

We want to express our sincere thanks to Georges Hoffmann, who took an avid interest in *Le Bonheur en Dieu,* for undertaking this translation. May he receive here all our gratitude and our appreciation. We are overjoyed to know that readers on the other side of the ocean will make the same discovery of the reality of the Trappist life and will also seek to join the spiritual and brotherly experience lived in the monastery. Their brother and sister monks and nuns, who pray for them in the Trappes of the whole world, walk with them on this life path, where "our hearts and bodies prepare for the battle of holy obedience to his instructions" (RB Prol. 40).

Br. Guerric Reitz Séjotte
Abbot of La Trappe
May 2017

FOREWORD
TO THE TRANSLATION

During one of my business trips to Europe in late October 1995, I visited my parents in Brussels, Belgium. As was often the case during such visits, my father went to sleep around 10 p.m., and my mother and I stayed up to chat about family and work back in Atlanta, Georgia. The television was set on the France 2 channel. At 10:30 the literary program *Bouillon de Culture* came on, presented by the French journalist Bernard Pivot. The program featured famous philosophers, actors, authors, and politicians discussing their most recent books. It was immensely popular. That night Pivot had invited two monks. Dom Marie-Gérard Dubois, abbot of La Trappe, was interviewed about his recent book, *Le Bonheur en Dieu*. He was there with a younger monk.

While it was not unusual to have theologians and religious pundits appear on television, it was rare to see a monk, especially a Trappist, appear in monastic habit to talk about the essence of God's call to his choice of a monastic life. Happiness radiated from these two monks throughout the whole program. Because of the popularity of this TV program, the book sold very well in France. I read it at different times when my spiritual journey was taking side roads, not to say dead ends. Each time it led me back to that elusive call of God. I believe that there was no coincidence in my visiting my parents that night and our watching that program.

Moving forward twenty years. After many detours, my spiritual journey brought me to the Trappist Monastery of Our Lady of the Holy Spirit in Conyers, Georgia, and its group of Lay Cistercians. After reading some of the monastic authors, I thought that the reflections of Dom Marie-Gérard could still be an inspiration to all of us listening to God's call today.

These are the words and reflections of an abbot relating how he and some of his brothers encountered God's call and discovered the Cistercian answer to this call that led them to enter the walls of a monastery. It is also the story of the Trappist Order laboring through the post-Vatican Council II reforms as told by one of the leading forces behind these reforms.

The last question Pivot asked Dom Marie-Gérard in the 1995 interview was, "What would you like God to tell you when you get near heaven's gates?" Dom Gérard answered: "Come on in. Let me now watch over those you took care of." I suspect that God told Dom Marie-Gérard Dubois exactly that when on July 2, 2011, he called him home.

***

I am very grateful to Dom Guerric Reitz Séjotte, abbot of La Trappe, for his enthusiastic approval and support of the translation of this book and for having written the Preface to *Happiness in God*. My sincere thanks and admiration to Jean Truax, PhD and Independent Scholar in Medieval History, for having generously given her time and knowledge to review the translation and the footnotes. To both Dom Guerric and Dr. Truax my most sincere thanks.

Georges Hoffmann

A Note on Notes

A glance at the bibliography for this book will show that Abbot Marie-Gérard Dubois was a well-read man. He sprinkled his memoir with quotations from a variety of sources, ranging from "a thirteenth-century Cistercian manuscript" to Martin Heidegger. Feeling that some readers will want to explore further, we have replaced Dubois's footnotes to French editions with references to the latest English editions where possible.

Many of the documents of the Cistercian Order, both ancient and modern, are readily available in the Resources section of the official website, http://www.ocso.org/resources/. This includes the current *Constitutions* of the Order. References to the *Constitutions* are abbreviated Const and are parenthetically embedded in the text. Encyclicals, conciliar decrees, and other papal documents can be found on the Vatican website, http://w2.vatican.va/. The documents of Vatican II can be found at http://www.vatican.va/archive/hist_councils/ii_vatican_council/documents/. The Rule of Saint Benedict can also be found online at http://www.osb.org/rb/text/toc.html#toc. References to the Rule are abbreviated RB.

We have also done our best to provide sources for the quotations that Dubois did not footnote. Sometimes we have not given specific page numbers because the statement is not a direct quotation, but rather Dubois's own summary of central ideas contained in the work. In other cases, we have not been able to supply any information beyond the author's name given in the text, and we believe that these are Dubois's reflections based on his familiarity with the authors and his own thirty years' experience as a monk, abbot, and member of various commissions of the Trappist Order. The text also contains a number of explanatory footnotes on historical figures and events, some written by Abbot Dubois and others by Georges Hoffmann. All of our notes, both bibliographical and explanatory, are enclosed in brackets {}.

Before I had the good fortune to join Georges in this project, my knowledge of the Cistercians pretty much ended with the twelfth-century fathers. Now, after having encountered one of the great voices of the modern Order, I can truly say that Dom Gérard and his colleagues are worthy successors to Saint Bernard of Clairvaux and his contemporaries. I will be eternally grateful to Georges for introducing me to them.

Dr. Jean Truax

Chapter One

The Two Faces

That night in his cell, a monk was about to complete his earthly journey, but no one knew. A monk who dies slips away quietly. He is laid in the ground, without a coffin, and no one speaks of it. His first name is inscribed on a simple cross with the date of his death. No last name, no birth date, no date of entry into the monastery, no titles or obits in this small cemetery within the walls of the cloister. Nothing, except that the word *priest* is added if it applies to the deceased. The cowl that he wore as a monk, the long white choir vestment with the hood of the Trappists, will be his coffin. I have seen so many of them go this way. I have thrown so many shovelsful of dirt on the bodies.

This monk was so quiet you might have thought he was passing into death as through a veil. Brother Jean-Baptiste was one of our elders at La Trappe. He had been following his path of prayer and detachment for a long time. Step by step he reached the end of his journey, so far away and with so much peace and confidence, that he never looked back to ask for our help or to give us a sign. But we were all surprised.

He experienced his transition without any agony, maybe without even realizing it. Death was a simple and easy act. We didn't expect him to die then, to start his transition that evening. Our world was already touching eternity without our seeing it. There is not far to go from this earthly life to infinity, and Brother Jean-Baptiste went there in the same way a person walks from one room to the next, without any ceremony. He went through a fog or through a light, barely a thin screen in passing the threshold into this other world. A curtain, that's all.

He didn't warn us. He sat down in his chair and that was it. The monk who was taking care of him in the infirmary was just coming in to get him ready for bed. "It is not going very fast" was Brother Jean-Baptiste's response to his brother's greeting. He passed while talking to the other monk. Nothing easier, in the blink of an eye, his sentence barely finished.

It was Thursday. At La Trappe we had never witnessed the celebration of the perpetual vows of one monk and the funeral of another on the same day. In two days' time a monk who had been living among us for five years was scheduled to make his solemn vows. It would be a great celebration, with many people coming to the monastery church. Among them a good number were coming from his village of Cauville, close to Étretat in the region of Caux. They were about to leave on the two-hundred-kilometer trip with the new monk's close family. I was thinking about this celebration, and at the same time I was thinking about our brother, who had just left us so suddenly and so quietly. Everything had been ready for a long time for Brother Aelred's vows. Our neighbors from around the abbey were about to arrive. What to do? It was impossible to postpone the funeral and keep the body in our midst in the August heat. It was obvious to me the celebrations had to be linked.

A burial in a Trappist monastery is one of the most impressive events one can witness, but so is a celebration of perpetual vows. I had already been struck by this at the age of eighteen, when I first attended the burial of a monk. I didn't know what to expect at all. The monk was a former superior of La Trappe, and I didn't know then that one day I would succeed him. When he became ill, he resigned and was sent to the Cistercian Monastery of Mont-des-Cats, close to Lille, where I had entered a couple of months earlier. The chants and the ceremony at the cemetery, while the body was laid without a coffin at the bottom of the freshly dug grave, made me feel that I was accompanying him on his entry into Paradise. The Easter-like character of this burial touched me so much that I trace back to that very moment my interest in the liturgy, especially the burial liturgy, as well as any reflection relating to death.

I intended to preside over the funeral on Saturday afternoon, since the vows were planned for Saturday morning. The time that Brother Aelred would spend close to us and close to our deceased brother would be particularly poignant and solemn. I just had to add a homily for the funeral to the one that I had already written for the vows.

We Trappists do not hide anything about death. If we show it, notwithstanding its horror and incomprehensibility, it is because we give it a celebratory tone of triumph over death. The community first gets together, as close as possible to the place where the monk, in this case Brother Jean-Baptiste, finished his journey, to say the first prayers and to bless the body with incense and holy water. We ring the bells. Then the deceased is carried on a bier to the choir in the church, face uncovered and not trapped in a coffin. Two monks, if possible, but at least one, will stay with him constantly, day and night. He will never be left alone. The usual prayer services and the Mass will take place in his presence. To hide death and to leave the parents and the families to their grief is a modern attitude often absurd and cruel, which poorly hides a revolt against something that is beyond our understanding. In our monastery, we live and experience death together. We are bound during our lives, and we are united in this unique moment.

I knew that Brother Aelred was sufficiently prepared, but these circumstances reminded me of a decision we took three years ago for his simple vows. He didn't take them like the other monks in our chapter room, where, as in each monastery, the community gathers every day to receive spiritual teaching, instructions, and sometimes practical information. At the end of Brother Aelred's novitiate, a television crew led by Patrick de Carolis was preparing a program on monastic life for the magazine *Événements*, and they asked to film the ceremony. In order for it to take place more comfortably and with a solemnity lacking within our monastic cloister, we held the ceremony in our church during Lauds, our second community prayer of the day. Brother Aelred, absorbed by his commitment, barely took notice of the cameras. On the other hand, his parents had the joy of seeing him on television in their house in Normandy. Now at twenty-seven years of age, he would once more be accompanied, but in a different way, a more solemn way. Death would be there behind him. Young monks coming from other monasteries for a formation session would also be present.

We do not become monks for ourselves alone. Monastic solitude includes the presence of all those who walk beside us on our earthly journey. I was happy that so many people gathered on that day in our house, close to the cloister, which for the monk is already a reflection of Paradise. Monks are withdrawn from the outside world, or, better, they try day after day to be more withdrawn, but it is different from abandoning the world. It is to rediscover it, to live it in another way, and to take up the struggle. Brother Aelred had already intensely experienced this separation from the world for the last five years. His life had come to fruition, he told us. He had gambled it all in his search for redemption, in betting on the invisible.

When he was twenty years old, while he was wondering about God's existence, he had already observed these cloistered men. He thought that maybe their lives provided a silent answer to that question. Monastic life represented a challenge in his eyes. Monks not only stated in words that God was alive; their very existence constituted such an affirmation. It deserved, he thought, a closer look, and perhaps eventually following in their steps. At that time in his life, Christ did not really appeal to him. He had a number of criticisms for him. What about the church? What about God in all this? Was there something that could explain the existence of men, animals, mountains, stars? In his search for God, he didn't see how a man who lived two thousand years ago and whose existence was not sufficiently proved could be of use to him. And prayer? What was prayer? What were the monks doing behind those high walls? These were some of the questions of his youth.

Years had gone by. As is true for many of us, the perpetual vows were neither the most remarkable moment in Brother Aelred's spiritual journey nor his strongest awareness of personal commitment. To cross the threshold of the monastery or to take on the monk's habit is often a more decisive event.

Two days later, on Saturday, August 27, 1983, Brother Aelred woke up as he did every day at 4 a.m. and walked to the church for Vigils, which lasts one hour. The monks relieved those who had kept the vigil all night next to the body of their deceased brother, allowing them to go to their rest. The vigil continued. Nobody likes to get up in the middle of the night, to wake up from his sleep, to hurry up and enter a sometimes very cold church. This time it was an important day for Brother Aelred. It was his day, as it was for his elder brother, who had just passed away.

A strange although familiar feeling overcame him. He had already tried to suppress it without success, because this feeling doesn't let go easily—the feeling of ever-present death. It is there—the "scandal of death." This scandal arose again before him and within his heart on the very day of his perpetual vows. Could death track him down any more persistently? Could it pressure him any more at the last minute? Yes, the question he had originally had was "what do the monks do and what is their use?" He had answered those questions, but death was still so close and God was still so invisible—Faith! Only faith to take one more step and to sign the *cedula* of perpetual vows that he would then put on the altar!

Brother Jean-Baptiste rested among us. The presence of death remained and filled up the church. A summer night is never cold, even under stone arches. We waited for the bells to sound for the start of the first prayers, of the first shout that the monk directs early in the morning in faith to his God: *Lord, open my lips, God, come to my rescue, Lord, hasten to help me.* Yes, come to

my assistance. The monks raised their supplication to God and
to the whole world. The rustle of the white cowls and the soft
steps of those still hurrying to their wooden stalls before the start
of Vigils, the rustle of the pages of the song books as pages were
turned—everything showed that the community, even struck
with emotion so close to the body, was not shaken and did not
change its customs.

A Trappist, even on the day of his perpetual vows, can still be
scandalized by death. It is so close, so overwhelming, silent and
insidious, always wanting to lure us into nothingness and have
the last word. Today death is defiant. Isn't death invincible? Its
ultimate provocation, at the moment of Brother Aelred's perpetual vows, became insignificant, and far from scaring him off,
it convinced him that he was right to engage in the fight. Death
was an abject thing in his eyes. Together with Christ, he was
fighting against death, and he wanted to conquer along with
him. God did not create humans for death or for the absurd. And
Brother Aelred, like all contemplative monks, wanted to thank
God for his creation.

Now came the end of the morning's celebration, and he lay
down on the floor, in a gesture of complete surrender to God,
identical to that of a priest at his ordination. His hands were
crossed on his chest, his forehead touching the ground, his head
uncovered. The remains of Brother Jean-Baptiste were still close
to him. While the entry of a young monk into the monastic life
was taking place in the presence of death, the mortal existence of
the other was tipping over into eternal life peacefully and without
a sound, just as if death hadn't been there between the two of
them, just as if it had been pushed aside and already conquered.

In the audience, among the family members and the strangers
gathered to celebrate, a young man looked on. He was stunned
to see this monk facing the ground and behind him another one
facing up toward heaven. This picture touched him so much that
he saw in it a symbol of something grand, of all that he felt and all
that he wanted to express, just as if that scene were a summary of
life on earth and of entrance into heaven. It struck him so strongly

that it constituted, without our knowing it, the last stage of an internal evolution. This unexpected situation appeared to him to be filled with a rare spiritual value. At the end of the ceremony, he went to the park and sat down near the pond of La Trappe, where Bossuet[1] and Abbot de Rancé[2] exchanged their religious beliefs in these peaceful forests at the border between Normandy and La Perche. The young man came then to see me:

"I want to be a monk."

"How old are you?"

"Twenty years old."

"You have to think about it seriously. How long have you been thinking about it?"

"One hour."

"One hour?"

"I was touched by this celebration. I sat down next to the waterfall—and it happens to be my birthday—I've thought about it thoroughly."

He was about to start his studies to become a priest in Paris. He was registered in the Grand Seminary of Issy-les-Moulineaux for classes starting in October, but he had decided to do a retreat in our abbey first. I did not encourage him to change his plans; I only left the door open. The call to monastic life is always mysterious, and it can take many different roads. The decision at twenty years of age to shut yourself up behind those strange walls with the intention of never leaving them is only made after intense preparation. Wanting to become a priest seems to put someone on the way, but it may be an illusion due to a misunderstanding of monasticism. You don't switch from one call to the

---

1. {Jacques Bossuet (1627–1704), French priest and preacher who became the tutor of Louis XIV's eldest son, the Dauphin. His eulogies were famous. He used his talents to speak up for the rights of the French church against the papal authority. See also p. 294, n. 19.}

2. {Armand le Bouthillier de Rancé (1626–1700), abbot and reformer of the Trappist monastery of La Trappe and one of the founders of the Strict Observance of the Cistercian Order.}

other as fast as you change clothes. The life of a diocesan priest is totally different from the life of a Trappist. The priestly vocation is completely different. The idea of becoming a Trappist in the monastery of Rancé can send chills down your back.

The young man's voice had a certain self-assurance and enthusiasm. He explained to me that at the end of August he would meet with Cardinal Jean-Marie Lustiger[3] to decide what direction he should take in the seminary. I encouraged him to go to that meeting. On the day he had agreed to come back to the monastery, he arrived fifteen minutes early, but it was simply to inform me that he was entering La Trappe.

Two years earlier, in November, he had spent a couple of days in the guesthouse of our monastery. He was then a senior in high school. It was freezing, and he hadn't met any of the monks yet. During that first visit he was bored out of his mind, he explained, but he noted in a diary that two things struck him, the smiles of the monks, which seemed to reflect a sincere joy, and their personal poverty. Together they could use all the goods belonging to the whole community, but they did not own anything individually. Even though the joy appealed to this potential postulant, the prospect of individual poverty scared him a bit. He would be poor and without any social standing, giving up everything until his last day.

No, entering La Trappe was not what made him dream. This was not the way he envisioned a successful life, one useful to others. In fact, he had a lot of friends in Paris and did not want to leave them. Why isolate himself from them and from his family? Why never travel again? He wanted to finish his studies and serve the community, imagining that in the distant future, fifteen or twenty years from the present, he might finish his life sheltered in a monastery. He still had not decided to withdraw

---

3. {Aaron Jean-Marie Lustiger (1926–2007), archbishop of Paris from 1981 to 2005. He actively defended Catholic education against secularism and was an outspoken opponent of racism and anti-Semitism. He was born to a Jewish family and converted to Catholicism at the age of 13.}

from the world so young; taking on the habit and integrating into a community still scared him a little.

He still had these feelings during his following visit. When he entered the church he saw one monk face down on the ground, face hidden, and another one looking up at the heavens, his face illuminated by all the lights. The former in the shadow was looking at the earth, the latter was radiant with the mystery of God when I pronounced these words: "There are only two moments in life where you can meet God, the present moment and the moment of death—these are the two moments mentioned in the *Hail Mary*: 'pray for us now and at the time of our death.' "

For the young man, this liturgy led him into an impressive spectacle of sound and light, where the beginning and the end of human destiny meet, and it was a shock. He had never interpreted the prayer to the Mother of Christ in this way. The present moment was symbolized by this monk face down toward the earth and the moment of death by his brother on the bier. He thought that if one really meets God in the present moment and at the hour of one's death, it might be better not to further delay his desire to become a monk. This idea came to him, dazzling, and it did not leave him.

He watched Brother Aelred celebrating his vows just as if death, arrogant and impenetrable, weren't trying to tease him. Death sat on Brother Aelred's shoulders, of him who thought that if he persevered in his vows, one day he would be in the same place where his dead brother was lying. For him, death was still inconceivable and inadmissible. He didn't understand it, but he lined up his footsteps with Christ's footsteps, and his hand was in Christ's hand, walking toward a triumph that he could not yet envision. Faith was to believe that it was possible; faith was to risk his life for it. It was to trust the invisible and to know that our desires would be fulfilled beyond any expectation. Pure faith was to accept as authentic what our eyes did not see. As was the custom, Brother Aelred knelt down in front of each monk, asking him, "Pray for me." When he got up, each monk embraced him, and then he moved on to the next stall. It was a celebration for the community to welcome a new member, but there was no shortage of sadness, thinking of the brother who had just passed away. All these contrasts were joined and illuminated in the Easter candle lit in the middle of the assembly.

The young man understood that the present moment was a moment in eternity and that it was sufficient for him to take the first step toward it. The gift had to be in the present and not in the future. I received the commitment of Brother Aelred. I told him that he was not fleeing the world or the responsibilities that he would have assumed by marriage and work, but that he was now carrying out a gesture of more complete poverty by abandoning the intention of serving the church and others that was still burning within him when he entered the monastery. To let everything go, that is what a Trappist is called to do—to abandon even what appears good, even what appears to be the best, even a secret dream of sacrifice and prayer for the world, of a life hidden under heroism or love. The greatest challenge for a monk is the total abandonment of himself to God's will. For the best among them it is no longer a personal project when someone else takes it upon himself to show him what to do. I spoke to the assembly of this total self-abandonment to the Father, of this monastic life, which means assuming no new responsibilities, no penance or punishments, no harassing constraints, no reaching a sublime ideal by using supra-human or non-human means, but an act of poverty and liberty. While I said all this, the body of the deceased lay among us on the bier. Our eyes could not completely get away from it. He had completed the journey that another was starting that day.

It was the first time during a profession of perpetual vows that I had had to explicitly address the subject of death. I spoke about a new birth arising out of death. But who was I talking about? The one who closed his eyes to this world and transitioned to eternity or this young monk who, by committing himself, died to the world, so to speak? This is really what the vows imply, a self-abandonment and a renunciation of certain legitimate activities in order to experience true happiness, the submission to the discipline of the community and to a superior, to the communal will of a group of men or women, entrusting themselves completely to God until the end of their earthly lives. A crazy project if the earthly existence ends up in nothingness, a completely useless project for anyone if God does not exist. Folly of the cross, folly of the faith. Mountain climbers, also called the "conquerors of the useless," can gain some media glory, sportsmanlike satisfaction, and money if they're lucky. But monks?

That afternoon, with death still present, in the middle of prayers for forgiveness for the one who, like each one of us, was a sinner, we sang songs of hope and of triumph. The family of the young professed monk stayed, and I appreciated the discreet happiness, which, notwithstanding the pain, accompanies most Trappist funerals. We always insist on our faith in the resurrection, and this paschal aspect of the liturgy is essential, as I said in the beginning. The large candle lit at Easter is again lit next to the body. The songs recall the exodus of the Hebrews out of Egypt, the crossing of the Red Sea, and the pillar of fire guiding them, while the procession goes to the cemetery, with the bells tolling. The cemetery is not a simple collection of dried-out bones. It is not intended to be a place of death. It is the waiting room of heaven. It symbolizes Paradise to a certain extent. We lead the body to the kingdom of life. It awaits the resurrection, but the spirit of the deceased enjoys the vision of God and eternal life, perhaps after a certain trial period, if—as theologians state—it was not sufficiently purified at the time of death. The spirit participates in the joy of heaven, and that is what makes us joyful, really full of confidence.

A monk carrying the candle, symbol of Christ, leads the way. The bier is carried by four brothers. As abbot, I follow them. Then come the priests wearing their purple stoles. The other monks, wearing their white cowls, follow in order of seniority, and then come the faithful. Everyone follows the deceased brother, who precedes us and guides us. At one point, close to the grave, we have to stop while he continues his journey. We will entrust him to God in a last *adieu*—"on the threshold of the house, our Father awaits us."

In the first prayers, we call upon the angels to come and meet the one who is leaving us. The liturgy picks up on ancient themes of the Christian tradition, like the account of the agony of an old monk of the Egyptian desert in the fifth century. Surrounded by his companions, he suddenly saw Abraham and then the martyrs, the apostles, and the angels running towards him. "I see Abraham," he said. "I see the martyrs." They came to fetch him, but he asked them to grant him one more moment to do penance. Everybody told him that he was a saint, so "Why wait one more moment? The angels are ready to take you." The old monk answered that he realized that he hadn't started to serve God yet. This revealing story concludes with Jesus himself coming to fetch the soul.[4] The liturgy reenacts this very scene, in which we ask the angels and the celestial world to come for the brother who just left.

Some bodies have a peaceful appearance, others look tormented. We don't hide them; we don't conceal anything. That's what death is all about. If it is hot, the body will give out a distinctive smell. It is said that incense was adopted to cover that up. But can one totally erase it? The smell is there, for it is part of death. Our society wants to hide death, cheat it, avoid thinking about it. We do not wipe it out; we do not erase anything. The brother infirmarian simply washes the deceased and adjusts the clothing. Certain bodies remain in good condition, others do not, and the impression is different each time.

The practice of burial without a coffin was originally not specific to the monks. The poor also laid bodies directly in the earth. It was common, and we have kept that custom as a sign

4. {A story similar to this is found in the *Lives of the Desert Fathers*, except that the dying monk is given three years instead of only one day to amend his life (*The Lives of the Desert Fathers: The Historia Monachorum in Aegypto* 10:17–19, trans. Norman Russell, introduction by Benedicta Ward, CS 34 [Kalamazoo, MI: Cistercian Publications, 1981], 84–85).}

of poverty and the fact that we represent very little in this world. The brother infirmarian goes down into the grave to receive the body and to lay it down. He pulls down the hood and puts a veil on the face to protect it from the dirt. I throw the first shovelful of dirt. Other brothers follow me, without haste, until the body disappears. A last prayer, a last goodbye, and a very beautiful litany in which we chant the supplication "Lord, have mercy on this sinner." And then we entrust the deceased to God and the celestial world. Just before that, the grave is blessed with a prayer recalling the three days Christ spent in the tomb and his resurrection.

Until the last minute, the face is visible. He is present and we can see him. Contrary to what one might think, by doing it this way the process is much more human than if the face were masked. I attended the funeral of my brother-in-law in Cachan, Val-de-Marne, on March 6, 1993. He was a well-known journalist, a member of the Bayard-Presse group, Étienne Camelot, nephew of Father Camelot, who had published numerous books on theology. He was a member of the city council, and he fell ill as he was on his way home from a meeting. He had barely made it home when he collapsed at my sister's feet. The day of the funeral, I went to the hospital, where he had been transported without ever regaining consciousness. His body was kept in a side row of the large funeral room. I made it there just in time for the closing of the coffin. The lid was half closed and we could hardly see him. Without paying too much attention to us, probably out of decency, the physician simply unfolded the sheet, adjusted the lid and sealed it, and left. Since Étienne's face appeared twisted, my sister didn't want the children to come close a last time, so under those circumstances I didn't approach him either; the last time I saw his face was thus a few months earlier when he had come to La Trappe. Everything was dignified but felt cold. The closing of the lid was a quick and painful formality, almost reduced to a legal verification that it was he and nobody else. The deceased was hidden. I tried to say some prayers, but the mood seemed sad to me. Of course, hospitals do what they can, and my point is not to blame them. Our funerals at La Trappe are less dramatic. I am not talking about our belief in immortality, but about the human aspect and the sequence of events.

I was present in the funeral home only as a family member and not as a priest. Because of their dwindling numbers, priests don't have the time to attend either the preliminary rites of death or those at the cemetery. They can only handle the church ceremony, and barely that. One can regret this and wonder if it is acceptable. The death of a loved one is an important event in the life of a family and an opportunity for evangelization not to be ignored. Luckily, in more and more cases, lay Christians assume this ministry of accompanying the family in its bereavement, for it is essential that no one end up grieving in solitude, facing the absurdity of death, which remains disconcerting, revolting, and incomprehensible. Our whole being resists death until our last breath. But for the faithful, death is only a transition, and the moment you have to capitulate is precisely the moment at which you conquer. But you have to be conscious of it. It is difficult for everyone involved.

We know that Saint Bernard was torn by the death of his brother Gerard. He described the scene vividly, saying that Gerard "was dying while singing and singing while dying."[5] These are the two faces of a funeral: the sorrow of those helplessly witnessing the departure of the loved one, and the hope that this passing is for the deceased an entry into true life. Regarding the passing of Saint Bernard's brother, there is a Cistercian document of the thirteenth century that doesn't hesitate to proclaim, "We are using you, O death our enemy, to go towards happiness, although you are the mother of sorrow; opponent to the glory, we are serving you up for glory; we are using you, gates of hell, to enter into the kingdom; from you, grave of distress, to find redemption."[6]

---

5. Bernard of Clairvaux, *On the Song of Songs II*, 26.11, trans. Kilian Walsh, CF 7 (Kalamazoo, MI: Cistercian Publications, 1983), 70.

6. {Dom Dubois provides no further information about this document.}

It is true. Transition from life to death is in fact a transition from death to life. We leave this world to transition into a world both richer and larger. Death is a birth, but a painful one; this transition can be agony, even if it ends up in light and peace. Jesus triumphed over death by going through it, not by avoiding it. Transition to life is often accomplished with great suffering, perhaps for the one leaving, but more so for those who surround him and remain as pilgrims of misery in the world that the loved one has left. We in monastic life can be torn by the deaths of our brothers or sisters to the same extent as with the deaths of our own parents and friends. I have cried at the passing of some of the monks that I had known. You don't live next to each other year after year without being affected. How could I have not recognized my sister's sorrow?

No, faith does not prevent grief. But what does it mean to be in mourning? Does mourning someone mean that we finally accept that he is no longer as he was yesterday? Our instinctive temptation is to fixate on the past by remembering him with nostalgia, but in fact we should cut this stage short and live in the present moment, finding the loved one who remains mysteriously present with us. "Why do you seek the living among the dead?" (Luke 24:5), the angel asked the women who were running to Christ's tomb. Maybe we need to learn another language to communicate with the one who has transitioned into the next life. This is the meaning of mourning. We saw that the risen Christ was not immediately recognized by his disciples. It took Mary Magdalen to be called by name in front of the empty tomb for the contact to be re-established (Matt 28:1-7; Mark 16:1-7; Luke 24:1-7). We have to bring silence into our hearts to hear our loved one calling us by name.

The ancient monastic tradition recommends keeping the thought of death before our eyes. You should not prepare for the transition as if it were a distant event that will take place in a vague, undetermined future, or even something—you never know—that might not happen at all. It is not to be observed from far away with binoculars, like the coming of God. It is by living in the present moment that we ready ourselves. Like many others, I have said that in each life there are only two important moments: the present moment and the hour of death. To tell the truth, it is when it coincides with the present moment that death becomes relevant to us, and we will be ready if we live each present moment correctly. One should not misunderstand this statement. We give up the attitude of the child, who wants everything immediately and locks himself up in the present moment. Children have to learn through education to control their immediate impulses.

Culture in that sense means to go beyond the immediate. Man appears, said Heidegger, as the "being of infinity."[7] He is the creator of history, he has a past and a future, but, just as a circle only meets a tangent at one point, our life revolves but only meets God in the present moment—a moment that is part of a history, but that we need to live fully, since it is the moment of our encounter with God. This concept is a source of dynamism in our monastic life, in which identical days follow one another, causing us to run the risk of falling into a routine. Neither vacations nor resting weekends break the daily monotony. But can we talk about monotony at La Trappe? You don't need to wait for the main event, which might happen tomorrow or in ten years, because it is in a present moment, which he will decide, that the encounter with God will take place. That encounter is the main event, in the present moment.

There was a large crowd in the desert of La Trappe on April 16, 1990, when a twenty-year-old man, who had been struck by the two faces of life and death as he observed Brother Aelred's final vows, made his own perpetual vows and received a solemn blessing from the Church under the name of Brother Hugues. The whole Church, and, interestingly, often those who do not

7. Martin Heidegger, *Being and Time: A Translation of* Sein und Zeit, trans. Joan Stambaugh (Albany: State University of New York Press, 1966); Heidegger, *Introduction to Metaphysics*, 2nd ed., revised and expanded translation by Gregory Fried and Richard Polt (New Haven: Yale University Press, 2014).

belong to the Church, are fascinated by a man "leaving for the desert." In the assembly, another young man, or even an adult man, observing the celebration, may then come to the abbot to tell him, "I want to be a monk." If it is not at this time, it may be at another, like all the other opportunities that have perpetuated the monastic life for centuries, for two millennia, under a multitude of forms.

Brother Hugues still looks back today at the double celebration he witnessed as a seminal event that continues to nourish his spiritual life. If you would meet God now, you need to live the present moment completely.

Sick with an illness that would lead to his end, Christian Chabanis,[8] whom we welcomed in La Trappe, calls out to death in a poem.

The monk, contrary to what some people think, is not closer to God than others, but he puts God before anything else, and he collects what is in him and around him to present to God. He lives in the heart of the city and in the world, while being in the desert. He is not a stranger to other people; he often lives like them, but he knows that his face, without being turned away from the earth, has to be turned towards heaven, even though at the moment of Christ's ascension into heaven, the apostles were rudely brought back to earth by the angels, who asked why they were staring at the heavens (Acts 1:11). Monks have a duty to keep their sight on the heavens, reminding everyone how to stay on their true course.

---

8. Christian Chabanis, *"La Mort, un Terme ou un Commencement?"* (Paris: Éditions Fayard, 1982), 438.

CHAPTER TWO

ONLY ANGELS HAVE THE RIGHT TO FLY

At the beginning of this book, when I had only told of the burial of one monk and the perpetual vows of another, and related a family event, I wondered, should I continue to tell this story or not? A Trappist doesn't talk. A Trappist doesn't tell his own story, and he talks even less about other Trappists. I knew a monk in Italy, who, during his ministry as a chaplain in a convent of our order, met a sister who would be beatified by Pope John Paul II in 1983. As a very young man, Father Lambert, a Swiss, had entered the French monastery of Mont-des-Cats, close to Lille, where I would later enter. Sent to Italy, he brought the consecrated host for four months to Sister Gabriella in the infirmary of her monastery, Grottaferrata, close to Rome. There he also met another sister lying next to her, Sister Michelina. The abbess told him, "I have two saints in the infirmary, but I don't know which one is the more saintly."

One of the two sisters knew that she was terminally ill, and she died a year later in 1939 at twenty-five years of age.[1] Father Lambert never thought that she would be beatified. She didn't

---

1. Bernard Martelet, *La petite soeur de l'unité: bienheureuse Marie Gabriella 1914–1939* (Paris: Médiaspaul, 1984).

really play any role in his life, and their frequent encounters did not make any strong impression on him, even though they were roughly the same age and belonged to the same monastic order. Sainthood is not necessarily something that you can see, and it is not always necessary that it can be seen.

Each monk, each sister, is entitled to say, "This secret is mine, it is my secret," as Isaiah repeated in a formula that Saint Bernard applied to the spouse that he mentioned in his *Sermons on the Canticle of Canticles.*[2] Why tell what can easily remain within the silence of a Trappist monastery?

A few nuns at Grottaferrata, now transferred to Vitorchiano, close to Viterbe, Italy, still remember their sister Gabriella. Tourists, believers or non-believers, are allowed to enter a room with pictures and artifacts belonging to the young woman. The Cistercians, as the Trappists were originally called, have quite a few saints recognized by the Church. But in the silence of a monastery, not everything takes place in such a way that the merits, albeit extraordinary, of a member will be disclosed one day. In fact, nothing is done with the intention of talking about it. Acts of heroism or sainthood, weaknesses or temporary lapses, routine events in the daily life or in exceptional circumstances, complete or incomplete vocations, being raised to the unknowable or remaining in laborious immobility—we do not expect that such facts, great or small, will be disclosed.

This lack of disclosure is not for the purpose of hiding or concealing the facts because they could be embarrassing, or because the outside world would not understand them. The fact is that it is difficult to talk about such things because of their very nature. Trappists do not talk because their life takes place in an inner world. The silence surrounding them favors their search. How can one tell what happens in the depth of one's soul? Nothing remarkable happened in the life of Sister Gabriella. Our Trappist brother who went to her room to bring her the holy sacraments

---

2. Isa 24:16; Bernard of Clairvaux, *On the Song of Songs II*, 23.9, trans. Kilian Walsh, CF 7 (Kalamazoo, MI: Cistercian Publications, 1983), 34.

only saw a courageous patient, kind and lonely. There were no long discussions about God or faith, no sublime statements on the Church or the world's salvation. Nothing. Only simple faith under the simplest of appearances. In short, a life like anyone else's, allowing for differences in personality and spirit. The same patient was in the same infirmary week after week. When the young priest, born—he liked to tell us—one day before Pope John Paul I on October 16, 1912, and ordained the same day as he was on July 7, 1935, left four months later for another mission in our Order, he had nothing special to say about Sister Gabriella. Not that he hadn't noticed the quality of her soul, her intense faith, and her disposition always to search for complete perfection, but since he himself was fervently searching to live on a similar level, this quality of soul escaped his notice.

Sister Michelina, whom nobody mentions anymore, was not so different from her companion. The three of them were, I believe, too close to the heart of their religious vocations for a passing observer to notice anything remarkable about them. It is really difficult to talk about contemplatives in general. It is stronger than the desire to keep secret what happens behind what we often call the "high walls of our monasteries." That is why I wondered if I should go further in describing and analyzing our lives at La Trappe. The danger is not of saying too much or too little, but of being unsuccessful in showing what is the best or the most important. What matters most is precisely what makes Trappists silent and contemplative, what leads them to question the world and some of its values, to distance themselves from it with the intention never to return.

Nevertheless, new circumstances were about to occur.

When I was appointed superior of La Trappe in November 1975, I left the abbey of Mont-des-Cats, close to Lille, where I had been a monk for more than twenty-five years, and went to Normandy, more precisely to Le Perche. I was elected abbot a year later, on February 2, 1977. While abbot of La Trappe I had been asked to take an interim position as *superior ad nutum* at the Abbey of Cîteaux (Côte d'Or) for a couple of months in 1993. I had to make many round trips between La Trappe and

Cîteaux, which were about 350 miles apart, spending about two weeks in one abbey and two weeks in the other. I felt that I could not refuse this assignment in the first house of the Order. The abbot, Dom Loys, had resigned after twenty-three years in office. The abbot general of the Order had conducted numerous discussions and surveys, which convinced him that conditions were still not optimal for holding an election at that time. Certain events had troubled the community, and it needed to get its confidence back. It needed to examine its future on the basis of new information, as often happens when a new abbot is chosen. It needed a new maturing period that would take place in peace and dialogue.

Nevertheless, it was not reasonable to leave Cîteaux without a superior. The task was perhaps delicate, but because of the quality of the community of Cîteaux, everything fell into place faster and better than I could have hoped. Six months after I had appointed him as prior—that is, my first assistant—Father Olivier was elected abbot on August 5, 1993, just in time for him to participate with the other abbots and abbesses of our Order in the general chapter held in Spain in September of that year.

It was in that context that Father Olivier, still prior, received a phone call that he shared with me. A publisher and an author showed interest in introducing our Cistercian way of life to the general public. We made an appointment to meet at Cîteaux with Charles Ronsac, well known in the publishing world, and Michel Damien, who had published long articles in various books. I reflected on the consequences of such a commitment. They told me that producing such a manuscript would require a lot of work. Monks do not like to talk about themselves, and so again I hesitated. Nevertheless, I was conscious that for many decades I had been a privileged observer or actor, sometimes in the modest role of secretary in a commission in our Order, and had witnessed important changes that shook the monastic world as a whole and the Cistercians in particular in the second part of the twentieth century. The abbot general encouraged me to accept: "Ultimately it is your generation that did everything. Why not tell the story of this adventure of the Spirit in a book?"

This great adventure, which required some monks to get heavily involved in looking for new paths at the risk of not being understood, was indeed worthy of being told. The history of this period would allow us to highlight spiritual blessings without embarrassing anyone. Moreover, it was not appropriate that the only people talking about the monastic life to the general public were individuals who had left the cloister after a few years for some reason. Their memoirs satisfied the desire of their readers to know what happened behind our somewhat mythical walls, but were they really the best people to express accurately what was going on there? Why would we not listen to someone who felt strengthened in his vocation and who had closely experienced the evolution of the Order?

That is why I agreed to take on this endeavor. However, that agreement did not resolve the problem of time or of access to personal data that I didn't totally control. I authorized Michel Damien to participate in the monks' life as one of them for a period of close to two months, and I directed the monks to answer his inquiries to the extent that our common research required it and to the extent that respect for our community life allowed it. He was free to move around within the cloister, and no one refused the discussions that he requested. He had known of Cîteaux before this project and had gathered a lot of information. Each of us, according to his position, received confidences that enabled us to refine our opinions. I was no longer alone in going forward.

In addition to retracing my personal journey, this book recounts a monastic adventure lived by all of us for decades. It is neither a log nor one entirely devoted to my life—why my life more than anyone else's? Instead it describes a monastic universe rich in important changes. It would not make sense for an abbot to put himself forward more than for a simple monk in such a project. It would be contrary to our way of life for a Trappist to decide to recount his own memoirs. His life has to remain hidden, anonymous, for a monk does not seek notoriety. I have only agreed to be the main thread of the story to comply with certain literary constraints of the collection that welcomes it. If I sign this book as the abbot, showing my face and providing some biographical indications, it is not to suggest that others have not contributed to this book, even though their identities are not always revealed. The names appearing herein are mentioned with the approval of all concerned members of the Order, at least those who are still alive.

In a way, each monk is unique, with his own history and preferences that are his and that define his personality. All these increase the value of the community. One day at Cîteaux, a monk knocked on my office door, located at the top of a monumental staircase of white marble dating back to the eighteenth century. I didn't know him well yet. To receive the charge of a new community is a terrifying privilege and a formidable mission. It enriches the experience and deepens it, but it requires first to be able to listen, to read unknown faces, and to decipher the demands of the hearts. He announced to me that he had been invited by Air France to sit in the cockpit of a new giant and hyper-sophisticated plane, the Airbus A340, for a free round trip from Paris to New York. He hadn't won at a television game, for monks do not gamble and do not watch television. A television camera would be present during the flight, and a broadcast on France 2 would show him piloting the plane. He left it up to me to decide if he should accept the offer.

His passion for flying was unquestionable, and I listened to him attentively. Before entering the monastery, he had been an airline captain on international routes, the director of the pilots' training center at Air France, and the president of an airline pilots' union. He was not a newcomer to this specialty. As a young man, his exploits earned him a place in the elite corps of fighter pilots, the toughest of all pilots. He became a hero in World War II, earning the Legion of Honor for his combat missions. He had had a wealth of adventures, just like Mermoz[3] or Saint-Exupéry.[4]

3. {Jean Mermoz (1901–1936) was a French air force pilot who was the first to fly the route Paris, Dakar, Buenos Aires. He pioneered night flights over the Andes.}

4. {Antoine de Saint-Exupéry (1900–1944), a French pioneer commercial pilot who opened and flew the dangerous airmail routes in Africa and South America. A writer and poet, his novels *Night Flight* and *The Little Prince* earned him worldwide acclaim.}

He was a true ace, who sometimes watched the planes flying over the monastery with emotion written on his face. This monk knew the heavens, both the one that our eyes can see and the one that our spirit seeks. He hadn't left Cîteaux for years, and this invitation from the journalist could only thrill him and—maybe—also be agreeable to our community. The tickets were reserved, but we needed to think about it together.

"Father Baudouin, doesn't this trip mainly bring publicity to Air France for the inaugural flight of its new plane? Is it really the place of a monk to sit in the cockpit?"

This man was experienced and sensible, knowledgeable about the world and about business. He had had time to evaluate the advantages and disadvantages of this invitation.

"I doubt that anyone would think that I am still capable of flying. These planes have so many electronics now. Still, the opportunity will probably never present itself again. It is too unbelievable. A monk in this situation, isn't it an opportunity to talk about the religious life?"

"Or about the planes. What will the viewers get out of it, if they only let you talk about the planes? Are you sure that they will put what you want on the air?"

"I would like for Cîteaux to be known—"

"Me too, I understand! But I know that deep down you are thinking the same thing that I am. They ask you to be on a stage. Nothing is free in this world, or very little."

There we were touching on the essence of the question. Was this in accord with his vocation as a monk? He was experiencing a small disappointment faced with a refusal that he knew was inevitable, but he was no fool. You only ask for permission from a superior when you are honestly convinced that he can grant it to you. Otherwise, the monk would not be responsible for his own actions. The point is not to come back to rigid prescriptions or childlike obedience. We grant each monk a fair amount of freedom, the freedom to decide for himself, in consultation with the superior, if it is important, what needs to be done with a view to achieving a more complete gift of our self to God. Obedience is not the easy way out, and in our lives there are quite a few

sacrifices that we need to make. But the ultimate goal remains
the gift of love. We will only be able to escape from this tight
network of perpetual sacrifices and from the inherent severity
of the Rule once we draw near to Christ from the heavens' side,
where only the angels have the right to fly. Father Baudouin
knew of which heavens we were talking, just as he understood
the totally different meaning of a surprising phrase he had heard
on Christmas night in 1946.

That year he was head pilot of Air France's continental network, in charge of the supervision of the young pilots just out of
flight school. I was then about to enter the monastery, and nothing suggested that our paths would cross one day. On December
23 he was to reopen the flight from Paris to Madagascar, which
had been interrupted during the war. The DC-3 plane had had
some technical problems, thereby delaying the departure by one
day. Few airports were then open for night flights, and there were
stops scheduled in Tunis, Cairo, and Nairobi. The sky cleared up
during the flight and became glorious. He asked the passengers
if they were willing to extend the night flight to Cairo in order to
make up for lost time. A week earlier he had flown through El-
Adem, the necessary refueling stop, and he knew that the airport
was open at night. El-Adem was a military airstrip belonging
to the Royal Air Force, close to Tobrouk, in the middle of the
Cyrenaica desert, where, I was told, the events portrayed in the
famous war movie *Taxi for Tobrouk* with Lino Ventura and Charles
Aznavour took place. The passengers gave him their approval.

He crossed the gulf up to Benghazi, where a continuous layer
of low stratus clouds started to hide the ground. While the mechanic tried in vain to contact El-Adem, he thought that the radio
lighthouse would enable him to find the landing strip. But it also
remained silent. After about three and a half hours of flight, he
guessed that he had reached El-Adem and started to circle. The
mechanic couldn't reach any other tracking stations and issued
a distress signal, but without any success. It was a catastrophe,
for there wasn't enough fuel to reach Tripoli, and they couldn't
wait for dawn because there was less than forty-five minutes

of fuel left. He kept circling above the position, which might or might not be correct. Soon the engine would stall and he would plunge into the darkness and crash on a sandy hill. How many days would go by before the rescuers would find any possible survivors? The inquiry commission would certainly conclude that the pilot had been reckless in attempting a night flight. That thought offended this man, accustomed as he was to being in command. He would have time to notify the passengers at the last minute, and so he didn't tell them anything while the flight attendant (he remembered her name was Janine Lançon) was serving a Christmas Eve dinner.

Having already begun his descent, fifteen minutes before the fuel ran out, he suddenly noticed a little light between the clouds, a weak glimmer through the layer of clouds concealing the ground. It was the El-Adem landing strip, which had remained lighted after all. It was a miracle to have guessed its location within a mile, without any marker, after a trip of over seven hundred miles! Despite having initially known perfectly well that finding a landing strip was unlikely, he nevertheless descended and touched down on the runway. He saw a British airman stumbling across the runway towards the plane, having just celebrated Christmas. Immediately he unloaded onto him all the fears that had taken hold of him for the last hour. The soldier answered him phlegmatically: "But sir, it is Christmas night. Only angels have the right to fly!"

This reply threw him off. He walked to the officers' mess, where the whole base had gathered, to have a drink and totally forget planes for a while. The next morning, he left for Madagascar. Don't ask me to talk now about his conversion, which took place amidst the dangers and successes of a career that he loved.

In my office at Cîteaux, he didn't tell me that much that day. When he understood that I was not in favor of his accepting the invitation for a brief outing to make the Paris-New York trip, he left quietly. I found him moments later in the church looking collected and peaceful and preparing for the liturgy that was about to start. The hardest is always hidden and tucked away in the heart. Planes . . . hmm . . . planes!

On March 15, 1947, the flight from Paris to Nice disappeared in the Alps. A plane was readied to search for the wreck, with Captain Bernard Cordier, the future Father Baudouin, as commanding officer. Sitting next to him was Henri Ziegler, Director General of Air France. As they flew over the mountains surrounding Grenoble, Henri Ziegler asked to fly the plane. Since he was coming too close to the mountain peaks, the former fighter pilot suggested that he increase the altitude to avoid the down drafts. The director refused, stating that he was quite familiar with mountain flying. Repeatedly his companion had to take over to get back to a safe altitude, which seemed to offend the director. Tension grew in the cockpit between the two men. Once the rescue crews found the wreckage of the lost plane they had been seeking, the rescue effort began. The plane had touched a ridge, provoking an avalanche that carried all the bodies down the mountain. Long iron rods used to probe the snow, by coincidence, enabled the future monk to be the first to locate the body of the pilot. The next morning, Cordier was sanctioned for having displeased the director, who accused him of being "excessively careful." The blame was so severe and affected him so much that it made him think about the vanity of such worldly things and consider the call to another life.

About half a century later he received from the airline the gift of a free long flight at the helm of its best plane. In the monastery, community prayers followed each other, accompanied by the sound of the bells. Life at Cîteaux continued as if no invitation had ever come. Bells again, meals, work, *lectio, oratio*, library, stairs, hallways, cell, cloister—no large space or spectacular clouds for our brother.

But a couple of months later Father Baudouin completed, without a warning, his earthly pilgrimage. We found him on the morning of September 16, 1993, unconscious on his bed, stricken by a heart attack, with a book of Thomas Merton and a few other books of Cistercian spirituality next to him. He had taken flight with the angels for a much loftier journey. Finally, the heavens had allowed him to fly.

How does one become a Trappist? Why does one remain a Trappist? There are as many types of conversions as there are converted, as many circumstances as there are postulants, as many moments to question oneself and make a decision as there are hearts to listen to an inner voice. Despite the collective dimension of the life at La Trappe, each one of us follows an entirely personal course and remains a different person from the others, totally unique until his last day, whom nobody replaces when he passes and whom no postulant will cause to be forgotten when he takes his own place in the choir or the dormitory.

Father Baudouin had asked for my permission to tell his life story,[5] and he had penned some notes that were nearly destroyed years ago. I consented to his request, thereby softening his regret at not being able to fly to New York. His story could certainly measure up to biographies that highlighted social success, connections, and the spirit of adventure. It would definitely be as good as the stories told by journalists or writers, who, whatever their talent might be, evaluate things from the outside, or the stories sometimes written by those who have left monastic life. They offer, generally speaking, only a limited point of view, not to say a biased one, marked by an experience that wasn't always positive. These writings do not completely fill the needs of those who wonder about actual concerns and are looking for answers in a modern language. I had recently been personally disappointed by a book that a former Benedictine monk I knew had just published under an alias. Wouldn't the assignment that Charles Ronsac and Michel Damien had just offered me enable me to give the general public a more accurate story?

Monastic life lends itself so well to misunderstandings, and clichés are so widespread that a famous member of the Academy of Science recently asked the following of one of his friends, who told it to me after having spent some days in one of our abbeys:

---

5. {Bernard Cordier, *Dans le silence des étoiles: Pilote de ligne devenu moine à Cîteaux*, Editions Parole et Silence (Paris: Les Plans-sur-Bex, 2002).}

"So, have you seen them dig their own grave every day? Is it true what Chateaubriand said about them?"[6]

I have never dug my own grave, nor do I have the desire to lend myself to this morbid folklore. Léon Bloy[7] noted that if it was true that monks were digging up one shovelful of dirt each day for their graves, these would have reached depths never seen before in drilling for water on earth.[8] The essence of monastic life cannot be expressed, because it belongs to the invisible, and what can be revealed is only secondary. But what is secondary

6. {François-René de Chateaubriand (1768–1848), a French aristocrat who survived the revolution by traveling to America. Upon his return he joined the Royalists, leading to a new exile to England. He was one of the founders of romanticism in French literature. While the intelligentsia of the time was largely anticlerical, Chateaubriand wrote *Génie du Christianisme* in support of the Christian faith.}

7. {Léon Bloy (1846–1917) French writer who went from an agnostic youth to a committed Catholic devotion. He wrote extensively against the anticlericalism of Victor Hugo. Having made a retreat at La Trappe while struggling with tension between a possible religious vocation and a romantic involvement, Bloy later recounted his impressions of two contemplative orders in his autobiographical novel *Le Désespéré*, including the description of a funeral, but the detail cited above does not occur there (*Oeuvres de Léon Bloy*, ed. Joseph Bollery and Jacques Petit, 15 vols. [Paris: Mercure de France, 1964], 3:91–150). In 2013, Pope Francis surprised many by quoting Bloy during his first homily as pope: "When we do not profess Jesus Christ, the saying of Léon Bloy comes to mind: 'Anyone who does not pray to the Lord prays to the devil'" (*Missa pro ecclesia* with the Cardinal Electors, Sistine Chapel, Thursday, March 14, 2013; http://w2.vatican.va/content/francesco/en/homilies/2013/documents/papa-francesco_20130314_omelia-cardinali.html).}

8. What is true is that once upon a time when deceased monks were buried immediately, a grave was kept ready in the cemetery half dug up. It only needed to be completed the day of the funeral. It is not surprising that, at a time when death was experienced as a tragedy, a custom grew to meditate in front of that grave. Is this particular to monks? Certain people determine their place of burial: Chateaubriand himself did so! Isn't that what happens nowadays when people maintain family vaults? On that theme, read Anselm Dimier, *La Sombre Trappe: Les légendes et la vérité* (Saint Wandrille: Editions Fontenelle, 1946).

is not insignificant, and it can lead to the essence, which is the only thing important to the monk, provided that the secondary is not transformed into the ridiculous.

On certain nights only angels have the right to fly—forgive me for trying to do the impossible by undertaking this endeavor.

Chapter Three

"Beware of the Trap"

In 1937, I was eight years old. Our neighbors across the street had recently gotten electricity, and their windows lighted up at once. What surprised me was the speed at which light surged forth. I tried to do the same with gas light, dimming and lighting it as fast as I could to make them believe that we too had electricity. I wanted the people across the street to believe that we were as privileged as they were. I sent them signals, but the flame flickered and was slow to show our affluence. We didn't have central heating, either. We lived in a rental house with a very small garden. We were living in cramped quarters, with seven children and our parents in three bedrooms. Not that we were really poor, but we were not so well off as the neighbors.

My father built locomotives, designing them at the factory as an industrial draftsman. But to play with locomotives I had to visit a friend. During our vacation we played with his electric trains, and I dreamed that maybe one day I would have one just like his, if my father made enough money with his own locomotives. My father enlisted at the beginning of World War I at the age of eighteen and was sent to the Balkans. He returned from there having suffered from the German gas used in the trenches. His brother had died in that war, and since another brother had previously died at a young age, my father was the last surviving member of his family. Because of the war he couldn't become an engineer, as he had wanted to, so he remained an industrial draftsman. His salary barely enabled us to belong to the lower middle class of Lille, the very low bourgeoisie, where often one does not earn enough to make ends meet. At that time, he was forty years old, and my mother forty-four. I knew that he worked hard when he left in the morning to design and draft parts manufactured by the plant located outside the city in Fives-Lille. Aunt Marie, whom we called Aunt Ninie, one of my mother's three sisters, had married a physician, who was the celebrity in the family. They lived in a house surrounded by a large garden.

On my tenth birthday, as I was walking down the street alone, proud to be grown up, a lady recognized me and asked me my age. I was happy to tell her:

"I am ten years old."

"You are so short!" she told me. "My God, you are short for your age—"

Then I was really disappointed and annoyed. For many days, her surprised look kept coming back to me, and I really wondered, "Am I that short?"

At home there were kids shorter than me. I was the middle child of seven, three older siblings and three younger ones. One sister and two brothers on one side of me: Geneviève, André, and René, and the same on the younger side, Antoinette, Michel, and Stéphane. I was born on November 26, 1929, and the position of middle child put me in a peculiar position with respect to the rest of them, for I often felt that I needed to play mediator. If I didn't always succeed in reconciling everybody, as the family grew I realized the privileges and frustrations of my position.

The war broke out when I was ten, and we lost everything. The little we had disappeared in a flash, just like the light in the house across the street when you turned off the switch. No one imagined the complete disarray into which our family would be thrown. There had been small events that had given me some idea, like a chimney fire that made us fear that the house would burn down. This time we had to leave it while it was still standing. Another type of fire had been lit all over Europe, one that would not be extinguished with buckets of water. As a precaution, my mother wanted us to leave the city in June 1940, while my father remained at the factory. Moreover, we were told that we were only leaving for a couple of days, and it wouldn't be long. We traveled with very little luggage towards Saint-Pol-sur-Ternoise, a small neighboring city in the Pas-de-Calais to wait for the fire around us to be under control, so to speak. Everything fit in one piece of luggage and a few small bags that the children carried. My brother Stéphane was four years old, the oldest one sixteen. I didn't take a scarf with me, since we would be back way before the winter. In my haste I left my Erector Set boat on the mantel.

The Germans were breaking through on every front. They were everywhere. We fled with the refugees, first on foot, then by train. In Abbeville, there was a bombing just as we arrived, but it didn't last long. On the piece of luggage, my mother had written *Rouen*, because her goal was for us to get there. We did not leave the train when it stopped in Elbeuf, because we didn't think that we had reached our destination. Unbeknownst to us, the luggage was unloaded and lost. The train departed. No Rouen. An aunt lived near Le Mans, and we planned on joining her there. It was not until we set foot on the platform there that we realized that the luggage had been lost.

"Wait for me here," said Mom.

My mother talked to the employees of the train station to try to find our belongings while the seven of us anxiously huddled together in a corner. People scattered left and right, and the train station was soon empty.

A French officer walked towards us and seemed to take pity on us.

"What are you doing here, children?"

"Mom is coming—"

He waited with us. We were huddled together like little ducks watching for the return of their mother duck. When she came back, he questioned her. He didn't think we could reach our destination at this late hour, so he offered to take us to his place, a small rented bedroom in the city. I was lucky to have a spot in the bed with the three youngest ones. The others slept on chairs like the officer, or on the floor. What would we have done that night without him? It was a risk for my mother to accept this offer, but it was luck, an "angel's visit."

Our aunt was not at home, but two of her children welcomed us, just in time to inform us that they too were getting on the road, because the Germans were getting closer. How could we hitchhike in this chaos? Nevertheless, we reached Angoulême. We stopped there because it was useless to try to escape further, for the Germans had already overtaken us!

As I watched the troops passing by, I wondered where we would go. My mother wondered the same thing. At least they were not chasing after us. We were directed to a boarding school run by nuns. During the school holidays, the students' dorms were empty and were made available to refugees. We camped there, trying to hold on to the privacy of our family as best we could. When the school year started again, my mother registered us in schools in Angoulême. Later we learned that my two older brothers had gone to the same school where François Mitterrand[1] had been a student.

The teacher terrorized me. That is the only thing I learned from him. He made us cross our fingers so that when he hit them with a ruler it would hurt more. His voice, his eyes, his movements terrorized me. I always expected a disaster, whatever the subject was. He embodied terror for me, and I was totally lost in his class. I was not close to any of the other students, being too perturbed by the uprooting and separation of our family. In the morning, I left home because I had to, burdened with anxiety, and once the school day was over, I went back home without any regrets.

Luckily, the nightmare didn't last very long, but it remains etched in my child's mind as one of my earliest memories, to-

---

1. {François Mitterrand (1916–1996): a French socialist politician and statesman who was President of France from 1981 to 1995.}

gether with another adventure I experienced at three or four years of age. One day I went with my mother to get my brothers and my sister from school at the end of the afternoon. I walked next to her, refusing to hold her hand, because I was grown up now. She picked up the two older ones and left. She walked along the sidewalk and I followed her, totally lost in my thoughts. Two streets further on, she made the wrong turn, which surprised me. I looked up and discovered at that moment that it was not my mother but another woman whom I had been following by mistake. I was able to find our house, little man all lost that I was. I stood on my toes at the front door to ring the bell, but it was too high. A man working on a house came down from his scaffolding to help me. Nobody answered, and the door was locked. I left right away, in panic, looking for my mother. But she had to walk into another neighborhood to pick up my older sister at another school! Luckily, she had notified another woman of my disappearance, and that woman recognized me and caught up with me. Finally! From then on I did not play the braggart anymore.

In Angoulême, we waited for news of my father. He had told us when we left that if he had to leave Lille, he would go to Givors, in the Rhône region, where his factory had another plant. My mother wrote letter upon letter to City Hall to inquire if M. Dubois, industrial draftsman from Lille, had arrived in Givors and registered with City Hall. But instead of answering the mail, City Hall just left it piling up. One day my father became worried and went to City Hall, where he discovered the pile of mail from his wife.

"Why didn't you give her my address? I had specifically left it with you for that purpose."

"Because there were no stamps for the answer."

My mother took steps to travel from the "Zone Occupée" to the "Zone Libre,"[2] where Givors was located. Once we were all

---

2. {The *"zone libre"* ("free zone") was a division of France established in 1940 after the French troops had surrendered to the Germans. It was the southern part of the territory administered by the government of Marshal

together, we should in principle obtain a *laissez-passer* to return to Lille. In the meantime, we all packed into a rather old apartment. In fact, we had to wait for two and a half years for that *laissez-passer*. I was quickly sent to a boarding school in Saint-Chamond run by the Marist brothers, seventeen miles away. I resigned myself but was full of anxiety about making this trip because I would be arriving in the middle of the school year, in November. My two older brothers and I, poor refugees from the North, were placed in different classes. I was in the seventh grade.

"Two weeks is a long time to wait for you," I wrote my mother in December 1940, in letters that she kept meticulously. I found them fifty years later, experiencing all the emotion that an adult can feel toward the eleven-year-old child that he had been.

"Sometimes I am discouraged by my work, for I can't do it. Next week, there is a test in ancient history about which I do not know the first word, not a single one. I have never studied that subject before, and from what I did study, I don't understand anything. In one word, I don't know anything. And then there is also a test in geography and sciences, all that at the same time. You understand if I cry, I cry, and I cry. Mom, I beg you, pray and pray even more for these tests. I am crying about this, even now. It is a long time to wait without talking to you, without hugging you, without seeing Dad or Stéphane, or the whole family, or even the cabin [our refugee housing] with its large room, which will seem very small when I come back compared to this dorm. Pray well, very well, pray very, very well."

Two days later, on December 7, 1940, I wrote to my mother from Saint-Chamond: "We are at page 100." I hoped that she would ask the people in charge of the boarding school to exempt me from the history test on materials that my previous teachers had neglected to teach me. "How do you expect me to learn

---

Pétain, based in Vichy. To the north was the *"zone occupée"* ("occupied zone"), where the Vichy government had limited powers. In November 1942, the German and Italian armies seized the *zone libre;* both zones remained under German administration until 1944.}

100 pages at a time? If only I could understand something, but nothing. I have a two in math. You see, my math teacher does not understand. I almost always have a one or a two out of twenty because he keeps asking questions on subjects I have never been taught. My knees aren't cold, but it hurts behind my knees. They really hurt, because there are chapped cracks there and I cannot move my legs anymore. I serve Mass in the large chapel. They give us blue cassocks with white surplices and "canailles" (sic!) as they call them, blue with white velvet collars.[3] The chapel is beautiful with rugs and trees and totally lit."

The Marists were more lenient than the teachers in the school in Angoulême, and I soon had friends. I wanted to reassure my parents, so during the following summer holidays, when they sent me to a mountain camp, I repeated on page after page that I was happy and satisfied. I added to the emphasis by underlining, the first word once, the second twice, and the third three times: "I am happy, happy, happy!" And on August 23, 1941: "I have seen Mont Blanc myself. We went to the *Mer de Glace*, and we saw the hoodoos and the cheminées de fées."[4]

When I was about twelve years old, after I had been observing the Marists for some time, like five or six of my boarding school classmates, the vague idea of becoming a priest came to me, even though I was unable to make sense out of it. We watched these priests and told ourselves, "We could live like them." We were a small group sharing the same desires. This was nothing special in this environment, and our conversations reverted to that subject from time to time. During a retreat in preparation for our confirmation, I was so struck by the words of a young priest, Father Pierre Chièze, that I opened up to him about my

3. {*Canailles* is probably a term used by the altar boys in that boarding school, as Dubois indicates with his *sic!* Not knowing what it meant, we leave it here, as he did in quoting this letter from his childhood.}

4. {In France hoodoos are called *demoiselles coiffées* ("ladies with hairdos") or *cheminées de fées* ("fairy chimneys").}

intentions. Later on, before traveling back up North, I asked to meet with him in Sainte-Foy-les-Lyon, where he resided. He accepted without giving me a set time, thinking that it was a courtesy request that I would not follow up. He would tell me one day how surprised he was the next day to find a thirteen-year-old boy talking to him about his vocation.

Nevertheless, I didn't think that I wanted to be a Marist. But those years made a strong impression on me, as they did on many of us. One student, ten years our senior, Pierre Waton, entered Cîteaux; a younger one, Maurice Coste, joined the Trappists in Tamié, in Savoie, where he joined another alum, Jean-Marie Escot, who would be their prior for a while.

Early in 1943, we returned to the Zone Occupée and found our way to our house in Lille. It had been requisitioned for a long time by the Germans, but thanks to a "collaborator"[5] we were able to get it back. Strangely, his name was communicated to us by our uncle, who we later learned was a member of the Resistance against the Germans. We went to play from time to time in this uncle's huge garden, where we met a young boy whom our uncle introduced as "a nephew from the other side of the family." After the war, we learned that he was a Jewish boy whom my uncle was hiding. My uncle was known by many as the doctor of the poor, and he could not disguise his name behind a pseudonym. This inconvenience would turn out to be a blessing. A member of the Resistance was arrested and interrogated by the Gestapo:

"Do you know Dr. Defaux?"

"Yes, he is my wife's physician."

This good answer, given by reflex, saved my uncle, and he was never suspected. I would get to know him better later. Before

---

5. {A collaborator refers here to a French citizen who cooperated, usually willingly, with the German occupier. Most collaborators were tried for treason after the end of WW II. The most notorious trial involved Marshal Pétain, mentioned above, who was tried for treason by the High Court in June 1945. He was convicted on all charges, and the jury sentenced him to death. Because of his advanced age his sentence was commuted to life in prison.}

the war, he was what we called "a social Catholic," a member of the *Sillon de Marc Sangnier.*[6] He faithfully attended the Social Weeks, a large traveling university, which provided for enriching exchanges in most diverse encounters. He was president for the North Region of the Popular Democratic Party,[7] so he naturally joined the Resistance as early as 1941. After the war, as County President of the M.R.P.,[8] he was first elected to the City Council and then became Deputy Mayor of Lille. He sat on the General Council of the North Region, of which he eventually became the Vice President. But at that moment in 1943, I only knew him as my uncle the doctor, an uncle with good connections.

When we returned to our house, I rushed to see my boat that I had left on the mantel, but of course it had disappeared. The rooms had been emptied, and no furniture was left. During the following weeks, my parents got tables, chairs, and beds here and there. Very soon I was registered in the ninth grade at St. Joseph High School, a Jesuit school, because my parents wanted my brothers, sisters, and me to have a religious education. Once more it was a trial to start school in the middle of the year without knowing the program. I had the feeling that the curriculum provided by the Jesuits was more demanding than the one provided by the Marists. You had to hunker down, I noticed after two years, when I had finally become a good student without too much effort.

I joined Troop "V Lille, Groupe Lyautey" of the scouts. I didn't much like the marches and the group games, where you had to

---

6. {Marc Sangnier (1873–1950), a French politician and Catholic activist. In 1894 he founded a Socialist Catholic organization called "Le Sillon" ("The Furrow").}

7. {The Popular Democratic Party (Parti Démocrate Populaire, PDP) was a French political party, Christian in the largely anticlerical Third Republic.}

8. {The Popular Republican Movement (Mouvement Républicain Populaire, MRP) was a political party created after World War II to support General de Gaulle's coalition to govern France and to counter the influence of a well-organized Communist party.}

march almost the whole time. But in doing so, I came out of my cocoon and played sports. We accomplished more than group games in the woods, for we were operating in an atmosphere of reflection and mutual assistance, and I liked that shared ideal. Nevertheless, I came across as not very sociable and as an introvert, even though at home I was outgoing and a tireless joker. The scouts didn't think that I was very resourceful, but though the scoutmaster saw me as shy and awkward, nevertheless I became patrol leader, I don't know how, since I never proved able to be anything but awkward. In my new responsibilities, I did more myself than I expected others to do. Everything I didn't dare ask of others, I did myself. It was faster, and I avoided complications that way. If ever there was someone who was not a leader, it was me! Although later I had to be a leader on many occasions, my first thought was always to do everything myself, so that I didn't have to show how incapable I was of giving instructions to others. I had a hard time training my patrol and getting them interested in any activity, which really frustrated me. I would have loved for it to be different. Why don't I have that ease and that dynamism that others have? But I learned to deal with it.

I was an odd patrol leader, not at all a leader or a responsible person, but on the other hand, I was a good talker. My uncle told me that later I could be a good lawyer or a good preacher. People also told me that I looked serious and that this inspired confidence in another way. Maybe I was too serious and often looked ill at ease, but in my heart I was joyful. I practiced the harmonica and the reed pipe, happy to come back home and play the instruments by ear and sing what I learned in the choir, since I couldn't read music.

Life was not easy. Nevertheless, I felt capable of accomplishing a great deal and showing others what was in me. I felt confident I could do well if I applied myself. Around that time, I made a public argument that surprised my Jesuit teacher. Our entire P.E. class was punished by being assigned to discuss as a group the famous Latin sentence *Mens sana in corpore sano,* a healthy mind in a healthy body. Our teacher probably expected that all of us would support that aphorism in favor of sport. But I argued with passion that to have a healthy body was neither a necessary nor a sufficient condition. All of a sudden, my classmates discovered me. I explained at length that you could be someone great even with a handicapped and totally disfigured body. I gave many examples of patients transported to the beach at Berck-Plage in chairs and in casts. Or on the other hand, you could possess a strong body and have a deficient mind in many ways, but there I did not give any examples. The goal was to reach internal success. My speech probably saved the poor hiker that I was because it was in part a self-defense of someone who did not excel in sports. It also gave me an opportunity to think about internal life and about what I would like to say, even to a Jesuit. He provoked me and he got my point of view. Although skinny, I was never sick.

When I was fifteen years old, I participated in a large yearly summer camp. When it was finished there were still some weeks of vacation left. We didn't have enough money for me to go somewhere else, and I was prepared to spend those last weeks at home with my brothers and sisters. But then I ran across someone on the street who would help decide the course of my life. The scouts' chaplain saw me and asked me all of a sudden,
"Why don't you come with us to Mont-des-Cats?"
"I didn't know that you were going."
"You should come with us. We leave tomorrow."
In school he was also in charge of a small Marian congregation to which I belonged. From time to time he organized a short stay for its members in that monastery, where I had never been. It was a Trappist monastery located about twenty-five miles from Lille. The monks lived together and spent their days in liturgical prayer, work, and spiritual study, without leaving their convent, their "trap," as we said.[9] Although some of them were priests,

---

9. {In French "une trappe" is "a trap or trapdoor." Dom Dubois puns on the word throughout this chapter.}

they didn't go to parishes and were not involved in ministries, except for the hospitality they offered in a building adjacent to the monastery, which was called the guesthouse. That was where the scouts' chaplain invited me to go.

Later I would learn that the Trappists followed the Rule of Saint Benedict, written in the sixth century. They were Benedictines, but as the centuries passed, different groups of Benedictines developed, because this sixth-century rule was sufficiently flexible to allow diverse interpretations. Sometimes reforms came about to correct a certain way of life that over time had distanced itself from the original spirit. One of these reforms took place at Cîteaux in 1098, and the Benedictines that followed it called themselves Cistercians, after the name of this abbey. The Trappists are Cistercians. So where did this other name of Trappist come from? This name was given to the monks because of the great influence that a Cistercian abbey located in a place called La Trappe would have during the French Revolution. I will come back to the different twists and turns of this story in another chapter. I didn't know that story that morning when I met the scouts' chaplain in the Rue de Lille, and, frankly, I didn't care. I had other worries because I had to consider the cost of accommodations for three days.

"I don't have the money." I told him, "The scouts' camp ate up all my savings."

"Come anyway," he insisted. "The money that your parents would have to spend at home for you will be enough to pay for your stay. Tell your parents not to give you more!"

His offer surprised me. I went home and explained the encounter to my mother, who was as surprised as I was. She agreed, and I packed my bag, happy for the unexpected outing. The priest had told me, "Five o'clock p.m. at the train station."

The next day, I arrived at the train station early. A train was scheduled to leave around that time, but I didn't see anyone from my school. Time passed and I was still alone. The train was about to leave. Where were they? I was getting worried, but I left anyway, somewhat confused. In fact, the appointment was not at the departure train station, but in Baillieu, the arrival station, so that we would go on together to the monastery. The others had left a long time ago for the five-mile walk. On the platform in Baillieu's train station I met another boy who hadn't understood the instructions any better than I had. He lived in the city and we wondered what we should do.

"It is a two-hour walk to get there. That's a long way," I said.

"The monastery will be closed."

"We won't be able to turn around before nightfall."

"Come to my house. We'll leave tomorrow morning."

As we left in the morning, he warned me, "We must beware of the Trappists. I heard that, if you enter in the abbey through the wrong door, you can never get out."

A mile further on, he told me again, "Let's not get in through the wrong door! Beware!"

He repeated this to me the whole way, and by the end I was as scared as he was. After a while both of us imagined ourselves stuck behind a door that wouldn't open anymore. This was not encouraging. I was watchful, and we cheered each other on to be diligent, determined not to be caught in that trap.

The monastery is built on a little hilltop about 450 feet above sea level. It is not high, but it overlooks the large northern flatlands. You can see the coast from Ostend to Cape Gris Nez from the gardens of the abbey. The cranes at the port of Dunkirk pierce the horizon, twenty-five miles away. At night, you can see all the harbor lights. When the weather is clear, it is said that from the attic the monks can see the belfry of Lille, twenty-five miles away in the other direction. I was not sure if they climbed up there very often, or what they would have been doing up there. We knocked on the door, intimidated and on our guard.

The brother guest master welcomed us to the guesthouse, which is part of the monastery. Once settled down in my room, I thought of introducing myself to the retreat leader, a Jesuit just like our chaplain. He asked me what I would like to do later.

"I would like to be a priest," I told him.

"Why not a Jesuit?" he asked me.

"What advantage would that give me? I would have to obey even more. What's the point?"

"And why not Trappist?"

"Even less than a Jesuit. I don't like that at all."

What I knew about it didn't stretch very far. Except for the brother guest master, whom I saw briefly, I had never met a Trappist before. What I did see was that dark little staircase, close to the office of the Jesuit father, which led to the scary depths of the monastery. I glanced at it before entering his office. This black hole made me think of a dark and gloomy trap. Oh no! Not Trappist, not in there! I didn't want to fall into this trap, which at this time did not appeal to me.

I went to my cell and started thinking about writing down the reasons why I envisioned becoming a priest. Suddenly the question came back to me. Why not a Trappist? Something unexpected happened then. It only lasted a fraction of a second, but it would orient my whole life. The question arose all of a sudden, like a light flashing in front of my eyes. No image, no symbol, no face. The light was in front of me, and I felt that if I wanted to say no, I shouldn't look at it, because if I looked at it, I wouldn't be able to look away, and I would have to follow it. But I felt totally free not to look. I could have closed my eyes. But at the same time, I didn't want to look away from that light. I couldn't avoid looking at it. I understood in a fraction of a second what the theologians have such a difficult time explaining: the coexistence of man's total freedom with God's almighty power to get what he wants. At the same time free and enthralled, I watched the light while being totally at peace. And I said yes. "Why not be a Trappist! Others have chosen this course; why not me?" That dual impression of the power of divine grace and of my total freedom remains vivid in me. One thing is certain, always the same truth: if I look at the light, I cannot avoid following it; I am free not to look at it, but I cannot prevent myself from doing it. It doesn't impose itself on me, and I could close myself away from it. The choice is mine, totally mine, totally personal. But it is stronger than I am.

Everything happened very simply. From then on, my mind was made up. I would be a Trappist. The turnaround was as complete as it was sudden and unexplainable. What I had been avoiding a couple of minutes ago, I now knew was right for me. My course was set from that moment, and I would never be able to push away this light that attracted me. Even in moments of darkness, I would keep going in the direction of that light. I had already started to go forward; I had made the first step.

Suddenly somebody knocked at my door. A fellow student dragged me from my thoughts. He had been tasked with asking each of us if we would like to talk to one of the priests who had been assigned to us while we were on retreat. I chose the name of a monk, Father Yves, at random from the list. Later I learned that he was a distant cousin of mine. He came a little later and asked me the usual question:

"What do you want to do later on in your life?"

"I want to be a Trappist!"

He was surprised by how forceful my answer was. No introduction, no detour—I was determined. Nevertheless, I still had not met a single Trappist. He was the first Trappist that I had ever talked to in my life, except for the brother porter, with whom I had exchanged some polite greetings.

Later on when I looked back on this essential experience, I confronted the explanations from the theologians. We have a tendency to place humankind and God on the same level, in competition with one other. If one is perceived to have done something, the other is assumed to have had no part in it—either God or humankind, never both. We can understand that some people reject what looks like a takeover by God, which prevents humans from exercising their free will. In fact, one is never as free as when one answers what feels like a call from God. All those who, like me, enter religious life had that experience one day or another, even if it was not so sudden and decisive the first time. The process is sometimes long, tortuous, tormented, and hesitant, but in the end there is that experience of giving in freely to an appeal. This is the decisive element of a vocation, but it doesn't prevent us from wondering about someone's aptitude for the monastic life, for that also comes into play.

Those who get married do it because they love each other. That doesn't mean that before committing to each other they don't have to think about each other's tastes, orientation, and temperament, in order to increase their chances for success. But the dynamic that drives them comes from somewhere other than analysis.

After my answer at Mont-des-Cats, Father Yves notified the novice master, who met with me and questioned me.

"One doesn't make that decision lightly," he told me. "It would be preferable to put on a piece of paper the reasons for and against that choice, by writing them in two columns so as to compare them."

I found it normal that he tried to understand this better, and I tried hard to do what he asked me. As far as I was concerned, I had for the moment only reasons in favor of that decision. But so that I would appear serious, I looked for drawbacks. I wrote "manual labor"! Who loves to work? In any case not me!

Right after our conversation, I felt embarrassed in front of the others. I found myself in their midst and not wanting to talk to them about what had just happened to me. They would not understand. A moment ago, I would not have understood either. They felt that I had something in the back of my mind and that I was hiding it from them, for I was no longer like I was before. They knew me as someone like themselves, but now there was something different. The atmosphere was no longer the same. I didn't tell them anything, since they would be informed soon enough. My secret made me feel that I was being observed like a stranger.

I went to the abbey church for the first time, and the surprise gave me another shock, because I didn't imagine a monastery church like that at all. It looked nothing like a parish church. There were no benches or chairs, but instead stalls and lecterns along the walls. I looked over the place from a balcony reserved for visitors and retreatants. The monks were far away from us, occupying a large space below us. The ambiance, the architecture, and the disposition of objects were all totally foreign to me. It was a different world that materialized before my eyes. "That's a monastery's church?" I wondered.

Nevertheless, at the same time, I seemed to recognize the place. I observed in silence.

"That's strange. I have seen this somewhere. I know this place."

This was strange, because it was the first time that I had come to Mont-des-Cats, but nevertheless I recognized this place. Was it already mine? I was having a type of fundamental experience, without ever having thought about it, which was to recognize the place, to identify the location where someone has to live in order to feel at peace. For me, this was it.

"Write in two columns, on one side the reasons for entering the monastery and on the other side the reasons against," the novice master, Father Francis, a smiling man, had told me. He returned later and asked for my paper. I gave it to him, shaking inside, wondering what his impression would be.

"But," he said, "you did not draw any conclusions or indicate which column wins?"

"Me? I don't need to draw two columns to know what I want. It is for you that I completed this assignment."

He smiled and told me that he would talk to the father abbot.

That evening and the whole next day, I reflected on the series of coincidences that had led me to this unforeseen course of events, from the Jesuit whom I met in the street, to the missed train, and to the buddy who kept giving me his advice for two hours: "We shouldn't take the wrong door—Oh no, we shouldn't!" And in the end, the question from this priest preaching the retreat. The others realized that I was troubled and maybe attracted to the religious life. I was the one who fell, where I had been warned that there was danger. But I didn't see any obstacle anymore. They spied on me discreetly. The father novice master told me that there was a substantial difference between becoming a Trappist and becoming a priest.

"These are two totally different things," he explained to me. "The monks' way of life may not suit all priests. But we will have time to think about the appropriate direction for you."

He wanted to test and try me. Back home, I couldn't wait to return to the monastery. It started to matter in my life, and I thought about it often. It was love at first sight. I was not yet sixteen, and already I could not envision my future without it. When I was working on a task, my mind wandered to the monastery. And when I was not working on something, there was always a detail, a word, or a confused feeling that made me think about it. The monastery comforted me and, most of all, invited me to search deep within myself for what was hiding there. Why was it so important to me? It relieved my loneliness, it brightened my days, and it gave me a feeling of security and wisdom that I did not find anywhere else. Every time the thought of Mont-des-Cats and the monks crossed my mind, I experienced a feeling of happiness as if I had just uncovered a treasure.

Many months went by before I got the opportunity to go back to the monastery. The first time was the following year at the start of Lent. I joined another group going on retreat, and I asked to stay one more day by myself. But without the group activities, I was bored out of my mind. The charm was broken. I couldn't stay in one place, nothing appealed to me anymore, and the decor and the monks all made the time seem endless. An abbey is not exciting. I should have left with my buddies instead of trying to be smart by staying all alone like a poor soul.

This Ash Wednesday, forty days before Easter, in accordance with the custom of the time, the monks walked barefoot into the church to receive the ashes on top of their heads: "You are dust, and to dust you shall return." From the balcony, I observed the perfect choreography of their movements. I was impressed, and something struck me again and seduced me during the service of Compline at the end of the day. The captivating chant of the *Salve Regina* resonated beneath the vault.[10] A solo voice started to

---

10. We know that the famous painter Alfred Manessier found faith and his own truth when hearing the *Salve Regina* at La Trappe an evening in 1943.

sing the first words, and the whole community followed with incredible power, fifty voices calling on the Mother of Christ in our valley of tears. Only the statue of the Virgin was lit, and all eyes were drawn to it, with everything else remaining in shadow.

I could barely distinguish the monks. I presumed they were all standing, turned towards that light, strange, white, and motionless shapes, impenetrable, singing and praying. Where had they come from? What personal adventure brought each of them here? I saw men who had given up everything and who continued to do so, raising the clamor of their hope towards heaven from their earthly exile. I was moved. Then nothing! Everything stopped! The light was turned off and everything went back to an even deeper mystery. The great monastic silence overtook everyone and everything, even as the inimitable tones of the last chant echoed. The Trappists left in single file and disappeared behind the walls. Where were they going? Which life goes on?

When I returned home my reflections continued with a deeper consciousness. You can get bored in a monastery. You are certainly bored there if everything is not centered on faith. Did I believe during the days I was there? I went back to the monastery another time, attracted by something that I could not explain. I was invited to come down from the balcony and sit in the choir with the monks. I discovered that the atmosphere was a new one for me, formed by their presence and the strength of their voices. The stalls were different from a bench. These trials told me something more about their customs. The novice master did not hide from me the fact that it is never easy to undertake this journey. The dreams were always overtaken by reality. The beautiful light of that first day could not hide this from me.

I carefully told my parents what I was doing at the monastery, and it didn't take them long to understand my intentions. They were not opposed to it; on the contrary, they respected my choice, perhaps being proud, but also conscious of the sacrifice that they would have to make. "We won't see you anymore," they said.

I talked mainly with my mother. We didn't see much of our father, because he left early for the plant, and we went to sleep early in the evening. Nevertheless, he insisted on coming home for lunch, and we had to hurry to sit down as soon as he parked his bicycle in the hallway. He often left without touching the dessert.

One day I visited the scouts' chaplain, who sometimes criticized me for being too withdrawn socially and not much of a leader. I told him of my intention to become a Trappist.

"So that was it!" he shouted. "Now I understand! You are following your temperament."

Is that bad? No, but temperament does not explain vocation. Not all those who have the same personality traits that I have become Trappists. Others who are very outgoing do become Trappists.

My sister Geneviève got married in October 1945. I was almost sixteen. Her radiant happiness forced me to wonder once again about my future. "Do you want to renounce that whole life?" I asked myself. "Do you want to renounce the joys of matrimony? How can you be sure that you won't regret it?" That wasn't all. My brother-in-law twisted the knife delicately, approaching me with self-assurance, like someone who knew life: "Your project is a first-class funeral!" he grinned. "Poor buddy, do you really want to bury yourself there?"

I tried to argue with him a bit, but my heart wasn't in it and my reasons did not get through to him. Why would I want to bury myself? What a thought! I wanted to live, and I felt that one could do this fully in a monastery. Ultimate paradox: as time went on I traveled much more than he did. But we didn't know that then, neither he nor I. A few months later my oldest brother also decided to get married. Was my ideal not based on illusions? Was life not going to bring me back to reality? Always, always, the memory of the white light, so soft and attractive, followed me, a symbol of freedom and grace, but it did not reappear. I didn't talk about it with anyone. But after that moment, I didn't see myself anywhere other than in a cloistered life, of which I still knew almost nothing. Inside, I was ready. Everything in me answered that call. Where was the idea of sacrifice? It was a joy. Others decided to give up everything to pursue a different vocation. For me, my vocation was God and the search for God in this particular condition.

A few days after my brother's engagement dinner, I entered Mont-des-Cats, the evening of September 28, 1947. My parents, afraid of being too emotional and probably out of respect for a vocation in the face of which they felt very small, let me go alone. My uncle the physician, who had a car, accompanied me to the doors of the abbey. The one who leaves pursues his dream; he is full of hope, even if he suffers from being separated from his loved ones. His intention creates in himself a dynamism that carries him forward; he flies. But the parents do not have the dreams to comfort themselves, so they experience the departure of their child more painfully, because they only experience the separation side of it. We impose on them a sacrifice that is harder to endure. Was it the son or the father, Abraham, who was more tormented, when they walked for three days on the way to the mountain to which God was calling them for a heart-breaking offering, the sacrifice of the son by his father's hand? Luckily, the sacrifice, as we know, never took place (Gen 24). Similarly, our parents seem to find us all over again when they come and visit us. Sometimes they feel even closer to us. God cannot be outdone when it comes to generosity.

CHAPTER FOUR

THE GATES OF SILENCE

When I passed through the gates of the monastery, I knew inside that I would never leave. What made me happy was the belief that I had found my path. Oh, yes, I was happy—the community could still reject me, but I barely thought about that, and I was determined to do whatever it took so that they would never consider it. I felt as though I was already fulfilled, as if I had just earned a high grade or a reward.

Luckily, I was still totally unaware of the details of the Trappists' way of life, because if I had been familiar with it I might have been frightened. I might have started doubting, if not for the overly optimistic presumption that I would be able to face them. These details might have been scary from the outside, but they could only be understood inside the cloister, for which they were conceived, and I really had not been warned about them. In the meantime, what pleased me was to be there, and I savored each moment that I was there, barely troubled by my shyness. The unfamiliar surroundings troubled me less than I had imagined.

"I was also impatient for happiness," said Father Francis, the novice master. "Why did I become a monk? I wanted to be happy." I felt the same way. He didn't say anything more. I hadn't thought about it, but that was exactly it. We understood each other about that word. Impatient for something. One does not enter the monastery to be unhappy. My parents felt sad and were afraid for me. Were they right to let me go? The author Pascal said, "Everybody wants to be happy, even those who are about to hang themselves."[1] In my mind, God was linked to the possibility of feeling happy, on this earth and forever. Now and forever.

"Yes, it will work," I repeated to them. I was sure I would be fine in the abbey.

They didn't hesitate anymore, convinced of my determination by my insistence on talking about it. I was not looking for problems. I did not want to complicate my life with ascetic exploits. To meet God without further delay, that's what I wanted, a God of happiness and joy who is waiting for us now. I put all my confidence in a confused and maybe naïve intuition, which the novice master kept examining as he did during our first meetings.

"Each evening we sing these words of the psalm in the liturgy of Compline: 'Many, Lord, are asking: Who will bring us happiness? Let the light of your face shine on us. Who will bring us happiness?'" (Ps 4:6).

Father Francis was still a young man who didn't intend to abuse me with penances and interrogations. He commented, "Saint Benedict only asked one question of the future monks, those who still didn't know that they would become monks but were anonymous in the crowd: 'Who is the man who loves life and wants to see happy days?'" (RB Prol. 15).[2] I was that young man who loved life and only wanted happy days.

The mystery of his experience touched me, but he would only tell me a few words about it. Our only goal in the *trappe* was to live before God. This truth made me happy because it was an absolute. I talked about that with him. Everything looked easy

---

1. {Blaise Pascal, *The Provincial Letters, Pensées, and Scientific Treatises,* trans. Thomas M'Crie, W. F. Trotter, and Richard Scofield, Great Books of the Western World 33 (Chicago, London, and Toronto: Encyclopaedia Britannica, Inc., 1952), 169–352, no. 425, at 243–44.}

2. {Saint Benedict, *The Rule of St. Benedict in English* (Collegeville, MN: Liturgical Press, 1981), 58.8. Also available online at http://www.osb.org/rb/text/toc.html#toc.}

to me beforehand since I was there for God. I still didn't know anything about the mysteries and the battles, the joys, maybe the regrets or the illusions that existed behind these walls and these gates, these fences, and these windows. Nevertheless, I believed that if I walked without fear, I would discover what I was looking for. I was impatient to learn. A penitent who wants to suffer? That was definitely not me. I was way too delicate, or even sensitive, to expose myself to extraordinary dangers that attacked everybody's body, mind, and imagination. Moreover, I had no desire to draw attention to myself. I would be a postulant for a month, wearing my own clothes, among the novices and the temporarily professed. I didn't feel as though I was confronting a test or a challenge, but rather coming home and feeling good. Why would I think about getting out of this?

At that time, I did not understand what was happening to me very well. I let myself be guided in the monastery. Yesterday I was at home with my parents, and today I discovered myself transplanted to another universe, hoping, maybe hastily, that it would be forever. I took the step, the big leap that separated me from the world. Most novices, if they are not where they belong, will notice it sooner rather than later and leave during the first months. I could not imagine that this dream of perfection and union with God would end with me holding a piece of luggage because of a disappointment that would force me to leave. They would show me the door mercifully. No, unthinkable. It would be as if heaven were driving me away.

But if I stayed, everything would happen two years from now. On that day, a monk would ask me to leave the chapter room, where the whole community was gathered. The fifty brothers would vote. According to a custom meticulously described in the *Book of Usages of the Order of Cîteaux*, which I would get to know, the father abbot would instruct the prior to distribute three balls of different colors to each monk. The white one would be a vote for my admission for three more years, the black one for an immediate rejection, and the gray one for those who had no opinion or did not want to express it. The prior would tip over the urn placed on the table, showing that it was empty. Then, in order of seniority, each brother would drop his vote into the urn, trying not to show which ball he had chosen.

In those days, we believed that a monk did not have a past anymore. All those brothers with whom I would spend time should remain partially strangers to me. I would ignore their exact origins or maybe certain past personality traits. If I wanted to talk, it would be only with the novice master, the sub-master, and the father abbot, or, in his absence, with the prior. My past, my life, and my intentions were nobody else's business. I was only introduced briefly. Nobody explained to me who all these monks were. It was inconceivable that we would exchange impressions or disclose our tastes or thoughts. Silence was dedicated to God, prayer, and meditation.

Everything was mysterious in this house: the customs, the clothing, the schedules, the tasks. Was it because life there was turned towards the mystery, and that life's end was a mystery? I couldn't explain what attracted me the most, or fascinated me more or caused me to worry, and I did not make the effort to question myself every half hour. That wasn't what interested me. There was a road, and I wanted to follow it. I would also have to learn how to communicate with hand gestures, just like a deaf-mute, by using a coded language to say *table, eat,* or *rain,* and to avoid by any means the buzzing of words that traveled in the rooms or hallways, as well as any other noise. As soon as you passed the door, you could feel that the silence and peace of the cloister were totally offered to God. The anxieties and apprehensions that I might have had disappeared when I passed the threshold. Here, nothing bad could happen to me.

I was stripped of all objects coming from the outside world. To keep a book or a letter, we needed an approval. From then on, nothing would belong to me anymore. If I wanted to write I would need authorization, and if someone wrote to me, the letter would be given to me already opened.

The sub-master, Brother Sébastien, who was thirty-two years old, helped me not to get lost and initiated me and the other novices into the customs, which were mostly common sense:

"Here are the desks where each monk puts down some personal items, books, notebooks, letters," Brother Sébastien explained to me. "This one will be yours."

"I didn't know that we were entitled to one."

"Discipline is very strict in that regard. A monk who opens someone else's desk to take out a book commits a serious offense, even if it is only to know the title or the subject. For the novices, it might be a cause for dismissal."

"What is true for books is even more so for personal writings," he added. "If you find some anywhere in the house, you need to bring it to the superior without reading it. You absolutely don't own anything personally, and our personal writings are shown to the superiors if they ask for them. We can only use the things put at our disposal. Even with words we will never claim anything as ours. We won't say *my book* or *my table*, but rather *our book* and *our table*."

He looked at me to gauge if I understood well, reassured that he only had to give a simple example.

"We will not say *our head* or *our hand*, or that *we have committed* that offense if you are the only one who has committed that offense."

He led me to the father master, after having shown me the scriptorium, a common study room with long tables and school desks without drawers, like those I had known in high school, with shelves alongside where only the most useful books for our formation were kept. The novice master was one of the few monks who had a desk with drawers. On the way, we passed a brother with his hands tucked in his large sleeves. The two greeted each other in silence by bowing their heads ever so slightly and smiling, and I too answered the greeting.

"Every time we meet, we greet each other like this," Brother Sébastien told me later. "Not during the great silence of the night, which lasts from Compline until the next morning around 7 a.m. No greeting in the church or the refectory, nor in the dormitory or in the workplace. Since we are in a community, you will see that there are a lot of places where we pass each other. A monastery is so big."

I was not sure if I should ask him for his evaluation of my greeting of the monk whose name I didn't even know, but he reassured me before I could open my mouth: "It wasn't exactly how it's supposed to be, but don't worry."

What is essential is different. It becomes second nature. You seek to reach a state of permanent prayer while at the same time accomplishing the necessary acts of your daily life without thinking about it. Every minute is set, every situation is planned. It is not a yoke of obligations, but it is the certainty that you will neither be distracted nor surprised whatever may happen, that you will never wander away from your prayer. The Rule provides for everything to lead to God. Remember always that we are here only for God.

When it came down to it, that's what was wonderful. I was drawn into a movement leading to the invisible, and when I disliked something it did not stop me, for I was convinced that others before me had faced the same trials and confronted them if they had any significance.

"A light bow with a slight shoulder movement is appropriate in certain cases," he added. "There are two kinds of bows and three kinds of prostrations. The light bow is just a slight bow of the head. You do this, for example, when hearing the name of Jesus or Mary, except if you're kneeling in the church. The deep bow is done by crossing the arms on the knees in front of the abbot or the Holy Sacrament, or at the end of the psalms when we mention the Holy Trinity."

Sometimes we bowed deeply on the "articles." I didn't understand very well what that meant. It is an old word that means the finger joints: you kneel with your hands on the ground.

The bell sounded suddenly to call us to the office of None in midafternoon. Brother Sébastien explained to me that I would have time, if God called me, to discover the rest later. He did not hurry to get to church. The bell rang five minutes in advance, so we were not late.

"I will teach you how to kneel, how to sit in church with a cloak when you have received yours in a couple of weeks, and how to make the Sign of the Cross," he continued while sorting out envelopes:

> You also need to know how to kneel for a long time, with a straight upper body, without leaning too much on the stalls. I saw that you were using the hand opposite the altar to lower or raise your seat. You always need to use the other hand. The little board under the folding seat we call the *misericord*, which enables Benedictines to sit while appearing to be standing up, but not us. We only lean on it in certain bows. Think about all the hours of wakefulness it has represented over the centuries in order to have earned that name. The misericords were generally beautifully sculpted and sometimes represented a devil, the only one on which you can sit without scruples! Out of mutual respect, we don't say *the father* or *the brother*, but *my brother* or *my father*. You will be my Brother Gérard.

In the cloister, my new brothers headed without any hurry toward the church. My Brother Sébastien left me to take his place in a stall, and I sat in a stall in the lower choir where the novices were gathered. "The hand on the side of the altar to raise and lower my seat. Touch it only when I sit down," I told myself as I watched those across the nave. I could not seem to find the correct page in the large book laid out in front of me. I was embarrassed to let my neighbor show me the correct prayer. With my concern about what to do, was there still time to pray? I had a quick look at the tabernacle; that would be my prayer for this fifteen-minute office. Already, the monks were leaving, and they carried me along in their precise and skillful movements, the workings of which I did not understand. There were muffled sounds of woolen cowls and innumerable soles. They walked in single file on one side of the cloister, while the novices went up to the novitiate, where they were assigned their work. There were about ten novices.

After a couple of days, I had confirmed that all that had been said about the austerity of the Trappists was at the same time true and false. I already knew that from my previous stays at the monastery. Contrary to what the legend said, the monks did not say to each other while passing in the hallways, "Brother, we have to die." They didn't talk to each other. They didn't meet up to discuss this or that. That was not the case for Father Francis, who needed to talk to me a lot and listen to me even more to make sure that the taste for solitude that brought me to this desert was not generated by a lack of reflection, or by frivolity, or by something too human. He pointed out the questions I needed to ask myself.

"It is not good to look down on earthly things," he said. "There are some excellent and precious ones. They simply have an end. Even a beautiful face carries the signs of its own frailty, of its own obsolescence. Even a love that is said to be eternal will end sooner or later at the end of time. The rich are only rich temporarily; geniuses die as do idiots. Nothing can resist this. Everything human is branded with an end. How could we not be sent back to somewhere else?"

Our one-on-one conversations were simple and intense, but I obeyed everything, and they were conducted with confidence. If I can say anything I want, if I have to say it, I realize that these conversations centered more and more around the description of the Rule and the Cistercian tradition, as well as the steps of the inner spiritual journey.[3] During these conversations, I learned that

3. Later, this spiritual journey will be described in the Constitutions of the Order (Const C.3.): "Through God's Word the monks are trained in a discipline of heart and action to be responsive to the Holy Spirit and so attain purity of heart and a continual mindfulness of God's presence . . . . The monks follow in the footsteps of those whom, in times past, God called into the desert to engage in spiritual warfare. As citizens of heaven, they become strangers to worldly behaviour. Living in solitude and silence they aspire to that interior quiet in which wisdom is born. They practise self-denial in order to follow Christ. Through humility and obedience, they struggle against pride and the rebellion of sin. In simplicity and labour they seek the blessedness promised to the poor. By generous hospitality they share with their fellow-pilgrims the peace and hope which Christ has freely given. . . . The monastery is an expression of the mystery of the Church . . ." {OCSO website: http://www.ocso.org/resources/law/constitutions-and-statutes/.}

Father Francis loved to sail and read André Gide. Notwithstanding the purity of its language and a certain spiritual dimension, Gide's *The Fruits of the Earth* made him remember, dissatisfied, a phrase from the prophet Isaiah: "As when a hungry man dreams he is eating and awakens with his hunger not satisfied" (Isa 29:8).

Except for a few moments of hesitation and clumsiness, of fear of getting lost in the hallways or of not being up to par, I came to a new conclusion: life was in front of me, with an endless number of precious hours and minutes that I would spend in a context, an atmosphere that suited me, and at a rhythm that was compatible with my nature. I did not feel that I was a prisoner of God, or that I had subjected myself to an avalanche of boring duties, or renounced my liberty, but rather that I was incredibly lucky to be able to do what corresponded to my deepest desires.

The amazing thing that was offered to me within the confines of the meticulously maintained buildings was the opportunity to take part in the life of a community in which everything was organized to help me move forward in my inner search. Nothing here would ever be mine, but I was welcome to have everything here at my disposal. What more could I ask for?

"Some enter the monastery in doubt and affliction," the novice master told me:

> They hang in there for months or sometimes for years before being sure that they can persevere. Nevertheless, their vocation is not any less strong than that of others who sang or flew but had a deep-seated anxiety. To a certain extent, you're lucky to adapt so quickly, but you will have to hold on for fifty, sixty years or more. Are there stages in becoming a Trappist? Do you accept little by little going from an easy and free life to one of obedience and austerity, or does it happen all at once? There are no rules. Each case is different, brutal conversions, sudden transitions from one extreme to the other, very slow adaptations. Most often the monk passes through a number of stages and usually reaches a more advanced level each time. But there are also short-lived failures, discouragements, sometimes setbacks. That happens in every Trappist's life, and it is part of a normal

spiritual life. You will have to learn how to manage these problems with me and later, if you become professed, with other monks who will be walking next to you in these trials. They cannot be avoided. There are no exceptions.

The picture was not encouraging, but I could not envision these troubles. Instead of confronting trials head on, I only had to look around me to realize that there were treasures to enjoy. If there were difficult moments to come, studies to complete, sacrifices to make, so be it: I didn't take these as challenges. I only needed to strip myself progressively of all these worries. The end would be worth it.

"Six hours of prayers a day, sometimes seven, then the *lectio divina*, as we say, which means an in-depth reading of the Bible and of spiritual authors for three more hours. Manual labor varies, depending on the season, between four and six hours a day," continued the novice master. I noticed how his softness contrasted with this harsh program.

He looked me deep in the eyes.

"That's what is waiting for you if you stay," he told me.

That was what was waiting for me.

"Until the last day," he insisted.

Nothing else to hope for until the last day, no novelty, no improvement. No social progress here, no revolution. About ten hours a day were devoted to prayer in one form or another, in a group or separately, in the church or in other places, including reading, *lectio divina*. You had to do what it took, if you wanted to become a contemplative. A great fast had just started two weeks before I arrived on September 29. It started on September 15, the day after the Feast of the Exaltation of the Holy Cross, and lasted until Easter, six or seven months depending on the year. I was immediately immersed in it, notwithstanding a slight dispensation from the food and the schedule because of my youth.

"Until they reach twenty-one years of age, novices only get up at 4 a.m., and receive one more portion of food in the refectory," Father Francis confirmed to me. "In the morning, we eat about three ounces of bread with coffee or chicory, sometimes grilled barley in some monasteries. It is called the *frustulum*. The brother refectorian uses a balance to measure the portions. Not that long ago, in the nineteenth century, we had only one meal a day in winter, but in the middle of this twentieth century we may be weaker. I have known some old Trappists who withstood deprivations for their entire lives that today would knock us out. Since you are still young, you will be getting 'relief,' meaning that from time to time you will receive some butter or two eggs."

They had already given me some. I tried hard not to rush to swallow, but I was quite happy. I didn't know if the others were watching me while eating their smaller portions, but I didn't think so. You didn't look up while sitting at the table, and my neighbors didn't seem to bother with my dish, except at the beginning to make sure I was not missing anything, and I did the same for them. On Sundays, the *frustulum* became *mixte*, meaning that the portion increased to six ounces of bread, carefully weighed by the brother refectorian. I also got milk.

Already, I was back in the church, and already we left the church. Then the bell called for us to return to church, and I realized how fast time passed by. I thought that I would finish a chapter of a book assigned to me, and already it was time for manual labor. Noon. Meal after a twenty-minute liturgy. The monks left the church behind the abbot and walked in single file slowly toward the refectory. I took my spot in the single file, without a word, serious, meditative. You only heard a rare squeaking of the shoes or rustle of the habits. I had only talked to a very few Trappists. I didn't know who they were, but I quickly learned some first names. All these faces and these silhouettes were still mixed up in my mind. If someone had asked me for my impressions, I would have said that the community existed, that it was alive, that it walked, that it sang, that it loved me (I thought), that it welcomed me as one of its own, but that it still appeared to me as a new world, of which I still needed to discover the secret. I suspected that many surprises were awaiting me, and I walked with confidence among all these monks.

From the long line of peaceful men, walking towards the refectory without any hurry, without one passing the other, all with their hoods on their heads, emerged a strange simplicity and power, undefinable, which contained something even bizarre, something supernatural, just like the Gregorian chants that they had just finished, which were still resonating inside my head, notwithstanding the silence hanging over the whole abbey. I felt like a child among them, but they were like children with the power of men, of humble men who sang inside and who played and ran in their hearts. I soon noticed that a number of them had a sense of humor and could laugh, while others were more reserved. I couldn't read anything in their faces. I couldn't say that the silence here during the day was the same as the one you would encounter at night in other places. I was struck by the peace that was present everywhere. These monks seemed to walk with measured steps from a world of prayer in the choir to another world of *oratio* in front of their dishes.

Before entering the refectory, we first washed our hands, or rather the tips of our fingers. These gestures were not improvised, but were carefully considered, defined by the Cistercian usages. Each one took his place and made a simple bow toward the large crucifix hung on the wall. The superior made a discreet nod to the cantor, who started the *Benedicite,* which we all continued until the *Gloria Patri,* during which we bowed. Those strong voices conveyed the feeling that nothing was more important at this moment than praising God. Whenever they raised their voices, they insistently expressed the same thing. The sound was not identical to the one that vibrated in the nave of the church or in the choir, but it struck me just the same. Father Abbot blessed the reader, one of the monks who walked up some steps to the lectern to read a passage of the Gospel, and then from another book while we ate. We had dinner at lunch time and supper in the evening.

We sat down with our hands on the edge of the table, our large sleeves covering them up. It was still not time to eat. After the reader read the first sentence, the abbot gave us another nod. Everyone looked left and right to make sure his immediate neighbor wasn't missing anything and then unfolded his napkin. A monk cannot ask for anything for himself, except for bread, water, or salt. I tried to observe the ceremonial without being seen to avoid committing any mistakes, with an appetite much tempered by these intimidating beginnings. But this wouldn't last. Years later I heard some stories that will make you smile. One story told of the monk who found a small mouse on his dish. His neighbors didn't seem to have noticed. So he made a sign to the brother refectorian and told him, "My neighbors do not have any mice!"

In the refectory, every detail was set. When we drank, we held the bowl with both hands by the two handles. Holding it with only one hand would be a lapse in discipline. At the end of the first day's meal, I was somewhat behind the others. I was so preoccupied with putting away my dish and silverware that I knocked over the bottle of vinegar at the very moment when the father abbot walked by me. I started to believe that after this embarrassing moment, nothing else so regrettable could happen to me, and so I was cured of my shyness forever, having reached such a pinnacle of clumsiness on the first day! They were lenient, and I didn't receive any penance. Later on, if I dropped something during a meal, I would have to walk across the refectory in front of everybody and prostrate myself in front of the superior, and while nobody would see or comment on anything, dozens of eyes would follow my every movement. This ceremony seemed to infringe upon my spontaneity, but it would enable me slowly to develop my inner freedom.

After the meal, we returned to church with our hoods up while singing Psalm 51: "Have mercy on me, God, in your goodness; in your abundant compassion, blot out my offense." The rigor of that observance struck me less than the serenity of the monks, always this serenity that transformed the movements and the silence. They all looked happy. In the songs, in work or study, they looked like people who had just heard good news. Were they really happy? Or were they forcing themselves? Were they putting on an act? That idea came to me vaguely, but I was too involved in my formation to make a distinction between what is felt and what is the result of the will or the routine.

"Attending the offices regularly plays a major part in asceticism," the novice master explained to me. "It is a work, a great work, says our father Saint Benedict, a service, a *pensum* that requires effort but also brings joy" (RB 19–20).

I couldn't imagine very well what standing up or kneeling down for an extended time could have to do with emptiness in our hearts or with the distress of our whole being, and even less with what the old manuals on the ascetic life called the "disgust of God," in which one's being seems to be abandoned by heaven even though stretched to the limit by its efforts. I couldn't imagine what it would be like if our being suddenly didn't know what it was doing or where it was going, where the brothers didn't look like brothers anymore, and where God seemed to betray his own call. I listened with enchantment to the praises in Latin. I didn't have the impression of being among saints, but among men at peace who would not want to leave the *trappe* if they were asked. You would have to throw them out, and then they would crawl back through the windows again. Of course, you needed to have the vocation. A missionary who attended our long liturgies for November 2, All Souls Day, told us that it was more exhausting than being bounced around through the jungle.

"I would like to know if it is contemplation that gives them that appearance," I said one day to Father Francis. "I feel good here."

Contemplation! Am I a contemplative? How many among us are? I have almost always had duties that were time consuming. With regard to contemplation I've always felt like a man thrown in a swimming pool with slippery sides, where he can't hold on to anything, doesn't have footing, and cannot swim. The only way to manage it is to take care of others. So as not to drown, you need to enter resolutely into Matthew 25:31-46 on acts of mercy. The monk is a man of solitude always surrounded by others, all the others he meets in the monastery. The first signs of true contemplation arise out of this fraternity, which offers unlimited opportunities to lose your egoism, your individualism. God doesn't ask us to look him in the eyes until we can grasp the look in the others' eyes.

Father Francis seemed to have drawn from a long-term observation of the monastic life a knowledge that intrigued me. I was even more puzzled when he told me that one of the first tasks of a monk is to forgive, forgive everything. How could men so dignified and wise have anything to be forgiven? I would discover over time that we were no angels. Our characters conflicted with one another, and weaknesses were hard to avoid. "After so many years," Father Francis would confide at the end of his life, "I am convinced that the vitality of a monastic community is measured neither by the quality of its liturgy nor by its apparent influence or following; it will be measured by the quality of the reconciliation and the relation among brothers. What God has in his heart has to come into ours: mercy."

"Our father abbot will decide if you can be admitted to the novitiate," he warned me one morning with a confident look in his eyes. "You will have to do a full eight days' retreat."

He held a new book in his hands and offered it to me like a sumptuous gift.

"Father Abbot Combes has just published a critical edition of the letters of Saint Thérèse of Lisieux.[4] Her Carmelite sisters are only giving out advance copies, maybe incomplete ones, but you will discover the spirituality of the saint in what are probably the best words written about it today."

I read these letters from cover to cover during my retreat. I had the sense of recognizing my own aspirations in certain passages in which the author, until then totally unknown to me, described her love for God and her desire for union with Christ. Her language was so simple that the pursuit of perfection in

---

4. {Saint Thérèse of Lisieux, *Collected Letters of Saint Thérèse of Lisieux*, ed. André Combes, trans. F. J. Sheed (New York: Sheed and Ward, 1949).}

the smallest things of daily life seemed to be within everyone's reach. This was the first great author I encountered at the *trappe*. Later Saint Thérèse would introduce me to the doctrine of Saint Bernard, because their evangelical teaching was similar, although worded in culturally different terms.

On the day of my taking the habit, November 1, 1947, Father Francis made me wait at the door of the chapter room where the community was gathered. I was very moved. He told the superior that a postulant wished to become a novice in the Order and then came and got me. I walked forward shakily, with everyone looking at me, and then knelt down and prostrated myself in the middle of the room.

"What are you seeking?" asked the abbot.

"The mercy of God and of the Order."

He received me, and when I had gotten up, he addressed me with an exhortation:

"Are you prepared to follow the Rule and to persevere in your vocation?" he concluded.

"Yes, Father," I said in accordance with the formula I had learned, "with the grace of God and the help of your prayers."

"May God finish what he has started in you."

Part of this dialogue was in Latin, and the community punctuated it with a powerful "Amen." All of them stood up, heads uncovered, while the abbot received a white stole from one of the religious and blessed my future vestments, which were lying on a table between his seat and the seat of the prior. I knelt down. The cantor started a canticle that the two choirs sang in alternating parts as they took off my jacket, in a symbolic move, and put on me the white habit and the white cloak of the novices, the latter being a long coat of the same color. This change of clothing signified the change that was supposed to take place within me.

"May God make you devoid of the old man and of his actions," said Father Abbot, "and may you take on the new man created by God in justice and sainthood."

I kept the name Brother Gérard but changed my patron saint, replacing the one of my birth, Saint Gérard Majella, an eighteenth-century Redemptorist who died at the age of twenty-nine, with a monk of our Order, a brother of Saint Bernard.

The gentleness of the father novice master and his warm attention in all circumstances did not seem to fit his duty, as written in the Rule of Saint Benedict, to warn me of "the hardships and difficulties that I will face leading to God." I got along well with him, and there was a mutual sympathy. We understood each other. He explained to me little by little everything I had to know. The "painful and austere" realities described in the Rule, which enable us to reach God, were still a mystery to me. While insisting on these realities, the Rule also says that as we move forward, the heart expands and we start running in the infinite sweetness of love. I rejoiced that they hadn't made me wait four to five days at the door of the monastery as Saint Benedict suggested (RB 58.3).

Saint Benedict did not shy away from harshness in putting vocations to the test: "Do not grant newcomers to the monastic life an easy entry. If he has shown himself patient in bearing his harsh treatment and difficulty of entry, and has persisted in his request, then he should be allowed to enter and stay in the guest quarters for a few days" (RB 58.1-4). It has always been the monastic tradition not actively to look for candidates or to do any promotion. Even today, if inquirers about this life are welcomed with kindness, our constitution points out that we shouldn't give them "easy entry." Regular visits to the monastery enable them to get acquainted with the community, but they will only be received if they show sufficient maturity, a spiritual disposition, and also good health, which is required for community exercises.

The principle has not changed since Saint Benedict: "After two months have elapsed," he says, "let this rule be read straight through to him" (RB 58.9). The Rule has a prologue and seventy-three short chapters, of which the last provides that the practice of sainthood is not set out in this Rule (RB 73.6). Benedict says that if the candidate promises perseverance in his stability, he is to be taken back to the novitiate (RB 58.11) and again thoroughly tested in patience, meaning without conceding him anything but without going beyond his strength and his spiritual development (RB

58.11-12): "After six months have passed, the rule is to be read to him, so that he may know what he is entering" (RB 58.12). If he accepts, he is taken back to the novices, and then four months later, the process starts all over again. At the end of this new reading, if "he promises to observe everything and obey every command given him, he will be received into the community" (RB 58.14).

In practice, these steps are spread out over many years. A few months as a postulant are followed by two years in the novitiate. Then follow the temporary vows, which last at least three years. During the novitiate, the candidate takes part in the monastic life, and the community observes him to see if he has grown spiritually. If "he truly seeks God and is zealous for the Work of God, obedience and humiliations, and is suited for living correctly, in solitude and silence, the community relationships that constitute Cistercian life within the Order, as prescribed in our constitution" (Const C.51), the abbot may admit him to a new step, the temporary profession.[5]

Even if certain things were hard for me, nothing seemed to be able to stop me. The consecrated life as a priest, which would not be an absolute and total gift of myself, seemed bland to me. I didn't feel that I was made for half-measures, and I never even considered it. As I would write to the abbot in my official request letter, "It seems to me that if I were in another less austere Order, I couldn't bear the idea that I was not offering everything to the good Lord." It was neither a feat nor a painful sacrifice, but an act in harmony with my inner self. My life was offered to someone, to God, to Jesus Christ. If I had to offer myself up, if I was called, then I wanted to do it without any concession, without any restriction. Behind the smiling and severe face of my novice master hid the imposing face of Saint Benedict, which I was able to discern better and better. It fascinated me and didn't scare me. The only thing I desired was to be his disciple.

5. {Simple vows and solemn vows: If after two years in the novitiate a candidate is accepted in the community, he pronounces simple vows and makes a temporary profession. After three years, if the community agrees, he will make a perpetual profession pronouncing solemn vows (Const C.51).}

Listening to my Father Francis was like listening to the patriarch of the Western monks and to all those who for the last fourteen centuries had collaborated in transmitting his experience to us. That experience fascinated me, and I wanted to know all about it, to live it without pulling back from any effort. Efforts? To tell the truth, it is important to let things happen, to let yourself be molded by the style of the monastic life itself. The goal is not to acquire something by force, but to consent to be conquered by love, by the grace of God who calls us.

You also need to learn to know yourself. The novice master was there to identify my good qualities, my weaknesses, and my motivations, and to teach me to see clearly in this bubbling and this fervor. "You don't become a monk," he said, "without knowing yourself, without controlling yourself, and without blossoming under God's sight. Persevere always. You might think too easily that you've already made it! Nature suggests so easily that it is gliding on high while our feet are still in the trenches!" Father Francis talked to me of the journey, but I didn't realize how long it would be. I had no concept. I was proceeding with an overflowing enthusiasm, almost like a ball bouncing down the road. Even if it didn't show, I was only trying to do well, and my only fear was not being able to do everything well that was expected of me.

Some jokes are told among the monks about those who embody mystical and ascetic lives without looking like it. The story goes, young monks look like saints but aren't. Middle-aged monks don't look like it, and in fact aren't, and old monks don't look like it anymore, but are! Notwithstanding their apparent faults, they have the true smile and the look of those who have walked with God for a long time and therefore appear so happy and light that everything looks easy to them.

On Monday, Wednesday, and Friday we took classes about the constitution and history of the Order, along with our usages, ceremonies, and sign language, with the goal of better understanding the Rule and the elements of our spiritual life. We occupied premises separate from those of the professed. The novices did not get assigned activities that might distract them from their formation or take all their time. But the formation program was neither scholarly nor academic. It was mainly concerned with teaching the novices how to integrate themselves into the life of a community that wanted to live a life dedicated to the search for God. We journeyed together, as a community. We didn't live as savages. We were in the monastery for God, not for the purpose of establishing an association of old bachelors. The fraternal cohesion was important and required an apprenticeship.[6]

What bothered me the most was perhaps our life in the dormitory. Each of us had a kind of alcove. They were lined up in two rows, each about seven feet long and five feet wide, with walls of plaster (or wood), barely higher than a monk standing up. No doors. Just a simple curtain to close them off, each one identified with a number and a name. The snoring noises traveled without hindrance, and—of course—those brothers always fell asleep first. However, you had to sleep fully dressed, as provided by the Rule, so that at two o'clock you could get up quickly and go to the church through the poorly lit cloister. For me this was really the most dreadful penance, especially in the summer, after days working in the fields and perspiring abundantly. This custom would be eliminated in 1969, and I wouldn't miss it. In my early days, the dormitory was not heated in the winter, and it often happened that the water in the font, placed at the entrance of our alcove, froze, despite the salt poured in it when it was blessed.

On the other hand, I was not troubled by the usage that we called the "Friday discipline." In the dormitory right after Vigils, we used small whips consisting of five ropes, each with five

---

6. The spirit of the Order is described in our Constitutions: "Since all the brothers are of one heart and one mind, they have everything in common. By bearing one another's burdens they fulfil Christ's law, participating in his sufferings in the hope of entering the kingdom of heaven" (Const C.3.1). "Each brother is to contribute to the upbuilding of fraternal relations especially by sharing with others the spiritual gifts he has received by God's manifold grace" (Const C.14.1). "The preservation of unity among the brothers depends on a sincere and mutual effort towards reconciliation" (Const 15.1).

knots, to hit our shoulders. We did this for about two minutes, the length of time needed to recite the *Miserere*. It warmed you up in the winter and enabled you to exercise a bit in the summer while bare chested. The practice, which dates back to the Middle Ages, was eventually abandoned and then picked up again in the nineteenth century. It was meant to unite the monk with the flagellation of Christ. But was it really a gesture of penance that helped us to get rid of our egoism and our pride? Too superficial and concerned with outward appearances, this practice would be abandoned once more. As Saint Peter Damian recommended in the eleventh century, "Rather scourge your spirit."[7]

Almost every week after his explanation of the Rule, the abbot held the chapter of faults in the chapter room. In this gathering, the members of the community confessed both their own shortcomings or mistakes and those of their neighbors. It did not cover their actual sins; it was not a confession that would normally happen in secrecy with a priest. Rather it concerned clumsiness or shortcomings as defined by customs or the Rule. We had to say where we erred, straightforwardly and without any vague allusions. But we had to conceal the deeper motive for that action. Certain blunders, like breaking a glass for example, could be the consequence of a simple distraction, irritation, or animosity. We didn't take these differences into account. The brother just said, "I broke a glass." By this custom, which conveyed both a certain solemnity and a constant examination of one's own conduct and that of the others, the community got to know, to test, and to improve itself. In the language of the *trappe*, to report someone was to point out to one's brother one of his shortcomings in front of the community. This monastic observance was meant not to satisfy someone's own rancor, but to carry out an act of mercy, a brotherly correction grounded in faith. Nevertheless, it could be offensive, because not all monks are thick skinned. Since Vatican II we have tried not to

---

7. {Peter Damian, *Letters* 2.56, trans. Owen J. Blum and Irven Resnick, Fathers of the Church, 7 vols. (Washington, DC: Catholic University of America Press, 1989), 61–68.}

remain on that trivial level, but it would take some time for us to find new forms of brotherly support that at the same time are more profound and more respectful of the other person.

When I was a novice, everything was regulated, from the place where you were supposed to stand to the way you moved around. In the cloister, a large square hallway built around a courtyard, where silence is absolute, you could not walk in the middle of the hall, but only along the walls, except when the community proceeded in a single file. Then the usages specified that we were to keep our hoods up, as well as in the dormitory, the refectory, and the bathrooms. Someone who doesn't have a vocation only wonders one thing, "Am I still allowed to breathe?" He is hemmed in on all sides. If he wonders this instead of having a feeling of incomparable freedom to run in the steps of the Lord without risking getting lost, it is probable that he lacks a vocation. He'll probably be worried, since he feels asphyxiated, strangled by the Rule, and he may think that he is being forced to confess mercilessly what he still doesn't know about himself but that he will discover sooner or later.

In fact, it is not brainwashing. The Rule leads you to get rid of your own egotism and to build up another, more authentic personality, which expresses the most intimate depths of yourself, when everything has been cleansed away, purified, and restored, and everything superfluous has been discarded. It is a systematic destruction of everything in your own will that is egotistical, narcissistic, and vain, a getting rid of your own will in the sense of a self-centered ownership. The objective is essential, but is it necessary to cut off any and all initiative in order to reach it? One could wish to keep more freedom in the exterior behavior without losing anything essential, and that is exactly what happened in the post-Vatican II reform.

Sometimes you might see a monk eating on the floor. He would sit down in the middle of the refectory with his dish and silverware, his bread and water carafe, with his hood on, the napkin laid out on his knees. It was neither sad nor grotesque. The kitchen server for the week, who brought out the food portions and cleaned up the tables, would bring him soup or vegetables, his portion of water and a dessert, but only after all the other brothers had been served. At that time, punishments in the refectory were relatively frequent. The simplest one required a monk to prostrate himself at the door. The one who was being punished would leave the church a few moments before the rest of the brothers so that he could lie on the ground waiting for the whole community to step over him as they entered the refectory. Another punishment involved asking your portion of food in mercy, which meant begging it from all the brothers. One day I gave a spoonful of my share to a brother who stretched out his bowl with both hands. There were already a few potatoes in the bowl. He moved from one brother to the other, kneeling down before each and then getting up to bow down. I got up to return his bow. To a certain extent, I was as touched as the punished brother, and we both felt that we had taken part in the same task of self-control and humble submission.

When I entered the novitiate, these humiliations, within the context of how they were experienced, did not give me the unbearable feeling of mortification that someone looking in from the outside might expect. Translated into the ordinary world, they would have been intolerable and often totally unfair. Within our walls, the successive rituals became accepted and necessary activities, which you would not seek out for pleasure, but which did not cause you a crucifying shame. After Vatican II, they would be eliminated without losing anything of the essence.

We did not live haunted by mistakes and punishments, by time schedules, or by intellectual or manual labor. At most, you could say that we lived in a universe where poverty, asceticism, and abstinence produced a system with a rather strict military flavor, but with a lot more love. We were reminded of a visit of Marshal Bugeaud[8] to the *trappe*: "Our soldiers in their quarters are

8. {Thomas Bugeaud, Marquis de la Piconnerie, Duc d'Isly (1784–1849), was a marshal of France and governor general of Algeria.}

better housed than you are," commented the marshal in surprise when he visited the dormitory.

Paradoxically, I would really have to think hard to figure out what was so rigorous about our lives. Weeks go by. Christmas is here. Christmas is gone, without gifts or Christmas Eve parties. Our faith is our present from heaven, and it burns in our hearts. The Cistercian fast takes a short pause after Christmas but will soon pick up where it left off, in order to reach the summit of Easter, with spring and nicer days, with the great news for the monk: "Christ is risen, alleluia! He is truly risen!"

Added to the fervor of Holy Week was an occurrence on Good Friday especially for the younger novices, of whom I was one. On that day, which started at 2 a.m. like any other one, the monks recited the 150 psalms in sequence in Latin. It took roughly four hours. These four hours came on top of the usual liturgy of the hours and the solemn liturgy of the day. We remained in church until 1 p.m., when we had a lunch of bread and water. We had to hurry; the verses followed one after another; the youngest monks, who did not know Latin very well, swallowed part of the words, got some other words wrong, and could hardly hold back their giggles while exchanging funny looks with each other. I can almost say that I never laughed so much as on Good Friday! We left our shoes in the dormitory as a penance and walked barefoot almost the whole morning.

Each morning, those monks who were not assigned to a set task learned what they would have to do during the day. It was the case with the novices. The sub-master or "work director" distributed the tasks among us. We pulled up our robes with a clever system of cords, and, if there was more than one worker, we went to the assigned work place in a single line. The superior or the novice master walked in front, and an older monk walked in the rear. We all held our tools under our left arms or on our shoulders if there was more than one tool. The first day in the fields was a disaster. As a city boy, I could not see the difference between what I had to pull out or leave in the colza field that we were weeding. Was I going to destroy the healthy furrows we were cultivating and leave only the weeds? I tried to look at what my neighbors were doing, but they moved faster than I did. We weren't supposed to talk, except to the superior, and I didn't dare seek any help. How humiliating it would be if I was doing something wrong! For the first time since I entered the monastery, I understood that the humiliations that you don't seek are more mortifying than the other ones, programmed or predictable. I finally decided that the most numerous stems must be the good ones. So, I left them. What did I know?

"Pull out the beans, but not the green ones," they told us another time.

They all seemed green to me, these beans. It is true that I am a little color blind. How should I know? They should have told me: "Take the dry ones!" But I didn't understand it, and it was better not to inspect my crop too closely. It was quickly mixed with the crops of the other novices. Sometimes the work lasted longer, especially during harvest time, where we needed to bale up everything in the fields. Even if the bell rang, calling us to the liturgy, we remained in the field. At the superior's signal, we recited together the liturgy of the hour surrounded by nature, in two lines, trying very hard to maintain the setting of the choir. "The brothers," said Saint Benedict, "will really be monks when, as our fathers and the apostles did, they will live from the fruits of their labor" (RB 48.8). For some, agricultural labor was a joyous relaxation. I would have preferred to be assigned to the cheese dairy, a more industrial labor, rather than digging up potatoes, stooped over, row after row. And in the north of France the potato crops are important!

I learned how to say verbs and nouns with my hands. Some were obvious, but most of them made no sense, and you had to learn them like a Latin declension. We indicated the novice master by touching the left ring finger with the tip of the right thumb. The number one hundred was shown by putting the finger in the open mouth. For grass we shook one stretched hand after the other parallel to each other, but depending on the context, that could mean either the salad or dead leaves on the road. Misunderstandings sometimes came up if we weren't thinking about the same thing. One time I wasted about an hour of work because a wrongly interpreted sign caused me to wait in the wrong place for the person I was supposed to help. Some signs referred to other signs that in turn referred to other ones. There were 465 words in the official glossary. At the same time, it was both a lot and very little. We only used the most common ones, and sometimes we made up new ones.

The experts among us could sometimes hold real conversations about abstract subjects. Some good stories circulated about this. One told the story of the abbot watching two brothers gesticulating. He asked them what they were talking about. "I am explaining the Siege of Sebastopol during the Crimean War of 1855 to him," one of them answered. As you can see, the story is an old one. Today that custom is being lost, but I was pretty skillful at expressing myself in this way!

Small phrases marked my journey, and I wrote them down during my readings or my lessons. In the fourth century, Saint Gregory of Nyssa wrote, "Finding God is looking for him constantly."[9] Saint Bernard and many others repeated this. To find and to search are not separate moments with the search on one side and the discovery on the other. They constantly go together; they need each other, so that the formula could be reversed: To search for God is constantly to find him, because those who believe get what they believe in through their desire for it. The thirst for God is already to a certain extent its own quenching, and the greatest desire for spiritual things, a way to see God, is the only one given to us on this earth. After all, isn't God, and only God, endless and infinite? If our desire ceased, it would be the sign that we were not encountering infinity. Also, finding God does not conclude the search or the desire. The life of a Trappist

9. {Gregory of Nyssa, *The Life of Moses*, trans. Abraham J. Malherbe and Everett Ferguson, pref. John Meyendorf (New York, Ramsey, and Toronto: Paulist Press, 1978), ¶¶219–55, pp. 111–20, especially ¶239, p. 116.}

does not consist in always thinking of God, but in searching for him everywhere and in finding him everywhere. It is the way to constantly live with him.

But these lofty considerations need small material aids. If some improvements didn't take place in our lives as beginners, we would not be able to cope. Still too young to stand the full Trappist treatment, we would otherwise spend our days dozing off and feeling hungry. We would rejoice in the simple fact that we remained upright while watching ourselves fading away. We would have empty heads and stomachs with tearful hearts. What would be the purpose of all this? The goal is not to suffer or to become skinny carcasses, but to strip ourselves of everything that is not indispensable. Adaptation was necessary, and I was all too happy to comply with the instruction not to get up from my straw mattress at 2 a.m. (solar time)[10] and to accept the relief granted in the refectory because of my youth.

On the day of my military board of review, I was allowed to visit my younger brother Michel in the hospital, where he had been in serious condition for six months. He was suffering from tuberculosis and meningitis and was really in pain. I left his room, shaken up, to visit my parents. Everyone expected the worst.

"And you, how are you?" my uncle, the doctor, Jules Defaux, asked me.

10. {Dom Dubois appears to be alluding here to the ancient method of calculating time, which was based on the initial assumption that there were twelve hours of daylight and twelve hours of night time. This of course means that daytime "hours" were longer in the summer when there was more daylight. In the sixth century, Saint Benedict acknowledged this fact in his Rule, which states that the number of psalms to be said during the various offices had to be adjusted according to the seasons (RB 9–10). Monks could be considered the first timekeepers, because the Rule required them to pray at established hours. The monasteries had sundials, or hourglasses with sand or water, to keep track of the time. The bell calling the monks to the church would be heard in the neighborhood, which also gave the surrounding community an indication of time.}

"Father Abbot is very good to me. He allows me to eat more and to wake up only at 4 a.m."

"What? You *only* wake up at 4 a.m.? And you talk about a privilege! That is the world upside down. What are you doing that early?"

The monks spend two hours in church when they wake up. First a short office to the Virgin Mary that lasts twenty minutes. Then there is half an hour of personal prayer, which we call *oratio*. Then they pray Vigils and Lauds one after the other. That is when I wake up, to continue the day with them. It is the time for private masses by the monks who are priests, which the other monks serve. Then follows a second morning office, called Prime, and after that a meeting in the chapter room, in which Father Abbot comments on the Rule or gives us spiritual instructions. Only after that do we have breakfast, which we call either *frustulum* or *mixte* depending on the days. By then it is about 7 a.m.

My brother was fourteen years old when he died on December 1, 1948, a few days after my visit. We were all devastated. This was a distressing test for my parents, especially for my mother. She told me that if she didn't have faith she would jump in the canal. For the first time, I found myself in a different place before God. What did he want? What were we here on this earth? It deepened my faith. Why was I here? Yes, I believed, and I only wanted to go further to meet him in the invisible, where everything was taken away onto the bruised face and tortured flesh of the Man-God put on the cross with his soul pierced with all our pains and sorrows.

My current life surprised most of those who knew me before. One of my brothers said, "Gérard is with the Trappists; he is no longer interested in our problems. The world is of no interest to him anymore; he can't understand it. He is over there, far away from things; what happens to us is of no concern to him—what does he know of our lives?" Perhaps he had the wrong idea. In fact, I was interested in their lives, our lives, and I was there for that reason. Later I would learn that another one of my brothers, on the contrary, clung to what I was: "If Gérard has chosen to be a monk, God should mean something to us."

You are not a monk for yourself alone. A monk who wants to be a monk only for his own salvation or for some kind of privileged relationship with God will not be a good monk. You become a monk out of love, even if you are not able to express everything contained in that word. I pray for everyone, those I know and those I do not know, those who implore God and those who do not implore him or do not do so anymore, those who do not want to hear about him, and those who have said no once and for all and who may not be wrong from their point of view, but that is not the only one for me. I have never again seen the light that lit up for me once, just once, in that guest house bedroom, but its memory still illuminates me, and the more I move forward—sometimes in the dark—the more certain I feel about the journey.

One night I had a dream that made a strong impression on me. In the Abbey of Mont-des-Cats, one of the front towers of the church has a spiral staircase that ends up in the novices' quarters. I climbed this staircase many times a day, and I knew it very well. During my first year in the novitiate, I dreamed that I was climbing these steps and that I saw Saint Benedict waiting for me there. He was a large character, who filled up the whole place with his sizable stature. I was surprised. He put a ring on my finger and made me a promise that I heard very clearly:

"What you have, you will keep forever."

I woke up, shaken by that apparition full of light, and I thought about its significance. My unconscious self projected clearly in this dreamlike scene all the intensity of my desires as well as my need for reinforcement and security during this time of probation. But I came out of it reassured and happy. I will never forget that dream. What did it mean? Should I understand that no one will ever take away my monastic identity, or anything that relates to it, like the joys and torments? I was so shaken that I talked about it with the novice master. At that moment, I was not sure if the natural elements did not merge with the supernatural acts. A new link with Saint Benedict was fondly woven, and I applied myself to learning more about his Rule, his life, and his example.

He was born in Italy about seventy miles from Rome around 480, eighteen years before the birth of Clovis. When he was twenty years old, he interrupted his studies to live as a hermit in a cave in the mountains of Subiaco. After a few years, some disciples started to follow him, so he set up some small communities, each containing a dozen monks. Around 525, fleeing the opposition of a nearby priest, he left Subiaco to establish a monastery at Monte Cassino. He got inspiration from the monastic rules written before him, and, relying on his coenobitic life experience, he wrote his own rule before dying in 547. It is this rule that the coenobitic monks of the West follow, so we can say that he is the father. It is nevertheless striking that the only vision the Lord gave him of the future of his work was the impending destruction of his monastery by the barbarians. God leads his people in the darkness of faith.

In fact, the Lombards invaded Northern Italy and the monks fled Monte Cassino thirty-four years after the death of Saint Benedict. Nevertheless, the foundations of coenobitic life had been laid for centuries to come. An extraordinary balance of life is contained in these few pages, which has appealed to thousands of men and women: "Listen carefully, my son, to the master's instructions" (RB Prol. 1). These are the first words of the Benedictine Rule, in which the author almost assumes the authority of a Saint Paul speaking in Christ's name and commanding others to follow him. Then: "This message of mine is for you, then, if you are ready to give up your own will, once and for all" (RB Prol. 3). We are starting on our way, following Saint Benedict, the master, who rejects excess and laxness. He warns us that "the good of all concerned, however, may prompt us to a little strictness in order to amend faults and to safeguard love" (RB Prol. 47). He tells us not to be "daunted by fear and run away." The road that leads to salvation, he reminds us, is bound to be narrow at the outset (RB Prol. 48). That does not scare him away from "intending to establish a school for the Lord's service . . . . We hope to set down nothing harsh, nothing burdensome" (RB Prol. 45-46). As he requires of the abbot, it is necessary that the strong have something to support them in their journey without causing the weak to flee in discouragement (RB 64.19).

Months went by, with study punctuated by important liturgical celebrations, by the bells, manual labor, and *oratio*. Although we were not allowed to speak to each other or to establish familiarities or friendships in groups that could become closed cliques or potential centers of conflict, some privileged contacts were created through signs, looks, the undefined presence of one person which is different from the other. If monastic life does not favor private encounters, on the other hand, it does not prevent friendships. It does not eliminate the psychological traits or the affinities of taste that grow over time. You feel better with some than with others, even if you can't explain why. For months I had been getting along well with a fellow novice. We shared a joyous rivalry. One day he lost his enthusiasm; he was no longer the same. What was going on with him? He didn't believe in what he was doing anymore; he forced himself to attend the liturgy and to participate in the exercises.

I could not communicate with him, but I learned that he was leaving our community. The news hurt me. Was it possible to have believed in God's call and then no longer believe in it? For the first time, I discovered that a monastery looks somewhat empty when one of its members leaves. His spot in the stalls in front of his antiphonary, the huge book of Gregorian chants, is deserted, and then another novice replaces him. A community is composed of faces, expressions, and voices. You get used to a thousand little things and to all these presences without any warning. This failure made me think about the fragility of our temporary commitment. I was probably the most shaken by this departure, but the others did not find it unusual. A young man tries, he doesn't like it, and he leaves.

I felt strangely safe within these walls that were as impressive as they were reassuring, more convinced day after day that my brothers were interested in me for what I was. I didn't consider myself more courageous or intelligent than the others, those who come to the monastery, those who do not come to its doors, or those who leave. Nor did I think that I was closer to God than my parents, my brothers and sisters, my teachers or my old high school buddies. I thanked God from the bottom of my heart for revealing to me the road to follow amid the pitfalls and the jungle that is this world, in this "valley of tears," as it is described in the *Salve Regina*. I thanked God for showing me that I was loved in this monastery. Still, I felt that I belonged to a privileged group.

We have been called the front line of the Church Militant. Is the monk a soldier of Christ, a knight destined for great spiritual fights, who undergoes an initiation before storming onto the battlefield? At the time of my entry into the monastery a book about the Order of Cîteaux was published by Dom Anselme Le Bail, the prior in Scourmont, one of our monasteries in Belgium. He noted that above asceticism, Christ "proposes to an elite a higher calling: he gives it a status in his Church; he specifies the practices that go along with this status."[11] But it is a status based on the heart, on evangelical teaching, fasting, separation from the world, and especially on prayer, repeated over and over, deepened and lived.

Later on, words like these were substantially nuanced, because there are no higher categories of Christians in the church. Vocations differ. There is religious status in celibacy, and there is commitment in marriage. The significance of each of these statuses is probably different—one may be more prophetic than the other—but that does not imply any hierarchy of values, as if religious celibacy were higher than marriage. Nobody would sustain the argument today that the basic Christian should be satisfied with trying to practice the apostolic commandments while the others, such as monks or priests, should pursue the more sophisticated and more elite demands of Christ. In fact, what was called "evan-

11. {Dom Anselme Le Bail, *L'Ordre de Citeaux: La Trappe* (Paris: Édition Letouzey et Ané, 1947), 7–8.}

gelical teaching" is offered to everyone, but each one responds to it in accord with his or her vocation or life situation.

Life continued peacefully and harmoniously at Mont-des-Cats. My novice master introduced me to authors about whom I knew nothing. He was a forward-thinking person. At first I had not appreciated how open minded he was in an environment where everything seemed so well established and set for centuries. He taught me how to reflect on the meaning of our usages and customs rather than following them blindly.

"All this wasn't done in one day," he said. "To understand our life, you need to go back to the sources and read the first Cistercian authors. We don't do it enough."

His spiritual approach left a deep impression on me. Among his revolutionary initiatives at the Abbey of Mont-des-Cats was his encouragement to read Saint Bernard. In 1947 this was one of his most substantial contributions. Saint Bernard entered Cîteaux around 1112, a few years after the foundation of the monastery. He was quickly put in charge of a group of monks that left to establish a new Cistercian community at Clairvaux in 1115. His influence on the history of the growing Order and on the life of the Church in his time was dominant. His spiritual writings contain precious teachings on the monastic life, but they were written in Latin, and at the time of my novitiate, they were not often read in our monasteries. They hadn't been translated into French yet, except in nineteenth-century publications that were outdated and off-putting. Bernard was a faraway figure whose words didn't speak to us. Nevertheless, he was the starting point of a whole school of thought, and I quickly learned the names of the most important of its representatives: William of Saint-Thierry, Aelred of Rievaulx, Guerric of Igny, Isaac of Stella, Adam of Perseigne, and Gilbert of Hoyland.

"The most important one is Saint Bernard," Father Francis advised me once. "Read him!"

This recommendation was given to me in the spirit of friendship, but it came from someone who was well read and who could sort through the thousands of volumes in our library. I could not yet measure the audacity of this recommendation, which would leave its mark on me throughout my whole life. The education given to novices usually did not explore these avenues. Our abbot trusted our good and attentive Father Francis to do what was best. He had total confidence in him. In return, Father Francis, instead of teaching in a moralizing and sanctimonious style on the Rule and its sanctions, invited us to enter into the spirituality that lay at the origin of the Cistercian movement and that had been a beacon for many centuries. I discovered his free thinking and his freshness, so natural and obvious to me, through this connection with a spiritual universe that he made enthralling to me. His teachings already contained the seeds of a renewal of the monastic life that was waiting just over the horizon. However, it was too early in our strict observance of the usages and customs to perceive this clearly.

Before my novitiate was completed, Father Francis Decroix was summoned to Rome to become an adviser to the abbot general. Later he would be elected abbot of the Italian monastery of Frattocchie, where the community of Our Lady of the Catacombs, which had been founded by monks of Mont-des-Cats in 1883, was transferred in 1929.

Of all he taught me, I think that what I remember most is the need for humility, a humility so deep that you cannot ever be offended. At the end of his life, he left a beautiful testimony: "We didn't want to offend anyone, but we did. You can make up for an injustice, but you cannot force a wounded heart. You have to wait as a pauper. As a pauper possessed by the desire to rekindle the relationship, who continues to love when he is being offended. Better yet, we should be so poor that we can't be offended anymore."

On Monday, November 21, 1949, five days before turning twenty, I made my temporary profession at the same time as Brother André Louf, who followed me by one month in birth date as well as in entry into the monastery of Mont-des-Cats. Strong bonds of friendship grew between the two of us as we passed through the successive stages of formation together. One day he would be elected abbot of Mont-des-Cats. We had one little disappointment mixed with our awaited joy, because Father Abbot had to attend the funeral of another superior and the election of his successor, our father immediate. Instead of postponing the ceremony and disappointing us in another way, Father Abbot delegated his authority to the prior so that he could receive our commitment. This was Father Yves, the first monk who had listened to my determination to become a monk. In our hearts these were already perpetual professions taken in the family intimacy of our community.

Buffeted by the uncertainties of his functions and traveling over hills and valleys, Saint Bernard exclaimed one day, "I would not want to be an ant stuck to a large cart.[12] . . . I am the chimera of my century. I act like neither a cleric nor a lay person; I embraced the life of a monk, but I really don't behave like one."[13] I too, like others before me, felt like a little ant laboring in a large endeavor, and, even though I wore the habit, I was not yet fully a monk. I was three years away from perpetual vows, three years that were getting harder. I was holding onto the memory of the promise, given by Saint Benedict one night deep in a dream, claiming a victory behind these gates of silence.

12. Bernard of Clairvaux, *The Letters of St. Bernard of Clairvaux*, no. 347, trans. Bruno Scott James (London: Burns and Oates, 1953), 424–26, here 425.
13. {Saint Bernard of Clairvaux, *Letters*, no. 326, pp. 401–2, here 402.}

CHAPTER FIVE

LEARNING HOW TO SPEAK
IN THE CLOISTER

When I entered the monastery, I didn't know how to speak in public. Like all the monks, I had to express myself in front of others, and well before being elected abbot, I had to do so more and more often. It may be paradoxical, but it was in the cloister, a place representing silence and meditation, solitude and peace, that I learned how to speak. When your deepest being confronts itself and others, the words arise that express what you really want to say. There is no chatting in the cloister. Or better, there should not be any chatting. There, words are only spoken to convey your true self, and sometimes those echoes pierce through the walls. But this effort took place over time, and I didn't learn anything in one day.

Time is precious for the monk. He always has something to do and does not waste the moments that are granted to him. Fénelon[1] observed mischievously that God never grants two

---

1. {François de la Mothe-Fénelon, *Meditations on the Heart of God,* trans. Robert J. Edmonson (Brewster, MA: Paraclete Press, 1997), 71–72, chap. 36. Fénelon (1651–1715) was a prominent figure as a writer, religious confidant, and preacher in Louis XIV's entourage. A friend of Bossuet, he wrote extensively in defense of the Catholic faith and human rights.}

moments at the same time. He takes back the one that ends and offers you a new one without your ever being sure that there will be a third one. He is completely and totally in the present moment, and you would look in vain for him anywhere else. Over time I noticed the encounter with infinity in this short time lapse, this particle of eternity where we breathe, where we see, where we hear and smell, and where we are conscious of existing. This notion of the fundamental value of the present moment, beyond what it humanly holds as positive or negative, as pleasant or indifferent, moved me along over the years, and, without my clearly noticing it, moved me closer to a theology of the present moment, a really fancy name for a reality that is so short and that we find in abundance with each step. It probably does not deserve such an impressive official name, but the notion of the precious and irreplaceable moment more than anything else carries weight in the monastic life, sanctifying everything in its own way and making everything sacred from dawn to dusk, the small moments like the important events. One minute is never secondary; it is never to be wasted. Postulants are always amazed at how fast our fragmented days go by. Time is not to be wasted in the monastery. Out of what is perishable in this succession of fleeting moments arises our contact with eternity.

Nevertheless, the Trappist has all the time in the world, though you would think that he was running short on time. You see him getting up early in the morning and hurrying to church. You see him continuing his day as if his whole salvation depended on it and falling asleep without granting himself needless rest, because he hasn't figured out how to regard that one hour as less important than the next one. The monk and time are two inseparable companions. They fight against each other. They also keep each other company enough to be accomplices. The monk's struggle ends up being outside the present moment, there where the fleeting moment leads to something that remains.

Everything goes fast in a monastery, contrary to the image one might have of a rigid life, maybe a dead life, where nothing happens. Punctuated by the liturgy of the hours, which regularly brings us back to the church, the day goes by almost unnoticed. Except for manual labor, rarely does an activity take longer than one hour, and we quickly get to Compline, the last prayer of the day, which ends with that unique song *Salve Regina* and the blessing by Father Abbot before we go to the dormitory.

And finally one day, after all these days, a moment arrives that leads directly into eternity. But there are also other moments where the world catches up with us, a moment that pulls the monk one way or the other to remind him until the end, as it has done ever since his temporary profession, that he belongs to this century and to this society. The world enters into the cloister in multiple ways.

I was pursuing my classes in philosophy and theology with a view to preparing for the priesthood when I received the call-up for the draft. "Brother Gérard," they told me that morning, "you're leaving for Algeria."

I left in October 1951 wearing my Trappist habit, as was the custom then. I was a big hit in the first barracks. I almost didn't notice my first four years in the monastery go by, and I didn't completely realize how the world was. At that time, we didn't have newspapers at Mont-des-Cats, and we didn't listen to the radio. We only knew what the superior considered important enough to tell us. Since nobody told us anything more, that meant that it didn't concern us. The purpose was to avoid being stressed by the immediate moment and to allow the rhythm to start all over, unchanged, indestructible, centered around the three main activities of prayer (*oratio*), spiritual reading (*lectio*), and manual labor (*labora*).

My orders instructed me to go to the military school in Cherchell, close to Algiers. The trip took three days. My monastic tonsure was eliminated just before my leaving the monastery, but I still had a closely shaved head. I was thankful to my superiors for having taken away that kind of halo. It would have been even worse than it was, for the conscripts laughed at my outfit, and even the most lenient among them were curious. "What kind of job do you have? It's strange to be dressed like that."

When I met two seminarians in cassock, we were able to form a small, less vulnerable group, and we protected each other as best we could. Some people were surprised to observe that my outbursts and my language got blunter as the days went by, a sign that I was getting progressively but quickly integrated into this new environment.

When I got there I had to take a physical test, which I failed miserably. You might have thought that I would not dread the early morning bugle, but I quickly picked up the habit of waking up "late" again, and I was not adverse to staying in bed whenever possible. Since I could not remain in the Reserve Officers School because I had failed the physical test, I was posted to the 9th Zouaves Division,[2] which had staff headquarters located in Algiers. I did my basic training in this elite group for six months, learning to use machine guns and mortars. Almost every one of us feared the captain, an irritating man. In the evening, when he went home after the dismissal, we all started to breathe. Military discipline is not monastic discipline, and the efforts have a different meaning. I was promoted to private first class and assigned to kitchen duty. Our tent encampment—the Lido—was located on the beautiful bay of Algiers, and the sea was not far away. I spent my time getting supplies from Algiers and keeping the accounts for the meals and the kitchen. That brought some relief to my sergeant, who appreciated me because I gave him my ration of cigarettes since I didn't smoke; in addition, the accounts were always accurate.

On certain Sundays, to take a breather, I went to Maison-Carrée, where the mother house and the novitiate of the White Fathers is located. Further south, close to Medea, I also discovered the Trappist monastery of Our Lady of the Atlas in Tibhirine. It was recently—in 1947—elevated to the status of an abbey after being

---

2. {Zouaves: infantry regiments who were part of the French army between 1830 and 1960. They were first used in North Africa and then in the imperial guard. They were largely recruited from Algerian and Moroccan soldiers and wore a uniform inspired by their North African roots.}

in existence for ten years. From 1934 on, monks from Slovenia sought shelter in Algeria; they were joined in 1938 by other monks from Aiguebelle, and all of them settled at the present site in the foothills of the Atlas Mountains. The region was easily accessible by train, and during the eighteen months of my military service, I visited there nine times, ending the trip on foot through the mountains. Each time, sixty miles away from the capital, I melted into this community and felt at home, with a known atmosphere and *horarium*.[3] France was too far away for us to spend all our leaves there. The first time I went to Tibhirine was to celebrate Easter Vigil in 1952. I got there at night, just before the celebration, which thanks to Pope Pius XII had been returned to its correct nocturnal time. Having barely slept one

3. {On March 26, 1996, less than a year after the original publication of this book, six monks of the monastery of Tibhirine (including Br. Luc, mentioned in Dom Dubois's note, below) and a visiting monk were kidnapped. They were murdered, and their bodies were found two months later. The exact circumstances of their deaths and the identity of the perpetrators are still unknown, although the Armed Islamic Group (GIA) claimed their kidnapping. There are no longer any monks in the monastery. (For more information see Dom Armand Veilleux, "The Witness of the Tibhirine Martyrs," *Spiritus: A Journal of Christian Spirituality* 1, no. 2 [2001]: 205–16. The movie *Of Gods and Men* [2011] tells the story of the last months of these monks before their kidnapping.)}

{The following note appeared in Dom Dubois's original volume.} The situation of this monastery is currently very delicate because of the political events that are taking place in that country and what looks like a civil war. Our monks are well integrated in the population, which may enable them to stay. Since he settled there, a Trappist doctor, Brother Luc, now in his eighties, has healed patients of both sides. He has been the shield of this monastery since the war for independence of 1956–1963. That didn't prevent armed militants of a certain side from visiting the monastery twice. But the brothers have decided to remain among those who in any event cannot leave, "honoring," as they say, "the meaning that our neighbors were able to find in our presence, along with the daily sharing and the solidarity that most of us have practiced with the best of our personal and community charisms" (letter of November 1994).

hour, I fainted during the initial hymn *Exultet* and collapsed—a strange way to be welcomed.

The mix in social classes and temperament in the military camp brought me out of myself, but what I didn't do was go out to have fun with my buddies.

"Why don't you come with us? Your life is strange! Come and have some good laughs with us? Why are you depriving yourself of all kinds of things that don't harm anyone?" They were chasing girls, and I let them go on weekend leaves by themselves, since I did not want to have the kind of civilian life that I would soon abandon.

A sergeant told me, "Take advantage of military service to have a try, to see how it is with a girl! You will be able to judge afterwards. You may change your mind." "But if I try, I may not want to go back to the monastery. There's a risk I might just like it." "You're right! Yes, it might be better for you not to try."

The only thing I wanted to accomplish by presenting him with this very human motive was to give him a reason to leave me alone. He could not understand why someone would lock himself up in a *trappe* and renounce marriage. My explanation was not a good one, and the proof that he didn't get it was that he accepted it. I didn't give my real reason. Nevertheless, a hundred days before the end of my military service, I let the others drag me to a bar to have a drink—the only time I ever crossed the threshold of a bar. Conversations of a religious nature never went very far with these guys, and I wasn't looking to preach. Being a Trappist was my business, not theirs, and I didn't have to justify myself to anyone. The choice to live in a monastery was already one of solitude. This was not new, and it didn't worry me. The situation did not add any bitterness to what I had felt when I couldn't explain to my family or my teachers why I chose to be apart from the world. More than anything, I avoided going on a crusade to persuade them that there was another way of looking at things.

"What is the purpose of being a monk?" the wiser or more curious ones asked me. "It doesn't serve any purpose. What does it accomplish to spend all your time saying prayers in church?"

Always the same questions. Where does the contemplative vocation come from? How can you explain it? Why me and not someone else? What was I going to do in the monastery? The religious will tell you that there are natural faculties on one side and God's call on the other side and that the conjunction of both factors produces the vocation. But how can you prove God's call? Impossible. A real monk feels as naturally at home in monastic life as others do when they are exercising their vocation in a society where their choice does not cause any surprise.

The monk does not object to the additional constraints, though that does not mean that he does not have to struggle with all his strength to do his duty. But isn't that the case with any and all vocations, and also with many professions pursued without any vocation? What long-lasting result do you achieve without any effort? The person responding to the monastic call possesses first and foremost the natural means to accomplish it, a truth that is often overlooked. At the onset, these means exist under the surface and are probably present since childhood. A monk "is like that," and not otherwise. Most of the time, but not always, it is hard to deny that psychological aptitudes converge.

In fact, monasticism exists outside Christianity. God acts within our psychology. Spiritual reality is not independent from our psyche. The discovery and fulfilment of a vocation never take place outside the psychological being of a man or a woman. On the contrary, it translates into this psychological being. God is waiting for us there. This natural dimension is a field of research for the humanities and social sciences. In that sense, a psychologist could completely take apart the history of a religious vocation and explain all the choices, the attraction, the call, the developments, the hesitations, the sacrifices, and the devotions. Humanly, everything can be analyzed and justified without ever having to call on any *deus ex machina*. And still!

"We agree on that," I tell a buddy, "but there is more than that."

"What else? Why would God choose some and not others? What is it to him? Did he create them to live locked up?"

To call upon only natural dispositions does not account for the essential. These only form the fabric into which the essential is woven. The discussions I had during my military service showed me how difficult it is to go to the heart of the matter. After all, my sister, who upon my return from military service announced her engagement to Étienne, would never be able to tell me why she chose him.

"There is more than that," I always say, without ever being able to go further.

When I look inside me, I am sure that my past does not totally account for my present or for the future to which I am heading. No theory on the causes of the monastic condition holds water if it only takes into account the psychology of an individual. But how could I argue God's action in my desire to become a Trappist without being able to prove God's reality? We are going around in circles. We are explaining the unexplainable with the inconceivable, or a mystery with another mystery. God acts within the temperament. "Ah, now I understand!" the chaplain of the scouts shouted out when he learned of my desire to enter a monastery. He knew me as being reserved. But what did he understand? The outward expressions of my character weren't sufficient to explain that specific choice.

For the believer, a spiritual life is a place of confrontation between grace and freedom. It is within a person's freedom that grace comes to life. All monks experience something profound that enlightens them, or that has enlightened them, be it even just for a fraction of a second, but it lasts forever. How can we account for that? What marked them so strongly? Why do they often say that they can't talk about it? The humanities do not have the ultimate explanation of the inexpressible. Can they pretend to have it? Why would we believe them when they assert it? What are they putting forward so that we would believe them? And what is the inexpressible, the divine, the supernatural? It is God talking to us in our hearts: only the believer understands it.

But because of our fundamental freedom, the vocation is never a predefined phenomenon that can be discovered by resorting to fortune tellers. Once more, it is not that I was not really free! Simone de Beauvoir[4] has published pages on the subject that caricature freedom and our choices. Her protest against a simplistic vision of a vocation and of an obedience to God that consists in an anxious deciphering of a scenario prewritten in heaven that we then need to reproduce are both well-founded. But she imagines that this concept is the only one that allows faith in God, and she logically concludes that therefore she cannot have faith. Within that perspective, I wouldn't be able to have faith in God either. The Christian concept of divine Providence cannot be conveyed by these narrow views. For us Christians, God acts in our whole freedom; he saves us with our freedom and leads us with it. We write the scenario together. If I go right, God is on the right; if I go left, he is on the left. To a certain extent, I am the one who decides where I meet him, even if in that game of grace

---

4. See for example in *Mémoires d'une jeune fille rangée* (Paris: Gallimard, 1958), 226: "at that time I was quite happy to do without God, and if I made use of his name it was only in order to designate a void that to me had all the splendor of the plenitude of grace. I still had absolutely no desire to know of his existence, and it even seemed to me that if I had believed in him I should have detested him. Groping my way along paths whose every twist and turn he knew, buffeted by the chance winds of his grace, petrified by his infallible judgment, my existence could only have been a stupid and pointless ordeal. No amount of sophistry could have convinced me that the Omnipotent had any need of my miserable life, or if he did, it would only be to play a joke on me. In earlier days, when adults' amused condescension used to transform my life into a puerile piece of play acting, I would be convulsed with rage, and today too I would have refused no less violently to let myself become the ape of God" (*Memoirs of a Dutiful Daughter*, trans. James Kirkup [Cleveland and New York: The World Publishing Co., 1959], 241). The ideas that I develop here are not my own. See for example the short article by Michel Rondet, "Dieu a-t-il sur chacun de nous une volonté particulière?" *Christus* 144 (1989): 392–99. {Simone de Beauvoir (1908–1986), a French author and philosopher who promoted a feminist existentialism in her novels and biographies. She was involved in politics and social issues with her lifelong partner Jean-Paul Sartre.}

and freedom that I like to call to mind he can attract me where he wants to lead me.

I was released from military service in March 1953 and returned to Mont-des-Cats. On June 6, 1954, exactly ten years after D-day, I pronounced my perpetual vows on the feast of Pentecost. I was twenty-four years old. In the church, I prostrated myself at full length during the great prayer of blessing chanted by the choir. Then I knelt down in front of each monk in his stall to ask for his prayers. Each one answered me in Latin: "*Dominus custodiat introitum tuum et exitum tuum.*" The prayer is inspired by a prayer of King David: "May God protect your comings and goings," meaning protect you in all your steps (Ps 121:8).

Each monk then helped me up and embraced me, and I went on to the next stall, very moved but incapable of really thinking about it. It is one of the most impressive moments in the life of a monk, right after his entry into the monastery. The abbot reminded me of my commitments and asked me if I was determined to remain faithful to them until the day I died. When I had given my consent, the whole community knelt in front of the altar singing the *Veni Creator*. I signed the *cedula* ratifying my promises and put it on the altar.

"Lord," I repeated three times, reciting a prayer from the psalms, "accept me as you promised and I will live; do not disappoint my expectation!" (Ps 119:116).

God knows that I was happy! Twenty-four years is an age at which many people get married. My brothers and sisters took that road at that age, and now I was entering into my new condition with feelings of happiness probably similar to theirs, with a lot of hope and love. How can I explain it? I was not shriveling up at the *trappe*. Life was there, and my dream was to live it fully, like them, but in a different way. The simple vows were kind of a family affair celebrated in the chapter room. The perpetual vows were pronounced in the church to affirm them in public in front of the altar. It was like a wedding day for me. The feast was a success, and the wedding was performed. The homily was given by my old chaplain, the one who had teased me about my desire for a contemplative life. He drew parallels between my commitment and the one I had taken nine years earlier with the scouts. He invited me to serve as a knight "without fear and without reproach."[5]

I wore the ample white cowl over the black and white habit of the professed monk, and the monastic crown.[6] My hair was buzz cut leaving a one-inch crown around the head. It went completely around, and (theoretically) each month a brother monk trimmed it to even the crown out. So it was, at that time, in all our monasteries, that you could easily find a monk skilful at using the clippers. Maybe he had learned it in mowing the grass in the yard or in cutting the flowers with a pair of shears—on scheduled days his "salon" was full, but silence was also observed there as in the cloister.

Three years later, on July 15, 1957, I was ordained a priest by Cardinal Liénart in the abbey, together with two other monks. It is neither a second marriage nor the highest point in the monastic life. My parents were surprised when I told them that the ordination was in one sense less important for me than the perpetual vows. "You can consecrate the bread and wine, that is something for a Christian," they told me. "Why aren't you more moved?"

I was moved, but this is not the same for a monk as it is for a seminarian. Priesthood is a function that implies a consecration to God, and we have already consecrated our lives to God on the day of our perpetual vows. You can neither do this twice nor consecrate yourself more, for consecration doesn't increase. In that sense, the ordination is not the crowning of a monastic

5. {*Sans peur et sans reproche*, originally applied to the French knight Seigneur de Bayard, also known as the Chevalier de Bayard (d. 1524).}

6. To tell the truth, I had worn the crown for the last three years. I was among the last ones to be dressed like that. Now only the cowl is received at the perpetual vows. With regard to the crown—it is now reserved for heaven! {The monastic crown (*la couronne monastique*) is what is in English called the tonsure.}

commitment, and a lot of monks are not priests, not to mention nuns. Seminarians have not made a similar commitment; they live their ordination as their principal consecration to God, and on a human level this sets them apart more than it does us. On the general level of the church you cannot reduce priesthood to a specific *ministerium*, because it involves a consecration to God. This consecration for the monk is connected primarily to his solemn vows, and priesthood in our monasteries is linked to a function to which we are called in the community.

"Wouldn't you have preferred being only a priest?" some ask me.

"No, because as a priest I would have experienced a lifestyle with functions that do not fit my choice."

In itself, monks do not need to become priests to fulfill their vocations. They nevertheless need priests in the monasteries to administer the sacraments and to provide spiritual services to our guests and to the nuns of our Order. Instead of calling on the diocesan priests, already overworked, certain brothers of the community receive the priesthood. But they should not be put in charge of parishes, because that would divert them from their vocations.[7]

From 1955 to 1958 I studied at the Gregorian University in Rome to improve my theological formation. I lived in the Generalate on the Aventine heights, where the abbot general of the Trappists lived, as well as the six monks who made up his coun-

---

7. Canon 674 of the Canon Law Code (1983) indicates that the contemplative life, because of its important "spiritual sacrifice of praise to God," prevails over "any urgency of the active apostolates' needs." In fact, if all the monk priests in France, who are clearly a minority in the monasteries (about eight hundred), left the monastery and joined the thirty thousand parish priests, it would make only a minimal difference in the French dioceses. The solution to the crisis in vocations does not lie there. On the other hand, the monastery churches could be a place of prayer and Eucharist taken into consideration in the organization of certain parishes.

cil.[8] There were nine students in the building for the first year of
my stay there. We wouldn't remain such a small flock, because
the Holy See had published a document requiring monks to
have an academic degree to teach in their monasteries. Our constitutions at that time forbade Trappists to complete university
studies anywhere but in Rome. Students from all over the world
flocked to the Eternal City. The following year there were so
many of us, about thirty, that the Order decided to build another
Generalate. In the meantime, we had to squeeze in, and it felt
like camping out. The arrival of monks from the United States,
Holland, Spain, Australia, and Africa made me discover through
this amazing mix of backgrounds the existing resources of our
Order. I would see some of them again later as priors or abbots.
The distance that some of them had to travel was so huge that it
would have seemed more reasonable to authorize them to study
in a university closer to their homes. Centralization was carried
to the extreme!

One day, shortly after my arrival in Rome, I was walking alone
on a sidewalk. Every Thursday afternoon we had to take a walk
in Rome. We discovered the monuments, the church frescoes,
the Christian art, and its symbolism thanks to a fellow student
monk who knew these masterpieces very well. This time I was
walking alone from the university, wearing a black hat, as was
customary in the fifties. There was nobody on the sidewalk. Suddenly a noise caught my attention, and I looked back to see in
the distance school children gathered on the side of the road. I
couldn't make out what they were doing, and I was about to walk
on when, all of a sudden, I heard motorcycle policemen escorting
a car. The convoy got closer, and I saw a figure dressed in white,
who was blessing me. It was Pope Pius XII coming back from
Castel Gandolfo, his summer residence. I had just seen the pope
without realizing it. Stunned, I remained motionless with my hat

8. {There are today the abbot general and five councilors, plus several
others, in the Generalate, which is located in a southern suburb of Rome.}

on. As the car drove away, I said to myself, "The pope just went by and I kept my hat on my head!"

The pope must have thought that this seminarian was impolite and disrespectful. I still thought about it a long time later, and it made me smile. I saw him again later in Saint Peter's Basilica when I was attending impressive ceremonies that made us resonate with the rhythm of important dates and solemn events in the church.

The bachelor's degree in theology required us to speak Latin, because all the courses were taught in that language. In the beginning I didn't understand a word, for I was immersed in a brand-new universe. I watched for the moment the teacher pronounced a word that I could understand; when a Frenchman talked, at least his Latin was not distorted by an American or German accent, which threw me off. It was only twisted the French way! I laughed when I heard the others laughing, so as not to look stupid, but often without understanding why I was laughing! After about two or three months I started to get the hang of it. As was the custom then, the courses required more memory than thought. The final exam for the bachelor's degree was completely in Latin. It required us to know one hundred theological theses and be able to defend them. Essentially that meant remembering the reference for each authority supporting one point of view or the other. One day I wondered, "How can I remember this mountain of numbered data? I have to find a solution." A clever way is to dissect the sources in which all the arguments originate, for example the letters of Saint Paul, and understand the structure. Slowly I was able to understand them by and for themselves. Then it was easy to go back to them to support a certain thesis. The repetitive memory was then superseded by the thinking process and inward knowledge, and I could synthesize the material more easily. That was also how I got acquainted with the history of the fathers of the church, learned to identify them, and remembered all their unique characteristics.

These efforts made me discover an aspect of things that I wasn't expecting. I was not the only one to discover it, of course.

I think that everyone who studied this at the same time as I did understood it. Later, it would enable me to understand what happened to the church in the 1960s. I started to realize that the church had evolved, and that the church could evolve further. This discovery of the historic dimension of the dogma and of the liturgy was the most important concept that I took away from my studies in Rome. For me it was an incredible revelation. Nevertheless, I believed that we were still in a rigid religious universe, and I didn't see how that would change in practice. For years we had been used to following the Divine Office and our monastic customs without ever thinking that a single detail could be modified. But now these practices became relative for me, since I had learned that they had not always been as they were now.

I also discovered what the Tradition was: not the immutability of a concept dating back to the apostles, but a slow unavoidable maturation, in which men and women had a role to play. People of all eras have shaped it by leaving the mark of their personalities, their intelligence, their agreements, and their disagreements. I continued my studies, fascinated by this concept of change within Christianity, and I observed that the life of the Church is like that of a large organism, as alive as I am. It unites us all in a prodigious adventure, in which each of us is called upon to be saved but also called upon to act. Yesterday, people intervened and left their mark on our spiritual heritage. Today other men and women, in the same faith, continue to think. This is what they once found, and this is what their successors suggest, on the basis of their experience of new circumstances. It is not a revolution but a slow evolution, a consultation, an uninterrupted research: in a word, *Tradition*.

The liturgy has also evolved. Until then this fact had never come to my mind because the liturgy we celebrated seemed cast in stone, forever unchangeable, as if it had fallen from heaven in one piece. As the young people we were, it was almost unthinkable that the rituals of the Mass and the monastic offices had ever been different. Here in Rome we realized that it was simply not true. The reasons for their evolution, the process, and the possibilities for innovation came to us slowly. For the first time the sources of our Cistercian and liturgical traditions were accessible to me. I was becoming aware of the historic dimension of the Church's thought process and structure. Later I would better understand the fundamentalists, who had not completed such studies; they thought that what they knew had always existed and was eternal. This is one of the reasons for their error. Years of study have taught me that the rituals of the Mass, to which fundamentalists remain attached, are not the ones that were always practiced.

In June 1958, I returned from Rome with a degree in theology, and in October I was appointed to instruct the young brothers in the monastery in that subject at the same time as I was put in charge of the choir. On the ninth of that month Pope Pius XII died.

"We need to prepare the chants to pray for a good election of his successor," I was warned.

Oh, my God! It was the first Mass that I had to conduct and rehearse. Not only was the function of cantor new to me, but nobody was really at ease with these melodies, which were rarely used, in which we prayed for the unknown person who would be elected by the cardinals. Pius XII had been elected nineteen years earlier! Our present cantor had left the monastery with a group of monks to found a new community in Madagascar. He had been one of our founders, and we needed to replace him and appoint others to fill the vacancies.

"He has never done this," everyone said in surprise. "How is he going to conduct the choir?"

My superiors' choice in entrusting me with a prominent position during the choir prayers was somewhat surprising, because I was young, and they did not know yet what type of service I could render to the community. In fact, when I had been participating in the chant I was mentally following the beat without showing it while the choir master was conducting. In this way I had acquired some limited experience, so I did not feel too uneasy about it. In the beginning, I had problems finding the right pitch, but over time my voice carried. I especially liked this position because it touched on the liturgy.

I was nervous about leading the rehearsals, so I prepared them carefully to avoid mishaps. Surprises could always occur, so I identified the trouble spots that the monks might encounter. Fearing that the eyes staring at me might paralyze me, I was inclined to write down the comments that I would have to make to the choir at the next rehearsal, so that I would only have to read what I had prepared in advance. Nevertheless, I was dubious about this approach, because there was a risk of remaining a prisoner of that method all my life and of never being able to speak freely. I would be the hostage of my written notes in other circumstances when I would have to talk in public.

While I didn't realize it then, this was one of those little turns that decides the rest of your life. I had observed that the superior of a certain monastery, although intelligent and full of wisdom, was incapable of talking to a group without reading his paper. "How sad," I thought. "What he says loses ninety per cent of its impact. If that is asked from me, I will have to do it differently." In our existence, in which everything is programmed and tightly bound in a web of obligations, there is still room for a sense of responsibility. I gave up writing the comments I intended to make during the rehearsal of the chant, even though I still prepared them in my head. Instead of helping me to feel more at ease, my piece of paper had become a hindrance. If it hadn't been for the election of Pope John XXIII, I might only have understood that fact later, but I needed to get rid of that fear of public speaking.

For each one of us, internal formation is carried out in small steps, with small, similar actions. The later you start, the harder the hill is to climb; you must leap forward. That doesn't mean that you don't need to prepare what you will say or have a paper in front of you. You can in certain more delicate circumstances make use of a completely prepared text. But you need to establish a relationship with your audience, to cross the stage, as they say in the theater world, and not be a prisoner of your text. You get trained in each one of these small, daily opportunities.

When the choir chanted out of tune, I risked becoming irritated and blaming myself. On the contrary, I told myself, "Calm down! Chant peacefully yourself without being concerned with the others." I tried my best to follow this resolution, and I had the impression that the choir was improving, which was not always just an impression. Our state of mind influences others and makes us listen in a particular way. While chanting, I had been expressing my anger or my irritation, which aggravated the others. If you're irritated, you chant in an irritated fashion, and you irritate others. Conversely, you soothe by chanting serenely. These chain reactions are complex and can have some serious consequences in a monastery where people constantly live together.

The philosopher Alain noticed that you can see in other people's eyes the judgment they have made about you as well as some of their feelings. When he talked to someone, he tried to never judge that person, even under his breath, he said, because that person might feel it: "unconsciously you communicate with each other."[9] That observation made me think for a long time. I compelled myself not to judge or look down on the person sitting before me, convinced that it could alter our interaction, even if the person wasn't aware of anything.

It was in this context that, having been appointed sub-novice master, in charge of instructing the youngest monks in what we called the "service of the church," I faced a new dilemma one day. My task was to clarify for them the complicated rituals and to show them how to move around the altar, light the candles, switch the lights in a set sequence, present the thurible, and in general carry out what was necessary for the liturgy. I used notes with precise headings to help me out. Some were specific to our monastery, and the sub-master was, to a certain extent, the keeper

9. {Émile-Auguste Chartier (1868–1951), better known as Alain, was a French journalist and influential teacher of philosophy. He was known for short, pithy essays, many of which have been collected by topic and published in book form. For two essays reflecting these thoughts, see "Kindness" and "Good Wishes" in Alain, *Alain on Happiness*, trans. Robert D. and Jane E. Cottrell (New York: Frederick Ungar Publishing Co., 1973), 192–94, 218–20.}

of these rituals. One day I misinterpreted a text and taught the wrong movements to a novice.

"You'll do it that way, because that is the way it has to be done," I told him with complete peace of mind.

During the celebration, the well-informed brothers were very surprised. The novice was not acting as usual. What was he doing? He should have moved, but he refused to move. The ones standing next to him nudged him without any reaction on his part. He was convinced he was right because the sub-master had explained it to him.

When everything was finished I re-read the text carefully, and surprise! I realized my mistake. For a moment, feeling embarrassed, I was tempted to change the instructions to match what I had told the novice. After all, I had enough say in the matter as the sub-master. A new crossroad: if I ran away from my responsibility I would be taking the wrong road. To change the instructions so that I would not have to acknowledge my mistake would be to refuse to take one necessary step toward becoming an adult, and that would turn out to be a handicap with serious consequences. I had to take the plunge; otherwise, that progress wouldn't take place despite all appearances. The mistake was neither serious nor shameful, but I experienced it that way. Why was it so hard at this point? Wasn't it because confessing my mistake meant acknowledging that the others were right and therefore victorious over me? I felt the typical humiliation of a loser, and that was unbearable. I had to resolve this dilemma.

A confession has neither winners nor losers; it restores the truth of the matter and leads to forgiveness. Too often, we think that the other person's gaze only expresses condemnation and contempt. Interpreting another person's thoughts is one of the most formidable traps of the monastic life, as in any human relationship. We are inclined to twist and amplify them. There was one certainty deep within me, and I felt it resonate in my conscience: "If you don't take that step that is so hard for you today, you will be miserable and embarrassed all your life when similar problems occur. You will never be able to acknowledge your mistakes, and you will fall deeper into lies, hypocrisy, and even paranoia. Hurry up and get out of this trap!" At the next chapter of faults, I made a public acknowledgement of my mistake, and this confession, almost insignificant for my brothers, was a bitter sacrifice for me, but it became a decisive event in the exercise of my freedom. The important thing is not having committed the mistake, but being able to acknowledge it.

I experienced a newfound feeling of freedom that I would never have experienced if I had given in to my temptation to cheat. The freedom to choose exists everywhere. You can close your eyes to so many things! The simplest way to conquer evil is not by refusing to see it, because then it will come back more insidious and dangerous. The only way to conquer it is by recognizing it. You throttle it then, with the forgiveness that you can only receive if you admit that you are a sinner.

In the theology classes I taught to the young monks in formation, I rarely used the notes I brought back from Italy. I wanted to expand on them by turning to men of the renewal, like Father Yves Congar,[10] one of the greatest theologians of the twentieth century, and Father Henri de Lubac,[11] whose qualities would be rewarded—somewhat late, it is true—by their appointment as cardinals. I studied their works and felt at ease with these minds so filled with the Tradition of the church, but far from being

---

10. {Yves Congar (1905–1995) was a French Dominican priest who promoted ecumenism in the Roman Catholic Church and the Church's opening to Eastern Orthodox and Protestant Churches. He was critical of the Roman Curia in the 1950s but was still selected by Pope John XXIII as an expert to prepare Vatican Council II. In 1994, seven months before Congar died, Pope John Paul II named him a cardinal.}

11. {Henri de Lubac (1896–1991) was a French Jesuit who taught fundamental theology and became a very influential theologian. His critical writings on Sacred Tradition and the church fathers, and his support of the "competency of the laicity," earned him a decades-long suspension from teaching, but, as was the case with Yves Congar, Pope John XXIII selected Lubac as an expert to prepare Vatican Council II. In his later years Lubac became a conservative theologian. In 1983 Pope John Paul II named him a cardinal.}

petrified, they merely called for certain changes in our way of behaving and reacting. Father Congar especially appealed to me. One of his articles on the sacrament of the Eucharist gave me a principle for understanding what we call in Christianity the history of salvation, and also of all the sacraments, human experience, the role of Christ, and spirituality.

There is a principle that always sustains me: our journey aims toward God; we have to rise up toward him with all our human resources, but we can't reach that far. The journey cannot reach its end. Then the end of the journey becomes our quest: God becomes man, taking over basically the whole of human history, condensing it and bringing it to its end through his act of obedience to the Father. He becomes our journey and leads us into God if we surrender to his action and allow ourselves to be led in his return to the Father. It is somewhat hard to understand, but suddenly I felt that I was holding an essential key to the understanding of the spiritual life. The studies of Father Jean Danielou on the ancient authors brought maturity to my thoughts, like the studies of many others, including Father Mersch, Father Durrwell, Father Lyonnet, Father Liégé, and Father Bouyer. All of them gave me a better understanding of what the Church and its liturgy are.

La Trappe enjoyed a far-reaching prestige in the middle of the twentieth century, but beginning in the fifties, a number of its monks had started to wonder if certain customs were viable and whether we should embark on a fundamental reform. But by whom? How? For what future? We didn't see it then, or we didn't know yet if we should only think about it, but slowly a movement took shape. The great wave of transformation that would wash over the whole church was already reaching us, but nobody realized how significant it would be.

Chapter Six

Different Journeys, Same Call

The roads that lead to the monastic life are many. Some people, like me, enter the monastery at a young age, with a rather blank past, you could say, just like their criminal record. Others have experienced a professional, social, or romantic life for a shorter or longer period of time. Each case is individual. I could have told the story of a nun who, after fortuitous circumstances and before entering the novitiate, spent three years at the court of the Shah of Iran teaching French and piano to his niece. She is now working in the secretariat of the Generalate of the Order in Rome, where I met with her often. But I am sure that others, whom I don't know, have even more remarkable stories to tell. Some have had a glorious military past. If I elaborate on three of them in this chapter, it is because they pretty well represent a phenomenon that we encounter in our communities. It is not human sympathies, converging political opinions, or some kind of common taste or affinity that unite us. We do not have any of the characteristics of a club of good friends, a political party, or a sect. Our communities are colorful, filled with diverse personalities united only by God's call and engagement in the same spiritual combat, the "service of a single Lord," or the same "school of divine service," as Saint Benedict said (RB Prol. 45)—in

113

short, one and the same community, oriented toward the search for God and structured by monastic observance.

This reality implies a reaching beyond one's own feelings and interests to meet and love each other on a different level, which Christians call "brotherly love." We do not look for God as hermits, but in a community, as cenobites. It is remarkable to note that Saint Bernard, when he talks about the "journey back to God," always provides for a space to encounter the neighbor, the brother. He always reasons from the point of view of indivisible trilogies, which at the end of the day relate to the me, the other, and God.[1] Modern authors also know that there is a link between the alienation of one's self and of the other and that there cannot be any reconciliation with one's self without reconciliation with the other, and vice versa. We could add, without reconciliation with God, and vice versa. A sure sign of our reconciliation with God is given to us by the parable of the Pharisee condemning his brother the publican (Luke 18:9-17). He is neither saved nor justified, even though his moral behavior seems perfect. We are not going towards God by cutting ourselves off from our brothers.

My time as superior of Cîteaux enabled me to become better acquainted with Father Baudouin, whom I introduced in chapter 2. He was a captain for Air France, who entered the monastery on April 3, 1950. The second person I mention in this chapter preceded him at the monastery, entering on July 19, 1949. I had the opportunity to meet Father Baudouin during some psychology sessions in which both of us participated in the years between 1965 and 1968. I was happy to see him again after all these years, the same brother I had known in Cîteaux.

The paths of these two brothers could easily have crossed before they chose the monastic life, even though they were going in opposite directions. The first path, chosen by Father Baud-

1. {Bernard of Clairvaux, *On Loving God* 8.23–25, Analytical Commentary by Emero Stiegman, CF 13B (Kalamazoo, MI: Cistercian Publications, 1995), 25–27.}

ouin, was that of the Resistance in World War II and victory. The road taken by Father Thibaud at a certain point in his career was darker. Without a certain manipulation of information, the young man of twenty-three, as he was then, might not have been freezing on the Russian front or fighting in the woods wearing a German uniform before being seriously wounded. Before the war of 1939–1945, the two young men did not know that they would be fighting under the command of leaders at war with each other before serving later side by side under a monastic rule and an abbot in the same community, searching together for Christ.

One day in 1940, the future Father Baudouin, who was not yet thinking about Cîteaux, sat down at a table in the airbase of Orconte, close to Vitry-le-François. With his squadron, he had just shot down a German Heinkel bomber. Suddenly he saw a name carved with a knife in the wooden table: Antoine de Saint-Exupéry, who had just been on the Orconte air base with his squadron and had sat at this very table. He would disappear over the Mediterranean Sea four years later.

"It was not in flight that we got the most scared," Baudouin explained later. "You had too much to do. It was on the ground that we realized that our days were numbered if the air combats continued with that frequency and if the war did not end soon. In my squadron of thirty pilots, ten had already died. Five were wounded, and another one had been taken prisoner. And we were only in 1940. Carving your name on a table seemed somewhat ludicrous, but you took your mind off of things any way that you could."

His parents were affluent. His father was a criminal court judge in Dijon and belonged to a long line of judges in Franche-Comté. His mother had pinned to his crib the genealogy of the Marquis de Montrichard, an old family dating back to the Crusades, which had allied itself with the family of Saint Bernard. In memory of that fact, he was named Bernard when he was born on March 3, 1912. The family lived in Neuilly, and everything pointed to a happy future supported by the family's wealth.

But that turned out to be a fragile and fleeting future. His father caught the gambling fever and lost his fortune, leaving behind huge debts. Bernard flunked the Baccalaureate at sixteen, and given the material disaster into which the family had been plunged, he had to find a job with an American pneumatic-drill manufacturer, while his mother was forced to take on manual labor for the first time. He became a substitute in different departments of the company while thinking anxiously about what he would become ten years in the future. Maybe in twenty years he would be at best a department head.

Two years later, his life changed because of one question: "Why don't you take the test to become a pilot?" one of his cousins asked him.

The Air Force financed a private school. He passed the test, and after fifteen hours of training in dual command, he completed his first solo flight, close to Clermont-Ferrand. He now had only one desire, to pilot the excellent Morane 230 plane, designed for acrobatics.

He hid above the clouds or behind Puy-de-Dôme with a piloting manual to try loops and barrel rolls. For the last flight of the school year, his demonstration earned him first prize. At nineteen he joined the prestigious fighter squadron in Istres, sharing his dorm with the future aces of the war that was about to start. His taste for danger and the recklessness of youth pushed him to place foolish bets, to execute loops just above the tree line, and to bail out of a spin at the latest possible moment, with a blackout at ground level, so that he wondered for a few seconds if the plane would make it or crash. He realized that he needed to conquer the fear of death if he wanted to become a good fighter pilot. Soon to reach the rank of senior corporal, his joy knew no bounds when he was sent to Le Bourget to join the acrobatics squadrons that performed during the visits of foreign heads of state. The Bastille Day parades and the flights low above Paris were accompanied by orders to crash in the Seine in case of a technical breakdown.

"It was better not to make any moves to the side on takeoffs, when forty planes, close to each other on the field, all took off together with a deafening roar," he remembered.

Ambitious and self-assured, he knew that he was among the best and held the others in contempt. He was quite proud to be at the controls of such a sophisticated plane. His first accident took place around that time. Close to Strasbourg, his engine stopped suddenly. He found a field, but the wheels didn't touch the ground, and at the end he hit an embankment, which tore away the landing gear. He was thrown into the canal but did not lose consciousness. He freed himself and swam to the bank, where a crowd was already assembling. All of a sudden, he remembered that orders had to be followed in the event of a forced landing in the countryside. The notice with the orders was still in the cockpit at the bottom of the canal, so he dove in again to go and get it. Then he realized that he had forgotten his parachute, so he disappeared into the water again. Back on the bank he remembered his luggage that had stayed behind, so he dove in for a third time, much to the amazement of the spectators. "It was a beautiful accident," remarked a reporter, who ran off and published a lengthy account in *Les Dernières Nouvelles d'Alsace*. The cause of the accident was that a pipe had gotten crushed by mistake during an overhaul, so that it prevented the tank from filling up properly.

The plane was equipped with an 850-horsepower engine and could climb to an altitude of 30,000 feet. Nevertheless, the plane didn't have a radio for navigation, and it was difficult for the pilot to determine his location when low clouds hid the ground and he was 80 or 150 miles from the base. The only way to orient himself was to fly the plane below the clouds, look for a railroad, and follow it until the next train station so that he could read the name. Bernard was named sergeant, and the report read, "Exceptional subject. Has exceptional ability to keep cool under pressure, endurance, and skill. Absolutely perfect morals." Specializing in high altitude flights, he wanted to keep flying further and faster, and to control the most modern, high-performance equipment. His ambition was to become a test pilot for an airplane manufacturer, and to be rich, famous, and admired.

Air France was created in 1933. Bernard was twenty-five and had about eight hundred flying hours when he joined the company.

After many reconnaissance flights on all the continental routes from Berlin to London and from Prague to Bucharest, he became captain on the Lyon-Geneva flight in May 1938. "The interest in that flight was that it had great restaurants at both ends," he noted.

The following winter, he was assigned to the Paris-Cologne-Berlin route and watched the Nazi troops holding parade after parade along streets covered with red flags bearing swastikas. He was in Berlin the night of Kristallnacht, November 9–10, 1938, and witnessed the fury of Hitler's militants as they broke the windows of the Jewish stores before looting them. On board the planes he noticed numerous Jewish passengers showing their happiness when he informed them that they had just crossed the French border.

He was promoted to second lieutenant the day of the mobilization in September 1939. He asked to join a combat fighter unit with a friend; they were sent to the "Tom Thumb" and "Red Devils" units, equipped with American Curtis P-36s, based in the Vosges.

At the same time, on the other side of France, a twenty-year-old boy, whom Bernard didn't yet know but whose destiny would be linked to his, was about to enter the elite cavalry school at Saumur.[2] He had worked very hard to be accepted into the Military Academy of Saint-Cyr[3] at eighteen years old, and he was now a second lieutenant.

"An important fact that determined part of my life," explained Father Thibaud, looking back, "is that I am a 'Victory Child' in that I was conceived in the joy of the armistice of November 11, 1918. I was born in August 1919, and I reached adulthood, then

2. {Saumur, a town in western France, is the location of the National Riding School, home of the famous Cadre Noir display team.}

3. {The Military Academy of Saint-Cyr (referred to as Saint-Cyr) is the most prestigious military academy in France. Founded in 1802 by Napoleon, it counts the most decorated French military leaders among its alumni.}

twenty-one years old, right after the armistice of 1940. This is how my youth fits into European history."

When he was around seven or eight years old he felt a strong call from God to enter into his service.

"The first call is often something that you shouldn't define as vague but rather as indistinct," he said. "I remember that it happened for me on a Saturday under a pear tree in a small garden, between the Seine and the house where I was born. Did I mention it to my sister, who was sitting next to me? I don't remember, but it was a precise and complete call from the Lord. Inwardly, it was very clear. Either I was going to die young, or I was going to be something like a priest. The way it was going to take shape, I didn't know just yet."

In 1933, the year that Hitler came to power in Germany, Thibaud spent his summer vacation in the Jura with one of his cousins. The two young people told each other, "There is no doubt! With all that is threatening us, we will have to join the military."

Slowly the thought of becoming an officer took shape. He would have liked our country to show its strength, and he favored standing up to the enemy. But the French government only showed its weakness, just as in 1936 the British and the Americans seemed to him not to do any better when Hitler occupied the Rhineland. In a philosophy class at Stanislas College in Paris, Thibaud took part in a retreat organized by this Catholic institute. He wanted to take advantage of this opportunity to decide between a military career and a monastic life.

There was not much information about monks available to him. "If you need to pray all day long, that is not for me," he told himself. He didn't know that the constant prayer of monks did not mean reciting formulas without end. To him, contemplation called to mind Hinduism, and he was not about to dedicate his life to that. "Oh no, no, this is not for me," he decided, and so off he went to the military!

After many tired nights, he finished his infantry year at St.-Cyr before starting a cavalry year with about thirty companions: it would be the last squadron of St.-Cyr riding on horseback and motorcycles. Almost every month they brought back a seriously injured soldier from the obstacle course. They were lucky not to have any deaths that year, but the infirmary always had a cavalry student as a patient. Thibaud had broken his foot during the previous year and entered the squadron limping.

On the weekends the soldiers relaxed with their friends, both boys and girls, activity that brought them out of their family cocoons. The girls were no longer just playmates, but women. They thought about these women sometimes, even if that didn't go very far. At that moment, it was the military service with all its risks that mattered to them.

Thibaud had barely arrived at Saumur in 1939 when he discovered an aspect of the Soviet reality that would always be in conflict with his views: Stalin had just made a pact with Hitler. Saumur, for which he had yearned for so long, would only last a week. The twenty-year-old second lieutenant would soon be confronted with the armored units of the future Field Marshal Erwin Rommel.[4] Before commanding the Afrika Korps, Rommel led the crossing of the Meuse River and the race to the Channel.

"I was thrown into the war with a total lack of information about many aspects of these misleading alliances and an obvious lack of maturity," Fr. Thibaud observed.

At first, he was in command of a motorcycle unit, which was part of the armored unit of the cavalry. His unit had modern mechanical equipment. They reached the province of Liège, in Belgium, where the Germans had just forced their way over the Albert Canal. What followed was a retreating fight, culminating in the battle of Arras on May 21, 1940, and the evacuation from Dunkirk to England. He embarked on a boat as German bombs started to fall on the docks. By way of Dover and Weymouth, he ended up twenty-four hours later back in the harbor of Cherbourg, France. After picking up new equipment in Paris, he re-

---

4. {Erwin Rommel (1891–1944) was a field marshal in the German Wehrmacht during World War II. His great success in commanding the German tank divisions, from the invasion in France through the North Africa campaign in 1941, earned him the nickname of "Desert Fox," *der Wüstenfuchs*.}

sumed the fight in retreat from Louviers, in the Eure region, just south of Angoulême. The general collapse appeared complete, but his unit, still in fighting condition, did not feel defeated.

Meanwhile, in the Air Force, where Bernard was fighting, panic was starting to set in. He turned white as a sheet when he received an order to take off at 5 a.m. The airfield had just been bombed for the first time. "Go and intercept a formation of a hundred bombers protected by fifty fighter planes," the order read. The enemy was pouring in, and he was left to confront them all by himself at that very moment, in a suicide mission that he had no time to dispute. He and his teammate headed towards the Saverne Pass, where the German formation was spotted. At all levels the authorities seemed to have lost their minds. Luckily, by the time they reached the pass, the German bombers had already crossed it. His teammate, whom he had known since their days in the "Tom Thumb" and "Red Devils" units, later died during another mad mission. The French anti-aircraft gunners shot more often at their own planes than at the Germans. These gunners were incapable of recognizing the nationality of the planes and shot at everything with wings. There was also some bad luck. Once when Bernard was returning to the base, he braked on the muddy ground, and the plane hit a large water pond and overturned. He hung upside down in the cockpit, his seat belts holding him in place with a burning hot engine below him. A very strong odor of fuel told him that the plane could blow up at any time. A prisoner of metal and belts, he expected to burn alive. After ten minutes of terrible anxiety, the rescue crew turned over the plane.

He knew then that his life wasn't worth much, but he didn't think of God or of defeat at that time. In his first air combat he encountered a powerful unit of four Messerschmitt 109s. Although he was locked on one of them, he couldn't pull the trigger, because killing was so abhorrent to him. Here he felt lost in a plane that was about seventy mph slower than the enemy's, but he made hairpin turns as soon as an enemy plane came up behind him. Suddenly, they got discouraged and disappeared without realizing that a simultaneous attack in front and back would have put an end to this cat-and-mouse game.

On June 9, 1940, Bernard had his first victory, and on June 11 his second one came after a fierce fight. By this time, he had fifty-five hours of combat flight, but everything was danger and absurdity on the ground and in the air, where there was nothing but explosions, machine-gun fire, panicked planes, yells, and contradictory rumors. Was this Messerschmitt pilot wounded when he flew away in a straight line at reduced speed towards another battle? Bernard caught up with him and fired in bursts, until the plane fell like a stone and crashed. He then attacked a heavy bomber protected by a large squadron of fighter planes and shot it down. He was awarded the Croix de Guerre with two citations: "Has distinguished himself with courage, energy, and audacity . . . brilliant officer."

At that time these two officers—Bernard and Thibaud—had one and the same enemy. How did their journeys diverge? The first one, Bernard, left for the Near East in December 1940 as captain of an Air France plane. He had rejoined the company after being demobilized. The second one, Thibaud, had landed a month earlier in the capital of Lebanon, assigned to a Spahi cavalry unit.[5] From December on he was under the command of General Dentz, high commissioner and commander of the troops in the East. The two future monks did not know each other yet, but their paths were slowly getting closer. To tell the truth, their destinies could still turn around, and until the end no one knew who would do what or how. As the Spahis successively assumed three surveillance posts at the border with Palestine, Bernard, now receiving orders from Vichy,[6] had to deliver—to his

5. {The Spahis were a cavalry regiment of the French army, largely recruited from the local population of Algeria, Tunisia, and Morocco, as were the Zouaves (see above, chap. 5, p. 94, n. 2).}

6. {Vichy: the city where the French government was located during World War II. Headed by Marshal Philippe Pétain, it collaborated with the German forces occupying France. Pétain and his government had control over the

great dismay—French planes to the Germans before he could go on to Syria to start his civilian post. At this crossroads different directions were possible. The human soul is in its own way the crossroads of all possibilities.

In the East, the situation was getting distressing, even grotesque. An Air Force officer in Syria took Bernard to task when he was put in charge of a Dewoitine 338 to fly the shuttle route between Athens and Aleppo, which was occupied by the Germans: "All Air France officers are cowards."

The officer's statement was unfortunate, since he didn't have any personal victories on his record. Bernard refused to take on this little battle in the midst of the larger war. It was nevertheless at this moment that he made a decision that he would regret for the rest of his life. After about twenty British pilots shot down by French fighter planes[7] were made prisoner, they boarded his plane to be handed over to the Germans in Athens. Above Cyprus, one of the British pilots came to the cockpit to implore him to fly them to Cairo instead. Bernard hesitated. There was no good way out of his predicament. There was an armed escort on the plane to guard the prisoners, and he did not know the signals to approach Egypt without being attacked. Moreover, he was singlehandedly responsible for the support of his entire family, his father, his mother, and his sister with two children, whose husband had already rejoined General de Gaulle in London.[8] If he diverted the plane, how would the escort react? What would

---

Free Zone in the south (see above, chap. 3, pp. 37–38, n. 2) from 1940 to 1942, while the Germans controlled the Occupied Zone in the north. From 1942 on the Germans controlled both zones militarily and administratively.}

7. {As a part of the armistice signed in June 1940, the French Air Force planes, still useful for the Germans, were requisitioned together with their French pilots. These pilots had to follow orders from the German command.}

8. {Charles de Gaulle (1890–1970): the French general who from London led the resistance against the German invaders after having refused the armistice signed by Pétain in 1940. De Gaulle was the leader of Free France, and he headed up the Provisional Government after France's liberation. He was elected President of France in 1960 and remained in that position until 1969.}

the anti-aircraft batteries in Cairo do? What would be the consequences for his family? He refused and went on to Athens. Later,
when he was at an RAF airbase in Scotland on New Year's Eve,
a British officer came up to him, totally drunk, and insulted him
profusely. A captain intervened, whispering in his ear, "Don't
blame this British pilot; he was shot down over Syria, and the
French handed him over to the Germans!"

Bernard remembered and didn't say anything. His honor was
hurt. He had been forced by circumstances to obey orders that
had resulted in *de facto* collaboration without any intent. These
pilots were ultimately liberated under particular conditions of
the Armistice of St.-Jean-d'Acres.

Later Bernard traveled to Dakar and throughout Africa in ter-
ritories controlled by the Vichy government, an experience that
enabled him to bring back some supplies for his family. He was
part of the patrol in charge of the evacuation of Marshal Pétain
and his government after the November 13, 1942, landing by the
allies in North Africa. But the marshal refused to leave France.[9]

Everything then took a new turn for Bernard, who was thinking about joining the Resistance. A few days later he welcomed
Commandant Manuel, an officer who had secretly come from
London to inspect the Resistance network. With his sister, Bernard had planned to treat Manuel to a good meal at a black-
market restaurant near Marseille. When they arrived, Bernard
realized that the restaurant had just been requisitioned by the
Wehrmacht to serve as a mess for its officers, who were having
lunch. Without missing a beat, Bernard asked the owner if they
could be served in a corner of the room. The owner asked the
Germans if he could serve his three friends, and they agreed.
Commandant Manuel sat down, but he had lost his appetite!
Nevertheless, he put Bernard in contact with the Phratrie resis-

9. {When the Allies landed in North Africa in 1942, the Vichy government
collapsed, and Marshal Pétain was given the opportunity to flee to North
Africa, but he refused and remained in France. He was then a simple figure-
head.]

tance network, which stretched from Marseille to Nice, where Bernard would be in charge of everything that related to the Luftwaffe. Nevertheless, the total absence of discretion within the network, which held its meetings in a restaurant in Cannes, worried the new member, who decided to leave for London.

The Gestapo was very interested in the name Cordier, which was often mentioned in radio transmissions. They tried to find out who this Cordier was. In fact, that name was used as an alias; the fake documents of Commandant Manuel used it, as well as those used by First Lieutenant Sonneville. The real Cordier—Bernard—notified that the Gestapo was actively looking for him, went into hiding, changing domiciles each night. What saved him was his habit of never using elevators. One day he had an appointment with the head of a network on the sixth floor of a building in Passy. Through an open door, he noticed the long coats of the Gestapo agents who had come to arrest him. He tiptoed back down the stairs as fast as he could, passing the desk of the concierge as she was being interrogated by other Gestapo members, who did not see him.

In London, he joined the Royal Air Force with a friend. He joined Squadron 148, based in Brindisi, Italy. The preparatory courses of the RAF were so demanding that there were about as many casualties during training as during combat missions. In order to preserve the morale of the aviators, the squadron leaders did not let anyone talk about accidents or go to funerals. Toward the end of the war, Cordier watched as crews were sent on Churchill's express orders to drop weapons by parachute into Warsaw, which had prematurely risen up against the Germans and was now surrounded. They knew full well that they would not return from these missions, because the tanks of their Halifax planes could not carry enough fuel to make the round trip, so they would have to land in enemy territory. At the same time, French pilots were dropping equipment and weapons by parachute for the Resistance in Yugoslavia.

Demobilized in July 1945, Bernard rejoined Air France, where he led the center for advanced training of flying personnel. Then he became head pilot of the continental network and president of the airline's union, before being assigned to the Paris-Saigon route. But it was the Paris-New York route that interested him the most, because they flew Constellations, modern, pressurized planes that flew at an altitude of 24,000 feet on night flights, when he felt far above the earth and the ocean. Sometimes they could see the Northern Lights.

On January 18, 1948, during a heavy snow storm in New York, the airport was closed for takeoffs and landings. He noticed that the atmospheric pressure data given by the meteorologists showed a unique weather pattern along a circle that exactly covered the New York-Paris route. The tail winds were estimated at more than seventy miles an hour for the whole trip. He decided to leave after a discussion with the authorities. It was night, and the visibility did not exceed ten feet. As the plane rolled through the snow to the end of the runway, he regretted starting this adventure. Usually direct flights took fifteen hours with favorable winds, but it often took twenty-five hours with stopovers in Newfoundland and Ireland. The plane took off without any problem; after ten hours and fifteen minutes of flight Bernard landed in Paris, thereby establishing a speed record that he kept for as long as Constellations were used on that route. He was living in a studio apartment in New York and making a lot of friends at the time.

This is the point at which his whole life took a dramatic turn. Landing at Paris Orly airport one day, he clearly understood that three days before he had taken off from the same airport for New York and that there was nothing left of this trip. How many thousands of miles had he traveled? What was left of it? He was passionate about his job, and he was well paid. He frequented palaces and restaurants patronized by billionaires. He could boast of knowing almost every nightclub in the world. He was one of the best pilots in the fleet, and his colleagues had twice elected him president of their union. But as time went by the more bored he became, even though he had everything possible to entertain him. Religion? Not important! It didn't matter to him. It didn't do anything for him. In fact, he had moved further away from it, as a handsome young man enjoying many short-lived romantic adventures without any remorse. He thought about getting married, but he became too particular, and despite being surrounded by a bevy of attractive flight attendants, he didn't find anyone to his taste.

On August 15, 1948, Assumption Day, he stayed home alone. He closed the shutters and took himself out of the present with a couple of good books. In flipping through the pages of a book on the origin of the world and evolution, he was struck by a sudden thought. A certainty slowly overwhelmed him, one he couldn't even question: "God exists. He is real, and he is everything. I exist only through him; he loves me, and he knows me and loves me in a particular way." For a whole hour he remained caught up in an emotion he had never felt before. That was when he decided suddenly to dedicate his life to God. The reversal was sudden and complete, and he felt that it would last.

He gave himself eighteen months, until Easter 1950, to bring his gift to fruition, knowing that nothing happens overnight. At Saulchoir, the Dominican study house in Soisy-sur-Seine, he met Father Yves Congar,[10] who recommended that he spend some time at a retreat house next to their monastery. The house, called L'Eau Vive, used to be the property of the marquise de Pompadour. He got a room on the third floor in the house in the middle of a park. On the second floor lived the Christian philosopher Jacques Maritain,[11] with his wife Raïssa and his sister-in-law. The first floor was occupied by the future cabinet member Alain Peyrefitte, who had recently gotten married and converted.

10. {See above, chap. 5, p. 110, n. 10.}

11. {Jacques Maritain (1882–1973): a French philosopher who converted to Catholicism at age 24 after having been disappointed by Scientism. He and his wife Raïssa, a well-known poet, helped through their prolific writings to revive Saint Thomas Aquinas for modern times. The future Pope Paul VI was influenced by their writings and maintained a lasting friendship with them.}

The flights to New York continued. Between flights he read a lot and attended classes given to the young Dominicans. One winter day, as he was taking off from New York at 3 a.m. for Gander, Newfoundland, the last refueling stop before the trans-Atlantic portion of the flight, the engines lost power, so he had barely enough lift to clear the tree line. A thick black smoke filled the cockpit with a burnt smell. The fire, of the kind that often signaled the end of a plane, created a panic. Death was present again, threatening him on his journey. Assuming an electrical short, he shut off the electrical switches. He succeeded in bringing the plane back to its departure location without any instrument lights and without any radio communications with which to send a distress call or to request that the runway lights stay on.

He was tired of that lifestyle. When he went to the Col de la Voza in the Mont Blanc region to ski with some friends and some flight attendants, he realized that daily Mass was becoming necessary for him. In March, while night still covered the frozen Olympic slopes, he went down to the little church of Les Houches at seven in the morning. He shortened his vacation to visit the Abbey of Hautecombe, which looked sad and almost dead in the gloomy weather. A little later he brought a woman into his studio in New York. He glanced at the crucifix hanging above his bed and explained to her that something had changed in his life. When she left she might not have understood anything, but he knew that his new orientation was irrevocable. One day, after 8,700 flying hours, about a whole year in the air, he walked down Fifth Avenue in New York and stopped in front of a bookstore across the street from the Plaza Hotel, where he saw a picture of Thomas Merton, a monk of the Cistercian abbey of Gethsemani in Kentucky. Merton's famous autobiography *La nuit privée d'étoiles*[12] caused him to discover some aspects of a *trappe* that he had purposely ignored because of the austerity

---

12. {Published in English as *The Seven Storey Mountain* (New York: Mariner Books, 1998).}

that he thought was inhuman. He gathered information on the different monasteries of our Order. The one in Aiguebelle, with its twelfth-century architecture, looked attractive to him, but someone recommended to him the dynamic and welcoming abbot at Cîteaux, Dom Godefroid Bélorgey, who had also converted at age thirty after a fall from a horse.

The abbot welcomed Bernard at the guest house and invited him to attend a monks' retreat that would take place a few weeks later. On the appointed day in February 1950, he arrived at the Dijon train station and called the monastery to confirm his attendance. "It is our retreat. We aren't receiving anyone," the brother porter told him, since he hadn't recognized his voice.

Amazed, Bernard was tempted to leave and join his friends at the ski resort. He hesitated and climbed into a taxi, praying to the Virgin Mary to enlighten him. He was sure that if he didn't go to Cîteaux then, he might never go back. The misunderstanding was quickly resolved. Bernard was enthusiastic about the Carmelite father preaching the retreat. The superior suggested that he pursue this interest further and come back during Easter week. On that occasion, in the middle of about a hundred monks, he was transported to another world, reliving the passion and resurrection of Christ through the sacraments and prayers. In the face of his determination, he was accepted for a year as an observer, without any commitment and without being vested as a novice, because his late calling and his professional activities did not allow a vocation to be taken for granted at that time. His name became Brother Baudouin.

Among all the unknown faces, Bernard hadn't noticed a novice who had joined a couple of months before him. Brother Thibaud had been injured in the leg. This thirty-year-old had come back from another hell of fire and pain without any glory or medals.

"Brother Thibaud was wounded in the leg in Syria," the novice master told Bernard one day as a short summary, but he didn't have the opportunity to talk with Thibaud. Could they have imagined that their destinies had been so different during the war years? They didn't care; they offered themselves to God, thinking only about God and wanting only to please him. That was more than enough for them. But God would ask a tough sacrifice of Bernard—Brother Baudouin—to begin with.

The new Brother Baudoin did not get along with the novice master. This was his toughest test during his early days in the monastery. The antipathy he felt for him seemed to be reciprocal. Until then he had been trained to give orders, but at Cîteaux he had only to obey. This he could accept, but to obey someone who didn't understand him and seemed to multiply the obstacles on his journey just for fun—was that necessary? This novice master was thirty-one years old. He had entered the monastery in 1941 and had been a priest for the last five years. He knew Bernard's story and noticed that he was harder to manage than Brother Thibaud or the other twenty-year-old novices who had entered the monastery. To test Bother Baudouin's vocation, the Novice Master used means that baffled Bernard.

Baudouin was ready to suffer anything for Christ, and if they had asked ten times more of him, he would have accepted ten times more. But still, why such humiliation? At that time, in accordance with the rules then in force, a superior was allowed to read the correspondence received by the novices. The purpose was to help in their formation and not to abuse one's authority by showing a lack of consideration. Perhaps Brother Baudouin did not distinguish very well between an obnoxious abuse and mutual assistance, which was part of the formation. One habit of the novice master particularly annoyed Baudouin—waiting a few days before handing over the letters to him and also asking indiscreet questions about the details of these letters.

"We were only entitled," he remembered, "to one letter from our parents every three or four months, nothing more. I watched for the moment when the mail would come in, telling myself, 'Well, here you go, there is a letter from your mother today.' I was happy, but the novice master didn't give it to me immediately. He made me wait one, two, three, or four days—and still nothing. Then he would call me in, and I would see the open envelope with the letter unfolded on the table. He would ask me tons of questions about my family. He would have liked for me to tell him all about the letter that I had not read yet. I was hurt each time. For someone who had just left the life of a pilot with all its responsibilities, this test was hard and totally unexpected, and I would become absolutely furious. As soon as I recovered a semblance of calm, I would say, 'There, this is the test that the Lord sends me, having that novice master. There probably aren't two like that in the whole Order, and I had to get him.'"

Clearly, this young novice master was being excessively zealous; it was not necessary to dissect a letter in front of a novice or to submit him to invented humiliations to mold him to the Rule of Saint Benedict. Brother Baudouin was not yet capable of understanding the sense of these tests, but he looked for a way to regain interior peace. He extended his time of prayer in adoration, remaining fifteen or thirty minutes in silence, abandoned to God, giving everything to him, without any specific prayer, and often came away with an unexpected serenity.

On the other hand, he appreciated the abbot and did not understand how the two men, so different from each other, could get along and complement each other. While he had to show patience with some actions that he experienced as bullying, in the hallways of certain governmental agencies at the same time it was being proposed that he receive the Legion of Honor, Second Degree. Other novices reacted differently, accepting as natural in a monastic environment dedicated to contemplation and penance certain things that were not acceptable to this new monk, who could have been their father.

"My two years in the novitiate were only bearable because there was God. I didn't care about anything else. It was becoming less and less important to me. I felt perfectly happy with God."

He was so happy that, consulting the calendar, he made sure that he took his temporary vows on a certain day so that three years later he could take his perpetual vows on the Monday after Pentecost, so that his family and friends would be able to attend. He was so sure that he would stay! Nevertheless, sometimes he was nostalgic as he watched planes fly by and said, "Since it is over, it is over." At his age, he knew what he was leaving behind and he had no regrets.

His life was Christ and following Christ. The hardest thing for him physically was to stay awake between three and five o'clock in the morning reading a book or a notebook in the library. Another thing was withstanding the cold. He served Mass holding the glass cruets tightly in his hands so that the water did not freeze. The two wood-burning stoves in the church were barely enough to warm a person up when he stood close to them, and the temperature often fell below twenty-three degrees Fahrenheit. These were extreme conditions. As Baudouin said, "Horribly terrible conditions." The food was Spartan, soup and a vegetable plate, never meat, fish, or eggs. And the silence, the ever-present silence of the monastery. As an additional trial, he did not understand any Latin, and he needed to learn it to become a priest. He was ordained at his old school in Neuilly on March 18, 1961. Many admirals and generals attended, including Generals Zeller and Challe, specialists in the Air Force, a few days before the Algiers Putsch of 1961.[13]

Meanwhile, during his initial years, Brother Thibaud also felt cold. He worked a lot and ate a little more than his brothers because he was considered weaker. He told his superiors everything he had to say, and Dom Godefroid Bélorgey, superior for sixteen years, welcomed him in searching to discern God's call. As a novice he didn't feel very proud of himself, and he had a huge need for reconciliation through Christ. What he found extraordinary about the monks was their unending forgiveness

---

13. {The Algiers Putsch took place in Algiers from April 21 to April 26, 1961. It was an attempt by four French generals to stop General de Gaulle's plan to give independence to Algeria; they aimed ultimately to take over the government in Paris. The Algerian war had been underway since 1954, and terrorist groups were getting more aggressive in France. The generals' coup failed when enlisted men rallied to General de Gaulle and refused to follow the four generals.}

for repeated offenses, both great and small. Life was hard for everyone in the novitiate, and those who lacked a real vocation left. Like Bernard, Thibaud too was enthusiastic about the superior, and he too had problems with the novice master. He did spectacular penances because of his violent offenses, but he never thought about leaving the monastery. He quickly realized that he was not a prisoner within four walls, because he could move around the large property and the buildings. The monks always had something to forgive each other for, were it only their illnesses or annoying habits.

"It was not pleasant for the others either," said Brother Thibaud, "to see a brother abandon his work station to go to the infirmary or to the doctor." The Rule of Saint Benedict specifically states that "sick brothers must be patiently borne with" (RB 36.5), both physically and morally. Perpetual reconciliation is one of the essential elements of the balance in our lives. We are brothers without being able to form a natural family. We are not simply buddies or colleagues. But reconciliation is permanent and constitutes an essential element of the type of life we live.

In 1941 the Spahis of Lebanon had been at a crossroad. Thibaud had been sent with his men to a post dominating the Jordan valley, on the old Silk Road going from Tyre to Damascus, south of the last foothills of Lebanon. A little further to the west, the men on watch spent their days observing the land towards Haifa with huge binoculars. One day in May, British troops with colonial helmets took positions along the white markers on the other side of the border. They were there about thirty feet away from each other along the same line, looking in opposite directions with equally large binoculars! The grotesqueness of the situation was equaled only by the tragic. No one knew who was doing what. The young Spahi officer ended up going to the British troops to ask them—if they didn't want any encounters with the French lookouts—not to cross the white marker line to get a better view of the scrubland.

"We are watching for the arrival of the Germans," the British officer answered.

"Don't worry, I'll make sure to notify you in time," the French-man answered, with humor.

This tragicomic aspect of the war surprised Thibaud. During the Lebanese campaign, the war appeared to him as a web of absurdities, and his companions were affected the same way. He was then twenty-two years old, and he seriously questioned the competence of those who led them. It seemed to him that they were getting into a war of brother against brother.

"One of the turning points in my life was getting involved in these absurdities," he acknowledged. "After the attack at Mers-el-Kébir,[14] there was Dakar, where General de Gaulle wanted to disembark with a British squadron. He was rebuffed by the governor, who had remained faithful to Marshal Pétain. And then there was the Levant in 1941. These events convinced me that even great leaders commit monumental mistakes."

Thibaud was repatriated from Lebanon to North Africa when he heard the call for volunteers for the "Tricolor Legion." Benoist-Méchin[15] and others were setting up an army that would be different from the one that came out of the ceasefire and the one that was active in North Africa. The project seemed crazy to Thibaud, but in 1942 he took some small steps in that direction just to learn more about it. "Why should I get into this?" he asked himself warily. He didn't really know.

---

14. {The Battle of Mers-el-Kébir is the name given to the July 3, 1940, bombing by the British Royal Navy of the French navy, which had remained under the command of the Vichy government and was stationed at Mers-el-Kébir, on the coast of French Algeria. The attack was the British response to Vichy's signing the Second Armistice with the Germans on June 22, 1940. Almost 1,300 French servicemen were killed.}

15. {Jacques Benoist-Méchin (1901–1983) was a French politician with strong pro-German opinions between the two world wars. He collaborated with the German forces occupying France in World War II by serving in the Vichy government and organizing the Légion des Volontaires Français, a military unit wearing German uniforms, which was set up to fight the Soviets on the eastern front.}

Once back in France he rejoined the barracks in Gueret and then the Caserne de la Reine in Versailles, where the headquarters were located for the French Volunteer Legion against Bolshevism, created in July 1941. The New "Tricolor" Legion wore German uniforms and had confused officers and a small group of soldiers, with few contacts with the French Volunteer Legion.[16] One day in October 1942, in the officer's mess, the colonel in charge made a dramatic announcement, much to everybody's surprise: "Well," he said, "we all need to join the French Volunteer Legion."

Until then this arrangement had been strictly prohibited. A great deal of discussion followed, revealing a strong reluctance on the part of some of the soldiers. So the commander created a simplistic myth that worked perfectly under these dramatic circumstances: "It is stupid to fight against each other for ever. We need to end these wars between the French and the Germans. We have seen Germans in the French Foreign Legion, but we have never seen Frenchmen join German units. Why?" This beautiful symmetry led to a request to end the series of wars with the hereditary enemy. The commander added: "You might lose everything, but you need to take this step, even if you do not fully understand it."

They had to decide within the hour. Either they left or they stayed. The initial organization was intended to compete with the French Volunteer Legion, but the reality was that its members would be absorbed by it. This meant the failure of Benoist-Méchin, who, as we all later learned, had already been sidelined a month earlier.

Aberration? Treason? Utopia? These were men who would risk everything, rightly or wrongly. Cowardice? A pitiful attempt at fraternization? A blind desire for reconciliation? They needed

16. {The Legion of French Volunteers Against Bolshevism (LVF) was a regiment founded by far-right French collaborationists in 1941 to fight the Bolsheviks on the Eastern front, alongside the German army. They lost half of their men in the battle around Moscow in November 1941.}

to give an answer immediately. Was it confusion after three years of war, or the need to achieve something useful, to serve? Rotten war! Thibaud needed to decide: he said yes.

First he was sent to a training camp in Poland, between Warsaw and Radom. A few weeks later he took part in skirmishes in the woods, in diversionary maneuvers behind the front lines with the furthest position in Briansk, in Russia. His new life was being transformed by this huge landscape, fighting against partisans, summer and winter alike. These battles were similar to those that some of his comrades would later fight in Indochina and Algeria under the French banner. Nevertheless, wearing the German uniform was so painful to Thibaud that he considered it a humiliation, a tragicomic calvary, but he still believed in the value of his commitment. During a confrontation close to Moghilev in Ukraine during the winter of 1943–1944, a part of his battalion was suddenly ambushed. As he was going to his commander for new orders, a stray bullet fractured his thigh. For him, everything was over—or better, everything was just beginning.

From February 1944 to May 1945 Thibaud went from hospital to hospital, where his thigh was broken once again. After many surgeries, he was convinced that he had come close to death. This realization made him think about the religious orientation of his life, which he had considered for the first time sitting under the pear tree. A German policeman hospitalized next to him made vague references to concentration camps. It was the first time Thibaud had heard about this. He was recovering in Austria when the Americans arrived and was brought back to France in a convoy of Alsatians—prisoners who had been drafted into the German army by force, along with a number of soldiers from Lorraine. Sometimes they had been forced to join the SS and sent to the eastern front. After the annexation of Alsace by Hitler's regime, about 140,000 were drafted in that way. The Americans referred to them as "the French of the Wehrmacht" and brought them to a triage camp with very little surveillance. In Strasbourg, Thibaud left the train when the locomotive was unhooked. He reached Paris in August.

Comrades found him shelter and subsistence. The French government demoted him from the rank of lieutenant, and his file started to circulate, like thousands of similar ones. He was more and more convinced of the stupidity of war as he watched the expedited trials going on after the Liberation. On both sides, men and women were all the same. He wondered, "What did I do for eighteen months while I was wearing the uniform of the Wehrmacht? I only discovered the human being in the Russian, the Pole, the German, the Lebanese, the prisoner, the wounded, the dead. It is always the same human being who suffers, under different attitudes and different faces."

From this time on, he lived a clandestine life. As years went by, he got increasingly tired of the situation, so he foolishly tried to cross the border and was arrested on Ash Wednesday 1948. It felt like a great relief, because it put an end to his clandestine life, in which he never stopped worrying about compromising those who were helping him. He waited for his trial in Paris; then it was moved to Limoges and finally to Toulouse. Like other prisoners in the same situation, he was incarcerated with common criminals and so discovered the hard job of the guards and the task of the volunteers involved in prison ministry. He had received the death penalty in absentia, but after the trial the sentence was reduced to five years of hard labor, which in turn was reduced to the year he had already served behind bars. He was pardoned in March 1949 and then freed after having paid his official debt to society. A few months of vacation with his family enabled him to find some balance in his life. He also inquired about the monastic life, which he wanted to embrace once again after having spent this one war too many as a "pre-postulant." He entered Cîteaux in July 1949.

His heart would be tested year after year, just like Brother Baudouin's. Good or bad, pure or impure, fair or unfair, the sheep or the wolf, all refer to categories that are not so well defined in the real world. Isn't it in our heart that we first confront right and wrong, friend and foe? Moreover, what does it mean to be right? If you pretend to be right, you put yourself in one camp. But aren't you then becoming wrong in the eyes of the other camp? Only Christ and the Spirit of Christ can justify us and make us understand the other side.

But Brother Thibaud drew another lesson from his adventures, that he had been partly the victim of manipulation, and he remained vigilant against anything that looked like that. As he commented,

> The manipulation of information is dangerous; it is a crime, and it often continues today concerning all the events happening everywhere in the world. It has become impossible to speak to soldiers today about obedience without addressing its limits, such as conscientious objection. Now our military codes include the right to refuse to obey an illegal command. The same question could be raised in monasteries about important matters. The formula "everyone is responsible" is definitely in fashion, but it only works under the condition of another formula: "everyone is informed." You cannot be responsible for what you don't know.

These are problems of personal environment; the essential requirement for men and women is to be true to God and true to themselves.

André Naël, another man who had been an adventurer, one day desired to be true to God and true to himself. Shortly after entering the monastery, he joined the other two veterans, but it didn't start well for him. His father had taught him to read in Saint-Pée-sur-Nivette, a small village in Basque country, seven miles from Saint-Jean-de-Luz, where he was born on March 22, 1917. He didn't like school. He later became a passionate, insatiable reader of Saint Paul, but as a child he didn't know his letters and numbers. He was all tangled up, and everybody felt sorry for him. When he was eleven he still could not tell time. One day, all of a sudden, he got it: "Ah, wow, that's the way it works!"

He experienced such a great joy that twenty-five years later he experienced a similar but stronger and growing joy when reading the biblical texts that had been inaccessible to him: "But this is obvious! Now I understand what they mean!"

André had a somewhat unusual childhood. While very young he loved running in the mountains surrounding the Nivelle valley. His father, from Brittany, had been orphaned at four years of age and at fourteen joined the merchant marines as a cabin boy. As a sailor on ships that sailed around Cape Horn before 1900 in search of guano for fertilizer, he went around the world thirty-six times or more. Not surprisingly, when he was at home he taught André geography. Recognizing the incredible risks inherent in being away from land for months and the possibility that they would never return, the sailors sometimes organized a feast before sailing. It was a life of misery.

André also came to experience the world's misery, though not material misery so much as misery of the spirit. Later he would say, "I was in the darkness," adding, "and in Satan's Empire." His parents, saddened by his life choices, suffered because of them. Shortly before her death, his mother reminded him that when he was twelve years old, he had thought of becoming a monk as he walked by a Capuchin convent each Sunday on the way to a rugby match. When at the age of eighteen he could not find a job, he joined the navy in Toulon and became part of a submarine crew, an occupation that wanted only volunteers. It was a dangerous life, confined at the bottom of an oceanic night that enabled André to discover humanity's dark side. He embarked on a very long journey to the end of this night. "If we have to sink, we'll sink," he thought. One day, when the submarine was diving off the Azores Islands, an officer explained a new technique for getting out through the lock in case they sank. But then he stopped: "In any case, this is pointless. Don't think for a moment that you can save yourself around here," he concluded. "We would all have been crushed, twelve thousand feet deep, before we could ascend."

When the pressure was too high on submarines that were submerged, the rivets exploded and water surged in, but thanks to safety partitions, the crew members did not always drown.

Instead they found themselves dying slowly of suffocation. They endured expeditions into the abyss of anguish, where they lived one on top of the other without any comfort, without water to wash in, getting as dirty as possible. They only emerged from the darkness at the end of two weeks, and, like the mine workers described by Émile Zola,[17] only to prepare during the following two weeks for their next dive. Sometimes André had the feeling that he would not survive the next expedition. So much the worse! He had learned not to be frightened anymore. One could even say that he was attracted by danger.

He was promoted to non-commissioned officer—chief warrant officer—but he felt no enthusiasm. He didn't know if a military career was his calling. Every time he had to allot a punishment, he felt embarrassed; he finally gave it up, considering that the life of these men was hard enough to be a punishment all by itself. The commanding officers were hard, and the risks were high. He wanted to change jobs. Three years later he joined the colonial telegraph operators, learning Morse Code and international communications.

André's base was at Montauban, where seventy-five percent of the specialists came from the navy and occupied most of the high positions in La Coloniale[18] throughout Indochina, Sub-Saharan Africa, China, and the Pacific. He was assigned to Dakar, Senegal, and was scheduled to ship out from Bordeaux on September 15, 1939. On September 3, war was declared and everything ground to a halt. He was not allowed to go to the front to fight, as he had

---

17. {Émile Zola, *Germinal*, trans. Roger Pearson (London: Penguin, 2004). Zola (1840–1902) was a French political activist and writer known for his theories on naturalism. Probably the most famous French novelist of the late-nineteenth century, he intervened in the "Dreyfus Affair," a case against a Jewish army officer wrongly accused of treason. He published an open letter in the newspaper *L'Aurore* beginning with the famous statement, "J'accuse!"}

18. {La Coloniale was a military regiment of forces recruited among the local populations of the French Colonial Empire from 1822 to 1961.}

requested, but was put in charge of instructing the new recruits. A few weeks later he protested and was sent to China, where he served as a radio operator at the French Embassy in Beijing before being sent to a post on the Great Wall of China.

Was he safer there than in the depths of the ocean? One of his comrades from Montauban was beheaded with a saber by a Japanese soldier who made him kneel down with his hands tied behind him. That happened at the border with Vietnam in Long Son, where skirmishes between French and Japanese forces took place in 1940 and where he would end up later. He didn't know how many others died on land or on the sea. Many submarines from the squadron that he had first belonged to were sunk in North Africa in 1942. What did all this slaughter mean? What was humanity doing? Where did all this violence come from?

He had never ceased thinking about the origins of humankind, after he strangely crossed paths in Beijing with Pierre Teilhard de Chardin,[19] whose lab was next door to where André was living. Chardin had participated in team research that in February 1929 in Chou-kou-tien discovered the Sinantrope, a prehistoric human about 500,000 years old. That discovery, and especially Chardin's writings, suspect because they were so innovative, made Chardin a world-famous personality. He was attempting to reconcile the scientific vision of the world with the Christian faith. His friend, Father Leroy, also a Jesuit, was a zoologist and

19. {Pierre Teilhard de Chardin (1881–1955) was a French Jesuit who taught sciences in a Jesuit College in Cairo, Egypt, and worked in the paleontology laboratory in Paris before World War I. He traveled to China to pursue his studies in human paleontology. Teilhard's unique understanding of paleontology and Catholicism enabled him to argue a progressive, cosmic theology based on evolution. Many of his writings were censored by the Catholic Church while he was still alive, but his book *The Phenomenon of Man* was published after his death. Pope Benedict XVI praised him, and Pope Francis cited his teachings in his encyclical *Laudato Si'* (w2.vatican.va/content /francesco/en/encyclicals/documents/papa-francesco_20150524_enciclica -laudato-si.html).}

the head of the laboratory. These two Jesuits transformed a building in the French barracks, located close to the embassies and left vacant when the officers and the troops left, into an institute of geobiology.

"Why don't we go see Father Leroy?" André suggested in 1943 to two non-commissioned officers who accompanied him. He and his friends walked the three hundred feet that separated them from the institute and knocked at the door. They discovered a staircase and saw Father Leroy standing at the top of the stairs. "Come on up," he said.

On the wall a large board hung, representing insects, tadpoles, birds, and a multitude of other species, with humans at the top. Father Leroy exclaimed,

"Behold man!" He then spent the whole afternoon explaining his research on biological evolution, what Teilhard and his colleagues called orthogenesis.

During the next three years, André regularly crossed paths with Chardin, who kept his residence in that house until March 1946. Each time André gave a military salute, the Jesuit responded with a smile, although he moved in circles of scholars and prominent people, a world totally different from that of these young soldiers. In December 1945 a message reached Chardin while André was on radio duty. General de Gaulle was asking Chardin to come back to France, because he was such a well-known scholar. André delivered the message to the embassy, but Chardin did not act on it, for he owed obedience only to his religious superiors.

These contacts with men of faith did not change André's opinion about the deeper realities. Faith did not do very much for him, and theological and scientific research did not upset his life. He wanted to complete his fifteen years of military service in order to collect his full retirement. Six years after his arrival in China, with the war having wound down, another one was about to start. He was told, "We are going to land in the Tonkin, and we need radio specialists." In 1946 he fought with the first marine division attached to the 821st battalion. Upon their arrival in Halong Bay they were the targets of Chinese guns, and the landing was a disaster. Many were killed on board the cruiser where he was the radio liaison with the flagship, where General Leclerc[20] was in command.

While André was in the Tonkin in 1949 he learned of the death of his mother. He had been in China when his father died in 1944. Now he felt lonelier than ever and was about to break down. "Is life that absurd?" he thought; "Is there no way out?" He was becoming an old veteran, maybe even a bit hot-headed. Bitterness overtook him when he heard that his parents had died without his having had the chance to see them again. Difficult moments came one on top of the other. Bullets shot by Chinese soldiers pierced the train compartment in which he was traveling.

Two and a half years later, André went back to China, where it was much quieter. He lived among telegraph operators, improving his knowledge of the Chinese language and visiting families of peasants. He was struck by their superstition, which he compared to the superstition of the French peasants he had met during his youth. Nevertheless, he sometimes lit sticks of incense. The prayer wheels of the Tibetan lamas he met in a monastery close to Beijing did not convince him. In fact, he didn't believe in anything. Even though he was a Christian by family tradition, he nevertheless did not have faith. What he had learned earlier remained foreign to him, as foreign as the prayer wheels and other rituals that he observed in the Orient.

Are some of the stories told in Genesis not preposterous? Isn't the creation of man on the sixth day of the universe in fact a crazy story? André laughed about this and wondered how someone could have written it. God created humankind, and humankind made some stupid mistakes, requiring God to send his Son to become a man to save humankind. Who can understand such a thing? Why would God in fact have created a man who

---

20. {Philippe Leclerc de Hauteclocque (1902–1947): a French general who served in World War II as the commander of the famous 2nd Armed Division (2ᵉ Division Blindée). They fought in Africa and in the Liberation of Paris in 1944. He was posthumously made a Marshal of France.}

committed stupid mistakes? It was wrong from the start. Who were they trying to fool? Nevertheless, one question kept coming up: why are humans violent? Who made the human heart? When he was with the Chinese, André also felt violent, just as he had for all those years, with a violence that did not express itself all the time but was nevertheless present. When he faced it, it troubled and scared him. Had he ever asked for such a thing himself? He was a patriot, but when he looked up, what did all this absurdity around him mean?

André left the army in 1950 after completing fifteen years of service. He worked for four years for Mazda as a material controller in Paris in the eighth district. He was unmarried and had more than enough to live on from his military retirement and his salary. That didn't prevent him from complaining when the company management took advantage of that situation and didn't give him a raise. He lived in a studio on rue Marc-Seguin in Montmartre with his girlfriend. Why would he deny himself this? But their frequent quarrels tarnished their relationship. One day he thought, "I could strangle her! This will not end well!" He might be capable of doing it: André, so impulsive, so strong minded, kept telling himself that. He was too violent and too much on edge to submit himself to a woman to whom he was not attracted by the purest and most touching love, but rather by lust and maybe also by a desire to escape his loneliness.

He thrived only on passion. Everything he did, he did with an internal fervor, a rage to devour the hours, the days, and the emotions: to become intoxicated by new things and to walk on the edge of the abyss. Humans are capable of everything, he thought. Then he looked at himself in his studio, a material controller, wondering why he controlled his inner impulses so poorly. Where did they come from? And why did they sometimes push him to do just the opposite of what he wanted? Where were these forces leading him? He realized that when a man is a slave to the flesh, it is terrible, but when a woman becomes jealous or a slave to a man, it is not any better. They could destroy each other with their conflicts. Violence was in him; violence was all around him. Nevertheless, a voice inside him kept telling him, "It will change, be patient!" What would change? This internal voice annoyed him. Time passed, but nothing new ever happened. Besides, what could change?

In 1954, at the age of thirty-seven he was struck unexpectedly in the manner of Saint Paul while reading Paul's works. Paul would remain with him until the end and would be his strength. He felt that what was called revelation contained the truth. No falling from his horse like Saint Paul on the way to Damascus, no voice resounding in a blinding light (Acts 22:6-11; 26:12-18; Gal 1:15), but an inner conviction. For three days, he was stunned and crushed by the inner knowledge that the divine word was the truth. He exclaimed, "Ha! Now I understand everything!"

What did he understand? This event was his conversion in tears. During these three days he wept; he did nothing but weep. And the more he prayed to God for the tears to stop, the more tears he shed. You could say that he was a mountain of wax on top of a red-hot oven. Everything melted. He was destroyed, liquified. He saw his youth again; he saw it all. Then the event stopped as abruptly as it had started.

André walked to a neighboring church and received communion daily. He visited every church in the area. He took the Bible and read it, read and read—"Was I intelligent before?" he wondered, "Was I able to read? No, my heart could not read." Nothing was of interest to him any longer, neither sports nor alcohol, not even a cigarette. He had been playing the horses at Longchamp. Sometimes he would win, but more often he would lose. Everything appeared to him as garbage. Then he asked himself, "And now, what am I going to do with my life?"

Irrevocably, he burned all bridges with the past. Everything connected very quickly. He had heard of Solemnes and of Cîteaux. At the end of 1954, he wrote to Dom Jean Chanut, abbot of Cîteaux. Dom Chanut answered him, inviting him to come and try out the community. When he got there, he was sent to work everywhere. In the dead of winter, he was sent to pull leeks with his bare hands. He did chores and was frozen with an aching back by evening. He didn't tell anyone about his conversion in tears; he wouldn't mention it for years. It was his most intimate secret. He simply asked to be a monk. Did he like monastic life? That was what people asked him. To tell the truth, moving horses around, loading manure into a wheelbarrow, or milking cows by hand, since the farm was not modernized yet, didn't really thrill him, but something else was of interest to him.

"Too bad! I didn't expect the monastic life to be like this," he thought, "but it doesn't matter. I will suffer; I accept the suffering. I want to give myself to God."

After three weeks, he asked if they would accept him.

"Come," they told him.

He took care of his personal affairs in Paris and notified his family, whom he had barely seen while he was in Asia. "I am joining a *trappe*," he wrote to a very Catholic aunt. She answered him right away: "Go and consult the best neurologist in Paris and have yourself committed immediately. You cannot be serious; you are sick." His cousins did not understand this turnaround either, even though one of them was a priest. They would not come to visit him for a long time.

"How was I able to live that long without knowing the Bible?" he wondered. He knew some prayers, but he ignored everything. When thinking about becoming a missionary, he pondered, "If a man wants to preach and God does not grant his grace to those who listen, what use are the words?" "Nobody comes to me except through the Father," said Christ (John 6:65). Why was this free gift granted to some and not to others?

Why are there differences among monks? When he entered the monastery, the novice asked Dom Jean Chanut to allow him to become a priest and a choir monk. The abbot refused and quickly sent him to the lay brothers.[21]

"I would like to study to be ordained," he said. "I have thought about it a lot." "The lay brothers' master will teach you your role."

---

21. See chap. 8, "They were Lay Brothers."

It was a terrible disappointment for the new brother, but he refused to turn back. The only thing of interest to him was following Christ. If they asked him to be a stable boy, he would be a stable boy. Nevertheless, he suffered because, as a lay brother, he didn't have time to read as much as he would have liked. He did not have the leisure to have his fill of the Word of God. He discovered it to be alive, to be precious, to be a delight. He persevered, but life was hard. But he was there for Christ, and he clung to his faith. "Our reading is to cling to Christ," he kept reminding himself. "This is the *lectio divina* of the lay brothers." He never forgot Saint Benedict's clarification of Saint Paul: "It is through patience that we participate in Christ's passion, and in doing so we deserve to participate in his glory" (RB Prol. 50; Phil 3:10-11; Rom 6:5). The goal is to give up ourselves to conform to Christ. The Rule asks us to obey for the love of God in order to resemble Christ, who was obedient until death. This changes everything. Spiritual obedience is at the heart of the monastic vocation. Patience is in fact suffering. Naël started and ended his days with that idea.

I have always been fascinated by the variety of destinies and temperaments that end up at La Trappe. For some of them you could have sworn that they would never present themselves there. Once they're here, though, it seems that they have been monks forever. We think that it is a miracle, and it may very well be one. We welcome their thinking that heaven is giving them a gift, but we are the ones receiving the favor. They are lions who became lambs. Willpower alone is not sufficient. Something else gives us the strength to go forward, something for which we deserve no credit. In the Apocalypse of Saint John (Rev 22:17) we read, "The Spirit and the Bride [the Church] say to the one who thirsts, to whoever desires, approach to receive the water of life without price." It is without price that we are transformed. It is also without price that we receive Christ, as it is said in another biblical revelation (Rev 2:17): "To him who conquers . . . I will give a white stone, with a new name written on the stone that no one knows except him who receives it." But the stones, as we know, turn into beautiful pebbles over time by rubbing against one another.

CHAPTER SEVEN

THE AGE OF REFORM

When they gathered in general chapter in 1965, the father abbots wanted to renew the members of the Order's commission in charge of the liturgy. My abbot put forward my name, even though I wasn't a specialist with multiple degrees. That was so true that early on nobody knew what position to give me within the new commission. Other members expressed specific interests and wanted to handle one or more of the areas that they had worked on. They were specialists; I wasn't. Dividing up the responsibilities went smoothly. Since there wasn't much left for me, I was told gently, "Well, Father Gérard, you will be the secretary of the commission."

In the beginning my task was to draft the minutes of the commission's meetings. Eventually I had to coordinate the work of the different members and present it to higher authorities. In that capacity I corresponded with the superiors of the Order, and I was invited as an expert to the general chapters. That is how, although I was a fifth wheel at the outset, I became one of the key people in the Order's liturgical reform. Later on I even became the president of the commission.

Our time was marked by Vatican Council II, begun by the good Pope John XXIII in 1962, which sought to bring renewal to the Church, and that renewal started with the liturgy. Pope John coined the term *aggiornamento*, which in Latin was *renovatio*. Was it a renewal of the vitality of Christians, or was it a reform of the structures and the institutions? To the extent that the structures were observances that we had to practice, they implied a personal commitment. To remain alive, this commitment required continuous internal conversion. That was the most important element! What was the purpose of changing the structures if it was not to live better? But on the other hand, did it make sense to pour young wine into old barrels? Could we maintain life in an unsuitable setting? Life called for adjustments; otherwise, we ran the risk of paralysis. The reform of the institutions could be an internal seed for renewal, a source of spiritual dynamism. In that sense, there was no point in opposing the letter and the spirit. On the contrary, we needed to unify them as much as possible. What would the spirit be without the letter? The observances were not an end in themselves; if they did not embody an internal vitality, they were useless and could even become a dead weight.

A reform is justified in many circumstances. One possibility could be to turn over a new leaf when there had been a decline. History has seen quite a few such reforms. Sometimes it is just a question of providing a fresh start for institutions that have not been able to adapt in a timely fashion and because of their rigidity have gotten out of touch with their surrounding culture. Therefore, they end up totally at odds with that culture. We should probably put the reform initiated by Vatican Council II within that category. The reforms carried out in the sixteenth and seventeenth centuries created a unifying framework, which didn't change much afterwards. That might have been useful, but a reframing seemed necessary in the late 1950s. The Holy Spirit was watching over the Church, and one might wonder what would have happened if the societal crisis of May 1968 had erupted like a hurricane in a church that had not experienced the Council: would the oak tree have remained standing?

The Order didn't wait for the Council to start some necessary reforms. We will discuss these when talking about the lay brothers. From 1953 on, a lighter *horarium* was introduced by simplifying the prayers. Of course, after Vatican Council II, the reforms took a more dramatic turn. Because of the central character of the liturgy, it was affected first. One could say with humor that the single voice of Gregorian chant had become a chorus of dissonances and false notes, to the point that it had turned into a cacophony. Let's not exaggerate, but we must acknowledge that there was, within the Order as in the Church, a reluctance that grew into honest complaints to the Holy See sent by monks and nuns whose deep convictions were troubled. It was their right to do so.

The reform was to be prepared by the team of specialists who made up the Liturgy Commission. This commission had existed for a long time, but until then, the efforts of its members, all prominent historians, leaned more towards reviving the liturgy of the medieval beginning of the Order. The perspective widened and changed dramatically after the vote by the Council on the document called *Sacrosanctum Concilium* (SC), whose aim was to encourage everyone's participation in a conscientious, active, and fruitful manner.[1] We needed to concentrate on the doctrinal and pastoral side of liturgical prayers and gestures, an aspect that required other competences. That is when the participants in the 1965 general chapter appointed other members to the commission, and that is how I found myself involved in that commission.

Without being a specialist, as I said, I had been interested in the liturgy since the beginnings of my monastic formation. I could have said, as Father Congar stated at the end of his life, "The liturgy revealed the Church to me."[2] My duty as a cantor had led me to propose some practical changes in areas where there was a certain freedom, like the reciting of the psalter on Good Friday. During my novitiate, this practice had provoked some giggling from me.[3] These small changes let us envision what a

---

1. SC 11. {The text requires that members of the Order "take part in full awareness of what they are doing, actively engaged in the rite, and enriched by its effects."}

2. {Yves Congar, *The Meaning of Tradition* (New York: Hawthorn Books, 1964), 125–32.}

3. See above, chap. 4, 78.

revamped service could look like, with modern language, more periods of silence, appropriate chants, and longer readings. This is what gave my abbot the idea of proposing my nomination to the commission in 1965.

I was only thirty-five years old and was quite intimidated when every morning I had to read my report of the previous session to the twelve-member commission, meeting for the first time in Westmalle, one of our monasteries in Belgium. I was sweating bullets. Slowly I learned how to prepare summaries and to express myself better and even to improvise, if necessary.

A few months later, the abbot of Westmalle, who was presiding over the commission, told me that he was tired and was resigning as chair. I was terrified when he asked me to organize the second commission meeting, which was to take place at Mont-des-Cats, where I was a monk. Since I was the host, I had to crawl out of my shell. This task put me at ease, and everything went better than expected. Since the discussion was utterly confused, the reports shed some light on the previous day's meetings, because I had trained myself to listen to everyone on the most diverse subjects and to bring the most important opinions forward in an orderly and harmonious fashion. After having read such a report, sometimes a member would tell me, "That is exactly what I wanted to say, Father Gérard, but you word it in such a way that I have the impression that I said something intelligent!"

I like to say jokingly that I go forward with other peoples' ideas. Over time I came to realize that an abbot should help each monk to take stock of his capabilities and improve instead of pushing something better onto him that does not come from within him. It is a skill that takes time to perfect.

One of the first questions we had to tackle was the choice of language for use in the liturgy. This could be the subject of a whole separate chapter: should we keep Latin or not? It was a rather technical question, but I want to elaborate on some details, because it touched on a sensitive aspect that defined the liturgical reform. I lived that moment very intensely, and, in fact, it was on this subject that the monasteries were the most misunderstood.

Since there was no clear provision prohibiting this, the Cistercian abbots determined in May 1965 that they had the authority to allow the nuns to sing the Divine Office in the local language. Vatican Council II kept the use of Latin for the clergy, but in article 101 of *Sacrosanctum Concilium* the Council authorized them to pray with the lay people in their own language while satisfying their duties. This ruling raised questions, however: shouldn't our communities, comprised of both clergy and lay brothers, read into this article the authorization to adopt the local language without any other procedures? Shouldn't we also take into account the presence of the lay faithful in our liturgical assemblies?

The work group in charge of preparing the liturgical reform for the whole church (called *Concilium* for short), under the leadership of Father Bugnini, had rejected that interpretation in advance in a letter dated December 16, 1964. His position was based on a strange theology that considered only the clergy as defining the whole monastic community gathered to celebrate the liturgy! It would take two years for such a mentality to change! In fact, the period seemed not that long. By considering only the clergy in our communities, the Holy See overlooked the real nature of a monastic community celebrating the liturgy, and its desire to maintain Latin at any cost seemed excessive to us. Nevertheless, the monks in mission countries were allowed to use the local language for the Mass and the Offices, provided that the majority of their community consisted of locals who had a hard time understanding Latin.

At first sight, it seemed difficult to go any further. On August 15, 1966, Pope Paul VI had personally addressed a letter, *Sacrificium Laudis*, to the superiors of all orders that had priests. In his letter, the Pope called on their consciences as guides and shepherds to consider further the dire consequences of abandoning Latin. The spiritual well-being of the Order and the Church were at stake, he said. He was troubled by their desire to use the local language and felt that he could not give his consent. The Cistercian father abbots, as well as the Benedictines and the superiors of other orders, reflected on it, but by a vote of 63 to 11 presented to the Holy See their request favoring the local language, a request that they considered to be based on their consciences.[4] Many monks had not studied the classics, including Latin, but wanted nevertheless to participate in the liturgical prayers of their community. There was no reason for this language to remain a point of discrimination between those who could pray in Latin and those who couldn't.

The unity of our communities and the desire of all to participate in the Divine Office constituted a strong argument for the transition to the local language. Gregorian chant remained an artistic and spiritual treasure that was hard to replace. Could it nevertheless be preserved in each monastery while ensuring that every monk could participate consciously and actively in the liturgy? "We know from personal experience that our most spontaneous and deepest prayer is said in our own native language," our father abbots wrote, before expressing their concern about future recruitment.

There was another reason: shouldn't the literary and artistic creation that would be necessary for the whole Church benefit from the sensitivity of contemplative life? For centuries monks had given inspiration to the Church's liturgy. Should they now be excluded from this vast endeavor that was about to begin: the transposition of a centuries-old liturgy to other languages and cultures?

Some criticized our request and branded it as a lack of obedience. Some went so far as to say that it would undermine the legitimacy of the authorizations granted. I do not pretend to know the deepest thoughts of Pope Paul VI, but, knowing his strength of character, I can hardly imagine that he would be weak and fail in his duties by granting the opposite of what he thought to be right.[5] I tend to believe that this convergence and the insistent

4. The vote took place on May 30, 1967, but the letter of the general chapter was only delivered to the Secretary of State during September following a misunderstanding about the proper delivery of such letter.

5. A study of his pontificate shows that Pope Paul VI could maintain his point of view when he thought it was necessary. In liturgical matters, "noth-

nature of the requests clarified the issue for him and led him to qualify his initial thoughts. His decision in principle was communicated to the Congregation for Religious Life by the Vatican Secretary of State on June 6, 1967. This was before our letter could have reached him and before the meeting *in Congresso* of all the Benedictine abbots in September of that year. The Dominicans had made their request before us and received a positive answer as soon as July 5. The Benedictine Congregation of Subiaco received theirs on November 14, and we received ours on December 14, 1967, after some minor procedural hiccups.

In an official letter dated July 28, 1968, Dom Weakland, the Benedictine Abbot Primate, who was later appointed archbishop of Milwaukee, told about a meeting he had had with Pope Paul VI. The Pope expressed his satisfaction that certain monasteries had kept Gregorian chant and Latin, but he acknowledged that "he understood well the essential demands of other monasteries that for a variety of reasons and circumstances could not continue exclusively in the traditional way. They are now searching for new allowable adaptations in the liturgy."[6] A later notification from the Holy See dated June 14, 1971, made the use of modern language generally acceptable both in the choir and in private, contingent only upon the approval of the bishop, the abbot of a monastic community, or the religious superior of a province. Some criticized the pope for having gone against the will of Vatican II, which had kept Latin for the religious communities. In addition to the fact that, as I mentioned, the texts

---

ing was decided—let alone promulgated—without Paul VI having been aware of it and, having received all the projects, commented on them personally, expressing his preferences and sometimes his demands or his refusals." (Aimé Georges Martimort, "Le rôle de Paul VI dans la réforme liturgique," in *Le rôle de G. B. Montini—Paul VI dans la réforme liturgique: Journée d'études. Louvain-la-Neuve, 17 octobre 1984* [Brescia: Istituto Paolo VI; Rome: Ed. Studium, 1987], 64).

6. Letter in Italian to the abbots and priors of the Confederation, translated in French in *Documentation Catholique* 66 (1969): 42.

of the Council contained a basis for his decision, a council never represents the end of the Church's history. Moreover, the pope has the necessary authority to take additional steps in the direction proposed by a council. As evidence, we can mention that the pope allowed the alternative use of four eucharistic prayers, as was not contemplated by Vatican II. Events would overtake the Council. The Church continues to live on, and nothing stops it, even if its march can sometimes be slowed down.

Other usages were reintroduced, such as taking communion from the chalice and receiving the host in the hand. These ancient usages were brought back not because of their archeological value, but because of their real significance. This was also the case for concelebration, meaning the opportunity for several priests to join together in the same celebration of the Eucharist instead of each one celebrating on his own. At Mont-des-Cats, as in other monasteries, the first concelebration took place on Christmas 1964, and it was then authorized once a month. On March 7, 1965, the new rite was promulgated permanently, at the same time as that of double communion with bread and wine. Until then, at the High Mass, where the community assembled, only the main celebrant took communion. The other monks who were priests had each celebrated their own Masses at an earlier time. The brothers who were not priests had received communion at the Masses they served, each in a separate chapel. In truth, about half of the community did not attend the mid-morning sung Mass, since the lay brothers were excluded. For those who have not witnessed that period, it may be hard to imagine the real change that occurred in the life of the community when it became possible for such a community to gather together around the same altar to participate in one and the same Eucharist, which became the focus of the monastic day.

It was around that time that Pope Paul VI expressed a desire for the monks to bring their testimony of faith to the first bishops' synod in 1967. He made that request to a Trappist of Frattocchie, a monastery close to Rome. An old leader of Catholic Action whom Cardinal Montini had known before being elected Pope, he had become a monk in that monastery later in life. The abbot of Frattocchie was my old novice master, Father Francis Decroix. He invited three or four other monks, among whom were Dom Porion, the Procurator of the Carthusians, now deceased, and the abbot of Mont-des-Cats. Thomas Merton, an American Trappist and best-selling author, sent a paper. Chosen as the secretary of the group, I drafted a proposed message from their exchanges about "the possibility of a dialogue between man and the ineffable God," which was presented to all the bishops meeting in synod in September 1967. We stated that the contemplative life, within the cloister, was in fact nothing more than a simple Christian life, but lived under conditions favoring the experience of God.

Contemplative people know that this experience is not esoteric, but rather typical of all Christian experience. They feel that they are placed at the very source of the Church. Their inner journey may lead them along some arid byways, which bear some resemblance to atheism. They may encounter the bitterness and anxiety of a dark night that would make them, like Christ in his agony, cry out, "My God, my God, why hast thou forsaken me?" (Matt 27:46; Ps 21:2). The temptations and trials that torment all people in their nights are their own. The world cannot understand God at his level; God's level cannot be reached by human instruments or calculations. God doesn't show his face, as is said in Exodus (Exod 33:20). He transcends human understanding.

The monk is used to this absent, almost nonexistent God and is not satisfied with a mere presentation of the infinity of the divine mystery that would reduce it to the level of a thing. Some Christians, driven by the desire to share their brethren's feeling of unbelief, advocate this unbelief as a basis for a thoroughly human sincerity: since we cannot reach this totally different and transcendent God, it would be sufficient to devote ourselves generously to the service of humanity in order to be a Christian. Like the ordeal of the night of the mystics, this temptation can be beneficial, if it leads those who are undergoing it to purify their imperfect image of God. If not, it would be incoherent, because the absence of the transcendent God is also paradoxically his immanent presence.[7] The monk knows that "God enables the attentive and purified spirit to reach him beyond words and ideas." The marvels of divine mercy exist in the heart of our revealed misery. A cloistered life is in itself a testimony to the possibility for the dark night of the soul to lead to a certainty and a victory. It attracts thousands of men and women in our time. Saint Paul tells us, "If it is for this life only that we have hoped in Christ, we are of all men most to be pitied" (1 Cor 15:19).

The monastic experience can only take place if the gift of this Spirit fills our hearts, in itself testifying to the fact that Christ died for our sins and rose again for us, as the apostle Paul writes in his letter to the Romans (Rom 4:25). Christian mystical knowledge is not only the obscure knowledge of the invisible God; it is that of a person, of the Word incarnate, who became like us.

Most of the 150 psalms that we sing in church are shouts of despair, cries for help, in which people from everywhere on earth and from every age can recognize themselves. They are overcome by illness, hunger, persecution, and misfortune. They come close to despair and sometimes succumb to it, barely holding on. They suffocate with pain, are frightened and pursued by the justice of their time or by injustice. They talk about the fear of death, of all the ills that eat them up, of sin. And like every human, they are convinced that they are on the right side and that others are on the wrong side. Sometimes they call for vengeance, which does not match the highest Christian values. Are we Christians so pure, so kind, so hospitable? Moreover, this is the cry of every human being, not solely Christians. Doesn't this cry often take the form of a cry for vengeance? In our prayers, we take on the

7. "In the torment of your absence, it is already you, Lord, who has met us. You are never a stranger, but the most inner host who reveals itself in transparency" (Commission Francophone Cistercienne, *La Nuit et le Jour* [Paris: Éditions Desclée/Cerf, 1973], 26).

cries of all humans, the good and the bad, of each revolt and each distress, to present them all to God.

Almost without exception, these texts are anonymous, because they have passed through so many human mouths and hearts. It is about the experience of a whole people and even of all peoples. That is their value. There is always someone on earth who is really suffering, as the psalm says, and we can make this suffering ours even if we aren't experiencing it at that very moment. It enables us to identify ourselves with the one speaking. There is someone with whom we absolutely need to identify, and that is Jesus Christ. Christ prayed all of these psalms. He spoke to the Father using the formulas of the psalms.

But with Christ we don't remain at the level of despair. He did conquer evil, and we share his victory. Most psalms, in fact, go from anxiety and a cry for help to hope and praise, thereby testifying to the healing received and the freedom experienced.[8] A certain holy alchemy takes place when our sufferings go through the heart of Christ. A saintly nun of the thirteenth century, Gertrude of Helfta, traveled throughout the world in her mind and collected all the sorrow, the suffering, and the anxieties of the world, all the pious hypocrisies, like the adulterated and impure love of all creatures. Like gold in a crucible, she purified them in the spiritual desire of her heart and offered them as a gift to her beloved Lord.[9] Gertrude's heart could only achieve this because Jesus had first conquered sin through his death, therefore embodying the resurrection. Such is the power of the intercession in Jesus—the cry of distress becomes the confident prayer of the Son: Abba! Father!

We had previously recited the psalms in Latin, and they gained a greater power of expression when we could sing them

8. On the psalms, see especially Paul Beauchamp, *Psaumes nuit et jour* (Paris: Éditions du Seuil, 1980).

9. {Gertrud the Great of Helfta, *The Herald of God's Loving-Kindness* 4.6.4, trans. Alexandra Barratt, CF 85 (Collegeville, MN: Cistercian Publications, 2018), 45.}

in our native language. But then we could not process as many as before. We needed smaller doses. We also needed to split them up, because we couldn't recite them one after the other over and over. That meant that we needed to review the general style of our celebrations. This was the sense of direction given by the general chapter in 1967.

A questionnaire had laid the groundwork for this direction. It had been drafted in carefully chosen terms so that the responses would not be conditioned by overly precise questions. It had been sent to all the members of the Order, nuns and monks alike, at the end of 1966. The questions were like this: "Do you have wishes to express about the Eucharist, the Divine Office, and the rituals?" You couldn't have asked for more open-ended questions. But they touched on all aspects of our lives. A sociologist mentioned that the worst outcome would be to have subjects come up that could not be addressed later. You can only inquire about subjects about which there can be an open discussion. The Order took some risks. The process of reviewing the answers took a long time. We were close to the opening of the first session of the general chapter on May 20, 1967, when we were at last able to identify the major directions. This chapter had special powers to launch the Order on the road to reform.

Within the Commission on the Liturgy, we felt from the start that we needed to grant the local superiors more freedom and decision-making authority, within certain boundaries. Our role was to clarify the boundaries and conditions of the experience we needed to undertake. It was no longer possible to settle all these details with one book of usages and customs that would apply to the whole Order, everywhere in the world, which only the general chapter could define further or amend. We were moving away from the beaten path, and we needed to be creative.

In 1967 the abbots approved by a vote of sixty-six to eight our proposal to leave to local authorities the final decision about subjects that did not touch the essence of the rites. This decision lent credence to the concept of a decentralized approach to the observances in other sectors. They also approved in principle the idea of more advanced experimentation on the structure of the psalmody itself and the liturgy of the hours. An exchange of correspondence started between the monasteries and the commission. I established relations with the nuns, who didn't set up their own commission. They considered that it would be best to have a healthy collaboration with the monks, one that turned out to be very fruitful.

One could have expected some turmoil in certain communities. Back in 1965 a few complaints had already reached the office of Cardinal Antoniutti, Prefect of the Congregation for Religious and Secular Institutes. At that time, the chapter had decided to eliminate the office of Prime, which duplicated the morning office of Lauds. In doing so, the superiors would have exceeded their jurisdiction. On February 10, 1966, the cardinal reacted by cautioning against insufficient consultations among the parties involved. Other interventions by the cardinal in the two years following the chapter raised quite a few eyebrows among the superiors. At the source of these interventions were a number of ambiguities in the exact sense and reach of the decisions of the chapter. We were still feeling our way toward methods and procedures to adopt. Together with the president of our commission, I was able to meet with Father Bugnini about that subject in Rome in September 1967. He was instrumental in the reform of the liturgy within the Latin Church.

As time went by, the projects did mature, and the exchanges and consultations among the communities increased, contributing to the acceptance of the reforms. On December 8, 1968, Pope Paul VI wrote a conciliatory letter to the Order,[10] in which he recommended prudence and reflection. He also recognized the need to move towards pluralism within limits that the Order had to establish. The turmoil subsided following the chapter of 1969, which reaffirmed the decisions taken at the 1967 chapter.

The "framework law" that the Holy See granted to us on May 24, 1969, as an answer to our chapter, enabled us to bring in some new, experimental choral prayers. Vigils, formerly known

10. *Documentation Catholique* 66 (1969): 452–55.

as Nocturns, were previously not sung but recited, chanted, except on Sundays or holidays. On these days, we would wake up a half hour earlier in order not to encroach too much on the day. Vigils included twelve psalms and short readings. They led directly without interruption into Lauds, which was normally a morning liturgy, when in fact daylight was still hours away. Some changes had already been made in 1955, because until then there was also the additional "small liturgy of the Virgin Mary" and on ordinary days an additional Office of the Dead. To conform to the Rule of Saint Benedict, who required that during Lent we wait until Vespers to eat, we had brought forward the evening liturgy to noon. This conformed to the letter of the Rule, but not to the spirit. All that had been taken care of in 1955. With the advent of the vernacular language, we had to provide for some more breathing room in the rhythm of the celebrations and the silent time. It was also necessary to reduce the breaks between the readings from the Bible and our Cistercian Fathers. We were entering an experimental phase that would last six or seven years.

Since any reform in the communities required a two-thirds majority vote, we put in place a process of exchange and consultation. This somewhat changed the style of brotherly relationship within the community. It was no longer sufficient to be hermits living side by side. We had to learn to listen to each other and to take into account other people's opinions. Needing more help from each other, the superiors started to meet on a regional level.

The liturgy was not the only area up for reform. The whole monastic observance needed to be rethought to allow monasteries to respond better to the growing need for more authenticity and inner freedom. The spirituality of usages,[11] as we called it, had produced saints in former times, and I had embraced it unconditionally during the first years of my monastic life, but it could no longer be applied. It assumed a certain uniformity among

11. {*la spiritualité des us*}

all the monasteries. In fact, this traditional principle, which was only pushed to its extremes in the nineteenth century, now had more inconveniences than advantages.[12] Had we not already seen these inconveniences brought to light in an observation of the general chapter of 1913? Certain exemptions had been requested by the community of Maristella in Brazil. It had been created as a refuge in case the Abbey of Sept-Fons fell to the French anticlerical laws of 1901 and had to leave France. The community had requested to be allowed not to wear the cowl on very hot days and to rearrange the *horarium* in order to take an afternoon nap. The participants in the chapter accepted the request, but only for a temporary period of five years. They also observed "that from now on we should avoid creating monasteries in countries where it would be almost impossible to observe our Holy Rule." Unbelievable statement!

Should we, for the sake of maintaining uniformity, give up the prospect of establishing new monasteries outside Europe? Should we reduce our Holy Rule to questions of *horarium* and clothing? How pretentious to link the monastic vocation to one certain culture, let alone to a climate or a variation in the thermometer, all in the name of a uniformity of usages that is very secondary! By contrast, in the twelfth century, the primitive customs of Cîteaux regarding the harvest that disrupted the ongoing monastic day were filled with modernity: "Each Church will decide in accordance with its local conditions and the dispositions of its abbot or its prior, because you cannot observe the same ways of doing things everywhere."[13]

The main question became one of a certain autonomy for the monasteries within their choice of the "living experience of the Cistercian life." The debate was fundamental. We had already

---

12. This was often contradicted by events. For example, from the fifteenth century on, many distinct congregations appeared. La Trappe under Abbot de Rancé had its own rules in the seventeenth century.

13. {*The Ancient Usages of the Cistercian Order = Ecclesiastica Officia*, trans. Martinus Cawley (Lafayette, OR: Guadalupe Translations, 1998), 84:32.}

initiated that debate with respect to the liturgy at the level of experimentation, but it quickly grew larger. Until then any small detail of the monastic life was uniformly codified by the general chapter. Could we continue on the same path, while the Order was expanding everywhere in the world, contrary to what the 1913 chapter would have liked? The United States only had three abbeys before World War II; nine more monasteries of monks and three of nuns were established between 1944 and 1964.[14]

The first monastery in Sub-Saharan Africa dates back to 1951. In 1972, the eleventh monastery was founded in Benin. In the meantime, the Order had put down roots in Madagascar, Latin America, Indonesia, New Zealand, Australia, and New Caledonia; it was also growing in Japan. Even if we look only at Western Europe, why would we force the Spanish monks to eat at noon, if in that country everybody else eats at 2 p.m. because of the local climate and customs? Should we apply to the whole world what suits Cîteaux, in Burgundy? But if we moved in this direction, how many customs would need to be reconsidered? Certain superiors argued that uniformity should be maintained within the Order, as it had been since its origin. Even one of the greatest innovators, Dom Gabriel Sortais, abbot general from 1951 to 1963, only envisioned his own attempts at reform within the framework of the strictest uniformity among monasteries, even if he understood that certain circumstances were unique. Therefore, he also considered regional conferences, where superiors of the same country met, as a threat of separatism and the formation of autonomous entities; he only tolerated them at the level of friendship.

The great turning point in the life of the Order was negotiated in 1969, when the superiors of the Order gave up the principle of uniformity. From that point a completely new situation had

14. {In 2018 there were ten Strict Observance monasteries for men and five monasteries for women in the United States; Canada had four monasteries for men and two for women.}

to be accepted by Trappists. They still wanted to hold on to their profound unity, but they acknowledged a real plurality at the level of usages. Were they going to achieve this? What would the Order be twenty years later? Wasn't it playing with fire, breaching dams, and letting loose floods that would engulf us all? I had the privilege of participating as an expert in this decisive moment at the general chapter. For the first time it was held outside Cîteaux, because of its distance from major airports. We stayed in Rome in the students' rooms at a religious institution, the Oblates of Mary. The theological college had enough meeting rooms, a dining room, and a chapel so that the abbots could pray together.

The plenary assembly was extraordinary, and the debates were very serious, for the stakes were high and deep divisions were feared. Remember that the chapter was meeting after years of tension in which the Holy See had intervened. Nevertheless, as the meeting moved forward, the participants sensed a deep unity among themselves, despite the confrontation of conflicting currents of thought and disagreements that seemed insurmountable during the first days of the meeting. This unity was clearly manifest in the decisive votes. One in particular, the *Declaration on the Cistercian Life*, was so characteristic of the unity and unanimity that it became a text of reference, along with the sixth-century Rule and the twelfth-century *Charter of Charity*,[15] the basic document of the primitive Cîteaux, which regulated relations between the monasteries and the Order.

"We Cistercian Monks feel a deep desire to interpret for our own times the traditions which our Fathers have handed down to us. . . . We are convinced that the best rules are those that follow and interpret life." We wanted more than ever to be monks before God, thereby refusing a legislation "that would determine observances down to the last detail." We saw in the Rule of Saint Benedict the concrete interpretation of the Gospel for us, looking for God by following Christ in humility and obedience. We

---

15. {For a text of the *Charter of Charity*, see www.ocso.org/resources.}

wanted as before to be monks before God: "With hearts cleansed by the Word of God, by vigils, by fasting, and by an unceasing conversion of life, we aim to become ever more disposed to receive from the Holy Spirit the gift of pure and continual prayer."[16] Another text, the *Statute on Unity and Pluralism*,[17] established some criteria or guidelines regarding the main observances but left to each local house the task of interpreting all the details. It was incumbent on each abbot to define his own community style in agreement with the brothers. The whole life of the monasteries was therefore going to be shaken up. The texts, approved at the chapter of 1969, defined the general direction for the updating of our legislation, at least regarding the observances. They led twenty years later to our new *Constitutions*, which regulate our Cistercian life in today's world.

By the time the sixty-second general chapter opened on April 15, 1971, about eighty-five percent of the monasteries had started experimenting. In matters of liturgy, the majority appreciated the lighter and more peaceful structure we had proposed for the Offices, more readings, and the freedom granted to each community to make certain choices in order to achieve a more fitting expression of the prayers. Two months later Father Bugnini reminded the Cistercians and Benedictines that the time for experiments was coming to an end and that we needed to reach a stable solution. The reports we had sent to the Holy See were taken into account, and the Holy See approved our choices on June 25, 1974. That was the end of a time of experimentation that had lasted for many years.

The Commission on the Liturgy of the Order passed the torch to the regional commissions that had already existed for some time in the Netherlands, the United States, Spain, and French-speaking Europe. We had to continue to help the communities

16. The passages are extracts from the documents of the general chapter. See www.ocso.org/history/historical-texts for the full Declaration.

17. {Statute on Unity & Pluralism: www.ocso.org/resources/law/statute -on-unity-and-pluralism/.}

to experience positively the reforms we had undertaken. The focal point shifted to the celebration itself, which was now held more often than not in the local language. That was why the commission was divided into several decentralized language subgroups. The *Commission Francophone Cistercienne* (CFC) was created as such in 1968. I was its initial secretary. In 1972 it became a nonprofit association according to the law of 1901, and I was chosen to be its president. This enabled the CFC to register with SACEM (the association of composers and authors) as the author of texts written for chants.

Gregorian chant was still used in certain circumstances, but it was necessary to write new texts in our common languages. We needed to have the ability to compose music for these texts, in order to "keep our liturgy perpetually young," as Pope Paul VI put it. Simply put, translating the Latin was not sufficient. Some Benedictine monasteries that also chose to do the liturgy in French experienced the same need. We started to collaborate within the CFC. About thirty of us got together at our general assemblies, Benedictines, Cistercians, monks, and nuns. We also collaborated with other liturgy specialists in France. Brother Pierre-Yves Emery of the Community of Taizé, Father Joseph Gelineau, SJ, and Father Didier Rimaud, SJ, were soon regular guests of our workgroup. Patrice de la Tour du Pin, who died prematurely in 1975, remained until his death a supporter, a faithful friend, and author of the foreword to the CFC's first collection of texts *La nuit, le jour*, in the form of a long letter to contemplatives.[18]

Some of us had met him at a meeting organized by the French bishops' conference in Villebon in February 1971. The purpose of that meeting was to draft texts. He was interested in our work in all humility, offering us his sense of poetry and liturgy. He knew how much the liturgy required "constantly new words and new images in the quest for the promised Face." He had hoped

---

18. In 1973, he inaugurated a series of publications similar to those of the CFC with Desclée/Cerf. {Patrice de la Tour du Pin, "Introduction," in Commission Francophone Cistercienne, *La nuit, le jour* (Paris: Editions Desclée-Cerf, 1973), 3–13.}

for the longest time that the contemplatives would take on that task. Monsignor Martimort, a great French liturgy specialist, had already told the Cistercian students in Rome in 1965, "Liturgical creation can only come from contemplation. Therefore, you have to take on an important role, much more important than you suspect, in your position as monks. Therefore, I throw down the gauntlet." That was one of the reasons that we requested the use of the vernacular language. More than two hundred hymns have been composed by the CFC.[19] Several were adopted by the French bishops' conference for the Liturgy of the Hours.

The musical questions were more complex. Except for the brothers of Taizé, nobody had experience with French psalmody for the office. Where could we find a decent repertoire of chants and melodies that we could use for the psalms? We had to learn everything. We first gathered all the songs that were already in existence at that time and set up musical formation sessions. Those responsible for the chants got into the habit of meeting within their regions to help each other. In France we were very lucky to be able to count on the collaboration of a number of musicians and choral masters. Speaking only of those who have passed away, we can mention in particular Jacques Berthier, who was well known for having made thousands of young people sing at Taizé and who was a real friend of the monasteries. He gave an authentic French sound to more than 120 of our hymns and other compositions. Of course, we needed to copy all these songs. In the beginning, I used an alcohol duplicator, which was much better than the original wet-stone method.[20] Then came

19. {During the Colloque Liturgie et Vie Spirituelle, organized by the CFC and held at the Collège des Bernardins in Paris in September 2013, Dom Olivier Quenardel, President of the CFC and abbot of Cîteaux, stated that there were now over 700 CFC-approved hymns used in the liturgy.}

20. The wet-stone method consisted of a plate with a kind of surface on which was written the negative of an original that had been written with a special ink. One then pressed individually however many copies of the original were wanted onto the negative of the text written on the plate.

the duplicator with stencils, with an electric stylus for writing the notes. Offset printing opened up other possibilities. What an improvement did we see when we were able to make photocopies on ordinary paper, with the possibility of enlarging and reducing the score. Now we are using contemporary music software. I am not sure if the quality of our music improved at the same speed as the technology, but if so we must be singing fantastically well!

An important effort was made to provide training in the basic principles of the liturgy, either through meetings of general interest or through the annual meetings of the CFC. *Liturgie*, the CFC publication, sought to spread these reflections and other studies to all the monastic communities with the goal of enlightening and harmonizing our practice, so that we might live the "liturgy in a more conscious, active and fruitful way" (Vatican II).[21]

During these sessions, I met a Benedictine monk, the delegate from his order, who later left it. I mentioned that he had previously published a book that had some success in the bookstores. In our eyes, it was full of errors and very insufficient. Did he understand anything of the monastic mystery? Maybe he was stuck at the human level. As our new *Constitutions* were later to state, "solitude, continual prayer, humble work, voluntary poverty, celibate chastity, and obedience are not human skills, and cannot be learned from human beings" (Const 45.2). The teaching of the abbot, the experience and wisdom of the elders, and the support and example of the community can only provide help in the tests and trials that are constant in the spiritual journey, a journey whose goal is described in the *Constitutions*: "the brothers so advance in the monastic way of life that they progressively attain the full measure of the stature of Christ" (Const 45.1).

21. SC 11. *http://www.vatican.va/archive/hist_councils/ii_vatican_council /documents/vat-ii_const_19631204_sacrosanctum-concilium_en.html*. It is impossible to provide many details within the scope of this book. For more information on liturgical reform in Cistercian monasteries, see *Liturgie*, especially nos. 10 (318–55), 51 (297–311), 63 (the whole number, especially 331–62), and 85 (124–47).

The groundwork of the new *Constitutions* aimed at codifying the reforms that had been put in place little by little during this time of experimentation, which had been spread over a period of fifteen years. The old *Constitutions* were built on the model of a hierarchical pyramid, with the government of the Order on top: the general chapter, the abbot general and his council, then the father immediate in charge of the canonical visits to the communities, and then the local abbot. The daily observance and finally the entry into the Order followed. This model did not correspond with the new sensitivity, which sought to emphasize life in community over the structure of authority, especially the central authority. Several new experimental projects were set in place.

A group of four individuals representing different continents was appointed to reflect on the pertinence of the new text. Did it take into sufficient account the ecclesiastical and theological renewal inaugurated by Vatican II? Did it pay attention to the signs of the time, and did it go sufficiently beyond the Western mentality to respond to all the sensitivities of an order spread all over the world? Did it also sufficiently express the Cistercian spirituality dating from the beginnings of the Order? Did it take into account the needs of the Order and the new legal requirements provided in the code that had just been published by the Holy See? The response, marked with ample and detailed criticism in the margins, allowed us to envision the work ahead of us, starting from this text. Faced with all these observations from a variety of sources, we chose to entrust the draft of a new project to one person so as to ensure the homogeneity of the whole. This third project, translated into Latin and the three official languages of the Order, served as a basis for the final draft approved at the general chapter in 1984.

After I was elected abbot in 1977, I attended the general chapters with a more responsible viewpoint. I was appointed president of the commission in charge of organizing the work of about a hundred abbots gathered for three weeks at the general chapter held in Mount Holyoke, Massachusetts, in May 1984. I was able to observe the moment at which unanimity was achieved and to note that this experiment felt like a fourth-down conversion,

to use a football analogy. However, this was not a foregone conclusion. The last document coming from Australia simplified
matters, but we had already received quite a few remarks and
proposed amendments even before the opening of the chapter.
How could such a large assembly work on one draft with such
a tight schedule?

When they arrived at Mount Holyoke, some were dubious
about the chances of reaching a consensus, while others feared
that we would reach a quick and mediocre decision just because
we didn't have sufficient preparation. It wasn't always easy to
channel the energies and reflections of such an assembly, in which
there were still disagreements. But the work method put forward
proved efficient, and we left with a document approved almost
unanimously. The following year the mother abbesses meeting in
the Escorial close to Madrid used our text as a base for their own
constitution as nuns. The final update of the two documents took
place at a joint meeting of abbots and abbesses held in Rome in
1987, the first such meeting ever held. We thought that it would
be easy, but for procedural reasons it took us more than eight
hundred votes.

Once the texts had been cleaned up, we presented them for
approval to the Holy See, which commented on certain points,
especially hesitating on the proposal whereby the abbesses would
participate in the election of the common abbot general. We had
to make some concessions, and the texts had to travel a number
of times between the Order and the Congregation for Consecrated Life. It took two more years for canonical approval to be
obtained—on the day of Pentecost 1990.[22]

It was the finish line of a long marathon, but at the same time
it was also a new start, the confirmation of an internal renewal,

---

22. Our *Constitutions* are published in *Cîteaux, documents contemporains,*
original texts and official translations (in French). Presentation of Fr. Marie-
Gérard Dubois, abbot of La Trappe (*Cîteaux: Commentarii cistercienses,* 1991),
{http://www.ocso.org/resources/law/constitutions-and-statutes/.}

one that affected each individual as much as the functioning of the institution itself. Each superior, like each monk and nun, was confronted with personal responsibility. As the liturgical reforms called for a more conscious and more engaged participation, the approved arrangements called for personal initiative and for efforts to love more, to communicate, and to understand. In fact, it means going back to basics.

The Rule of Saint Benedict leaves to the abbot a large part of the responsibility for determining what is appropriate in the different situations that the community as well as the individual monk encounters. The *Constitutions* define the way to live the Rule in accordance with the needs of different periods. They therefore change and enable us to better live the Rule, which remains unchanged. The changes are not aimed at making life easier for individual monks or nuns or at making monastic life more pleasant, since by nature it is a combat. They are aimed at enabling all monks and nuns better to express their vocation.

The usages that were partially abandoned, in particular the penances, which were getting to be folkloric, were nevertheless meant to express a value that should not be forgotten. They should not be reduced to rigid or strange habits. For example, if a young monk stood up when an elder monk sat down next to him, and only sat down upon a sign from the elder, it was not ridiculous; it reflected a respect for the elder, which is something beautiful. Did we want to see younger brothers passing their elders without greeting them? Or sitting down without checking to make sure that the elder had a seat? We had to be careful not to throw out the baby with the bathwater.

I strongly believe that we succeeded in this period of renewal, a period of *aggiornamento,* as Pope John XXIII loved to say. We had indeed evolved quite a bit, but wasn't that what enabled us to remain faithful to our tradition? Tradition is not a precious object from the past that we can carefully hand on from generation to generation without changing or breaking it. It is not like the Olympic torch passed along from runner to runner along the road. It is a life that we can only transmit by living it. And, of course,

by living it, we also make it evolve. A life can only surviv
evolves. Otherwise, it dies off. Tradition can only be transmitte
by passing through hearts, by being expressed anew, experienced
anew, and re-invented to a certain extent. Children always go
further than their parents, even if they follow in their footsteps.

Tradition is also transmitted by the documents from the past:
the Rule and, for us Cistercians, the accounts and charters from
the early beginnings of Cîteaux, and the spiritual writings of Saint
Bernard and of the other abbots, his disciples. But these texts—
even Holy Scripture—are not sufficient by themselves. Tradition
is the work of a living *magisterium*, a spiritual creation by people,
by real concrete communities. It is in them and in the living commentary they give and through the daily word from the abbot
that these documents from Tradition reach us and form us. Each
intermediary, because he is alive, leaves his own mark, each in
his own way, even if that mark is limited in time and in space.

Faithfulness sometimes forces us to know how to shake up
conventional wisdom and our own positions. God is a God of
beginning and a God of tearing apart:

> The close tie that the Bible establishes between the liberation
> of Egypt and the power "to start anew" is full of meaning.
> God created by "bringing forth." The image of tearing apart
> recurs frequently in the Scriptures. . . . One says of a mother
> who just gave birth that she delivered, but the child is also
> delivered. The end of dependence is the cutting of the umbili-
> cal cord, a sign of the autonomy of the newborn and of the
> mother. The beginning of each human being is also *libera-
> tion*. . . . The God who "brought forth" is an expression that
> applies to the exodus as well as to birth. We keep finding this
> in the New Testament. . . . The beginning only has validity
> if you accept starting all over again and again. From there
> comes the evangelical fracture, the tearing apart, which are not
> losses but gains. . . . Sin is the anti-birth, the sterilization.[23]

23. See Marcel Domergue, "Le Dieu des commencements," *Croire
Aujourd'hui* (1988): 29–74, here 51–72.

In that sense, true faithfulness is relative not to the past, but to the future, even with regard to one's own vocation. Of course, we need to remember the initial moment of the call, but not with nostalgia, as a distant golden age. God's call is always in front of us. It makes us new each morning. We are not marching to the beat of a past call that will fade away as we move forward. God precedes me; he calls me, "Follow me!" He walks in front: "Forgetting what lies behind and straining forward to what lies ahead, I press on toward the goal for the prize of the upward call of God in Christ Jesus" (Phil 3:14). A vocation is a growth in freedom.[24] Of course God doesn't make us change direction drastically every fifteen minutes, but the point is not so much to continue as to start—on the same journey, indeed, but each time in a new way. It is all the opposite of a routine, of a sclerosis. You cannot be satisfied by living in accordance with yesterday's decisions. You need to renew your decision every day.

This disposition enables us not to be disconcerted when the road takes unexpected twists and turns, because the Spirit is sometimes very unpredictable. It is the Spirit of continuity, of faraway preparations, but at the same time it is the Spirit of rupture. A certain young person who was being formed for some ministry and who dies in a car accident or of an illness touches on the mystery of the Cross, but also on necessary ruptures. The point is not to put one's confidence in the power of one's wrist, meaning one's organization and planning, even if it is necessary. It would be an illusion to believe

> that we are capable of knowing all that this commitment will require from us. No, the point is not to make a plan in advance, to draw up a quote or to sign a contract that we will only have to execute later, faithfully and honestly. No. To really commit is to sign as it were a blank check to God without knowing what he will write on it later, or knowing

24. See Jean Laplace, *Le Prêtre à la recherche de lui-même* (Chire-En-Montreuil, France: Éditions du Chalet, 1969), esp. 51–72.

that he will keep writing new things down. New perspectives will open up for you as you move forward. It will not be so much an invitation to do more as the urgent discovery of new conditions that are indispensable in order to remain faithful to the initial impulse. You are not allowed to stop because you completed the initial program set up at the start. When you hear the call for continuously renewed progress and you refuse that call, you cannot take pride in what you have achieved until then. You will regress to an ordinary and mediocre life. The one who wants to stop right there also renounces his initial commitment, because the real commitment is unconditional.[25]

The monastic profession, like a commitment to the priesthood, is not the same type of contract as the one that you would sign when moving into a boarding house. In the latter case, you comply with the *horarium* of the house, with the services to be rendered, as long as there is nobody loud next door. If at some point that condition is no longer fulfilled, you are released from your commitments. Some have reacted like that when confronted with the successive changes brought about by the *aggiornamento* of the Council. To the extent that these reforms took place in accordance with official rules and directives, this reaction is not acceptable. You have to follow the Church wherever the Spirit leads it. Pope Paul VI noted as much in his October 1976 letter to Archbishop Lefebvre:[26] "The Tradition is not a stagnant or

25. Yves de Montcheuil, *Probleme de vie spirituelle* (Paris: Éditions L'Epi, 1947), 107–8.

26. {Marcel Lefebvre (1905–1991), a French archbishop who took part in Vatican Council II as an active member of the conservatives. He refused to implement certain changes proposed in the conclusions of the Council. In 1970 Lefebvre founded the Society of St. Pius X in Econe, Switzerland. In 1975 he was ordered by the Holy See to dissolve the society, but he refused. In 1988, Lefebvre consecrated four bishops against the injunction of Pope John Paul II. The Holy See immediately excommunicated Lefebvre and the four bishops.}

dead letter. It is not an unchangeable fact that at a certain point in history would block the life of this active organism that is the Church, meaning the mystical body of Christ."[27]

27. Letter of October 11, 1976, *Documentation catholique* 73 (1976): 1058. See also what Pope Paul said in the general audience of August 7, 1974, when distinguishing between a deep-rooted Tradition and traditions, which are habits, customs, or styles and which "*must* often be criticized and reformed because of the ease with which human things age and become deformed and need to be purified and replaced. It is not in vain that we speak of *aggiornamento* and renewal, and you know *with what enthusiasm* we grant them such far-reaching applications" (*Documentation catholique* 71 (1974): 754–55 [italics by Dom Dubois]).

CHAPTER EIGHT

THEY WERE LAY BROTHERS

A round the time I started my novitiate at Mont-des-Cats, a man twenty-four years older than I entered the monastery of Cîteaux as a lay brother. He had definitely experienced different life events than I had, but his journey was far from ordinary. Why had he chosen the life of a lay brother? André Naël, another lay brother, whom I mentioned in chapter six, would not have chosen that life if the abbot had not imposed it on him. What did that type of vocation represent in the community at that time?

The lay brothers were established at the beginning of the Cistercian Order to carry out the chores that the monks could not perform because of their liturgical obligations, and also to maintain the link with the outside world. They didn't live inside the monastery and were not monks. The old texts, though, state that otherwise, "the monks would treat them in all things like themselves."[1] Over the centuries the lay brothers became progressively and completely religious, living within the monastery. They were nevertheless, from a legal point of view, not recognized as monks. They could not become priests and could

---

1. {"Exordium Parvum" XV in *Narrative and Legislative Texts from Early Cîteaux*, ed. Chrysogonus Waddell (*Cîteaux: Commentarii cistercienses*, 1999), 417–40 at 434–35.}

not participate fully in the liturgical prayer of the community. Until 1965 there were two types of religious: the monks who took care of the choral offices and who were called for that reason *choir monks*, and the *lay brothers* (also called *conversi*). This man who chose to enter as a lay brother was well known in literary circles. In a letter dated 1928, Jean Cocteau[2] had praised his talent: "Among the young writers, you possess a rare talent. If you would understand this, if you would write, if you would tell stories on table corners and on the back of envelopes and if you would send me your work to clean it up, you would be saved. I state this emphatically. . . . Be confident, your hour is coming—*but get out of the shadow so that your hour may recognize you at first sight* [Cocteau underlined this]. Write, write, write. Don't listen to anyone else but me, *because I am the oracle*. I would like for this letter to grab you by the neck and pull you out of evil. Kisses. Jean."

Yes, he would write, but he wouldn't come out of the shadow. On the contrary, he ended up suddenly diving deeper, into a Trappist monastery. Instead of writing novels like *The Devil in the Flesh* (*Le Diable au Corps*), by Raymond Radiguet, which Jean Cocteau had also encouraged, he sent out letters from time to time up until 1966. Many of those letters are literary and spiritual jewels, and they confirmed the intuition of Cocteau and the establishment frequented by the artistic and literary personalities of the turbulent 1920s. His name was Jean Bourgoint, and he became Brother Pascal. When he wrote from Cîteaux, he moved from one opinion to another about prayers and penances. Even when writing to a friend describing the cowshed beneath the snowflakes of a harsh winter, he could not keep himself from

2. {Jean Cocteau (1889–1963) was a multifaceted French artist, poet, writer, and *avant garde* filmmaker. His social circle included the whole French art scene, from Picasso, Gertrude Stein, and Coco Chanel to Stravinsky and Edith Piaf. His best-known works include the novel *Les Enfants Terribles* (1929), the play *La Voix Humaine* (1930), and the films *Beauty and the Beast* (1946) and *Orpheus* (1949).}

displaying that style: "All the cats at Cîteaux are outside and promenade in the snow looking prosperous and smiling. They look like the villains with fake mustaches in the old Mack Sennett movies. They have their bellies full of robins."[3] This man didn't read very much, since he had chosen to become a lay brother. Nevertheless, he knew by heart almost all the works of Proust, Saint-Simon, and Baudelaire and was very familiar with Dickens, Balzac, and Dostoyevsky.

Did Cocteau have a premonition? Did he really believe that he could reveal Bourgoint to the world one day? Did he want to interfere on the road where God was walking? In an undated letter—presumably from 1926—he had written to Jeanne Bourgoint, the sister of the future Trappist, "I am very happy about the good slope along which Jean is sliding towards reality. Because for him there could only be one reality: the heavenly one."

The reality was that at that time Jean Bourgoint was on drugs. He threw himself into opium. He sprawled in the paradise of poppy that became a chemical heaven without a God. As he wrote, the drugs transformed his life into a "scorched earth." The first day he met Cocteau, in Paris in February 1925, at the house of a young British man, the poet was smoking opium and introduced him to "winged tobacco." Bourgoint then also became an opium addict. Later, when mobilization was getting near, he feared that the military authorities would consider him demented and lock him up without any treatment. Drugs would ruin his life. He also tragically experienced his homosexual tendencies, which are clear from the way Jean Cocteau addressed his letters to him: "my beloved child . . . Jean, my dear angel . . . Jean, my little heaven . . . little blue teddy bear." He cooed and sent him kisses and ended up telling him on February 4, 1926, "I love

---

3. Jean Bourgoint (Frère Pascal), *Le Retour de l'enfant terrible: Lettres 1923–1966*, collected by Jean Hugo and Jean Mouton (Paris: Desclée De Brouwer, 1975), 52, #28. Jacques Maritain, who suggested the title of the work, encouraged the project until his death in 1973, and the monks of Cîteaux allowed it to be completed.

you."[4] What did Bourgoint answer? First to his mother, whom he wanted to spare: "Jean [Cocteau] has adopted me; he loves me as a son. . . . I have a lot of tenderness for him, as for an older brother."[5] Then to Cocteau: "I love you, my Jean: sometimes when you seem to forget me, I am angry in the depths of my heart, but nobody sees any of this."[6] Drugs and an attraction to men—he was not fooled by it. He wrote to his sister, "Mother thinks I hate to work; this is not true, I hate life." [7] In another letter, he mentioned that he lived in such a cloud of laziness and luxury that there was no strength left in him to lift a quill.

Could anyone have supposed then that he would ever become a monk? Nevertheless, he got to know Jacques Maritain[8] through Cocteau, who himself had wanted to meet Maritain in July 1924, when Cocteau despaired after the death of his friend Raymond Radiguet. Cocteau had expected Maritain to make him discover God. He had gone to confession and taken communion, but his conversion was fragile. Nevertheless, Cocteau accompanied Bourgoint to his baptism and was, as he would later say, his "terrible godfather."

Cocteau made Bourgoint the hero of his novel *Les Enfants Terribles* (*The Holy Terrors*), which he published in 1929. This book, together with those published by André Gide, has been credited with the emancipation of French youth between the two world wars. An essential work by Cocteau, this novel renames Bourgoint as Paul and his sister Jeanne as Elisabeth. It is a dark novel in which she kills herself at the moment her brother dies. The room in which the story takes place is totally closed in, as though set up for a liturgy without a purpose, without any hope. Cocteau got his inspiration from a room that he had visited four years earlier.

Jeanne had married an unattractive man, whom she very quickly pushed aside with the help of her entourage. After hav-

4. {Bourgoint, *Retour*, 45, no. 13.}
5. {Bourgoint, *Retour*, 46, no. 15.}
6. {Bourgoint, *Retour*, 55, no. 33.}
7. {Bourgoint, *Retour,* 46, no. 16.}
8. {See above, chap. 6, p. 127, n. 11.}

ing tried all kinds of pleasures and ways to forget that she was alive, she started to think about ways to stop living all together. At Christmas 1929, a few months after the publication of the novel, she swallowed two bottles of sleeping pills. On the night of December 24–25, her mother discovered her at her last gasp; she passed away at the Lariboisière Hospital in Paris at the age of twenty-nine.

Her brother had written her a few weeks earlier, realizing "to what extent all this was serious and what grave danger we faced. It is still lurking even if we don't want to see it."[9] He had begged her to change her behavior, if only because of their mother and the despair that would devastate her. Nevertheless, he also thought about suicide after a romantic disappointment. He would later write that what held him back was that he was baptized, and it would have been a deadly sin. Moreover, Cocteau was now more distant, having taken another lover.

Bourgoint dragged on for many years through all kinds of miserable stages, until one Christmas he wanted to go to confession, as he had never done in a confessional. He entered the middle compartment of the three before him, where the priest sat, quite startled. Bourgoint moved to the correct side and started his confession, not realizing that the grill was still closed, meaning that the priest had not finished hearing the other penitent's confession, and Bourgoint's turn had not yet come. The priest vaguely heard him reciting a prayer and opened the grid to notify him that he needed to wait. Totally embarrassed, Bourgoint forgot what he was coming to say.

In 1939, Bourgoint wrote to his mother that he had started a new detoxification program. Six years later he confided to his friend Frosca Munster[10] that the sight of a young German prisoner

---

9. {Bourgoint, *Retour*, no. 37.}

10. Born in Moscow, she died of cancer in Montpellier on August 22, 1963. She had always hoped to see Bourgoint again, but he could not come to visit her at the hospital where she was treated. He wrote to her from Cîteaux a little before her death. It was Frosca Munster and Jean Hugo, whom he met at Cocteau's home in 1930, who attempted to keep him from suicide.

waiting for his freedom, with whom he had sat on a bench and talked, had profoundly moved him. He was forced to confront himself with an attraction that he felt was inappropriate. He zig-zagged in panic between the absolute and the abyss. He sent the letter from the Mas de Fourques, close to Arles.[11] In November of that year he met a Dominican visitor, Father Ceslas Rzewuski, who realized that he was drifting away and tried to draw him back.

Fate intervened; a fire broke out in the house during the night because red-hot ashes were placed too close to a pile of dry wood. The flames and the smoke dragged the Dominican and Bour-goint out of their sleep and threatened the kitchen and the whole house. In an epic scene of contrasts that would have pleased Victor Hugo, the two men threw the books of the library through the window. The firemen arrived but had no water; however, luckily, the wind turned and the fire subsided on its own. The two men continued the conversation they had started the previous evening, and the young man shared his discouragement about the kitchen apprenticeship he was about to start in Marseille. On the spur of the moment, the priest invited the stranger to come to his monastery at Toulouse. At that moment Bourgoint didn't say yes or no, but he went.

From that point on his life changed. A sentence from the Gospel enlightened him: "Ask and it will be given to you," says Christ. "Seek and you will find; knock and the door will be opened to you" (Matt 7:7). He still couldn't resist the temptation of opium, which had made him ill since his latest detoxification. Nevertheless, he lived and worked in another Dominican monastery in Saint-Maximin. Suddenly he decided to visit Cîteaux. Remembering his past life, he was convinced that he didn't have a vocation to the priesthood, so at the end of 1947 he asked to become a lay brother. "My dignity as a human being was totally crushed," he would write later, until that blessed night of the fire, that *beata nox* that ended his tête-à-tête with death. The novice

11.{Bourgoint, *Retour*, no. 60.}

master opened the iron door to the cloister, where these words of Saint Bernard are written: "O beata solitudo, O sola beatitudo" ("O happy solitude, O sole happiness"). Seeing them, he felt that they had the magic power to free him from all anxiety. On Christmas day he was accepted into the community.

He kept his talent for storytelling and his ability to call up images: "There is a large iron bell at the door of our dormitory. I believe that it is cracked. Throughout the year, regardless of the season, precisely at 2 a.m. each day . . . this bell throws down upon our sleep a downpour of large pebbles mixed with scrap metal."[12] Yes, Cocteau was correct. That twenty-year-old angel who flew close to hell knew how to use his pen. Twenty roller-coaster years later, close to the abyss of the mystery of our being, he could still bend words to his magic, if only to send some news to his confidante Frosca on how Trappists wake up in the morning. J.-K. Huysmans,[13] who was fascinated with the Trappists at Igny, painted it with his own brush:

> When I hear Bourgoint talking about the morning wake-up call, sometimes it seems to me that I am an old boat sailing into the port of Liverpool in the nineteenth century after a difficult crossing in a fog. While I am laboring through the thick clouds, I hear a big bang from one side of the long hall to the other followed immediately by hurried footsteps. These are my Cistercian brothers, white and brown, jumping from their cots and hurrying to church, like sailors falling from their hammocks after an all-hands-on-deck call, or like firemen in an emergency call at night.

12. {Bourgoint, *Retour*, 116–18, no. 80, here 117. The following account of Bourgoint's life as a Trappist is taken from this letter, which he wrote to Frosca on June 20, 1948, about his first impressions upon arriving at Cîteaux.}

13. {Joris-Karl Huysmans (1848–1907) was a prolific French writer of novels that received praise for their extensive vocabulary and wit. He converted to Roman Catholicism and became an oblate at the Abbey of Ligugé. An expert in art, in 1898 he published *La Cathedrale*, analyzing the iconography of Christian architecture.}

Why didn't Bourgoint leave a body of work? Why so many years wasted? But answering this would be explaining our destiny and our liberty. Why hasn't each one of us done a better job than what we did? Why do so many monks renounce any and all earthly success to practice pure contemplation? I do not know any professed monk about whom you couldn't write a chapter or a book. That is La Trappe: a gold mine, a living spiritual treasure, a library of true stories. A man is a universe, but what about 150 monasteries! To speak about only one brother is to break up a galaxy, to isolate what only exists within the unity of the entire community. Nevertheless, when you watch the sky at night, two or three stars are sufficient to suggest everything that lies beyond.

During his novitiate, the verses from Cocteau haunted Bourgoint's memory. The worldly noises were not far away, but he thought that he had found the truth, God, "the secret of all secrets, the hidden secret that stares everybody in the face." His sorrow was that he could not participate in the choir prayers with the monks. While they were chanting the psalms, he stood on the side and recited Our Fathers, as was required of the lay brothers. He pitted himself against the four cows ("as big as transatlantic liners") he had to milk and compared himself to a boxer after a losing fight. Not in good physical condition after twenty years of opium use, he participated in the group's work but came out of it exhausted because he tried so hard. At 8 p.m., when it was still daylight in the summer, the bell ordered: "everyone to bed!" with its cracked iron sound.

Behind the curtain of his cell, he heard his mother tell him, just as she had before, but this time for the opposite reason, "What time are you going to bed, my little one? Your life is upside down!" His deprivation of the readings and the liturgy was hard on him. The absolute silence was difficult for him, as were the penances—even the "ugliness of our church," which had been built for juvenile delinquents after the French Revolution. His habits in civilian life were even more demanding mistresses, which had turned his life "into a stable of laziness, a room always in a mess at 6 p.m.: I had become the Bois de Vincennes after a godless Sunday." His life had become a waste, in which he didn't expect to be anything better than a newspaper seller calling out the front-page gossip on the boardwalk. He was happy to recall that lost time.[14]

Jacques Maritain attended the simple vows that Brother Pascal pronounced in 1950 in the chapter room in front of Dom Dominique Nogues, abbot general, assisted by his subprior for Cîteaux, Dom Godefroid Bélorgey. As Bourgoint entered the monastic life, he didn't understand the significance of the word *incarnation*, which he confused—without knowing why—with the term *Eucharist*. His father was a Freemason and a process server, who hadn't taught his three children anything about Christianity. Maxime, the oldest one, was also present that day in the chapter room with one of his cousins and Jean Hugo.[15] Beyond the theological vocabulary, the mystery of the incarnation of the Son of God in human flesh to live as a human being in everything except sin was now offered for the new Brother Pascal's wondrous amazement.

The work day of lay brothers started fairly early in the morning, at 5:30 a.m., after they had peeled the vegetables [for the day] between 3 a.m. and 4 a.m. In general, the lay brothers were in charge of the workshops, while the choir monks, when they were available, performed unskilled labor, mainly in the fields, which at the time required a lot of workers. The management of the community remained nevertheless in the hands of the choir monks. On Sundays during the liturgical offices the lay brothers stood in a section of the church reserved for them. While the choir monks sang in Latin, the lay brothers individually recited Our Fathers, each man for himself—the *patenôtres*, as Brother Pascal called them. They were not allowed to hold prayer books.

14. {Dubois here alludes to Proust's *À la Recherche du Temps Perdu*.}

15. {Jean Hugo (1894–1984) was the great grandson of Victor Hugo. He was a painter, illustrator, theater designer, and author. Born in Paris, he was part of a number of artistic circles that included Jean Cocteau, Raymond Radiguet, Picasso, Erik Satie, Marcel Proust, Jacques Maritain, and others.}

This division of labor might have suited the vocation of some, but Brother Pascal regretted that he was not allowed to chant the psalms like the choir monks. Some other secondary aspects of their lives, based on the fact that lay brothers were not legally considered monks, started to be less tolerated in the 1950s. Should the lay brothers be considered a special category, with fewer rights than the others? Only the choir monks, for example, elected the abbot of the community and took part in the important chapter decisions, like the admission of a novice or even of a lay brother.

In 1953, the general chapter tried to adopt measures to do away with what could be considered social discrimination. It took about ten years for the question to reach a global solution. At that time Cîteaux had a group of about thirty-five lay brothers, who reported to the father bursar for their work and the management of the workshops while reporting to the lay brother master for questions of monastic discipline, health, and spiritual formation.

Father Henri, a thirty-three-year-old monk, was appointed in 1955 as the new lay brother master. He would remain in that position until 1958, when he was sent to Africa. Brother Pascal chose him as his confessor, and they had a very close and confidential relationship. When Brother Pascal drafted his well-written letters, he talked about them with Father Henri and showed them to him.

Much later Father Henri said, "Brother Pascal was a real lay brother, with some weaknesses that you can understand when you know his temperament and the habits he had acquired a long time ago. Every life has its failings."

Everything started for Bourgoint in joy, real joy, not like what you experience in the world, he said, the one that you fear will not last, while "God's universe is always joy." With the innate feeling he had for the absolute, "he always wants to have his road be a straight line," down which you must run forward head first without ever looking back, the one used by those who do not have prudence in their heritage and never seek to acquire it.[16]

16. {Jean Menton, in the introduction to the collection of Bourgoint's letters mentioned in n. 1 of this chapter. Bourgoint, *Retour*, 19.}

In 1954 Bourgoint wrote, "You can only know God by loving him, for the very simple reason that he is Love. And the beginning of loving God is to believe this: that 'God IS love.' That is the essence and the foundation of the revelation of Christ that many Christians do not suspect. And once you love him, you have the overabundant and marvelous—but hard-to-communicate—proof that he exists."[17] Sometime later he wrote to Cocteau, who had just had a heart attack, "Experience also tells me that it is sufficient to immerse yourself in Christ to recover the youth of your soul, the vision of the Spirit, and the peace of heart. If you don't re-immerse yourself, the cleansing remains ineffective, for the same reason that it is not sufficient that bread have flour to be nourishing, or that it be perfectly baked—it also needs to be eaten."[18]

But the Lord would break the straight lines. There were plenty of tests at two levels, probably related: one regarding monastic observance and one regarding faith. Around 1963, Bourgoint's faith darkened, a fact that greatly disturbed him. Nevertheless, he didn't lose peace or confidence or the belief that grace was not an illusion. Six weeks before his death he was able to confide, "It is a beautiful thing to be able to freely live the present moment, which is the reality (with its joys as with its sorrows) in the light of God's today."[19] How can we not join him in his statement?

Brother Pascal suffered from the mechanization that was slowly taking over the agricultural processes and from certain work taking place at Cîteaux that seemed to damage the nature that he loved so much. To a certain extent, he said, faithfulness is trench warfare. Around August 1956 he started to wonder about the conditions of the lay brothers in a monastery where everything seemed to be conceived as a clerical society. It was a diversion, he thought; moreover, he was skeptical about the reforms decided at the general chapter of 1962. They would only bring about, he thought, "a cosmetic change, and not one of structure and mentality," since those seemed to be well entrenched. In

17. {Bourgoint, *Retour*, 148, no. 96.}
18. {Bourgoint, *Retour*, 158, no. 98.}
19. {Bourgoint, *Retour*, 294, no. 165.}

1959, he had already written to a friend, "Pray for me, because I am often tempted to change deserts, that is, to become a deserter. There is a certain behavior in religious orders towards lay brothers that God probably does not want, and neither, I suppose, does anyone in the Order."[20] He wrote to Father Rzewuski that it was possible that he would leave Cîteaux, "because of this lay brother question."[21] He was shaken in his vocation, and this was reflected in his faith, but this test would prepare him, he later acknowledged, in a negative fashion—in the depths, one might say—for all the graces he later received in Africa.

His superiors sent him to Cameroon to join a monastic foundation that Cîteaux had taken under its wing. Father Henri, his former master of lay brothers, was already there and was soon appointed superior. Brother Pascal would find peace close to him. Early in 1964 he was getting ready for his new life. He wrote that he went "to Dijon with the brother who will travel with me to Cameroon for a yellow fever shot. Departure is scheduled for the end of July or the beginning of August."[22] This travel companion was Brother Marie-Joseph, the old submarine warrant officer mentioned earlier in this book. He had now been in the monastery for nine years. Two different lives, two conversions in tears, who would join the former lay brother master in Africa. Brother Pascal said that one cannot enter into God's sight without tears in the eyes. Both left for new adventures, from which Brother Pascal would not return. Two years later, when he was sixty years old, he encountered "the lady with red gloves—but a red that is totally different from love"—the color of death.

As the two brothers prepared to leave, still wearing the brown habits of lay brothers, Dom Jean Chanut told them, "You have to wear the white and black habit of the choir monks to travel and live there." That seemed like an insignificant request, but it showed the tremors that were already shaking the Order. Brother

20. {Bourgoint, *Retour*, 199, no. 112.}
21. {Bourgoint, *Retour*, 280, no. 156.}
22. {Bourgoint, *Retour*, 239, no. 143.}

Marie-Joseph obeyed but wondered why his superior had asked him to change his habit. He suspected that during his absence the controversies on monastic customs would continue, and maybe changes would take place. He also wondered why Brother Pascal was seeking counseling from Jacques Maritain regarding personal matters. Dom Jean Chanut had authorized him to leave the monastery for a few days just to meet with Maritain. These problems might have been tied to the situation within the whole Order.

But curiosity was not guiding Brother Marie-Joseph, and he didn't have to wonder for a long time. The two lay brothers started to share their impressions. How did these two men form a team, notwithstanding their totally different views? Without realizing it, the two of them represented in themselves the problem of the lay brothers in the Order. They embarked from Marseille on August 9 on the cargo ship Sainte-Claire-Deville, owned by the Pechiney Company, traveling to Conakry. For the first time since they had lived side by side, they talked to each other. They talked a lot, about everything, without using the sign language that they had used in the monastery. While they knew each other from seeing each other and working together, Brother Marie-Joseph was happy to have a conversation with someone who had had a life experience somewhat close to his own, and Brother Pascal didn't hesitate to share with him his deepest thoughts and his fears for the future. They had an uneventful crossing while watching the flying fish and the porpoises. They took advantage of a luxurious cabin, though that didn't eliminate the swells, and they ate at the captain's table.

Both men regretted how slowly attitudes were evolving, and they agreed that they should be allowed to take a more important part in the monastic liturgy. They also agreed that their status needed to be changed. Soon Vatican II would support the changes that had already gotten under way in the Order. Nevertheless, the two did not see eye to eye on the best solution. Brother Pascal was opposed to the predominance given to choir monks who were priests, even though the status of monk was in itself a lay concept. He nevertheless wanted to keep the balance of life allowed by the status of lay brother, a life of humble labor close to nature. Brother Marie-Joseph was more sensitive to maintaining the unity of everyone in the community with an *horarium* that gave everyone access to the same monastic culture, each according to his capabilities.

They exchanged their points of view on the deck of the cargo ship, listening to the waves they had both loved a long time ago, watching the sunsets they had thought they would never see again. On the horizon loomed the idea of a general unification of the thousands of Cistercian monks in the world, a reform that raised numerous obstacles on both sides.

"Division is bad," said one of the men, while observing the seagulls in the sky.

"It's not desirable for all of us to do the same thing," said the other, "just as if we were all cast in the same mold."

"Look at all the wrangling, these arguments without end," Brother Marie-Joseph argued. "Is that good for the monks? What an example if people saw us!"

"This wrangling is taking place now; it didn't happen yesterday. I think that I will stay in Africa for twenty years, but I may not go back to Cîteaux if the evolution goes badly. I would rather leave the Order."

"Come on, Pascal! Who is putting forward these arguments? Aren't there some lay brothers who want to leave a situation that they feel is abusive? Aren't they the ones who run the material aspect of the monastery? But I don't share this resentment. I didn't enter the monastery to participate in quarrels. I prefer unity. There is a lot of hope now."

Brother Pascal confided, "I didn't enter the monastery to be forced now to do something different from what was planned in the beginning. I couldn't. This is not my vocation. There are many like me."

Brother Pascal's reaction raised a fundamental question. Is it possible to plan everything that might be asked of us later on? As I mentioned in the previous chapter, the monastic profession does not give you an insurance contract, but rather a commitment to a living community that will inevitably have its own history. It is comparable to what two young people experience when they get married. They are uniting for better or worse, even though no one is considering the worse on the first day. Can they foresee each other's evolution, life's hazards, unexpected events in their professional lives, illnesses, and setbacks? Even though they do not take this commitment lightly, the life that opens up in front of them will force them continuously to invent new behaviors if they want to stay true to their first love. They will have to accept the evolution forced on them by their mere existence if their union is not to be doomed to failure. Being faithful also supposes changes. The same life dynamic applies within the monastic life. Faithfulness does not mean being fixated on what was experienced at the time of the commitment or on what could be foreseen then.

The two lay brothers, on the threshold of important changes, took the train in Douala, Cameroon, for M'Balmayo. They went deep into the forest until they reached the monastery of Grandselve, about twenty miles away from Douala, close to Obout, arriving at sunset on September 2nd. Brother Pascal marveled at the contact with the villagers they had met during the daylong train trip. "From the bottom of my heart, I wished that the train trip had lasted as long as the crossing of the sea,"[23] he acknowledged. Butterflies of every color imaginable, what seemed like thousands of swallows swirling about, and the plumage of strange birds dazzled the two brothers. How beautiful! Trees and flowers surrounded the monastery with a dense natural landscape that stretched almost to infinity.

"But nothing is as beautiful as God's word," said Brother Marie-Joseph.

"Nothing is better than to be made for the uncreated beauty," responded Brother Pascal. "Those who possess a poetic gift and the habit of living for created beauty are naturally prepared to meet eternal truth, but they also can encounter dangers."

---

23. {Bourgoint, *Retour*, 250, no. 148.}

The landscape may have been grand, but Brother Pascal did not always see it that way; the monastery was small, and community life was strict. He experienced it as more austere than Cîteaux, where he had just gone through a serious personal crisis. He spent the first night listening to the thundering noise of torrential rain falling on the tin roof of the monastery.

Was everything going as well as he would have liked? The community of Grandselve was Cistercian, as Cîteaux was, and the Africans were not inclined to accept a second life style within the fraternal community that they were familiar with. The status of lay brother was not something they favored. Nevertheless, the atmosphere of the country was different, and Brother Pascal was captivated by its mentality. He stated that he would have preferred to be born in one of these villages in the forest rather than in the ninth district of Paris. In some respects, he had fled Cîteaux, and he went as far as asking Jacques Maritain if he should become a factory worker, hoping in some confusion to find a spiritual rebirth in a new environment. Here in Cameroon everything excited him; everything was possible. His dream of living near a leper colony was getting closer. He could see himself finding in a life with them the Gospel story that he would have liked to live out at Cîteaux. He thought of it as being cured of another kind of leprosy.

Nevertheless, Brother Pascal wrote, "Everything for me goes on as if I were losing my faith."[24] The first few weeks of the honeymoon didn't last. He loved the Africans and did not complain that he did not understand them. His search continued with other lights. His faith surprised him, but he thought that it brought him closer to Christ by pushing him to devote himself to the lepers. He bitterly criticized the Europeans who proclaimed the Gospel without inquiring if the Africans really understood them, never conceiving that they might learn or receive something from them.

24. {Bourgoint, *Retour*, 258, no. 152.}

One day he was headed for a leper colony deep in the north of the country. He was redirected to another one closer to his monastery and ultimately from there to another colony in the West, where he learned to make special shoes for the lepers. "Have among you the same feelings as were present in Christ Jesus," said Saint Paul (Phil 2.5). From the leper village in Mokolo, he commented that "the depths, the bottomless depths, of what is revealed in this short passage of the letter to the Philippians" is God's love for humankind, what he calls the "divine philanthropy." This had become for him the closest and most divine subject of the contemplation of God through Christ. "My whole experience of human life as well as of my religious life makes me feel the most leprous of anyone here."[25] He said this final word to a visiting Trappist: "I am a spiritual leper." And to Maritain he called himself "a leprous monk and somewhat a hermit."[26]

His situation with the Order of Cîteaux was not simple, but Father Henri, his superior, let him follow his special inclination and provided him with the material means to achieve it. He wrote to Dom Jean Chanut that he had never been as happy as here.[27] He explained that that fact meant that he hadn't been entirely happy anywhere else. He also understood that his fate was entirely linked to Cîteaux. He was a brother of Cîteaux, living with the lepers. Once he finished his apprenticeship as a shoemaker, he hoped to set up a shoe shop that would give him his independence. But in February 1966 he began feeling sharp pains in his stomach, and when the medications no longer had any effect, he was transported to the hospital at Garoua, where the doctor discovered an inoperable cancer. When he woke up, he was surprised to see so many people in his room. The bishop was administering the sacrament of the sick to him with great pomp; he received it in great pain. He didn't complain about anything and refused to be transported back to France. Father

---

25. {Bourgoint, *Retour*, 271, no. 154.}
26. {Bourgoint, *Retour*, 295, no. 166.}
27. {Bourgoint, *Retour*, 280, no. 156.}

Henri spent many days with him and celebrated the Eucharist in his room. They both brought up the marvels of God's mercy in his life, while praying very simply. The old master of the lay brothers regretted not having preserved the Our Father that Brother Pascal had transcribed in his own words.

"It was a masterpiece," he said, "as certain of his letters were, like the ones he dictated to me. Not a single word that wasn't pondered, personalized: 'Father Ours . . . .'"

"We talked so much on the boat. He had so many projects," Brother Marie-Joseph thought, overwhelmed when he heard the news of Brother Pascal's dying.

"'Father Ours . . . ,' said Brother Pascal in his beautiful prayer," added the superior. "It is this Father who held tightly in his arms his lost son who was found, alive and well in the light of eternity. This was our hope."

When he arrived back from Africa four years after he had left, Brother Marie-Joseph found Dom Jean Chanut waiting for him at the door of the monastery. His superior, who had told him to dress in black and white when he left for the trip, welcomed him with affection and asked him, "How do you want to be dressed?"

"I don't know. You are the abbot, you tell me."

Brother Marie-Joseph looked with astonishment at Dom Jean, who at this time was wearing the brown habit of the lay brothers instead of the habit of the choir monks, while Marie-Joseph had kept the black and white habit of his departure. What had happened in the community? The abbot's habit held the answer. "Wear the brown," he suggested.

The following morning some wondered about it and questioned him:

"Why are you wearing brown?"

"Because Father Abbot told me to do so."

"You should have remained in white with the black scapular."

"I don't understand anything about it. He told me brown. If he had told me red I would have worn red. I am above that. What does color mean to me?"

Without saying a word, he put on his cowl and walked towards the choir for the beginning of the liturgy.

"This is not your place," a choir monk told him.

"But yes, on the contrary, you can come," others confirmed.

"Father Abbot invited me to go to the choir where most of them were already," concluded Brother Marie-Joseph, "and I was too happy to join them to refuse. I had just come back from Africa, and I was not aware of the discussions."

The principle of the profound change had already been approved by the general chapter of the abbots. The remaining difficulty was that choir prayer was considered an integral part of the legal status of a monk. The positions of both sides had crystallized in the beginning around this point. Shouldn't the lay brothers participate in the liturgical prayer, the essential occupation of the monks, if we wanted to eliminate the two classes of monks in our monasteries and if the lay brothers were to be recognized as monks in the same way as the others? Some lay brothers didn't feel the call, especially since—at that time—the prayers were still chanted in Latin. Moreover, the choir monks, who had celebrated the liturgy since the beginning, sometimes watched with a critical eye as the choir was invaded by brothers untrained in the chants and unable to read Latin. They also feared that the participation of the lay brothers in liturgical prayer would not allow them to spend as much time on manual labor as before, with harm to the material life of the monastery and disruption to everyone's habits.

In December 1965, the Holy See had proposed a solution to this question in the *Decree of Unification* granted to the Order. The decree abolished any difference between the classes. From then on there would only be one category of monk. Nevertheless, it didn't force anyone to participate in the liturgical prayer. Each lay brother was allowed to remain in his previous status, while being allowed to wear the monastic cowl and take part in the election of the abbot. Those who agreed to joining the choir monks by signing the decree were still allowed to pray as they used to. In principle, everything could have taken place peacefully and freely. But unexpected factors came into play.

Some lay brothers, attached to their previous status, felt like the "last of the Mohicans," even though they were assured that they could enjoy their status until their deaths. They would not have descendants, as every new postulant would enter the monastery as a monk from the start. Would that mean the disappearance of the vocation of the lay brother? Yes, as a separate class of monk, but theoretically, according to the new status, it was still possible to achieve the essence of a lay brother's life, with a larger part given to manual labor, a simpler form of prayer (often on the work site), and fewer spiritual studies. This last point was confirmed by the *Constitutions* of the Order drafted in 1984–1985 and approved by the Holy See in 1990. These left to the abbot the task of determining for each monk according to his character, his formation, and his evolution the time he would devote to the Divine Office and prayer, to spiritual readings, and to manual labor.[28] Some who wanted to be protected by a special status thought, "Doesn't that leave everything to an arbitrary decision of the abbot? Who can assure me that he will respect my deepest aspirations?" In their general chapter meetings, the abbots reflected on how to address these problems.

It must be remembered that there was no unanimity among them. There wasn't even agreement on what the intent of the 1965 *Decree on Unification* was or what had happened since then. Was the intent simply to eliminate the class differences between the choir monks and lay brothers, which had become unacceptable, thereby making it possible for the lay brothers to participate in the liturgical offices? Or did we want to eliminate the vocation of lay brother, defined as the search for a simpler life, indeed a simpler prayer life, with more time given to manual labor, beyond the five or six hours provided for in the *Constitutions*?

The discussion that took place at the 1993 general chapter showed that some accepted the concept of this lay-brother vocation, while others disputed it. The latter stated that all monks

---

28. *Const* 14:2. See also 19:2.B.

lived this ideal of simplicity, which defined their vocation, or that the monastic observance, according to the Rule of Saint Benedict, included participation in the whole Divine Office, except in cases of dispensation or for reasons of work.

Since opinions differed, it was understandable that former lay brothers who wanted to keep a lifestyle centered in manual labor wished for the general chapter to take a position that would explicitly guarantee it. It was therefore not necessary to amend the *Constitutions*. The general chapter could approve a model statute that would clearly state what should be done.

The real question for the newcomers was not so much participation by everyone in the liturgy as it was the way manual labor and spiritual study were balanced in each monk's life. The liturgical reform accomplished with the momentum of the Vatican Council, and especially the gradual shift from Latin to the common language, made participation in the liturgy more desirable, especially for the more important services of the day.

There remained the fact that those who were attracted to the simpler work life, without much study time spent in *lectio*, needed to feel recognized as fully monks. Didn't the actual model and the whole organization of the monastery tend to make the lay brother appear more like the old choir monk, up to the *horarium* punctuated by the ringing of the bells? The group of lay brothers, with their own *horarium*, customs, and vestments, as well as their distinctive places in the refectory and elsewhere, did not exist any longer. The group had blown up, one might say, and this was inevitable and even good. A separate group could have survived as such for those who didn't sign the decree, but as things stood, it would only have lasted for a time and didn't have a future. In fact, a number of these "last of the Mohicans" became marginalized in their communities, where, happy in their fate, they continued to live their monastic lives very well, but in an increasing isolation.

The pluralism that resulted in each community had its advantages and disadvantages. It enabled each monk to better find his own way, and it prevented everyone from being forced into the same mold with the rigid structures that that implied. The communities ended up being freer and more alive. These were the fruits of the present *aggiornamento*. But the arrangement required more maturity and personal responsibility, which was good. It also made respect for outside discipline more difficult. It offered a more diversified appearance, but that could confuse those looking and listening to the call to the monastic life. From the outside, you saw a community that came together seven times a day for liturgical prayer. The postulant attracted by a life that gave more room to manual labor or to a simpler style of prayer, like that of the lay brothers of old, did not perceive from the start that this was possible. Some wondered if that could be a reason that this type of vocation was rarer than before.

One could observe—probably accurately—that this type of vocation occurred more often in a rural environment, which represented a decreasing percentage of the French population. The vocation of Brother Pascal was clearly an exception to this assumption. This situation varied greatly among countries. The protests of some of the lay brothers were stronger in North America, because they had been more recruited from among college graduates and professional candidates who had deliberately chosen this special lifestyle, which they didn't want to abandon. In other monasteries the unification took place successfully, and in Africa the question never came up. There it was unthinkable that a community could include two different types of vocations.

The present situation may still generate some discontent that a future evolution will probably alleviate, but it still can be painful for some. One of the challenges that our Abbot General Bernardo Olivera offered for our reflection on the eve of the ninth centenary of the foundation of Cîteaux in 1998 was this proposition: "The acceptance of authentically Cistercian vocations oriented to manual labor, lived as a type of service and search for God, could be an option more coherent with our monastic profession than hiring lay people to take care of our economic necessities and need for labor."[29] He knew the question of lay brothers inside out, since he himself had been one at the beginning of his monastic life in the monastery of Azul in Argentina.

His initial choice never seemed to be a mistake for him. In fact, he had felt that he was living a thoroughly contemplative life with the lay brothers, even if in canon law they were not monks. But what does canon law mean when faced with reality! That was really a monastic vocation. To those who denied it, Brother Bernardo would reply, "It may not have been a vocation in your eyes, but it was my vocation! I was called to that type of life." When he entered the monastery at age twenty-eight after veterinary school, he watched the choir monks, thinking like those who shared his work and *horarium*, "Poor souls! They have to use Latin and spend hours in church. We lay brothers are more gifted, and our monastic vocation is more complete."

The inner life of the lay brothers was as profound as that of the choir monks. Everyone acknowledged it, and nobody thought that choir monks were superior just because of their position under canon law. When the *Decree on Unification* was issued in 1965, it was applied slowly in Brother Bernardo's monastery, where he himself accepted it very well. He was also allowed to study at St. Joseph's Abbey in Spencer, Massachusetts, Azul's mother house, and was ordained a priest. But he understood that others didn't feel that they had to change status.

The unification process was implemented so well in Azul that Brother Bernardo's initial status as lay brother did not prevent him from being elected abbot of the monastery in 1984 and then being elected abbot general of the Order at the general chapter in 1990. In so doing he achieved a double first: not only did a former lay brother succeed Robert, Alberic, and Stephen Harding, the first abbots of Cîteaux, but he was also the first non-European elected to this position.

29. Letter to the Order, dated October 1, 1992.

When he was elected abbot general, Dom Bernardo was forty-eight years old. He was frightened for about one second, he said. Is it more difficult to be abbot general than a lay brother? "For me it is the same thing," he answered. "Because the problem is me. If I am pope or president of the republic, cook or house painter, it is always my own life for which I need to take responsibility."

To tell the truth, he hadn't chosen to be a lay brother. Since he didn't know Latin and couldn't sing, he was assigned to that category from the start. That's the way it was. Some tell the story of a novice master meeting newcomers with a tuning fork in hand. They had to be able to sing the scale before being admitted as choir monks. Some situations could be painful, with delicate human stories, hopes dwarfed, and wounds that never healed. It would nevertheless be wrong to generalize from this. Most former lay brothers, both those who changed status and those who stayed, were happy with their choices.

"Thanks to the reforms, I was able to publish books," said another brother. When he was twelve years old he went through the guest house at Cîteaux with a group of children from a vacation camp and declared that monks had absolutely no use. Much later, when talking to an agnostic student in an art school, he got the sense of how the contemplative life and the silent prayer of the monks might be more useful than the missionary life. He believed in God and reasoned that faith was not a given. What words could not do, maybe their inner life could obtain. It was the shock of his life. Everything suddenly became clear, and he asked to enter Cîteaux.

Soon afterward, at the end of 1944, he was admitted as a choir monk. Like others, he wanted to study, but after eighteen months, Dom Godefroid Bélorgey, the superior, informed him that he would only be allowed to stay in the abbey if he became a lay brother. Why? He had stuttered since his youth. The test was hard, and in 1959, thanks to the new ideas that had started to circulate, he was allowed to return to the choir monks, where he undertook studies and language training. He became so successful that he gave talks for the community. He was sent to different abbeys to lead spiritual conferences, while publishing books and articles about a new approach to the influence of Origen of Alexandria, a Christian philosopher and theologian of the third century, on our Father Saint Bernard.

"I feel very happy," said Brother Albert, who remained a lay brother in Cîteaux, not having signed the *Decree on Unification* in 1965. "Otherwise I wouldn't have stayed. I had some difficult periods, but in the end everything worked out." Knowing nothing about monastic life when he entered the monastery, he hadn't expressed any choice. His superiors sent him first to the choir, but he soon realized that this was not his calling: "Singing all the time is not a life. No, that is not for me. I am leaving."

During his studies in industrial engineering he had been accustomed, as most people are, to working from dawn to dusk. "You need a special vocation to recite over and over the same psalms in church, bowing and prostrating yourself," he explained to the novice master, as he gathered his belongings to leave. "If that is the monastic life, I cannot relate." "You could choose to become a lay brother instead of completely renouncing the monastic life," the novice master answered him.

That is how Brother Albert was still in Cîteaux half a century later. As time went by, he met Brother Denis, who could barely read and write but was an expert in wrought iron artwork. He, the illiterate one, was forging a wrought-iron lectern, telling in the metal curls and figures the story of the spiritual evolution of the monk, fighting his inner evil, reading, and producing a fruit symbolized by a bunch of grapes. It rose up to the Mother of God, who then handed the fruit over to Christ. The two brothers talked each morning in the shop. In principle, they weren't allowed to do that. Nevertheless, Brother Albert thought that "to only talk to the abbot or a superior was neither logical nor normal. Just because you entered the monastery didn't mean that you absolutely had to get along with the abbot and really understand each other. To talk there needs to be a trust and an understanding that cannot always be explained. Some abbots are more open and welcoming than others." He also observed that some monks were isolated because of their health or personal problems and did not automatically find the right conditions for a dialogue with their superiors. The new lay brother didn't want to follow that path. He spoke in total serenity about all kinds of subjects with the artist who was making music with wrought iron.

"The spiritual life of the lay brother is totally different from that of the choir monk," Brother Albert thought. "I can only take part in the liturgical prayer by continuing to live in the monastery in a way that suits my temperament. During the week, I go to Mass and attend some prayer services, and on Sunday I never miss Lauds or Vespers. Our spirituality has been grounded in manual labor for centuries. It consists in finding God in manual tasks. Years ago, the prayers were said at the workplace. We would stop and stand facing each other, as though we were in the choir, and we would pray in the middle of nature—something beautiful—or in the workshops. Of course, today tasks are more technical. I work at updating our library catalogue on the computer. You cannot pray in the same way when plowing in a group for a whole day among the beets as when you are working on a computer. You have to adapt to the economic conditions of your time. But it is the same one and only Lord that we are all serving."

Chapter Nine

Father Abbot of La Trappe

I have heard a politician referred to as someone who was "lazy but frustrated." That is a description that could easily apply to me. There are two types of monks, as there are probably two types of people—those who say all the time, "Why was I not chosen for that position?" and those on the other side, who say, "I hope they don't choose me!" Circumstances do not explain everything; there really are two types of characters. The irony is that often the latter, who didn't ask for anything, are chosen.

My character does not push me to seek responsibilities. Sometimes I say jokingly that the less I do, the better I feel. More accurately, the responsibilities came looking for me. At Mont-des-Cats, when I was thinking about the challenges that might come my way, I thought that the worst thing would be to be sent as superior to another monastery. By comparison, all the rest didn't seem to be worth getting upset about. In fact, when this duty was assigned to me, I took it on like any other one. To a certain extent, I am still waiting for my toughest and ultimate challenge. Before that hour comes, we don't have either the strength or the grace to bear that burden. It scares us, but when that moment comes, someone else is carrying that burden with us.

Since Christmas 1972, I had been the prior, that is, the number two in the community, just under the abbot. Before that, I had been the master of novices for seven years, and these duties appeared to me to be more than sufficient. A promotion, or at least what appears to be one, sometimes leads to problems and requires a greater humility. As in the outside world, some people within the cloister need to prove to themselves that they are worth something on this earth, and they expect recognition from others based on a higher position. The uninitiated lay person, who thinks that we abandon everything the moment we enter the monastery, might be surprised. Do you ever totally renounce your own character? The laws of human psychology are the same for all. It is not necessarily a fault or paradoxically a lack of humility, because it is not moral or spiritual. It rests on the need for the fundamental recognition that each human being needs to fully develop his or her character. The position itself is often less important than the idea that we have of it and the affective load it carries.

Sometimes young professed brothers keep up a correspondence for years after their vows with their college friends or former work colleagues. These friends are climbing up the career ladder and have increasing responsibilities, while the brothers keep doing menial jobs, like cleaning the bathrooms, raking between the vines, or painting a building. The working conditions in a monastery have changed from what they were forty years ago. Sometimes novices get more responsibilities quickly after they join the community. Nevertheless, they don't reach a level that they could attain in a company or in the government.

The problem is that in a monastery there are only a limited number of real jobs that could be a contribution to one's personal development. There is only going to be one abbot, one prior, one master of novices, and one bursar. We could set up a rotation of duties, but that would create other problems. The abbot, it is written in our Constitutions, "is to govern the brothers with reverence for the human person created in God's image, promoting their voluntary obedience and appropriately fostering their gifts of zeal and intelligence" (Const 16.3). That cannot always translate to entrusting higher responsibilities to each one of the brothers, and some could feel put aside or underestimated. On the other hand, not everyone is capable of handling each and every job. Some duties may require a specific training or a competence that cannot be promoted or simply assumed. Nevertheless, everyone has to find his space where he can grow and find himself while living in the search for God. One of the first monks of the Jura is said to have "painstakingly assigned to each brother tasks and duties for which he was more particularly gifted by the Holy Spirit."[1] That is what each father abbot would like to do. If the sixth-century biographer mentions this, it is probably because we do not succeed at it every time.

But the job duties do not represent everything. Are they even representative of the confidence others place in us? We may put too much importance on this for our own development. They represent services to be rendered more than a personal promotion to pursue. The only sight that could build up the inner me is God looking at me, he who created me and who saves me continuously with an unceasing love. To recognize God's glance, I need to see it through an intermediary, through the eyes of other humans. For each one of us, the sight of the Father, who loves and calls us, is essential. But we cannot always remain dependent on the attitude of the others, who may very well be struggling with their own problems and who are not able to give us that liberating look, because they are themselves waiting for that look. We need to assert and strengthen ourselves, whatever people think of us, by completing any task we assume, however menial or prestigious the task may be.

How many people in the city of men complete tasks that they don't like and that they did not choose? They devote themselves to it because they have to, and they do it in a cutthroat job market with a lot of competition! Despite all the handicaps I mentioned, the monk is privileged. He may have more chances to learn, as his master Saint Benedict said, to "live with himself in God's presence."[2]

---

1. {*The Life of the Jura Fathers*, trans. Tim Vivian, Kim Vivian, and Jeffrey Burton Russell, CS 178 (Kalamazoo, MI: Cistercian Publications, 1999), 3.149, p. 170.}

2. {Gregory the Great, *Dialogues*, trans. Odo John Zimmerman, Fathers of the Church: A New Translation 39 (Washington, DC: The Catholic University of America Press, 1959), 2.3.5, p. 60.}

I readily acknowledge that I am interested in everything without being really attached to anything specific. I could say that everything catches my attention, although I am not really engrossed in anything. It is not important to me if I don't get to do a task that I could have done, and if I get to do it, it will be done with dedication, although it is not indispensable to my life or my happiness. Maybe that is detachment, but it comes naturally and without any merit because it is part of my character of being "lazy but frustrated." It is true what someone who knows me well said: I don't always do what I want, but I rarely do what I don't want.

When you enter the monastery, you have made the fundamental choice, as in a marriage. It remains then to make other choices and to confront unpredictable situations. Not everything is achieved on the first try. The circumstances are generally not so turbulent as in the outside world, but they can be embarrassing or can generate delicate personal situations. Then there is nothing else to do but confide even more in Christ, to whom the monk has given his life.

My intention was to live in Mont-des-Cats forever, but in 1975 the abbot of La Trappe, located at the border of Normandy and the Perche, resigned. This community did not feel that it could choose his successor from among its own members. Its father immediate, as we call it, the abbot of Cîteaux, looked somewhere else to find someone who could be the superior. He asked the father bursar of the abbey of Tamié, Father Irenée, to fill this position. Four months after his installation in his new abbey Father Irenée died at the age of forty-six of a ruptured aneurism during the night. The community was shaken up, and, at a crucial and painful point in their history, I was asked to succeed Father Irenée.

The dreaded moment was upon me. As I was organizing all my papers before leaving Mont-des-Cats, I found some notes I had taken while reading the books of Father Congar,[3] whom I had

---

3. See above, chap. 5, p. 110, n. 10.

met some time ago at a meeting of novice masters at the Benedictine abbey of Saint Benoît-sur-Loire. Already severely handicapped and moving around in a wheelchair, this important
theologian came there to make a presentation. I thought, "Well,
maybe I'll write Father Congar. He doesn't like to be told how
much we owe him, but at this crossroads in my life, I can show
him my gratitude." He answered me graciously and humbly.

The abbot of Cîteaux drove me to La Trappe on February 1,
1976. It is a huge and sturdy abbey that looked like a little village. It was snowing, and the landscape was cold and humid. We
arrived around 9 p.m., because we had been delayed by the slippery roads. The monks had gone to sleep, and only the brother
porter and the prior waited up for us. I was introduced to the
community the following morning. During the first days, I had
to explore the place and get to know the people. I understood immediately the advantage offered by the outlying buildings over
the layout of Mont-des-Cats for welcoming guests, young people,
families, retreatants, and people in need. The space seemed large
to me. My sorrow at being uprooted was alleviated by the warm
welcome I received, and I knew that I needed to adapt. One cannot always live in the past or give in to melancholy. For a while
I walked around in the surrounding woods with some nostalgia
for the community where I had stayed for about thirty years. I
thought, "Heaven could be the Mont-des-Cats community within
this beautiful environment."

Daily tasks were calling and prevented me from thinking too
much about myself. I had to acquaint myself with my new duties.
One of the first questions that came up for the community was
somewhat divisive: the opening of the church to all the faithful,
men and women alike. The church was located well within the
monastery's walls. Until then access had been limited to men
who were spending a couple of days with us in the retreat house.
Nevertheless, on Sundays the church was open to other men who
wanted to attend Mass. Should we broaden this opportunity?

The monks had been pondering this question for a while and
had held discussions about it. Questionnaires had been circulating

to enable us to quantify the different positions on the subject. A large number of brothers feared that it would open the door, so to speak, to an invasion of the outside world that would be hard to contain or control. Our vocation, which we needed to preserve, was to live somewhat withdrawn from the world in solitude and silence. Some also felt that we should no longer maintain a position that was increasingly in opposition to the evolution taking place in the Church and in other monasteries. Was it appropriate to discriminate between men and women? In fact, I commented, it was one thing to let the faithful enter the church for our eucharistic celebrations in the part of the church reserved for them. It was another thing to let ourselves be overwhelmed with the spirit of the outside world, opening the cloister and sharing our lives and all our daily activities with people on the outside.

It is sometimes difficult to get along, especially among French people, when we talk about generic subjects, because we often wonder what the other person is hiding behind his or her statement. Therefore, as a first step I proposed a more concrete measure about which we could all agree: we would clearly define the limits of the cloister within the monastery. This would allow access to the church by the faithful on Sundays and to our families visiting us during the week. Later there would be other measures, probably relating to the guesthouse policies. I didn't hide anything, but we would decide each step with the same clarity and freedom as we do today.

"We will remain in control of the situation," I assured them, "even if we acknowledge that our decisions are a response to the desire of others and therefore to something of an outside pressure. We are not the ones who need this opening."

The reasons I put forward to support this proposition were twofold. First of all, our liturgies were not private acts, but acts of the church, which did not belong to us alone. We prayed on behalf of the whole church, of which the other faithful were also part. Why leave them at the door when we might be able to offer them something that they didn't always find in their parishes: a certain style of celebration, and also the prayers of the Divine

Office, based on reciting the psalms, like Vespers on Sunday? The reform of the liturgy suggested that much, and our bishop encouraged us.

"In addition," I said, "what image are we presenting to the increasing number of people who stop by our monasteries for a walk or for some other reason?" They hadn't had much contact with the monks until now except to buy yogurt, cheese, or postcards, which the porter handed to them through a narrow window shutter that fell like the blade of a guillotine. Behind these walls were men who prayed, interceded, and sang God's praise while being in communion with the whole church and in its name. Wasn't it important for those who walked by our door to perceive this? To share the products of our manual labor, yes, but why not share also in our prayers?

The proposition was accepted by more than seventy-five percent of the votes, and the community became aware that its unity was strengthening again in a regained mutual trust. That was felt intensely. Of course, some had expressed their disagreement legitimately. One of them expressed his appreciation for the frank and honest way the question was put to the community.

It is important that the whole community be involved in the mechanism by which important decisions affecting them are taken. It is nevertheless not a pure democracy. Once the decision is made, those who have a dissenting opinion and end up in the minority do not form an opposition party, constantly trying to revisit the subject. Normally, everyone joins in even if it is not easy or if it presents a conflict of conscience. After the community's vote, the ultimate decision belongs to the superior, and that changes the perspective.[4] We do not act solely on the proposal of a majority of the brothers, because sometimes that majority could be very slim and easily swayed. We have chosen to live in

---

4. In certain cases provided for in Canon Law, such as the admission of brothers to monastic vows or incurring major expenses, the abbot can act only if he obtains a positive vote of the majority of the members actively involved in the community.

obedience, and the decision taken by the superior in all legitimacy becomes the expression of God's will. "There where the Church is, is the Spirit of God," said Saint Irenaeus in the second century.[5] You cannot go wrong when you remain united with the community. A short time after our decision, I was happy to see a brother showing the church to members of his family, although he was one of the brothers who had wanted to hold on to the old observances and who had voiced his opposition to the proposed measures. He even went beyond what had been approved, but I made a point not to mention it to him. He wasn't stubborn about his own point of view.

In 1968 the *aggiornamento* of Vatican Council II started to bear fruit, and a societal crisis developed in France and in the world. Perhaps at that time the role of the abbot was not always well understood and respected in the community-based approach. He didn't have to resign from his responsibilities when he was confronted with a majority, especially if it was a slim one. Certainly he had to enlighten himself through exchanges within his community. It would not have been wise to proceed if he were faced with almost unanimous contrary advice, but he was the pilot at the helm. Communities may have been destroyed because the abbot did not commit himself sufficiently to following his own conscience. It was of course delicate and not reassuring for the abbot, but there lies exactly where his grace and his charism should reside, as we say. I believe that nowadays in our Order these ambiguities have disappeared.

In getting acclimated to my new community, I knew that I would probably not return to Mont-des-Cats. Except for major blunders or unfortunate incidents, I would be elected as the successor of the present abbot. There was no surprise in the election that took place a year later on February 2, 1977. I was at peace

---

5. {Saint Irenaeus of Lyons, *Against the Heresies*, trans. Dominic J. Unger, 3 vols. (New York: The Newman Press, 1992–2012), 3.24.1, p. 110.}

with that idea. There is suffering and joy attached to each position, and I knew that there were people unhappier than I was when I was entrusted with that charge, even if I was not exuberant. The election did not have too many uncertainties, since someone was pre-selected, as it were.

Sometimes elections are more laborious than others, and the selection of a new abbot can be difficult. Even in these cases, once the process is completed, all unite behind the one whom God entrusts with this mission and therefore with a new vocation. The abbot is the only one who is elected in a monastic community. The holders of any other duties and responsibilities are appointed by him. He makes those appointments after consulting with the brothers, at least for the most important positions, but he has the final word.

In accordance with our Constitutions, the abbot can be re-elected for successive six-year periods or for a period that is undetermined in advance. The understanding is that on his seventy-fifth birthday at the latest, he will present his resignation. He is not abbot for life, but only for the time that he can usefully fulfill his duties as an abbot. Once he is no longer able to perform his function adequately, whether he realizes it or the father immediate suggests it to him, he will offer his resignation. The same system applies to abbesses of the monasteries for nuns. Abbots and abbesses receive a special blessing from the Church through the agency of the local bishop, who gives them the crozier[6] and the shepherd's staff, the long-time symbols of pastoral care. According to Church law, the abbot has to be a priest. He is not a bishop, although he might wear a mitre. Nevertheless, he enjoys some powers within the community that are normally reserved for bishops. Although we are located within the local church and diocese, in many respects we are not subject to the pastor of this diocese. That is what in technical terms we call the

6. Why does this insignia only convey the aspect of authority conveyed by the sense of the verb *crosser*, which, according to the dictionary, can mean *to treat harshly or with scorn*?

canonical exemption. Instead we are under the authority of the structures of the Order and the Holy See.

This doesn't keep us from having good relations with the local bishop or from integrating, as is appropriate, into the ecclesial environment. When a new bishop was appointed in Sées, I insisted on inviting him for lunch. To give this visit a liturgical dimension, I looked for an early date with an important celebration in church that would precede the lunch. I asked him, "Why don't you come and administer the ashes to us for the start of Lent." "That sounds good. Agreed."

All of a sudden I froze. What was I doing? On that day at lunch we would only have bread and water! What a day to invite the bishop for lunch! He laughed but didn't want to change the date, despite my insistence. We would make it up later, of course, on other occasions, but it is not common to get acquainted with your new bishop by inviting him to fast on bread and water! In fact, nobody was surprised to observe in the new bishop's calendar "Ash Wednesday: La Trappe"—his reputation was already earned! Like others I prefer to leave the use of the mitre to bishops, to avoid any confusion and in accordance with our Cistercian simplicity. Abbots only received the privilege of wearing a mitre in the fourteenth century, while the usage of the staff dates back to antiquity. Other signs of respect dating back to my youth have also disappeared, but that does not mean that the role of the abbot is diminished by any measure. Other times, other customs. I like the way our Constitutions define the role of the abbot in his community: "The abbot exercises pastoral care of the flock entrusted to him. He shows to all the goodness and kindness of Christ, striving to be loved rather than feared. He adapts himself to the character of each, encouraging the brothers to run with a cheerful and happy disposition along the way God has called them. He is to pray constantly to God for each" (Const 33.2). The father abbot is not necessarily the spiritual director of each of the monks in particular. He can't be, because he doesn't have the time, and moreover, freedom of conscience has to be respected. Nevertheless, he exercises a spiritual paternity over the whole community as such.

Each community has its own style and spirit, and that is often the doing of its superior. He will influence the evolution of the community and the spiritual environment of each one of the brothers through his personality and his example. He can give direction to the community through his engagement and especially through his teachings and interpretation of the Rule and his choice of his closest aides. One should not underestimate the importance of that community context modulated by the abbot, if it is true that monastic life can be defined as a certain "controlled environment."[7] At that level the spiritual paternity of the abbot is real.

He represents Christ in his community, says the Rule (RB 2.2). The monks are fully aware of this role, but for the abbot this conviction of faith requires an inner strength and responsibility and should not lead to pretentiousness or superiority. If there is one thing he should never say, it is, "Obey me, I am the Lord." On the contrary, he needs to be as humble and humane as possible and to behave in such a way that his actions are easily understood by all. He should not act arbitrarily.

Saint Benedict insistently warned that the abbot would be held accountable to God: "The abbot must exercise the utmost care . . . , because it is not the healthy who need a physician, but the sick" (RB 27.1). If the abbot has to behave with the utmost humanity, the monks, for their part, have to put the spirit of faith first. One very astute observation in the Rule asks the sick brother "not to distress the brothers who serve him by excessive demands. Still, sick brothers must be patiently borne with, because serving them is like serving Christ" (RB 36.4). If each one observes what is pertinent to him, there will be peace, but if the brother infirmarian tells the sick brother, "Don't be unbearable, as the Rule mentions," and if the sick brother responds, "You must support me: the Rule says so," it will be hell! So the abbot

7. Dom John Eudes Bamberger at a meeting of the American abbots in 1968 (*Supplément à la vie spirituelle* [September 1969]: 424–25).

has to be as human as possible, and the monk has to see in his abbot the representative of Christ. Let's not trade each other's responsibilities!

It is also important not to lose your own personality beneath the position. If you are obsessed by it to the point of subordinating your own personality to the position, it will be disastrous. In case of failure or resignation, the feeling of having encountered a catastrophe or boundless humiliation could be overwhelming. This observation, based on good sense and human wisdom, is not limited to monastic spirituality. There would be more peace in this world if people would think about this more thoroughly. You don't want to lose face, you defend your honor, your position, and the idea you have of that position, you identify yourself with that position, and you start to believe that it would not survive without you. How many crimes have been committed on the basis of this confusion? Susceptibility is dangerous and we are—alas!—not exempt from it.

When I arrived at La Trappe, I had to make sure not to bring with me the ways we did things at Mont-des-Cats. The brothers here would not take kindly to something that looked like a colonizing attitude. A superior's previous experience may help to understand what there is to improve, but the community that he joins may not have the same needs or the same problems or history as the one he is coming from. There are numerous differences among communities. The location can influence the lifestyle, the buildings, their age, the accommodations offered, and even their aesthetics. The brothers and their social origins and their average age are elements to consider, as well as the economy and their commercial activities. Also, the specific tradition of that monastery and its customs, and the behavior of the previous superior will all contribute to establishing the "spirit of the house."

The celebration of the holidays and of the liturgy differs according to the latitude. So does the way daily chores are handled. Once you are used to it, you can recognize the unique character of a community. Monks that have started their spiritual journey in one monastery might not automatically be able to adapt to another. It can be compared to the way a wine or a cheese originated from one region develops a specific flavor. Each community has its own style and history. Good observation and perceptiveness are necessary when one arrives from another environment. This is also required when a father abbot does his "canonical" visits, or regular visits, as we say, in his capacity of father immediate.[8] The daughter abbey doesn't have to be a copy of the mother abbey that founded it.

What is true for groups of people is also true for individuals, and the abbot has to be very attentive to that. It is not always good to assume what someone thinks or wants on the basis of one's own desires. A dialogue is the way to discern what another person's point of view is and to move forward from there, while accepting being questioned yourself. Anger, said an old monk from the fifth century, is pretending that your own will has to be done.[9] That is not the way to bring out the true personality of the other person. Dom Savin Boinot, an old father abbot and friend of mine, mentioned to me that the other person is entitled to be himself and not only a poor replica of what we ourselves are. That also means that we need to look at him thoroughly to discover who he is and not just ourselves in him.

All too often listening only means gathering just enough of the other person's words to contradict him as soon as he is finished talking. It is not a dialogue when one talks while the other prepares his response. Then they switch roles, and when they separate, nobody has really listened to anything. To listen, said this father abbot, is to try to catch, beyond a sometimes-inadequate word, the truth of a self-searching thought looking for you to understand what is dear to him. You will never be the same

8. {Father immediate: the name given to the father abbot of an abbey that founded another monastery or has other monasteries of monks or nuns placed under its jurisdiction.}

9. {Abba Isaiah of Scetis, *Ascetic Discourses*, trans. John Chryssavgis and Pachomios (Robert) Penkett, CS 150 (Kalamazoo, MI: Cistercian Publications, 2002), 28, pp. 227–33 at 227.}

after such an encounter, because it destabilizes you, and that is why we fear it.

One should also perceive what the other is capable of bearing, while being able to encourage it. Saint Benedict has an admirable formula: "The abbot needs to arrange everything so that the strong people want to do more and the weak do not shy away" (RB 64.19). Antoine de Saint-Exupéry put it from a more human point of view: "What can I do with a friend who judges me? If I welcome a friend at my table, I ask him to sit down, if he limps I do not ask him to dance."[10]

When I arrived in La Trappe in 1976 the tables in the refectory were arranged in a horseshoe, and the monks sat on one side of the tables in order of entry into the monastery, without anyone sitting on the other side of the table. This arrangement presented advantages and disadvantages. Since at work we were more and more scattered and isolated, the only place where the community could mingle was the refectory. Not that we would be talking there! But to offer the elders the opportunity to mingle with the younger brothers and vice versa in a mutual service at a table for six could only be beneficial. That is what the community wanted, and I made this suggestion mine. I ate among them without a reserved seat. Each community organizes itself as it wishes in such an important matter, since we are not talking about a restaurant or a cafeteria where you only visit occasionally, but about a family table that traditionally refers to the eucharistic meal. As the Constitutions put it, "The common table both expresses and strengthens the unity of the brothers" (Const 13.1.A). At La Trappe, the evening meal is served buffet style, but still in the refectory and in community.

Like most western monasteries, the cloister at La Trappe is a large square gallery built around an interior garden. Along this gallery are located the principal rooms that define the life

10. {Antoine de Saint-Exupéry, *Lettre à un otage*, in *Oeuvres* (Paris: Gallimard, 1959), 404. For an English translation, see *Letter to a Hostage*, trans. Cheryl Witchell (Babelcube, 2016), 18.}

of the community. Our cloister measures 280 feet long by 10 feet wide. It has stained glass windows and capital arches. Close to the transept in the church is the tomb of the abbots, containing the remains of all those who came after the French Revolution. My preference, like that of two of my immediate predecessors, when the time comes, is instead to be buried in the ground of our cemetery among my brother monks. The general tendency goes to a spirit of simplification in the Order.

Walking along the cloister one can observe an amazing chapel with relics. I have never counted those relics, since they matter less now than before, with the exception of one. With a high degree of probability, one of these relics is a bone fragment of an arm of Saint Benedict. It came from the abbey of Saint Benoît-sur-Loire (now called the abbey of Fleury), established in the seventh century to receive the bones of the monks' patriarch, which audacious monks had fetched from the ruins of Monte Cassino in Italy. During the ceremonies of perpetual vows, we take out this relic and expose it in the church. Instead of owning objects of value like those lay people have in their living rooms or bedrooms, the Trappists keep these relics like treasures that history has entrusted to them.

In a different field, we have one particular work of art that is precious—the original painting of Abbot de Rancé, our seventeenth-century reformer, as painted by Hyacinthe Rigaud. As we might have expected, the "Sir of La Trappe," as he was then called, didn't want to sit for the painting. The mere idea that his facial features could be kept for posterity was unbearable to him. In order to catch them one needed either ruse or chance. Some attempts had been made, but without any convincing results. They needed an exceptional artist for that task. The great royal portrait painter under Louis XIV and Louis XV was going to fulfill that role, but he needed a strategy in order to succeed.

A twenty-one-year-old man, Louis de Rouvroy, Duke of Saint Simon, came up with the scheme. He visited Abbot Rancé frequently. One day he presented Abbot Rancé with the request of an officer, who was supposedly a stutterer, to sit in during their conversations. He would only be able to listen and watch. It was in fact the painter Rigaud. They organised three encounters, which never raised the suspicions of Abbot Rancé and which enabled the painter to fix the abbot's features in his memory. The details of these encounters that Saint Simon recorded in his *Memoirs* are intriguing.[11] Dom Gervaise, abbot of our monastery from 1696 to 1698, later mentioned that he had played an important part in the organization of these encounters and related that the painter had thrown himself at the feet of Abbot Rancé to get his blessing and to see his hands up close.

The visual or aural memory of certain artists is incredible. The witnesses of that time agreed that the work of Rigaud was truly lifelike. "A masterpiece!" Saint Simon shouted. "There was never a more lifelike or more natural portrait," confirmed Dom Gervaise. When Rancé learned how his portrait had been made, he was saddened and wrote to Saint Simon that, unlike a Roman emperor who said that he liked treachery but hated the traitor, he loved the traitor but hated treachery.

Copies were made, and Rigaud worked with his students on many paintings. Where is the first painting, the original one? In his handwritten will of June 6, 1754, Saint Simon, who had kept the original painting with him, bequeathed it to the monastery. But the Revolution destroyed the monastery. What happened to it? We know that on October 2, 1847, King Louis-Philippe came to La Trappe and could see the painting he had already admired in 1788. It seemed that the canvas had been hidden during the revolutionary flurry, but the research undertaken by one of our own monks, Father Lucien Aubry, to shed some light on fifty years of silence regarding the fate of that painting did not result in any clear evidence.[12]

11. *Historical Memoirs of the Duc de Saint-Simon*, vol. 1, *1691–1709*, ed. and trans. Lucy Norton (London: Hamish Hamilton, 1967). The Duc de Saint-Simon was a well-known French diarist with a sarcastic tongue.

12. Lucien Aubry, "À la recherche du vrai portrait de l'abbé de Rancé," Abbaye de La Trappe.

On November 18, 1970, the work received the official National Heritage classification, together with two busts of Rancé kept at the monastery. This classification enabled a restoration, because flaking was threatening the whole painting. A delicate transposition detached the coat of paint from the original linen so that it could be placed on a new linen canvas. Then we noticed that many layers had been added over the years to reinforce the painting. But when the original layer was uncovered, it had the signature of Saint Simon, confirming that it was the original. There was no longer any doubt.

The quality of the face argued for that interpretation. It was a more beautiful portrait than the other portraits of Rancé. It was not necessary to be an expert to notice this fact. We like his smile when we look at him in the Chapter Room. This is the room where we meet as a community to listen to the abbot's teachings or where we exchange views on decisions to be taken on our way of life. These meetings start with the reading of a chapter of the Rule of Saint Benedict. This traditional practice gave its name to the room and then to the assembly that took place there.

The church in the monastery is the central place of the monastery. Half of the nave is occupied by the monks' stalls. That is where we alternate the prayers between the *schola* and the whole choir seven times a day from 4:15 a.m. on. The morning service is a common prayer called *Vigils*; it consists of singing psalms and listening to readings, passages from the Bible and spiritual authors, ancient and modern. The rest of the time until 7 a.m. is spent in personal prayer and in *lectio divina*. The same pattern follows at other times of the day according to an established schedule.

At 7 a.m. the whole community gets together for the morning prayer that we call *Lauds*. This is the plural for the Latin word *laus* or praise, because the liturgy concludes with specific psalms of praise. The first psalms are rather penitential prayers: the passage from the confession of our status as sinners to the praise of a God victorious over sin evokes the cosmic symbolism of the sunrise and the triumph of light over the darkness. This morning liturgy includes the celebration of the Mass. Every brother takes part in the Mass, each according to his rank as priest or lay brother. I previously pointed out the power of this moment in the community, which is the highest point of our day.

At 8 a.m. the brothers go to their respective work assignments or, for the youngest ones, to formation. Work generally keeps us busy five hours a day, but certain tasks and functions require more time. I will come back to this later in the book. But for those who are able, in particular for the youngest and oldest brothers and for the priests, meeting in church three times a day, in the middle and at the end of the morning and then at 2:15 p.m. for a short community prayer of about fifteen minutes, reminds us that our lives must be dominated by attention to God and to prayer. We call these prayers the *Little Hours*. We identify them in accordance with the ancient Roman method, starting the day at 6 a.m., so *Tierce* (third hour) is at 9 a.m., *Sext* (sixth hour) is at noon, and *None* (ninth hour) is at 3 p.m.

The evening liturgy, which corresponds to *Lauds* in the morning, is called *Vespers* (from the Latin word meaning *evening*). It celebrates the transition from day to night by expressing our Christian hope founded on the Pasch of Christ that the light shall not be absorbed by darkness; a new day will dawn after the night. As the Lord promised Noah when he came out of his ark after the flood, "While the earth remains, seedtime and harvest, cold and heat, summer and winter, day and night shall not cease" (Gen 8:21). At the tragic moments in their history, the Jewish people relied on this promise as proof of love without fail from God. At 8 p.m. the community gets together around the abbot to hear his spiritual instruction. A last prayer in the church, *Compline*, concludes the day, before the brothers retire for their night's sleep of seven hours and fifteen minutes.

Trappists live a total and complete community life. They do not have a separate home where they can be alone during the day. Even for reading and spiritual study they gather in one room, where each has a place to keep his own writings. These are no longer long desk tables, like what I discovered when I entered Mont-des-Cats. They are now small individual desks, with drawers sufficiently isolated one from the other to provide some privacy.

It took until 1985 for La Trappe to be equipped with small individual cells in the dormitory. Other monasteries had made that transformation years earlier. It provided for much better sound insulation, which favored a healing rest. It also enabled the snorers to fall asleep peacefully, without suffering from a bad conscience because of disturbing their brothers, as they did before. We had previously renovated the infirmary by installing some utilitarian comfort in six rooms, where there had been no running water and no toilets, and where the floor was wooden and hard to maintain. Our sick brothers suffered quite a bit from these conditions. We added call buttons as well as security features. We also equipped them with video equipment, which enabled our brothers to watch and listen to the liturgy, the talks of the father abbot in the chapter room, and the readings in the refectory. This made those who were restricted by age or illness less isolated from the life of the community. This work was considered by the state a "renovation of a recently acquired building with a social purpose," the home for elderly people. This entitled us to obtain a state loan.

How was it possible for the monks to be considered recent owners? A historic event, which took place in 1978, resulted in the end of a century of conflicts. Anticipating political problems that were threatening France, a civil company was incorporated in 1872 to become the legal owner of the monastery of La Trappe. In 1912 this company filed for bankruptcy, and the property was sold, to be repurchased by a new company created with the aim of allowing the monks to survive. Over time the monks purchased the shares in their own name. Taking advantage of some favorable regulations, this company was transformed into an outside association benefiting the community. It was composed of generous people supporting the monks, some of whom participated in the abbey's committees. Nevertheless, the situation was not straightforward.

It would have been better for the community to own its assets outright. That only became possible under the Fifth Republic.[13] The laws of 1901 had effectively suspended the right for religious orders to exist and consequently to own property unless they obtained a legal authorization, which was usually refused.

It is hard to imagine today how strong the anticlerical climate was during the Second and Third Republics. Article 16 of the law of 1901 introduced the "crime of association," which criminalized any religious association that did not have prior approval from the government. Many individual religious and many communities went into exile. That was the case for the Benedictine monks of Marseille, who took refuge near Chiari, Italy. Later while among these monks the future Pope Paul VI heard God's call to serve him, and it was perhaps also there that he received the call to the monastic life.[14] Starting with the promulgation of certain texts announcing the crisis of 1880,[15] many skirmishes took place between the police and the faithful, who came to defend the religious when they were forced to leave or to submit to the inventory of their assets. The monks of La Trappe were expelled from their monastery for one month while their abbot was seriously ill, and in fact he died during that month. Demonstra-

13. {The Fifth Republic is the name of the present form of French government. This presidential republic was approved by referendum in 1958, with General de Gaulle elected as its first President. This republican system succeeded the weakened Fourth Republic, which had collapsed with the onset of the Algerian conflict.}

14. He himself confided that to a meeting of Benedictine abbots in 1973. In 1922 the Benedictines returned to France in the monastery of Hautecombe (Savoy) before transferring the community to Ganagobie (Alpes de Haute Provence) in 1992. {In 1993 the Community of Chemin Neuf, a Roman Catholic community with an ecumenical calling, took up the life of prayer and welcome at the monastery of Hautecombe.}

15. {Between 1878 and 1889 the French republic was shaken by many scandals and riots between royalists and republicans. The result was successive weakened governments.}

tors were summoned to appear in court because they resisted the police, who were opening the tabernacles. Pope Pius X published his encyclical *Gravissimo* in 1906.[16] At that time, the ownership of parish churches was transferred to the cities, while the ownership of the cathedrals went to the state. A happy consequence of these expropriations was that it is now incumbent upon the state to maintain our prestigious cathedrals and to restore them, while the budget of the church is no longer sufficient!

This anticlerical climate was foreseen by Victor Hugo in *Les Misérables*: "from the point of view of history, reason and truth, monasticism is condemned," he wrote in 1861, summarizing in fifteen pages every falsehood about the monasteries. However, with his visionary genius, he also summarized the elements that, strangely, would enable certain events to take place decades later. He compared a convent to one of those optical devices used by humankind to look upon infinity, finding in it both a hideous side, which he hated, and a sublime side, which he adored.

But his indignation quickly took the dominant place. One of Hugo's typical images was later coldly translated into administrative and legal language to drive the monks out: "The monastic communities were to the larger social community what mistletoe was to the oak tree and what a wart was to the human body . . . . If the monastic system was any good at the onset of civilization, useful for reducing violence with the spiritual, it is now bad for the manhood of the people. . . . The cloister has outlived its usefulness!" The fanaticism of the monks, he thought, needed to be pushed aside to save humans and their souls, and to protect the mystery against the miracle. It is necessary to "cleanse God from all these undesirable caterpillars and insects, the monks! We will clean out society and give more clarity to the divine light, if we perceive it!"[17]

16. {Saint Pius X, *Gravissimo Officii Munere,* http://w2.vatican.va/content/pius-x/en/encyclicals/documents/hf_p-x_enc_10081906_gravissimo-officii-munere.html.}

17. {Victor Hugo, *Les Misérables,* trans. Julie Rose, Modern Library Edition (New York: Random House, 2008), 2.7, pp. 422–32.}

In this environment, the Trappists won a strange privilege. They made a request for the "right to exist," but nobody answered them. Therefore, they did not receive a formal refusal, which would have placed them outside the law. They would not be expelled, except for one or two monasteries that would be forced to close their doors, like Chambarand, close to Grenoble. The silence of the government was the result of the meeting of two men, Dom Jean-Baptiste Chautard and Georges Clemenceau,[18] who then presided over the Senate's commission reviewing these requests. The former was the abbot of the abbey of Sept-Fons from 1899 to 1935. He wrote a book that sold more than 200,000 copies, *Soul of the Apostolate*,[19] which Pope Pius X is said to have kept on his nightstand. What did Clemenceau and Dom Chautard tell each other? The former had totally adopted the views of Victor Hugo, so common at that time: "You did render great services a long time ago, but today the whole country is cultivated, civilized. I do not see what role you can play anymore. You really are useless men, and even your example of a life removed from the intense activities of the country is not good. We really cannot approve you in this twentieth century."

Dom Chautard responded that the goal of the Cistercians was not to cover the country with schools or to devote themselves to hospitals, but to pray, adore, and remain in the presence of God in the Eucharist. "He is there, the one I adore as God," he said. "He is there, man and God."

18. {Georges Clemenceau (1841–1929): a French physician and politician who supported radical socialist and anti-republican views in the Chamber of Deputies. He was prime minister during the Third Republic (1906–1909) and again after World War I, playing an important role in drawing up the Treaty of Versailles (1919). He was the owner and editor of the newspaper *L'Aurore,* which published Émile Zola's open letter (see above, chap. 6, p. 140, n. 17) during the Dreyfus Affair and supported the staunchly anti-clerical policies of the early 1900s.}

19. {Dom Jean-Baptiste Chautard, *Soul of the Apostolate,* trans. a monk of Our Lady of Gethsemani (Charlotte, NC: TAN Books, 2012).}

He added an argument that grabbed Clemenceau:

> Doesn't this divine King, who is present among us, deserve
> a court to honor him? Every head of state on this earth has
> a court, a chosen few whose primary duty is to assist the
> master. Should the King of kings not have his? Wouldn't
> there be men and women who would consider it their su-
> preme honor to adore him, and would make it their voca-
> tion? Are we wrong? You were making fun a minute ago,
> Mister Chairman, of our long nightly offices without anyone
> attending them, of our solemn masses without witnesses,
> of our songs without any audience. You asked me what the
> use of this was. We only seek to honor Christ, who lives
> among us, who sees us, who hears us, and to whom we
> speak as if we saw him. When the row of honor in the Senate
> presents arms to the President of the Assembly when he
> enters the chamber, they do not do this for the public in the
> gallery, but rather to show respect for France, represented
> by one of its highest dignitaries. It is the same for us—when
> we sing or adore we don't worry about whether the public
> is there or not. The only person we think of is our God. How
> could you call that wasted time, for someone who believes?
> To tell the truth, it is not only faith that supports us when
> we stand guard for Him, it is love. To the one who loves,
> doesn't the time spent close to someone who delights him
> and is in every respect superior always seem too short?

Dom Chautard spoke with passion, and at the end of his fiery
tirade, Clemenceau was visibly moved: "Tell this to the Senate's
Commission with all your passion. I understand the ideal of the
monk. A French congress doesn't have the right to expel real
monks. Consider me your friend."[20]

---

20. Dom Jean-Baptiste Chautard related this conversation in a presentation he gave in 1931 organized by the Regional Direction of Cultural Affairs.
{Excerpt in Jean-Baptiste Chautard, *Les Cisterciens trappistes. L'Ame cistercienne. Une des conférences de D.R.A.C. donnée le 28 janvier 1931* (Dompierre-
sur-Besbre: Abbaye de Sept-Fons, 1937). No English translation is available.}

World War I saw priests sharing in the brotherhood of the trenches, which changed the public opinion. The religious who were veterans made sure that their rights were respected, and no criminal procedure could be pursued within this new context. During World War II the Pétain government signed a decree lifting the "crime of association" for the religious, because at that time they were still subject to prosecution. The Fourth Republic tolerated the existence of monasteries, which remained without any legal existence. The Georges Pompidou government (1969–1974) reintroduced the possibility of providing positive responses to communities requesting legal recognition pursuant to the Law of 1901 on associations.

La Trappe had already initiated the procedure for this request, so I only had to pursue it. The act of recognition of our community was signed by Prime Minister Raymond Barre in February 1978. The Real Estate Association of La Perche gave us back the property title. That is why I said earlier that the community was still "a recent owner" when we started the renovation of our infirmary!

La Trappe remains, with this recognition, under a legal tutelage that requires a prior prefectural approval for a number of acts, like receiving an inheritance, a disposition of real estate, or a sale of land. The system was set up in principle to protect the monks and to ensure that we are not taken advantage of. This fact shows that we are still not on an equal footing with other citizens. Nevertheless, the constraints are light, and we benefit from advantages like inheritance without paying estate taxes. It is rare that individuals bequeath us goods, but it happens. The predominance of European law over French law would also contribute to a certain evolution in the practices, since the right of association is recognized as a European right; from now on an association has the right to declare itself a religious association without the French state having to give its approval.

Confronted with such dangers and challenges, I often felt that I had come through without a scratch. I think that I was just lucky. Perhaps there is a certain way to face challenges. Each temperament may be like a sound box that can either multiply or absorb emotional shocks. I do not doubt that others in the monastery, as well as in the outside world, might be objectively shaken up, especially in unfortunate family or social situations like a painful death. I can easily understand their despair. I assume it in the counseling I can give them if they confide in me. But sometimes there may be nothing better to do than to listen or to pray to the Lord, begging him to come to their assistance and to console them. Sometimes I believe that I have been spared by God from personal problems so that I can better tend to others.

You don't choose your own challenges. Community life can create some that we do not seek, from brothers who are annoying to us or from services that we must render that we don't like, up to more important matters like health problems or moments of deep discouragement or even depression. These situations can be a better opportunity for us to step back from ourselves than penances chosen in advance. The real difficulty is peacefully to accept the challenge that we didn't seek but that nevertheless affects us. Sometimes there are intolerable or inconceivable circumstances that require us to go beyond what we are able to do. We have to go through a real desert.

Personally, I do not dramatize anything, and so I am just waiting for my real challenges, as I said. Not that nothing ever happened to me, but I took life as it came, totally trusting and abandoning myself to the Lord. I could easily adapt. Day after day one must live, go forward, and persevere. I tried not to feel overwhelmed and to make sure that problems did not prevent me from living and sleeping.[21] I didn't want to present the image of an anxious abbot, disappointed or dissatisfied. A community that watches its superior always complaining, whining, and dreading everything cannot rejoice. It is not energizing. I cannot give the example of discouragement. You need to try to live just enough

21. See "L'Hymne de la nuit," in Charles Péguy, *Le porche du mystère de la deuxième vertu*, in *Oeuvres poétiques complètes*, vol. 1 (Paris: Gallimard, 2014), 629–773 at 756.

in the present with wisdom, this present moment where you meet God and where he doesn't abandon us.

Apprehension can be disastrous and is useless. Thinking about the perpetually anxious, who lack confidence in life and in the Lord (and precisely there may lie their trials!), Saint Bernard wrote subtly, "For besides suffering from troubles which beset them day and night, they are tormented still more by troubles which have not yet fallen on them, and to such an extent that the day's trouble is not sufficient to the day, but they are overwhelmed by troubles which they will probably never experience. Can anyone think of a more unbearable hell?"[22]

I was also helped by others, who meant a lot in my life, and I never felt alone. They encouraged me and sometimes guided me. But if my temperament or other people helped me out, faith was there more often and won over the rest. "Oh God, come to my assistance," is the call that traditionally opens the prayers of the liturgy of the hours. If I had had the desire to become abbot and had maneuvered to get there, I would have had only myself to blame, but I didn't seek anything. I could turn to Christ and tell him, "You wanted this to happen; take up your responsibilities! If I am in a mess, it is your fault. I will do my best, but you sort things out." To sit down on the side of the road makes no sense when you know who is waiting for us at the end of this road, when you hear the call and understand the love of the one who calls us.

How can you reconcile this relatively easy way to live and overcome the challenges with the life of a monk, who by definition is linked to the cross? Tradition asks if this life could be anything other than the cross. I answer this: The cross is not a constant sense of pain. The cross is the experience of death that you have to live through to reach the true life, a death that supposes a certain renunciation. But this renunciation is not necessarily tied

22. {Bernard of Clairvaux, "Sermon 1," in *Sermons on Conversion: On Conversion, a Sermon to Clerics* and *Lenten Sermons on the Psalm "He Who Dwells,"* trans. Marie-Bernard Saïd, CF 25 (Kalamazoo, MI: Cistercian Publications, 1981), 1.3, p. 122.}

to a constant sense of pain.[23] It means rather forgetting yourself, not thinking about yourself. That does not mean that you have to misunderstand yourself. I would say paradoxically that the better you know yourself the more you're able to ignore yourself and therefore be useful to others. The life of the Trappists is not that different from what we imagine the life of everybody else is. It seems strange, misunderstood, and it is so in many aspects, but you can find the essence of the human condition in it.

Some people, especially nuns, say that what they missed because of their celibacy was not so much the love of a man or a woman as the absence of fatherhood or motherhood. On this point, luck was also on my side, since I was always in charge of the formation of young monks. This role, of course, does not replace fatherhood. But I think that it helped me to accept this renunciation.

Before I took on any particular responsibilities in the community, it was sometimes hard on me not to have any news of a sick brother whom I esteemed. At that time, there were a lot of events in the monastery that I was not aware of. Sometimes I was indifferent, but some other times it was hard. In hindsight, I realize that monks who do not assume important functions may suffer. I understand them better, although I don't see how to integrate them into the community in a manner more in line with their expectations. The ensuing human and psychological problems sometimes become a painful reality for those who feel pushed aside or underestimated. They don't have a mission that corresponds to what they feel they could achieve. This is almost inescapable in community life, because all of them could do something other than what they do day in and day out. When

---

23. "Not only does the love of God sweeten what is bitter, but it transforms the Cross in joy, because God is a God of joy . . . the merit of the Cross is not in its weight, but in the manner in which we carry it" {Saint Francis de Sales, *Consoling Thoughts on Trials of an Interior Life*, compiled by Père Huguet (Charlotte, NC: TAN Books, 2013), chap. 25, pp. 129–32 at 130.}

you choose the monastic life, you don't know what is waiting for you. Often nothing comes, except that Someone.

The notion of failure can also be very subjective. You may believe that you have failed and that you have been humiliated, while others do not see it that way and may even believe that you were successful. On the other hand, others can imagine that you are failing and think that everything is going badly at a time when you think that you are victorious. Never to be satisfied with yourself can sometimes turn out to be a trap, because self-hatred can in fact be pride. Sometimes you can judge yourself as worse than what you actually are, and at other times as better than reality. I was over the years the recipient of confidences of men who had a profound influence on the monastic world and whose names were well respected. They sometimes felt that they had constantly failed at everything and were good for nothing.

It remains necessary for the monk as for any person to learn how to live with his feelings and to put them in their rightful place. A sign of maturity is to be able to accept that you won't systematically succeed in everything you attempt. To the same extent you shouldn't feel overly exalted by a success. The distance that you put between yourself and your actions enables you to handle defeat as well as success and conditions you not to feel defeat as intensely. An old Egyptian desert monk asked in the fourth or fifth century, "Is contempt for you the same as honor? Is loss the same as gain, destitution the same as abundance? If you do not have that indifference, you have nothing." This is what Kipling in the modern age translates as, "If you can meet with Triumph and Disaster / And treat those two impostors just the same; . . . / Or watch the things you gave your life to, broken, / And stoop and build 'em up with worn-out tools; / . . . you'll be a Man, my son!"[24] We often balance between failure and success. Our pendulum needs to adjust slowly to maintain our equilibrium and stabilize us.

24. {Rudyard Kipling, "If: A Father's Advice to His Son." For the complete text of the poem see https://en.wikipedia.org/wiki/If%E2%80%94.}

What kind of failure can a monk face? We are not necessarily skillful in all our actions. We cannot always master the job we are asked to do, and some other less visible problems arise, like resistance to obedience. The monk does not always succeed in obeying at his first attempt. It is not easy. Life brings its share of annoyance, and I can sometimes give in to anger and miss a meeting with a brother. Some days, laziness, love of good food, and other temptations can lead me to actions that I will regret inwardly. More deeply, doubt can insinuate itself into our hearts, like certain disgust for spiritual things.

There were times when I was wrong, times when I was not proud of myself and when I even lost face, if only because of clumsiness or distraction during a celebration. The abbot is not immune to these things. There are many opportunities in life to lose face, and one should not dramatize this experience.

To the same extent, a monk is not constantly in a state of spiritual euphoria, and in fact he only finds himself there occasionally. There are periods of monotony. I had them. More than once I had to shake myself up and force myself to follow the Rule. I confess that if I were not living in a community where the bell rings at 4 a.m., I would not get up that early. Throughout the day I am involved in many duties for which I am not too enthusiastic. Monks do not live in a spiritual vision and in the knowledge of celestial realities that would free them from efforts common to all. They sometimes walk on the earth in pain. The journeys vary substantially, and some of us remain in a drought for long times. A thought has always helped me out when the weight of the observances, even the liturgical prayer, weighed heavily on my shoulders: How much would I be suffering if I were locked up in a concentration camp, for example, and were deprived of the religious offices of our monastery, and of the company of my brothers! I would be longing for that life that nevertheless today weighs on my shoulders! I tell myself then, "You have all of this now, enjoy it!"

It is a matter of spiritual formation. The young brothers who enter the monastery have a lot to learn. The master of novices and other monks provide them with a certain education that enables them to "enter into the mystery of Christ and of the Church as well as the Cistercian heritage," as our *Constitutions* state (Const 53). The main objective is to form them in the practice of the monastic life itself and to help them affirm their own personalities. This process happens on three levels: the one, more external, of observance, and those more profound and personal levels of integration into the fraternal life and spiritual experience. At the end of the day formation becomes filiation, creating a well-seated personality and discovering its own life wisdom.

I lived this experience with Father Francis during my novitiate, but the chain is not broken. It goes on from generation to generation. Everyone is born into the monastic life by fitting into a community and by becoming the disciple of a master, a disciple of the elders, the son of a father. The communities are generated one from another. They are mother houses and daughter houses, as provided for by our canonical language.

An abbot's prayer is filled with his responsibility, of course. I like to borrow the words of one of our most appealing masters of the twelfth century, the British abbot of Rievaulx, Aelred, spiritual son of Saint Bernard, whom we call the Doctor of Mercy. We know his *Pastoral Prayer*.[25] In it he begins by acknowledging his weaknesses and follows with a mild reproach to the One who has nevertheless called him to this responsibility of abbot, notwithstanding his weaknesses. He begs the Lord not so much because of his merits but because of his duties. Before interceding for those in his charge, he prays for himself, requesting more especially the wisdom and grace to serve his brothers well:

> All my thinking, all my speaking, all my resting and all my
> working, all my actions and all my thoughts, all my suc-
> cesses and all my failures, all my dying and all my living,
> all my health and sicknesses—all that I am, all that gives

25. {For more on Aelred, see Jean Truax, *Aelred the Peacemaker: The Public Life of a Cistercian Abbot*, CS 251 (Collegeville, MN: Cistercian Publications, 2017).}

me life, all that I think, all that I decide—let all this be be-
stowed upon them in all its entirety and entirely used up
for their benefit, for the benefit of those for whom you yourself did not consider it unworthy to be utterly spent.

O Lord, teach me, your servant, teach me, I beseech you,
through your Holy Spirit, how I can spend myself for them
and how I can give myself entirely to them. Through your
indescribable grace, O Lord, grant me patience in supporting their weaknesses, compassion in my love for them, and
discernment in helping them. Let me learn, let your Spirit
teach me, to console the sorrowing, to strengthen the faint-
hearted, to set the fallen upright, to be weak with the weak,
to be indignant with the scandalized, to become all things
to all people in order to win them all. Grant me a true and
upright way of speaking and an eloquence of mouth to build
them up in faith, hope, and love, in chastity and humility,
in patience and obedience, in fervor of spirit and devotion
of heart.[26]

Aelred also asks to be a teacher by example: "You are well
aware, sweet Lord, of how much I love them, how I have given
them all that I could from the depths of my being, how my heart
is soft toward them . . . . So answer my prayers, Lord my God,
answer my prayers."[27] That I might learn in the school of the Spirit,
said Aelred! Only the Spirit, only love can teach us the right attitude towards the other, within this responsibility as an abbot.
This is the motto that I wanted to take at the time of my election
to this duty, but I formulated it from a similar expression of Saint
Bernard that he found in the liturgy: *Unctione Magistra*, under the
guidance of the inner Spirit, following him, listening to him. The
point is to be conquered and convinced by love, a love that is God.

26. {Aelred of Rievaulx, *For Your Own People: Aelred of Rievaulx's Pastoral
Prayer*, critical edition, introduction, and annotations by Marsha L. Dutton,
trans. Mark DelCogliano, CF 73 (Kalamazoo, MI: Cistercian Publications,
2008), §7, 48–53.}

27. {Aelred, *For Your Own People*, §8, 52–53.}

CHAPTER TEN

THE ONE WHO LEAVES

Montmartre Cemetery in Paris is an amazing city within the city, where the structures belong to the dead and the windows open up to a heaven that is not of this earth. I was led to a small granite chapel, like what they built in the nineteenth century. It was one of the more modest tombs in this part of the cemetery. The key turned in the rusted wrought-iron lock and I entered; there was a plaque on the wall with an inscription for one of the deceased buried there. He had been a priest in a Trappist monastery. It could be surprising that a monk was buried in Montmartre. But the plaque also mentioned that he was married religiously. I didn't know this former monk personally—let's call him Father Louis—but I had heard about him, and being in the neighborhood, I wanted to say a prayer at his tomb.

If the departure of a man to the desert can often surprise, his return to the world, especially if it takes the form of a failure, surprises almost as much. And there are a lot of questions. A community where you took the vows of stability, meaning a promise to stay there until the end of your life, becomes a family for the monk. So what happened that he broke with that family? Does that breakup also mean one with God through the renunciation of the perpetual vows? Is it a sign of loss of faith? How can you fundamentally change faithfulness? What happens to the one who leaves? The plaque on the wall did not say whether Father

Louis had left the monastery in dignity or in shame, in anger or at peace, nor if he finished his life with a feeling of fulfillment or of failure. Did he have any regrets? Did his wife feel like a "Rival of God," to borrow from the title of a book?[1] In this present case, he received an official laicization from Pope Paul VI and was allowed to marry legally. Why? Others do not receive such permission.

With each such departure, which luckily does not happen often, the abbot and the community question themselves. Was the brother too isolated? Did we support him sufficiently? If he wasn't made for our lifestyle, why did we welcome him, and how was he able to stay among us for that long? Is he the only one responsible for his leaving? To witness a brother's leaving is never easy and may be painfully felt, especially by the father abbot who received him at his perpetual vows and placed all his trust in him.

Sometimes the problems become so serious that the departure is felt as a relief. This does not mean that the departure is not felt with pain deep in one's heart. Other times it seems surprising because, looking from the outside, it could not have been foreseen. The brother might have started his monastic life in a way that seemed good and normal. He may even have exercised a profound spiritual influence on other brothers. That was the case for the one buried in the Montmartre cemetery.

"I owe him my vocation," said one brother. He quickly added that he didn't understand why his elder had left and gotten married.

"He was an excellent teacher," another confirmed. "His classes encouraged me to study. He taught us theology starting from the Bible and deepened it following the Church's pathway."

"We were all astounded when we heard of his departure," a third brother added. "He was the last one that we would have imagined leaving."

Questions were asked, and answers were expected.

---

1. {Odette Desfonds, *Rivales de Dieu* (Paris: Éditions Albin Michel, 1993).}

Those who leave sometimes do give an explanation for their behavior. I knew Bernard Besret very well when we were in Rome during our early monastic life. I met him again later in certain sessions before he took a different path. He didn't leave silently, like others who later wrote books, as he did. Bernard Besret had his fifteen minutes of fame when, after being named prior of a small community of monks in Brittany at the age of twenty-nine, he led a large lay spiritual movement called the Communion of Boquen,[2] named after his monastery. He went way beyond what the authorities of the Order could allow by taking personal and partisan positions after May 1968. These positions quickly earned him a position among the loose cannons within the Church. He was demoted from his position in October 1969, and his movement, like the community that supported him, became bogged down and slowly disappeared. After leaving the monastery in 1972, he progressively distanced himself from the Catholic Church. He wanted to confront the world "in a different way than as a monk or as a man of the Church, even a protesting one."[3] Other departures have been less vocal than his and are rather experienced as a failure; the brother tiptoes away.

2. {The monastic community of Boquen housed the Communion of Boquen in the sixties under its prior, Bernard Besret. It was a center of ecumenical encounters among people of all faiths and among religious and lay people. The community was dissolved under Canon Law in 1973, because Besret went against many dogmas of the Church. Besret left the Church and became a Freemason. With the approval of the local bishop, Boquen welcomed first the Sisters of Bethlehem from 1976 to 2011 and then in 2011 the Chemin Neuf Community. The spirituality of this young Community is rooted both in the Ignatian tradition and in the experience of Charismatic Renewal.}

3. He has given an account of his evolution in several books, *Libération de l'homme* (Paris: DDB, 1969); *De Commencement en commencement: Itinéraire d'une deviance. Entretiens avec M.-Th. Maltèse et E. Milcent* (Paris: Seuil, 1976); and *Confiteor* (Paris: Albin Michel, 1991). The quotation is taken from the last book, 196. Besret is now Project Manager for the City of Science in Villette near Paris.

In this chapter, I would like to propose some answers to these questions in accordance with my convictions. I will not talk about those who during their probationary period before the perpetual vows very legitimately realize that they are not made for our lifestyle and change direction. Their departure may also be painful but does not constitute a particular problem. In general, their experience at La Trappe is perceived as a positive step in the development of their personalities. But why then do some others abandon the road they chose so totally and so generously? Each case is different, of course, but fundamentally you can divide them into three categories: either the monk and his superiors realize that there was an error in discernment from the start, or the monk progressively moved away from the road he chose, either because he changed or he was taken over by something else, or because at one point he thought that the conditions of his commitment were no longer those he had anticipated, and he refused to continue.

One of the dangers threatening the monk living in a community is that he progressively becomes isolated. Nothing is of interest to him anymore, and he crawls away to his own corner. Sometimes the duties that were given to him force him to be away from the community or prevent him from following the evolution of the community. There may also be a temptation. The support of the brothers is real. The love of our brothers carries us. But like every love, it has to be nourished and stimulated. You can hide from them or take refuge within a small circle of friends, which will restrict you more than it will let you grow. Solitude can then turn out to be wearisome and difficult, and you start to look outside, especially if you have maintained outside relations and the affective balance is not sufficiently grounded. If you don't pay attention, the inner drive weakens, a spiritual disgust takes hold, and you move away from community life. The boat progressively takes on water, and, if it is not bailed out, it quickly ends up sinking. A brother who is able to talk about his problems with his father abbot or another monk whom he trusts and who becomes his mentor or spiritual father will receive help and may be able to overcome his discouragement, but if he is alone he is in danger.

Father Louis came from a large family with numerous industrialists, veterans, judges, and politicians, a family that was proud to count priests and nuns in their ranks. Pope Pius X blessed his parents' wedding. He spent his youth in castles and luxurious second residences, taking part in parties where socialites related the exploits of their ancestors. Being an only son, he took violin lessons and later dance lessons from a private tutor. His education was very strict, and he was never given any reward, such as candy. His second cousin, who became a Jesuit, remembered, "His mother would tell us at 4 p.m., 'Go run, children!' We didn't really want to run, but each day at the same time she sent us out. Louis's education was very harsh. No mistake was ever tolerated. At that time in his life nothing indicated that he would become a Trappist."

Louis went to the Saint Stanislas School in Paris. He then decided, after having wondered about a priestly vocation, to join the prestigious military academy of Saint Cyr. He came out with the rank of lieutenant but again felt attracted by the idea of giving himself as a gift to God and more precisely to the Cistercian life.

His father threatened him: "If you become a monk, I'll disinherit you!" The twenty-three-year-old couldn't have cared less. He defied his family's advice and entered a monastery shortly before the war. He craved poverty, prayer, and selflessness. His formation was interrupted by mobilization and his captivity in Germany, but, suffering from asthma, he was freed after a few months and resumed his monastic life. Quickly he was given responsibility in the monastery. He was very close to the abbot and was one of his close advisors. When the abbot resigned and was replaced by another abbot, Louis went through a tough time, because he didn't get along with him. Faced with these new problems, after a few years he started to doubt. Had he committed permanently to this life because he was more fascinated by the influence of one man than by a real vocation?

Father Louis was sent to another monastery to perform some tasks and then as a chaplain to a monastery of nuns. He wondered if perhaps he was made for a life as a hermit, but he talked to a hermit who changed his mind about this route: "Don't have any illusions; solitary life is much harder than community life.

All the temptations are waiting for you there, sometimes as hallucinations. You need to resist with prayer and work." Slowly, he was distancing himself from the community. He experienced what older monks call *acedia*, a disgust for everything. God didn't talk to him and was of no interest to him anymore. If a monk goes through this trial successfully, he has a deeper knowledge of his real self, but sometimes with age he may renounce the effort and resign internally. That is what happened to Father Louis.

It is never easy to acknowledge a failure, even less when it appears as a weakness, lack of faith, carelessness, or a fault. You try to justify yourself, and you think you have good reasons for sharing the responsibility. That would be so much more reassuring! One reason for such a failure could be that after Vatican II our usages changed to such an extent that one could say that the contract was breached. I mentioned earlier what I thought of that statement. Nevertheless, when Father Louis wrote to his mother shortly before leaving the monastery, he referred to this view, mentioning that the evolution in the Order seemed to send him into a deeper solitude, a separation from the other monks. But he neglected to mention that he had never forgotten Yvonne, a woman whom he had met twenty years earlier.

During the famously harsh winter of 1954 a parish pastor drew the attention of the father abbot to the dire situation of a family with two children, seven and four years old, who lived close to the monastery. Father Louis as the cellarer of the monastery was in charge of helping the family to improve their situation. He talked to the father in his office and encouraged him to look for work and to pay his debt. "You must accomplish this through work, sacrifice, and affection for your children. You'll get there! God is there with you."

"Father, the situation is much more complicated. I spent two years in a hospital, and for this and other reasons that I cannot divulge to you I am not able to find employment. Moreover, when I got to know Yvonne, I was married to another woman, with whom I had three children. I haven't known their address for years."

"Would you resume living with her if you could find her address?"

"That is no longer a possibility. We talked about divorce. In 1946, I came with my new companion to the monastery to talk to the abbot, who was a friend of my father."

"Yes, I remember having met you in the guest house," Father Louis confirmed. "You went through some really hard times. But you have children; your duty towards them remains a priority. I know that a father and a mother cannot be replaced easily; you and your new companion must continue your parental duties. Nevertheless, as a priest I have to ask you to sleep in separate rooms."

The material problems were not improving; year after year the couple was suffering to the point of splitting up. To be honest, Father Louis had tried to find the address of the man's first wife. At that time, an irregular matrimonial situation was still frowned upon. Did he think that it was his duty to put an end to this, or did he act with ulterior motives? Even if over the years his correspondence with Yvonne became irregular, he never ceased to keep a discreet contact with her. When he felt isolated in his community, when boredom and spiritual disgust caught him, he went and found Yvonne, who was now alone. They decided to get married. Some of his former brothers thought that he wanted to repair the damage he thought he had done to the woman by separating her from her first companion. Who can tell? Wasn't it looking for a good excuse, and a somewhat strange one at that, for a marriage that may have had other motivations?

For a brief period of time, Pope Paul VI granted indults to priests leaving the priesthood, allowing them to marry religiously. Father Louis took advantage of this practice. Events leading to the turmoil of May 1968[4] created a situation that was difficult to manage. Quite a few priests and religious realized that

---

4. {May 1968: a period of societal changes in France that started with student unrest and occupation of universities. There was dissatisfaction on all levels with the de Gaulle government, and workers' unions organized massive strikes that paralyzed the country. After successful negotiations, the workers stopped their strikes, and the protests quickly ended. When elections were held in June, the party of General de Gaulle came out as a clear winner. Nevertheless, the societal changes reverberated for decades in France.}

their vocation was due to specific circumstances more than to a
really free and carefully considered choice. As young adults, they
had been formed in an environment such as a junior seminary
that encouraged them to follow a particular track. The errors in
religious vocations may have been numerous at a time when
social pressure and an active Christian life led some to choose to
become priests without asking themselves too many questions.

I do not think that this history automatically justifies abandoning the priestly or religious life. Somewhere I read an interview
with a priest who acknowledged, "In fact, as for my vocation, it
was my mother who had it. She put me in the junior seminary;
I took the classes and the road that opened in front of me." But
he added, "Well, now I am acknowledging my mistake. I am
successful in meeting God there as much as I would have been
somewhere else. I would not have chosen this path by myself,
but God is there as much as on any other route. I convert a mistake into a success in which I find my vocation after all." This
choice implies a strong and healthy psychology that enables a
person to accept oneself by taking responsibility for the unfortunate circumstances and the past errors about which one can
do nothing. In this case, it is my conviction that God gives the
necessary strength to follow that journey, which then becomes
a real vocation.

But not all of these priests had that level of maturity. A certain
tension within the institution of the Church developed, one that
Pope Paul VI tried after much thought to resolve with mercy. It
might be surprising that the Holy See would accept a situation
in which priests and religious left their primary vocation like this
while refusing the remarriage of divorced people. It considers
marriage as a covenant that cannot be broken, even when it is
clear that the spouses can no longer reconcile. Marriage is a sacrament before God. As Jesus says in the gospel, "What therefore
God has joined together, let not man separate" (Matt 19:16). The
Church has no authority over a sacrament; it cannot dissolve a
valid marriage. The only thing it can do is to declare a marriage
null if it is based on a fundamental error or tainted by certain

technical or formal defects. The marriage is then annulled, even if the spouses have lived together for a time.

In the same way, the Church cannot undo the ordination of a priest who was validly ordained. He is a priest forever. The Church can accept that a priest no longer acts as a priest, that he renounces the right to exercise the ministry of the priesthood, but the Church cannot erase the inner priesthood of that individual. This situation would correspond to the case of a couple who are separated without the bonds of matrimony being severed. But celibacy is not inherent in the sacrament of ordination; rather, it is a commitment requested by the Church from the priest, one that he has accepted. Therefore the Church can eventually release him from that promise.

The evolution of Father Louis might have surprised quite a few of his brother monks, because his outer demeanor and the duties he performed may have been deceiving. Other departures seem less dependent on the will of those who leave the monastery. Their health can break down so badly that it requires long absences from the monastery, and these absences become permanent. Sometimes it is their character that plays tricks. Normally, it is tested during the formation years, and only those who can integrate harmoniously into community life are admitted to the perpetual vows. But reality tells us that things are never that simple. The evolution of a personality is never a straight line, and certain faults only become important over a period of years. Sometimes with a novice, certain character traits may raise concerns or doubts, but how is he going to grow? Should we trust him? Should we be patient? Sometimes we overestimate the capacity of a young novice to integrate well into our community and to benefit fully from the formation that we try to impart to him. Certain character traits do not come out from the start. People are also unpredictable. It can happen that a brother is no longer capable of living peacefully with the others, and we are forced to provide separate paths, not without pain, but with a sense of realism.

Sometimes psychological dispositions degenerate and lead to anxiety and depression, which are difficult to control. Should the monk stay anyway? Is there a point at which remaining healthy trumps the vow of stability? Each case has to be considered separately. One can go as wrong in deciding to stay as in determining to leave. Leaving may very well not bring any help, just as staying may lead to a dead end.

Problems can also arise in the development of affectivity. The choice of celibacy implies a certain human maturity, which is not given in the cradle but which has to be acquired over time. It is absolutely possible to make a free and deliberate choice of celibacy for the kingdom of God based on other motives than a neurotic repression or a castration complex, for example. The real renunciation that such a choice implies has to be, on the contrary, the result of a healthy maturity. But who can pretend that he has evolved so perfectly that he does not experience any problems with his own sexuality? Formation is always ongoing. The probationary years are there to help a person have a positive rapport with other people and with himself. Normally, only those who can sufficiently master their problems in that area are allowed to say their perpetual vows. But there also, as I said about the character, certain evolutions are slow and surprising. One does not immediately see clearly. It sometimes happens that after the solemn vows certain needs or certain impossibilities manifest themselves, leading the monk to reconsider the chosen life orientation and to request a dispensation of the commitments.

Sometimes I have been asked if I knew of any cases of suicide in the monastery. They were rare, but I couldn't say that there were none. All in all, a person's psychology is not fundamentally different in a monastery than in the outside world. When it happens, it is always a drama for the people around him, be it a community or a family. It is also difficult to help someone in the community when you sense that he might be tempted to end his own life. Sometimes thoughts of faith may influence him, but they are generally insufficient, because the problem is not at that level. It is at the "psychological conditioning" level, which "so radically contradicts the innate inclination to life, thus lessening or removing its personal responsibility," as Pope John Paul II wrote in *Evangelium Vitae*.[5]

It may be really difficult to determine why and how people get themselves into situations like these. Objectively, these are failures or errors, eventually faults. The point is not to always feel guilty, even if you need to constantly examine yourself to verify your own reactions, to correct them if they are bad, and to prevent at all costs the worsening of the problems or the renewal of painful experiences. Sometimes you have only limited control over certain developments. A person's heart is a mystery. The brother in difficulty may end up not understanding himself anymore. What did he want? And why doesn't he want it anymore? Does he see it clearly? He may lose his usual reference points. Everything within himself may seem futile or hollow. He no longer understands what he thinks, who he is, or what he is capable of.

Above all, we must resist the temptation to judge another person. That would risk locking him up in his misfortunes or difficulties. Should we then consider what took place to be of little importance? No! To respond with mercy does not mean that you put on a blindfold. It is not trivializing the events, admitting the inadmissible, excusing everything, or just accepting it as a *fait accompli*. It is like Saint Augustine's expression, which Saint Benedict borrowed for his Rule: "hate the sin, but love the brother."[6] Condemnation reduces the other to his action, closes him off, and puts him down, while a look of mercy may free him by opening up a future for him. What is important is what the other person lives in the deepest recesses of his own heart: "only God probes the heart and the kidneys," as Scripture says.

5. {*Evangelium Vitae* 66. w2.vatican.va/content/john-paul-ii/en/encyclicals/documents/hf_jp-ii_enc_25031995_evangelium-vitae.html.}

6. {Augustine, *Letters*, trans. Wilfrid Parsons, The Fathers of the Church: A New Translation 32 (Washington, DC: The Catholic University of America Press, 1951–1956), no. 211, 5:38–51; RB 27.}

Saint Paul recommended to the Corinthians, "therefore do not pronounce judgment before the time, before the Lord comes, who will bring to light the things now hidden in darkness and will disclose the purposes of the heart" (1 Cor 4:5). What do we really know of what the brother went through and what he is going through now? In any case we need to continue to love him and to carry him in our intercession, even if he makes us suffer.

Those who leave must take responsibility for their decision and keep on living. For that they need to receive the Lord's mercy and ours. God is capable of renewing someone and giving him a new chance. It is sometimes hard for us to do so as long as the other person does not show us any sign of a radical change. You can understand this difficulty, although it is regrettable. At least, we ought not to label him permanently with the constant reminder of a past that he may have disowned or would like to disown.

God has the power to change our hearts. He always calls on the person, wherever he is, even deep in his own sin. He keeps opening up a future for him, even if the conditions are different from before. Nothing is ever hopeless for God. There may be irrevocability in our lives, but never anything beyond repair, except maybe sometimes the consequences of our actions. You cannot bring back someone from the dead, but there is nothing at the level of our willpower that cannot be repaired. The mark that Cain received on his forehead after the murder of his brother was not an indelible sign of his sin, like a sign of infamy, which would condemn him forever. It was the sign of divine protection, "lest anyone should kill him at sight" (Gen 4:15), thereby taking away any future for him. Victor Hugo was wrong: God does not confine anyone to his evil past.[7]

---

7. In his poem "La Conscience" (*La Legende des Siecles*, series 1, I.2), Hugo shows the eye of God pursuing Cain to the grave, where, pushed to the end, Cain buries himself so as not to see God's eye anymore, but, "The eye was in the grave and watched Cain."

One day when Father Louis was overwhelmed with regrets, he received a response from the bishop of the diocese of his former monastery, whom he had consulted: "Often God has a different view than men. He does not judge on the basis of appearances. You left. Is it possible to return to the monastery? No? So then what is the point of worrying yourself sick and listening to people here and there? You still have a long road ahead of you, with responsibilities to assume. Even what we don't understand perfectly may have an explanation. We need to trust in God, who knows where he leads us, whatever happens. Look ahead!"

The future of those who leave the life we have chosen is nevertheless not all rosy. Often the family does not understand and is surprised, and it doesn't always welcome back the one who left and is now returning to the family. For a mother, it may be suffering that is difficult to bear. Father Louis reflected for two years before committing to a marriage with someone he had known since the end of the war and who had resisted his advances. "I am not sure that I can give you the minimum desirable comfort," he wrote her. "Anything I will start at my age with my past is in many respects crazy. But what a joy to leave all these guarantees behind to live our love! My only support from now on is you and only you." Is this really happiness?

"And your family?" asked a friend.

"They don't want to see me anymore, and they ignore Yvonne. The silence that is imposed on me cannot last forever. My desire is to remain discreet, but I can't live a lie. Should I accept the fact that they refuse to help me, even though I left them a good part of my assets? Look at the small quarters we live in. It is so small."

"You need to earn a minimum to live decently."

Independent of the family, the Church and the Order also deal with this problem. If those who leave or are asked to leave do not have any claim against their monastery for past services rendered, the abbot shows them equity and evangelical mercy, in accordance with the language of our Constitutions. He is to "act with pastoral solicitude towards those leaving the monastery. Above all he is to act with disinterested concern for the welfare of the one who is leaving as well as for that of the whole community" (Const 59.1). It is not always easy to manage both without prejudicing anyone. With regard to retirement there is a system of assistance set up by different responsible entities within the Church at the national level so that all may receive a reasonable minimum amount.

Father Louis opened his eyes to some new realities. He visited one of his cousins, who lived in a large house. He had given it to him thirty years earlier and was looking to get a little parcel of land to build a small house. Following his cousin's refusal, he learned how to convert into concrete deprivation what had been until then, by his donations as a monk, just an abstract renunciation. To earn a living, he became a museum guard. When there were exhibitions at the Grand Palais in Paris he sometimes hid behind the beak of his cap so that he would not be recognized by people he used to know. When the head curator learned that a priest was walking the museum hallways among the paintings of Millet and Bacon, he hired him as his personal secretary in his office in the Louvre. He continued these duties until his retirement.

What happened later so that one of his children buried himself in all the theology books he could find when he came home from school? Maybe an aura of faith surrounded the former monk and reached those he met? Why did he never give up receiving the sacraments? This belonged to his new life, burdened with the trials of the modern world, up to the most paradoxical and painful one of not being invited to his own mother's funeral. He went anyway.

When illness struck, he tried as much as he could to visit the village church, responding to the bell announcing the Mass. It was his only reason to leave his room during his last year. "His intense gaze at the bread and wine I had just consecrated was impressive," said the pastor. "The last day he was able to come was the feast of the body and blood of Christ: 'Take this, for this is my Body . . . this is my Blood, the blood of the new and eternal covenant, which will be poured out for you and for many.' He had only acknowledged to me that he was a priest a year earlier." He died on the feast day of the Sacred Heart. On that Friday, by coincidence, a brother in his former community was ordained a priest, but . . . are there coincidences?

If at the crossroads I take the wrong road, God is still in front of me on that road, even if he was waiting for me on the other one, and even if that one would have been preferable for me.

In fact, it is within my freedom that grace, and thus God's call, plays an important role. I have alluded to it many times in this book, and I experienced it very strongly in my own vocation. It can give a certain reassurance to those who hesitate to commit because they cannot anticipate the long term and are afraid that one day they will regret today's steps if they turn out to be a mistake. It is said that young people have a problem with committing forever. Of course, the journey that opens up before them has uncertainties, but they can be sure that grace will be present whatever happens. The question for them is not, "Will the journey that I am starting today still be good for me tomorrow?" But it should be simply this one: "Is this journey good for me today?" Each day has enough trouble on its own! Don't worry about tomorrow; tomorrow will worry for itself!

"My vocation is in front of me . . . I find it each morning," said Jean Sulivan.[8] If you assume that discernment was not done properly during the novitiate and that objectively it would have been better if the candidate had not committed, if he commits anyway he can count on God's grace. In that sense, one can say that he had a vocation. That is one of the convictions I took from Father Joseph Fuchs, my morals professor at the Gregorian University in Rome. The Lord's will regarding my life is not written in the stars for me to guess at it haphazardly. It is decided in my heart between the two of us. Isn't that the meaning of the struggle of Jacob and the angel? (Gen 32:23-32). God knows where he leads me. He is the most powerful, but nevertheless he does not force me.

8. Jean Sulivan, *Le plus petit abime* (Paris: Gallimard, 1965), 122. {See the end of chap. 6, and chaps. 4 and 5.}

No vocation is worth less than any other. We are called to the joy of God. By committing to God, we are not alienating ourselves; we are sailing toward the high seas of happiness. The sea won't necessarily be peaceful. The ship will be shaken or even threatened by high winds, violent storms. The fishing may be fruitless. "Children, do you have some fish?" the risen Christ asked the apostles on the shores of the Sea of Galilee, after they had fished all night. They hadn't caught anything and were pretty sheepish. But a miracle took place, the meeting with the Lord who walked on the water and put them at ease, who himself had prepared some fried fish on the other shore. "Then their hearts did rejoice, and nobody was able to take that joy away" (John 21:1-14; 16:22; 6:16-21).

As Mgr. Rouet subtly mentions, joy is not to be confused with the exuberance of thanks and the action of grace. You give thanks for something that you have received, that is, for a gift in the past. Happiness is looking to the future. "It was born of the consent to hope. In that sense happiness is a passage, an exodus"—a hope that is not simply an image of the future based on an already known reality, but an expectation of "the One who comes in front of us, who approaches us from the what-is-to-come," and who always amazes us: "Forget previous events; do not dwell in the past. See, I am doing a new thing! Now it is bursting forth; don't you see it?" (Isa 43:18-19). What the bishop of Poitiers says of the priest, we can apply to the monk: "A monk is not simply happy *because* he succeeds in his function and his action. He is a monk *to be* happy,"[9] to find happiness in God.

9. Albert Rouet, "Moins de prêtres, plus de prêtres heureux, plus de prêtres," *Prêtres diocesains*, Jan 1995: 8–16; Summarized in *La Documentation catholique* (May 21, 1995).

CHAPTER ELEVEN

"SO, I AM STUDYING HEBREW!"

I had been abbot of La Trappe for two years in 1979 when a breeder and trainer of racehorses asked to be accepted into the community. He had Jewish origins. In the novitiate he soon wanted to learn Hebrew and meditate on the rabbinic commentaries on the psalms. I realized that this search for his origins and Jewish thought were important to him. I allowed him to contact people who were educated in the Talmudic schools to assist him in his studies. He did not know any Hebrew when he got here and had never paid any attention to the Jewish faith. This was an exceptional situation. We didn't push him with preconceived ideas, but in our community he went back to his roots.

How was he able to find his Jewish identity at fifty-four among Catholic monks? The monastic life reveals to us our inner selves; there may lie the explanation for this journey. To encounter Judaism in La Trappe is contrary to the image we have of what we can expect in a monastery. That could be because we are generally not aware of the surprises that the search for God and the soul baring can bring. Brother Jean-Pierre had no idea what to expect when he left his job as a business leader to knock on our door. He later confided that his journey back to the sources was linked to events that had marked him deeply and played an important role in his spiritual formation—the persecution of the Jews from 1938 to 1944. We had to take that into account.

He was arrested and held in custody three times and incarcerated in the Drancy camp[1] when he was seventeen years old. Before that, in 1940, he was first sent to Gurs, a camp of legionnaires in the Pyrenees, which had been set up for Spanish fighters and other foreigners. Three of his grandparents were Jews, along with his mother. He was born in Vienna in 1926 and had Czech origins.

Forty years after the end of the war, after he had entered La Trappe, he was visiting one of our monks in the ICU of the hospital in L'Aigle, a nearby town. The anesthesiologist on duty started a friendly conversation with him and said, "I often come to La Trappe, but they never let me visit. It is too bad." "Next time, call me," answered Brother Jean-Pierre. "I will show you around. But tell me your name."

"Marcel Galli."

"Marcel Galli!" he shouted out, dismayed. "Are you related to a Mr. Galli, who worked at the police department in Nice?"

The face of the anesthesiologist turned white. He stepped back and said:

"You were in Drancy!"

"Yes, but what is your family relation with this man?"

"He was my father."

"He arrested my mother."

"Was she deported to the camps?"

"He saved her life."

"How so?" he asked with relief in his voice.

During the large-scale round-ups at the end of August 1942, ten thousand Jews of the Free Zone[2] were to be turned over to

---

1. {The Drancy internment camp was used by the Germans in World War II to detain Jews and other people classified as "undesirables," who would later be transported to extermination camps. It was located in Drancy, a suburb of Paris, and was initially guarded by the French police. Between June 22, 1942, and July 31, 1944, 67,400 French, Polish, and German Jews were arrested and deported from Drancy, among them 6,000 children. The SS took over the camp in 1943; Alois Brunner became camp commander.}

2. See above, chap. 3, pp. 37–38, n. 2.

Hitler following an agreement with the Vichy government.[3] A three-day manhunt ensued. Brother Jean-Pierre's mother was abruptly released thanks to the intervention of the father of this anesthesiologist, whom he had just met in the hospital in L'Aigle.

"Your father was in charge of the Jewish question in the whole Free Zone."

"Yes. He died two years ago. What happened to you?"

I also asked Brother Jean-Pierre to tell us about these events, which had taken place fifty years earlier. It was an opportunity for us to remember this dramatic deportation and better to integrate it into our prayers. His adventure went beyond his personal case. It addressed the problem of the relations of the Catholic Church with Judaism as well as the responsibility of church fathers for the anti-Semitism throughout the centuries that led to the massacre of the Jews. He was almost a victim of that anti-Semitism, as many members of his family had been. Beyond this dark page of our Western history, both sides of us humans appeared, the one turned towards the darkness and the one lit up by a light. Often the same human being could have contradictory attitudes without being reduced to a simplistic explanation.

Jean-Pierre (his birth name) had had a very happy childhood. His mother, Lucia Gutmann, was born in Vienna. Like the large majority of assimilated Jews in the city, she had given up any religious practice, although she remained attached to Judaism. In her grandfather's generation it was traditional for the firstborn son to become a rabbi. The older brother of her grandfather, David Gutmann, was named Wilhelm. He was sent from his birthplace of Leipnik in Moravia to Hungary to complete his rabbinic studies. It didn't bring him what he was expecting, and so he changed direction. He turned to commerce and then to industry. He was immensely successful after in 1853 having with David founded the company Brothers Gutmann, with the symbol G.G. (Gebrüder Gutmann). Many businesses grew out of that enterprise. Wilhelm

3. See above, chap. 6, p. 122, n. 6.

became the president of the Jewish community of Vienna and David the president of the Israeli Alliance, while Lucia's grandfather was the head of the Jewish community of St. Petersburg. The brothers Gutmann were the founders of the Jewish Viennese Institute for Hebraic Theology in 1893. The name Gutmann was well known in Vienna.

Jean-Pierre's father, Kurt Ippen, was a Czech Protestant born of an old-school Catholic mother. She was the only one of his grandparents that Jean-Pierre ever knew. At that time in Austria, non-practicing Christians still wanted to give their children a Christian education. Jean-Pierre's sister, Ruth, two years his senior, remained Jewish and was sent to a Jewish school. He, on the other hand, was baptized and sent to a Protestant elementary school. Then in the sixth grade he went to a state high school, which in Austria was Catholic. He nevertheless followed the Protestant curriculum. After the Anschluss[4] of March 12, 1938, the students labeled as Aryan were separated from the Jews within their classrooms. Jean-Pierre spontaneously went with the Jewish children.

Soon after the racial laws of Nuremberg, which prohibited Jewish students from attending public schools, were enacted in Austria in May 1938, the principal came early in the morning to announce the new regulations. Then under the supervision of the teacher, the Aryan students stood up and kicked the Jewish children out of the classrooms. Jean-Pierre was among these and was actually very happy for these unexpected vacation days. He didn't understand why his mother seemed so affected.

In May 1939 the Ippen family finally got a visa for France and took refuge in Nice. When school started, the war had already

---

4. {The Anschluss was the forced union of Austria with the German Reich in March 1938, part of Hitler's plan to build a united "Gross Deutschland" of all the German-speaking countries. Very little opposition to the union occurred on either side of the border. The harassment of the Jews began immediately. This action ended in "Kristallnacht," on November 9, 1938, in which all synagogues were destroyed and six thousand Jews were arrested.}

been declared, and Jean-Pierre was not accepted in the state school, so his parents registered him in a Catholic school. Since it offered no Protestant curriculum, he received Catholic teaching. They used the manual written by Abbé Auguste Boulenger, which we today consider rigidly dogmatic.[5] Strangely enough, this teaching with its absolute and unnuanced certainties sparked Jean-Pierre's enthusiasm, because he had only known a moralizing reading of the Bible. He was looking for a logical basis for the articles of the Christian faith. He quickly figured out that Boulenger was following the three parts of Thomas of Aquinas's *Summa Theologica*. Over time he acquired the fifty booklets of the *Summa* in a youth publication. Every night he spent two hours avidly reading them. He hid this activity from his father, who, although not opposed to religion, still thought that moderation in all things was better. He only made peace with the fact that his son became a Catholic when his daughter converted and also asked for a Catholic baptism. He had always wanted her to become a Christian.

Because the validity of a Protestant baptism was not a sure thing at the time, Jean-Pierre was conditionally baptized in the Catholic church. The celebration took place in the convent of the Poor Clares in Cimiez on September 12, 1941. The date was significant—it was the feast day of the Holy Name of Mary, established in memory of the liberation of Vienna from a Turkish siege. Legend tells us that this victory was due to the praying of the rosary, which was promoted by the Dominicans. In love with the intellectual game of the scholastic, Jean-Pierre dreamed of becoming a Dominican, and for that purpose he kept learning Latin, which was necessary for his religious education. His more pragmatic father, though, was hoping that he would turn to science.

Comforted in his Christian faith and wrapped in his good conscience, Jean-Pierre was appreciated at school and felt perfectly safe

5. *Manuel d'Apologétique: Introduction à la doctrine catholique*, ed. Emmanuel Vitte (Paris: Lyon, 1928).

in the Free Zone. So did his family. His father had served under French command in the Czech army, adding to the certainty that he would be protected, whatever might happen. He had nothing to fear. Therefore he submitted to the census of the Jews without any afterthought, relying on the appeasing statements of the government employee.

On August 26, 1942, the BBC evening news broadcast on regular intervals coded messages that roundups would take place that same night in the Jewish refugee community of the Free Zone. His parents rushed to the phones to warn their acquaintances, then went to bed lamenting the lot of those they could not reach. They did not feel at risk at all. Jean-Pierre did not suspect anything. He was lost in his theological dreams. But at 2 a.m. he was abruptly yanked from his bed by a police officer. Half asleep, he didn't understand anything. He said to him, "Hello, sir."

Before he was able to ask the police officer what he wanted, he saw his pajama-clad father roughed up by another policeman, who ordered him to get dressed in a hurry. He understood that the situation was serious. A few minutes later, the whole family was led away to the Banquet Hall of Nice, just across the street from the hotel where they lived, Rossini Street. The room was still empty. Slowly other families came in, totally stunned. Around 6 a.m. they did a triage, sending those over sixty and those under sixteen home. Buses came to pick up the others. Jean-Pierre's parents and sister were taken to an unknown destination. He was alone and went back to the apartment. He waited until 8 o'clock in the morning and went to see the director of the school, a priest. Distressed by what he heard, the priest boosted Jean-Pierre's morale and wrote a long letter to the bishop of Nice, Mgr. Reymond, a classmate of Pope Pius XII. He gave the letter to Jean-Pierre, telling him to hurry up; the bishop could intervene effectively, he assured him.

When he got to the diocese, he was disappointed to learn that the bishop was not in Nice at that time. Another prelate came to the door. He had an impressive stature that reassured Jean-Pierre. The prelate only read the first couple of lines before turning towards him, saying: "My poor friend, let me explain to you what is going on."

He told a parable: "It is as if we were both on the boardwalk. You made one misstep, and you fell in the water. You were drowning, but I couldn't swim. Why would you want me to try to save you? Goodbye!"

Jean-Pierre was very surprised at this parallel and disappointed by the dismissive answer. He couldn't expect anything more from the religious authorities. So he went to the civil authorities. But his parents, who were refugees, didn't have any close connections with the city leaders. They were only on good terms with one shopkeeper, Mr. Vieil, president of the grocers' union. Jean-Pierre ran to the grocery. Mr. Vieil was scandalized by these arrests and declared in front of his customers that it was a shame not only to do these things but also to let them happen. He told Jean-Pierre not to worry about it, because he was going to take care of this situation. He called the police chief, who was one of his friends. He found him at his domicile. "I have something important to ask you." "Well, come over right away, I am available."

The grocer left his customers and went with the boy to the chief, who lived a couple of hundred yards from there. He welcomed them cordially and asked them to sit down in the living room. After a few courteous exchanges, he asked them what brought them to him. The police chief turned to Jean-Pierre and asked him, "Is your mother a foreigner?"

"Yes."

"Has she been in France for ten years?"

"No."

"Is she older than sixty years?"

"No."

"Is she Jewish?"

"Yes."

"And you tell me that she was arrested and detained?"

"Yes."

He turned to the grocer with a large smile and stated, "What more do you want? Everything is in order!"

The grocer got up, took Jean-Pierre by the arm, and went out, slamming the door behind him. Jean-Pierre then switched to direct action. He found out that the victims of the raids had been gathered at the military base at Riquier. When he left the hotel to take their identity papers to his father and sister, he noticed a policeman running after him when he crossed the Place Mozart. He recognized the policeman who had dragged him out of bed. He wanted to know if his parents had returned home. He then advised Jean-Pierre to hurry up to present the papers: "Don't waste a single minute. In three days it will be too late."

What did he know? At least his demeanor revealed that, notwithstanding the brutality of the arrests, his heart was not in his job, and he wished for the freedom of his victims. For Jean-Pierre's mother, who was Jewish, they needed a special intervention. His father and sister would have been able to go home on their own. Mgr. Bruno, his parish pastor, to whom Jean-Pierre went, was sincerely sorry not to be able to help. He didn't want to send Jean-Pierre away empty handed, so he wrote a letter to the Prefect of the Alpes Maritimes, without any illusions about the possible outcome. It was only a goodwill gesture. When Jean-Pierre got to Police Headquarters, the same scenario played out as at the diocese: "The prefect is actually not in Nice." Jean-Pierre was received by the prefect's secretary, a nice young woman who was moved by his distress. After thinking for long time, she told him, "Personally, I cannot do anything for you, but, if you don't tell anyone that I gave you this information, I can tell you that it is Mr. Galli who takes care of these files; you need to contact him and only him. He has complete discretion in this matter."

When the grocer heard that the man in charge was Galli, he jumped for joy: "No worries anymore! He was my best friend in school. There won't be any problem with him."

But at police headquarters they did not see it that way. It was impossible to get near the man. "Mr. Galli does not see anyone," they were told. "You're not allowed to let me in, but nothing prevents you from giving him my business card," the grocer suggested.

Three minutes later: "Sir, please come in."

"You too are coming for a Jewish matter?" Galli shouted, when he heard the purpose of his friend's visit. "If I had ever suspected that, I would never have let you in. I thought that you were coming for a grocery problem. Get out of my office."

"I would never have thought that you were capable of these horrible acts. I won't leave your office until you sign the freedom papers that I am asking of you."

The grocer told Galli all he had on his mind, and after five minutes of yelling, Galli allowed the file to be brought to him.

"You can tell your friends that I will go to the Riquier barracks at 4 p.m.," he said. "I will sign."

As promised, at 4 p.m., Lucia was freed. She was crying as she left her friends behind the walls. Two days later the train transport left without her for Auschwitz via Drancy.

Jean-Pierre learned later that this man who was in charge of the Jewish question in the Free Zone changed sides after the large raids of August 1942. He joined the Resistance and actively participated in the Liberation of Paris. This fact led to his not being prosecuted after the war.

The story that Jean-Pierre told gives a reliable account of what the atmosphere was like at that time and how complex the situation was. It allows all of us to wonder about the failures of civil and religious authorities[6] and about the reactions of people asked to help. We also wonder about the psychology of the executioners, the gendarmes, and the man in charge, Mr. Galli, who were neither innocent nor totally guilty. One should also remember that faced with despair, one should not be satisfied with saying that you cannot do anything. Even if you cannot objectively eliminate despair, a gesture or a smile can sometimes bring about unexpected miracles. The letter addressed by a priest to a prefect might have appeared useless. Nevertheless, it was sufficient that the letter fell into the right hands for a secretary

---

6. Later, in 1943, Mgr. Reymond asked the religious communities of his diocese to support to the extent possible an organization set up to save Jewish children. He worked skillfully to prevent numerous deportations.

with a good heart to provide information that caused the wheels to start turning and for a series of events to lead to the saving of a life. If this act of goodwill had not taken place in the beginning, nothing could have happened. First of all, it was necessary for Jean-Pierre to take the first step. We will never know on this earth what good or bad our actions and words have produced or all the good that our inaction may have kept from taking place. The secretary of the prefect never knew that she had saved a life.

"We cannot visualize the distant consequences of our actions," said Brother Jean-Pierre. We will only see later how we succeeded or failed. This may be one aspect of what we call the Last Judgment. He liked to remind us of a passage in Exodus, in which when the Egyptians were pursuing the Hebrews, Moses cried out to the Lord, who answered him, "Make them move forward!" (Exod 14:15).

God created a passage through the Red Sea. Nevertheless, the Midrashim, the rabbinic commentators, observed that God could raise the waters on the left or on the right side like a wall, but the children of Israel would not have been saved if they hadn't stepped forward. Everything comes from God, but if humans do not move forward, God cannot do anything. Christ multiplied food to feed the crowds in the desert, but it was necessary for a boy to bring five loaves and two fishes.

Later, during the summer of 1943, the Germans took over the occupation of the French Riviera from the Italians. The evening before the official transfer, the Germans sent a Gestapo patrol to take over the hotel where the Ippen family lived. The Italian Cease Fire Commission occupied the second floor. Upon the request of the SS Commander, the owner of the hotel gave them the names of all the Jews who were living there. When the Germans barged into the Ippens' apartment, they once again took Lucia away. Her husband wanted to follow her so as not to be separated, but the SS held him back. Nevertheless, he joined her in the lobby of the hotel as soon as he could. An SS officer made him climb the stairs backwards with a machine gun pointed at his stomach.

After the SS left with their prisoners, he took his daughter Ruth to safety with their friend the grocer. He then took a cab with his son to look for the location where the prisoners had been gathered. He had crisscrossed the streets of Nice in vain for an hour when, as he came up Boulevard de Cimiez, he noticed that the SS were guarding the entrance to the gardens of the Riviera Palace. No doubt that had to be the gathering place. He went to the guard, who recognized him. He turned to his colleague:

"He drove us crazy during the arrests. If he really wants to, let's book him, and we'll see what we do with him later."

Nobody was paying attention to Jean-Pierre. He followed his father, happy to see his mother again and thinking that she would be happy to see them coming. On the contrary, she was quite shaken. Almost immediately the group was taken to the train station. It was late at night when they reached Marseille. A truck took them to a dark building, the Saint-Pierre prison. They went through dark hallways dominated by iron watchtowers patrolled by soldiers with machine guns. They separated the men from the women before pushing them into already overcrowded rooms. Two weeks later they were taken to Drancy. The men were handcuffed two by two. Jean-Pierre and his father were able to remain together.

This trip lasted more than thirty hours, and Jean-Pierre did not handle it well. It was the end of September, and it was already cold around Paris. He only wore flannel pants, a short-sleeved shirt, and sandals, with a handkerchief as his only luggage. He developed a fever of 102 degrees that took him to the infirmary. This spared him from the questioning that each prisoner had to go through if they thought that they had some reason to be released. He would have been scared to death. The prisoners were punched or hit with an iron rod to force them to confess the falsehood of their allegations. Sometimes those who had legitimate arguments didn't dare to bring them up and preferred to be deported rather than to be exposed to the blows from Ernst Brückler, nicknamed "the Beast," the worst brute of the four SS men in the camp. The parents of Jean-Pierre waited outside the interrogation rooms. Through the door they heard the yelling and the moaning. At last, the prisoner being questioned came out, an ear half ripped off, and they went in. The room was stained with blood. The infamous SS Hauptsturmführer Alois Brunner[7] had become the head of the camp in June 1943, but he had established his headquarters in Nice to better track the Jews. Seated behind the desk was his substitute, Josef Weiszl, a SS officer from Vienna.

"You are Jewish?" he asked Lucia.

"Yes, I am Jewish."

He turned to her husband aggressively: "And you, you pretend not to be Jewish?" In order to leave Vienna in 1939, Kurt had applied for a German passport. For this he had to produce an *Aryennachweiss*, a proof that he belonged to the Aryan race. He had obtained false documents from the City of Sadova, where his father was from. Without saying a word, he put his German passport on the desk. Weiszl, surprised, shouted out: "We signed that document! No problem, you are free!"

"And what becomes of my wife?"

"She won't be deported, but she will be sent to a work camp."

"I do not want to leave her alone," her husband protested. "I can work in her place. That will be more efficient."

Weiszl, who had belonged to the Eichmann[8]-Brunner team installed in Vienna after the Anschluss, wanted to scare Kurt and told him in a contemptuous tone,

7. {Alois Brunner (1912–?2001) was an Austrian SS Officer known for his brutality and charged by Adolf Eichmann to execute plans to deport Jews throughout Europe to extermination camps. He was commander of the Drancy camp in France (see above, n. 1). After World War II he escaped prosecution and fled to Syria, where he remained until his death. The date of his death remains uncertain.}

8. {Adolph Eichmann (1906–1962) was a German Nazi commander and planner of the implementation of the "Final Solution," that is, the Holocaust. He reported on the progress of the plans for Jewish executions directly to Reinhard Heydrich at Hitler's headquarters. After the war he escaped to Argentina, where Juan Perón protected former Nazis. Subsequently captured by the Israeli intelligence service, Eichmann was tried and found guilty of war crimes and hanged in 1962.}

"You took advantage of Jewish money!"

"Without a doubt," he answered him.

"Why didn't you get a divorce after the Anschluss?"

"Because I had no reason to do so."

Weiszl thought about this for a moment and concluded: "That is true. If you had divorced, you would be a jerk. I will see if I can do something. Come back to the office tomorrow."

The next morning, he offered Kurt work as a translator. "That way you will be able to stay with your wife and your son, who will be assigned to the Category C1[9] to work in the camp. In fact, she will be exempted from work, and he will be charged with helping to clean the courtyard."

The three of them remained in the barbed-wire zone between the office of the Germans and the main camp. One day a visit by Brunner to inspect the camp was announced. All the interned prisoners were frightened, because they knew through the stories of those who had been there longer about the past and the perversity of this SS officer. Brunner was one of the three leading Nazis responsible for the implementation of Hitler's primary objective, the extermination of the Jews. His action was not limited to France. He had operated in Vienna, Berlin, and Salonica, and he would continue later in Bratislava after the liberation of Paris. He can be held directly responsible for the death of 130,000 people, with a particular relentlessness toward children. He enjoyed unlimited power, even over the military, and he liked to take advantage of his authority. Some SS members feared him, sometimes looked down on him, and hated him.[10]

Jean-Pierre and his parents were anxiously awaiting the decision that Brunner would make with regard to the "Ippen case,"

9. {After taking control of the Drancy camp, Brunner introduced a classification of all prisoners according to their competence and experience. C1 referred to prisoners with a certain level of education who were employed by the camp.}

10. See Didier Epelbaum, *Alois Brunner, The Inflexible Hate*, preface by Serge Klarsfeld (Paris: Callmann-Levy, 1990).

hoping that they would not have to meet him. The young man fetched soup every day from the camp kitchen. That day, when he was about to go out and before he could put his hand on the knob, the door opened and he was face to face with Brunner. The SS officer was furious that a prisoner was present in this forbidden area. In a contemptuous tone, he ordered the boy to explain himself. Jean-Pierre, terrified, stared at the famous whip that Brunner always held in his hands. He could already feel the whip hitting his head. Gathering all his courage, he answered as calmly as he could: "I am bringing a meal to my father."

Strangely, Brunner's demeanor changed, and his voice softened. He abandoned his harsh German accent, and without going into the vulgar dialect of his henchmen, he said with a reassuringly light Viennese accent: "I will get information on his case later." But the SS chief left for Nice without changing their situation.

Having learned a little later that the Gestapo had confiscated all his assets in Nice, Kurt was allowed to return to Nice to try to recover them. He wanted to assert that the process was illegal since he was not Jewish. He had to appear before Brunner at the Gestapo headquarters at the Hotel Excelsior. He recognized his own Citroën parked in front of the door. A guard told him that it was owned by the Hauptsturmführer Brunner himself. Once Kurt was led into the office, Brunner asked him if he had already found some of his assets.

"Yes," he said, "my car."

"Who took the liberty of taking your car?" Brunner shouted.

"I don't know who, but what I do know is that I have the honor of noticing that it has been placed in your personal service."

"Do you need it?" Brunner asked, stunned.

"Here is the registration," Kurt said, opening his wallet. "In Drancy, I do not need a car."

Brunner took the registration card and made this counter proposal:

"You work as an interpreter in Drancy and you're not incarcerated. I will tell our services at Avenue Foch to compensate you."

He offered a substantial amount that Kurt refused out of hand: "You know that I work in place of my wife, who is incarcerated. I do not want to be paid for that."

Brunner agreed, surprised.

"You are right. This work does not fit you. Find a job and housing. By Christmas I will stop in Drancy on the way to Vienna. If you have found something I will authorize the release of your wife and son. So hurry up."

Thanks to another incarcerated prisoner categorized as C1, who worked in the administration, Jean-Pierre's father got a fake contract to manage a racehorse stable in Maisons Laffitte. He rented a house near there. When Brunner came by Drancy he kept his word and signed the freedom documents, while warning Kurt, "The only thing I ask of you is to do nothing against us. You do understand that we end up knowing everything, and if you betray me by joining the Resistance, you will be the last Viennese that I pull out of the shit."

You can imagine the surprise of the Ippens when in April 1944 a van belonging to the General Union of Israelites of France, assigned to the incarcerated prisoners of Drancy, stopped in front of the gardens of Maisons Laffitte. André Kann, the liaison with the German authorities, announced to them that Brunner would come to visit the following morning at eight o'clock. Apparently he wanted to ride a horse. Surprise gave way to consternation and panic. What could be the real reason for this visit? Was the SS not rather coming to check on Kurt's "equestrian activities," which existed only on paper? If he became aware of the trick, he would have them all deported without a doubt. Kurt informed the trainer whose staff he was supposed to supervise. He rented a riding horse in a hurry and put it in the barn without deluding himself. If Brunner showed up in uniform, he probably had other ideas in mind.

Jean-Pierre left us the story of this unusual visit: "The next morning from seven-thirty on, I was at the window of the first-floor living room. My mother was on the second floor. My father sat next to me, reading the newspaper to hide his nervousness.

At eight o'clock sharp a black limousine that we knew all too well drove up our street. It was the car with a driver that the police prefect put at the disposal of the SS of Drancy. My father went straight to the gate to the garden. I stayed at the window. Brunner stepped out of the car. He was in a riding outfit. What a relief! Nothing prevented my father from leading him to the horse barn, since it seemed that he really wanted to ride a horse. Everything should be fine then.

"My father talked to Brunner at the gate. Instead of going to the barn, they both entered the gate and walked towards the house. I went to open the door, anxious about why there was a change of plans. My father reassured me immediately—Brunner had not had his breakfast yet.

"He was led into the dining room, and before he sat down, he told my father: 'You know, I don't think that I ever had the pleasure of being introduced to your wife.'

"Dismayed, my father didn't know right away how to react. Why was he making that inappropriate comment? After a brief hesitation he sent me up to fetch her. Brunner noticed how anxious we were. I went up the stairs without knowing how to announce this to my mother. Feeling awkward, I told her simply: 'Mom, you need to come to the living room.'

"I went down without waiting for an answer, or maybe instinctively so that I didn't have to give her any explanation. I waited standing next to the door to the living room. My father was standing next to the window, while Brunner was eating breakfast by himself. After a few minutes that seemed like an eternity, the door opened and my mother entered, pale but calm. Brunner got up right away and walked towards her and at a respectable distance greeted her with perfect courtesy. My mother didn't show any emotion. To avoid an embarrassing silence, Brunner asked her if she was enjoying her stay in Maisons Laffite. She answered honestly that she didn't really feel at ease. In our immediate neighborhood, there were a number of villas that were occupied by German officers. The Gestapo had an office close to us. Brunner in turn said, 'At least I hope that you are not missing Nice?'

" 'Well yes, in fact I miss it a lot,' my mother acknowledged.

" 'Oh Madam, believe me, you have nothing to miss,' he said cynically. 'Since we have been there, it has ceased to be pleasant to live there.'

"After a brief silence, without the slightest gesture, my mother turned around and left the room. There was a deep silence in the living room, but the atmosphere was not tense. Slowly Brunner went back to his seat and, gazing into the distance, started a long monologue. With a certain emotion, he mentioned his childhood in Hungary and his youth in the cultural climate of the Austro-Hungarian Empire of the time. You could not doubt the sincerity of his words. He painted a very accurate portrait of Austria after the defeat of 1918. We knew the background all too well: the virulent anti-Semitism of the Catholic clergy inculcated into the children from kindergarten on, and the popular piety, especially among farmers, who were filled with it. In the popular imagination, the devil's powers acted concretely through the Jews. Brunner mentioned the sufferings created by unemployment, the misery that had progressively taken hold of his family, and the deprivations that he had had to suffer before he joined the Hitler Youth. He made sure to mention that in his house, his school, his entourage nobody doubted that the Jews were responsible for all these calamities.

"Then, without any animosity and without showing the least hostility, he turned to my father and made clear that this popular opinion seemed to be confirmed by the fact that an important part of the economy of the country was in the hands of the Jewish upper middle class of Vienna. He added: 'You have to understand; it was with these convictions that I joined the Hitler Youth. How could I not have agreed enthusiastically with what they taught us?'

"As soon as he finished his argument, he got up and my father went with him to the stable. Along the way, he expanded on the theories of the Nazi regime to my father. The Jews were at the root of all the world's evil. It was necessary to get rid of them once and for all with the most efficient methods and without showing any weakness. In conclusion, Brunner observed that history offered other examples where moral and political authorities who were unanimously respected had used deceit and even cruelty to physically eliminate individuals or groups of people judged harmful to society. Upon his return from the stable my father felt very distressed by what he had just heard and experienced, but we were relieved that the danger had passed, and we wanted to forget this visit."

Jean-Pierre was never able to share within his family the impressions left by this encounter. Close relatives on both his mother's and his father's side had perished in the Holocaust, and he dared not touch on this subject. Of the fifty-nine people he shared his cell with during the two weeks he spent in the prison of Saint-Pierre in Marseille, fifty-three had been deported shortly after their arrival in Drancy. He had very painful experiences as he witnessed the drama of the deportations and the many convoys leaving for certain death. All this murderous hate marked him deeply and had for him one face: Alois Brunner.

He had a hard time believing what he had seen and heard in Maisons-Laffitte. It is obvious that we cannot minimize Brunner's culpability or grant him any mitigating circumstances whatsoever. How could we, when we think of his relentless and unceasing cruelty? There was nevertheless one nagging idea that grew in Jean-Pierre's mind and would never leave him: Brunner had also been marked by anti-Semitic propaganda in which—unfortunately—Catholics participated, even including some church fathers. Of course, these were their own views and not those of the Church itself. Jean-Pierre's story strengthened my conviction, shared by others, that the highest authorities in the Church should dissociate themselves from these acts and publicly express regret for the use that was made of the Catholic faith for perverse ends, which ultimately influenced the development of the Nazis responsible for the start of the Holocaust. Vatican Council II went in that direction, "deploring solemnly the hate, the persecution, and all anti-Semitic manifestations from whatever their authors or whenever time were aimed at Jews."[11] It is a source of satisfaction for us Cistercians to note that Saint Bernard in the Middle Ages rose up against the massacres of the Jews in the Rhineland in the middle of the twelfth century:[12] "Defend the grave of your Christ," he cried out to the crowds that he came to soothe, "but do not touch the sons of Israel and only talk to them with kindness, because they are the flesh and the bones of the Messiah. If you hurt them, you will hurt the Lord in the apple of his eyes."[13]

After being released from Drancy in 1944, Jean-Pierre had to pursue his schooling. He very much wanted to study philosophy in a Catholic institution. The closest one was the Saint-Erembert School in Saint-Germain-en-Laye. There were only a dozen students in elementary math, and he was the only one in

11. {See *Nostra Aetate, www.vatican.va/archive/hist_councils/ii_vatican_council /documents/vatii_decl_19651028_nostra-aetate_en.html*. In March 1998—three years after the original publication of this book—the Holy See's Commission for Religious Relations with the Jews published the document *We Remember: A Reflection on the Shoah,* Pope John Paul II, letter dated March 12, 1998. In this document the Vatican condemned Nazi genocide and called for repentance from Catholics who had failed to intercede to stop it (www.vatican .va/roman_curia/pontifical_councils/chrstuni/documents/rc_pc_chrstuni _doc_16031998_shoah_en.html.)}

12. "There are not words strong enough to condemn the monk Raoul, who would inflame the passions of the crowds: 'Oh monstrous science! O infernal wisdom, contrary to those of the prophets and enemy of the one of the apostles, subversion of religion and of mercy! Oh sordid heresy! Sacrilegious prostitution that, engrossed by a spirit of lies, conceives in pain and gives birth to injustice!'" (Letter 365). {Bernard of Clairvaux, *The Letters of St. Bernard of Clairvaux,* trans. Bruno Scott James (London: Burns and Oates, 1953), no. 393, 465–66.}

13. See, from the second half of the twelfth century, the chronicler of Bonn, Rabbi Ephraim, son of Jacob, in his *Book of Remembrance.* In the sixteenth century Joseph ha-Cohen of Avignon found inspiration in his Valley of the Sorrows. Joseph ben Meir, in a chronicle of these massacres in the Rhineland, mentions that the "wise and righteous man" had a strong voice and a disinterested mercy that prevented the projected evil from taking place.

the philosophy and literature section. His philosophy teacher, who also taught him religion, was an unconditional Thomist priest. They understood each other perfectly, and Jean-Pierre was completely happy. At the outset of the quarter a three-day retreat with other students in a monastery was announced. He was delighted, but his father rejected that idea categorically, sensing a danger in his attraction towards religious questions.

Jean-Pierre's strongest desire was to complete studies in theology at the Catholic University of Louvain in Belgium. That was totally out of the question, so he then chose political sciences. Since his father didn't want to deny him everything, he reluctantly accepted this plan, aware that his son was not making that choice for a practical reason. On the contrary, Jean-Pierre lived perfectly at ease in a dream, as if their situation had not changed because of the war. In February 1948 a thunderbolt brought him back to earth. The Communist coup in Czechoslovakia destroyed any hope that the family could recover the assets left behind there. The game was clearly over. They had to face the harsh daily reality, and Kurt applied for a license to train racehorses.

Jean-Pierre helped his father in these activities. Soon it became a full-time activity, because his father had to undergo critical surgery. Nevertheless, Jean-Pierre fully expected that one day circumstances would allow him to pursue his project of a religious life. He soon realized, though, that these plans would take much longer than anticipated, and he slowly gave up any thought of achieving something serious intellectually. Therefore he wondered if it would be wiser to envision a contemplative life in a monastery. He asked the question in 1958 of his old college chaplain, with whom he had kept in close contact.

"I cannot give you any advice," the priest answered. "You cannot envision that life style without trying it out first."

That was also impossible, because his parents needed him. His sister had married an Egyptian Jew and lived in Cairo. In 1964 his mother fell into a respiratory coma. She had suffered from emphysema for the last couple of years and was getting worse. She was rushed to the hospital. The verdict was terrible:

survival of a maximum of forty-eight hours without intervention or the possibility of resuscitation with a breathing machine,
with the risk of constant need for assistance in the future. The
family chose resuscitation. She regained consciousness, and for
the following three months she read, wrote, and listened to the
news. One day the respiratory specialist told them, "I need the
breathing machine for patients who can recover but can't turn
the corner without assistance. Take her home, it cannot last more
than three days for her."

Dismayed by this proposition, Kurt bought a breathing machine and had it installed at home. The doctor assured him that
it was crazy and that he had no idea what an adventure he was
embarking on. The use of such a piece of equipment was delicate,
and the doctor predicted a catastrophe.

"We are not risking a worse catastrophe than the one you are
proposing," Kurt countered. Lucia's condition required a constant presence day and night; for four years Jean-Pierre did not
leave the house while his father took care of the horses.

"That was my real novitiate," he said.

Lucia had only a couple minutes of respiratory independence
a day. She ate with the family in the dining room and spent time
reading and doing small tasks. These four years of constant intimacy with his mother marked Jean-Pierre profoundly. Both of
them lived in the far-away past, looking at photo albums as she
told him the circumstances in which the pictures were taken. She
would talk about family members on her mother's side whom
he had never known, especially those in Russia who for three
generations had played a major role in religious and cultural
affairs as well as in social action. Lucia accepted her condition
with good humor, because she knew that her husband and her
son were happy with her presence. Jean-Pierre felt that she would
have liked to know more about the Jewish faith. She regretted not
having been better initiated. Never did she make any allusion to
the fact that her son was a Christian, except once when she was
getting near to her death. She said, thinking more about him than
about herself, "I am concerned about you! I am afraid that you

worry about my salvation. I would have liked to reassure you by sharing your faith, but that is impossible for me."

She died on June 2, 1968, Pentecost Sunday. That year the Jewish Pentecost fell on the same day, as often happens.[14] Jean-Pierre was impressed by that fact and had an inscription made on her tombstone: her dates of birth, January 1, 1901, and death as well as the corresponding date in the Jewish calendar, "6 Sivan 5728." His father, who had been diagnosed with cancer in 1967, died three years later. The six years of Jean-Pierre's parents' illnesses caused the material condition of the family to deteriorate badly. Jean-Pierre was facing a difficult future. When the law gave him four months to accept or reject his inheritance, he remembered the advice of his old chaplain and took advantage of this delay to try a stay in a monastery. He quickly realized that he would always be blamed for trying to evade his problems by entering a monastery, not thinking that he was capable of earning a living alone. He had to wait again and take up the estate of his father.

A short time later he himself was hospitalized and diagnosed with Hodgkin's Disease, which at that time was still an incurable cancer. Humanly speaking everything seemed lost. Nevertheless, it was from his hospital bed that he concluded the greatest transactions of his life. The first groom of the stable came every day to report to him on his work with the horses and to consult about their management and their training. Thanks to the dedication of Alain Leclerc, his financial situation was straightened out. For Jean-Pierre it was as though the biblical story of Gideon had come true, in which God made Gideon reduce the number of his soldiers before a battle so that he would not imagine that he was responsible for the victory, so that he would understand that it came from the hand of God (Judg 7:1-8).

After many years of chemotherapy, Jean-Pierre was able to announce to our novice master, with whom he kept in contact,

14. {Since *Shavuot* occurs fifty days after the first day of Passover, Hellenistic Jews gave it the name *Pentecost*. According to Jewish tradition, Pentecost commemorates God's giving the Ten Commandments on Mount Sinai fifty days after the Exodus.}

that a new medication had defied the statistics and that the doctors had started to believe in his complete recovery. "You have to be able to make a decision," the father master wrote back to him, "and not miss the rendezvous that the Lord is giving us." He needed three more years to free himself completely of all the contracts that bound him. Such was his journey when I welcomed him to the novitiate in 1979.

He right away communicated to me his strong desire to engage in studies of theology and philosophy. He felt that he needed that education to lead a serious contemplative life, and he wondered if he wasn't too old for us to let him do that because the investment did not seem to make sense. I reassured him that it was not a question of return on the investment. The needs of a monk are a sufficient reason for him to receive instruction. My response gave rise to a misunderstanding. He understood that I promised him to let him do the studies he wanted, while I was only thinking about the studies to be completed in the monastery.

"After my temporary promises," he told me, "I would like to push my studies further for a better experience of God."

"The question must be asked on a more fundamental level," I answered him. "What relationship is there between an intellectual asceticism and a spiritual or mystical experience? Grace is always free and is never proportionate to our efforts. It is not by completing a course of studies that you compel the experience of God; you don't acquire that experience, you receive it!"

"Shouldn't we expand our knowledge as far as we can?" he argued.

"The only requirement is to do what is reasonably possible to avoid laziness," I added. "God does not reward laziness. The point is to find out what is necessary so as to define what is reasonable. It will depend on each person's capacity, temperament, or culture. In any event, the goal we pursue, the knowledge or the experience of God, will never be in proportion to the number of hours devoted to study. Everything will be a free gift from God and not the result of our efforts. An obsession about our formation might be the sign that we rely too much on secondary means that will always be inadequate. Study alone will not bring us the Lord. Almost everyone knows this or presumes it, but sometimes in our fervor we forget this.

"In religious life, you have to be ready to sacrifice everything, even what appears to be the best—even your asceticism or your studies if God asks for it through the circumstances. It will not be to the detriment of our spiritual life. The one who is not ready to sacrifice everything cannot get to know the Lord."

"It is very possible," I went on, "that after your formation we may have to entrust you with material responsibilities that would have you perform manual work. It may even involve more time than normal, like the duties of guest master or bookkeeper. Those people do not always have time to study as much as they would like. I cannot guarantee you the studies that you'd like. Do you think that the abbot is in a different situation? What matters is the inner availability."

He had been hoping to acquire this intellectual formation for so long that it didn't seem right to relegate these plans to the background now. He figured, moreover, that the prayers of a priest automatically had a higher value than those of lay persons. Therefore he was also disappointed to hear that I didn't envision the priesthood for him. Why did we seem to attach so little importance to it? His idea of the quest for God included an effort to acquire theological knowledge for a better contemplation of Christ's mystery and an engagement to follow in his footsteps in the priesthood. If La Trappe did not offer him either one of these ways to get to God, why would he enter it?

"You are taking away the objective reasons I had for becoming a Trappist," he told me. "Of course, I like your life style, but is this a sufficient motivation? I would have scruples about joining only to have a happy old age. If only I found some difficulty in it, it would be commendable! But not even that!"

"The difficulty of the monastic life," I assured him, "will come precisely from that inner availability I am talking about, from that self-offering to another, which is a more profound soul baring than an exterior life style or the asceticism required by the intellectual effort. Some from the very beginning experience our life style as too painful. On the contrary, others can immediately feel perfectly at ease, because they are escaping a bad situation or because they cannot adapt to their situation in the world. They soon experience problems integrating themselves into our community. Then there are the others with all kinds of nuances imaginable, of whom you are part. They need a time to adapt that can be shorter or longer. But you do not come here to mope or suffer. God wants people to be happy. The one who is not happy to be a monk is not in the right place here. In any event, merit does not come from the pain or the difficulty, but from the love that we put into each one of our actions."

He was going to discover—in fact—that by trusting the abbot one can reach whatever is essential to become oneself. It took him awhile to persuade himself. As the thought process of Paul Claudel[15] had not changed suddenly after the staggering moment of his conversion, close to a pillar in Notre-Dame in Paris, so also the thoughts of our brother only changed slowly over time.

During his novitiate, Jean-Pierre needed surgery on his hip. He wanted to take advantage of his recovery period to read the five volumes of the *Histoire de la Pensée* written by Jacques Chevalier. After the novice master, Father Emmanuel, refused him, he wanted to read the four volumes of the *Introduction to the Philosophy of St. Thomas Aquinas* by Father H. D. Gardeil.

"Even less," Father Emmanuel answered him, concerned for him first to finish his novitiate before authorizing him to start these studies.

As a last resort, and to ask as a joke for something totally incompatible with the novitiate, he requested: "So, can I learn Hebrew?"

---

15. {Paul Claudel (1868–1955) was a French diplomat with a successful career. After the war he became ambassador of France to Japan and to the United States. His writings conveyed his Catholic beliefs, having converted to Roman Catholicism at the age of eighteen on Christmas Day while listening to a choir singing Vespers at Paris's Notre Dame Cathedral.}

"Fine, learn Hebrew then," said the novice master to his great surprise.

Brother Jean-Pierre had never been interested in Hebrew. He was nevertheless quickly seduced by using a teaching method employing audio cassettes. His fascination grew when he realized that the sense of the Hebraic roots corresponded with what he sensed in the deepest part of his being. He became absorbed and dug into Gerhard Kittel's ten-volume *Dictionary of the Bible*[16] and the *Commentary on the New Testament from the Talmud and Midrash* by Hermann Strack and Paul Billerbeck.[17]

This time he discovered a totally different dimension to his reading of the Holy Gospel. He discovered that the Jewish exegesis was closer to Saint Bernard's and those of our other Cistercian Fathers than to a good number of current exegetes. His western formation was marked by a Greek spirit and an approach to the Gospel that wanted to be scientific. It was only in La Trappe that he realized how this approach was put against a background of reality and that this wasn't best suited to him.

His *lectio divina* was complemented by reading from rabbinic commentaries in Hebrew. He prayed the psalms in this language in the church while we were singing them in French. Truth be told, he could not sing, so he could use the Hebrew original for himself without any scruple. The psalter is one way to reach union with God.

Later Jean-Pierre was in charge of running the guesthouse for a time; there he would sometimes meet retreatants interested in learning the language of the Bible. He formed a group of fifteen people who met monthly around a teacher coming from Paris. I also authorized him to welcome international Hebrew sessions, which occupied our whole guesthouse for a week once a year. In

16. {Gerhard Kittel and Gerhard Friedrich, *Theological Dictionary of the New Testament*, 10 vols. (Grand Rapids, MI: William B. Eerdmans Publishing Co., 1977).}

17. {Hermann Leberecht Strack and Paul Billerbeck, *Kommentar zum Neuen Testament aus Talmud und Midrasch*, 2 vols. (Munich: Beck, 1922).}

1986 I entrusted him with the book section in our store. Among the four thousand titles offered to the public, a substantial number were dedicated to his specialty. He found joy in helping those interested in Hebraic studies at all levels to pursue their research with maximum pleasure and spiritual profit. He organized short sessions for that purpose. To present the rabbinic commentaries as they were understood in the living tradition of the Jewish community, he invited orthodox Jews who were deeply living this tradition. He also invited highly competent teachers who remained faithful disciples of their Jewish masters. One of them, Pierre Lenhardt, director of the Ratisbonne Institute,[18] a Christian center for Jewish studies, was a regular visitor to La Trappe.

"Why didn't you invite him to talk to the whole community?" I asked Brother Jean-Pierre when I saw this member of the Congregation of the Fathers of Sion leaving our abbey one day. Our brother was concerned that his passion would irritate others. He didn't like to talk about it, because he often wondered if his endeavor was really acceptable. It was probably not in the eyes of a Jew, because of his Christian faith, and from the Christian perspective, could his research into the rabbinic commentaries not bring up a certain suspicion? Would the discomfort of his endeavor not be a way for him to live his original unsettled Jewish condition, which means to be totally settled nowhere? Somewhere he also felt a certain discomfort in using a tradition that he had totally ignored during the persecution, so much so that he consulted a rabbi from the Consistory with authority on the subject. The rabbi did not discourage him from pursuing his studies, so Brother Jean-Pierre continued to do so without any scruple. Sometimes he wondered if the direction taken by his monastic commitment was the only response that he could now give to the echo of a voice that he perceived and that Fackenheim

18. {In the nineteenth century the brothers Theodore and Alphonse Ratisbonne founded schools in the Holy Land that were open to students of all faiths. For more information on the Ratisbonne Institute, see http://www.brothersofsion.org.il/Eng.asp.}

called "the prescriptive voice of Auschwitz." There are 613 commandments in Judaism, but a 614th was added after Auschwitz, forbidding any Jew to give a posthumous victory to Hitler by forgetting his Judaism.[19]

Brother Jean-Pierre realized that I was offering him all the means to get to know the Hebraic tradition. He thought about it and told himself, "By closing other avenues and by driving me to Hebrew, didn't Father Abbot lead me to my real identity? What I first experienced as a trial made me discover the real aspirations of my being. Finally, I would not have liked to become a priest and to get set in the narrow thoughts I had before entering the monastery." Before his perpetual vows, he asked for a meeting with me: "I had problems trusting someone I thought had deceived me," he confessed to me. "I think that for someone to commit to the monastic life and to promise obedience, it is good to have gone through the trial of Abraham."

From a human point of view, God had deceived the great patriarch by asking him to sacrifice his son, after he had promised him a large number of descendants (Gen 22; Heb 11:17–19). But Abraham's faith saved him. Brother Jean-Pierre added that it had been necessary for him to clear that difficult hurdle to understand in hindsight that he hadn't been deceived. By giving up what is not essential to our personal relationship with God, the trial sometimes appears indispensable to our own good, which is to become our self. He confided in me that it only became possible because his novice master had himself given up everything first.

19. {Emil Ludwig Fackenheim (1916–2003), a noted Jewish philosopher and Reform rabbi. *To Mend the World: Foundations of Post-Holocaust Jewish Thought* (Bloomington and Indianapolis: Indiana University Press, 1994), 10–14, 294–300.}

Chapter Twelve

New and Ancient Communities

I t would be a mistake to believe that the breath of Holy Spirit, which has moved men and women to establish or reform monasteries in past centuries, has now evaporated. New foundations are being set up today. I would say that there are two types of foundations, and I have been somewhat involved in the first steps of new foundations of each type. I was also a member of a committee, called then the "permanent committee," on which I represented the monks of France in the Conference of the French Superiors. We call them the "Major Superiors," because they are at a higher level of responsibility as the heads of provinces, and they enjoy special powers. That is how I came into contact with some realities of the life of the Church in our country. I participated six times in that capacity as a member without voting rights in the yearly Conference of Bishops in Lourdes.

In March 1982, right after he became archbishop of Paris, Cardinal Jean-Marie Lustiger[1] called me at La Trappe to ask me if I would be his representative to the new communities of men and women with monastic inspirations. His predecessor, Cardinal Marty, had favored their establishment around the church of

1. See above, chap. 1, p. 8, n. 3.

Saint-Gervais in Paris. They were created in response to Marty's call for prayer communities to settle in Paris and offer city dwellers a haven of peace and prayerful solitude. Monasteries, he said, were all located in the countryside in the provinces. Weren't there any city monks for the new era of bustling metropolises full of people in search of meaning in their lives, all too often left to themselves in a frightening spiritual emptiness—in a word, "monks for the year 2000"?

Father Pierre-Marie Delfieux, who had just come back from two years of solitude spent in the Sahara Desert, where sixty years earlier Father de Foucauld had lived, heard the invitation and in 1975 decided to establish such a community. His program was based upon the following principles: living in the city instead of the countryside; renting accommodations and working for a salary instead of owning real estate; living in consecrated celibacy in the middle of the city, the streets, the labor, and the liturgy; maintaining a spiritual cloister rather than a wall, with the monastery being the whole city; building silence in the middle of the noise and solitude in the urban zone; and being established as part of the local church, under the authority of the local bishop. In order to survive the rather demanding conditions of the city, the brothers and sisters would save one day a week, a few days each trimester, and one month a year for retreat. In that way they would blend into the rhythm of many city dwellers who feel the need to get away from it all from time to time. The Monastic Fraternities of Jerusalem, as they were named, already had about forty members.[2] The archbishop of Paris wanted a monk of an order with centuries-old traditions to assist the Fraternities in finding their way and drafting their statutes.

I did accept this assignment, because I thought that everyone would gain if a confident collaboration was established between

---

2. {The Monastic Fraternities of Jerusalem are now called the "Community of Jerusalem." They have about two hundred monks and nuns spread over their nine communities in Paris, Vézelay, Strasbourg, Mont-Saint-Michel, Florence, Cologne, Montreal, Warsaw, and Rome.}

the communities of the old ecclesiastical tradition and these groups showing a new vitality, an effervescence that for some might be a challenge. The new can be overly exciting, and it was especially this intoxicated excitement that was the question, just as when the crowd thought that the apostles were full of sweet wine on the day of Pentecost (Acts 2:13).

The excitement was there, yes. Sometimes lacking experience and looking to open new ways, the pioneers were heading off in many different directions at the same time, and it was not easy to determine which identity they were trying to take on. They were not leading a traditional monastic life, and they were entitled not to do so because they wanted thereby to respond to different needs of society and the Church. On the other hand, you can't invent community life; it follows rules that are well entrenched in human nature, and to ignore those could create difficulties that might confuse the issue.

My presence, which I wanted to be discreet and welcoming, was well accepted. I visited them from time to time, taking advantage of meetings that I had to attend in Paris, going once to the community of brothers and then to the small community of sisters, which seemed to need my services more, although they benefited from the assistance of the abbess of the Benedictine Abbey in Jouarre. I sometimes attended the general joint meeting of these communities in Sologne or once in Ganagobie, before the monks of Hautecombe moved back into that monastery. I reported my observations to Cardinal Lustiger and communicated his desires, remarks, and directives back to the brothers and sisters. When after five or six years one of his auxiliary bishops, Monsignor Rouet, was able to get involved more directly, I resigned my position without any regrets, grateful that I had gotten to know them well and had been able to forge close ties of friendship and brotherhood with them.

These new communities, like others that were created in the same spirit but that I was less familiar with, like the Fraternities of the Apostolic Monks of Aix-en-Provence or of Lyon, remained, in my opinion, within the traditional framework of the religious life. They were composed of single people of the same sex consecrated to the Lord. Granted, the legal structure set up by the Fraternities of Jerusalem included both men and women, but that was also true in traditional orders, ours in particular. Within our unity we had communities of monks and nuns. I will come back to that subject in the last chapter of this book. Each of these communities of only men or only women did devote their celibacy to the Lord. Father Pierre-Marie Delfieux[3] himself stated that he didn't believe in the possibility of a mixed monasticism.

Furthermore, these new creations drew their inspiration from ancient spirituality, finding there an anchor point in Saint Basil, for example, a monk-bishop of the fourth century, and in other spiritual authors writing within the classic monastic tradition. This was even more true for certain communities who declared that they wanted to fit into one or another religious tradition with a proven track record. This was the case for the Brothers and Sisters of Bethlehem, who, although settled in France, referred specifically to the teachings of Saint Bruno, the eleventh-century founder of the Carthusians. They preferred to live these charisms in a somewhat newer style, which the Carthusians were not prepared to adopt for themselves. This was the reason for their foundation.

Another type of community had started many years before, from what was called the Charismatic Renewal Movement. Christian men and women first met on a regular basis for prayer. Some wanted to create a closer community life among the members of the group. From there, new communities were created that included all the different types of people one might encounter in real life: unmarried people of both sexes as well as couples

---

3. {Father Pierre-Marie Delfieux (1934–2013) was a French priest who founded the Fraternités de Jerusalem in 1975 (see above, n. 2). After he told Cardinal Marty of Paris of his desire to be a monk in the city, Marty gave him the St. Servais church, close to Notre Dame, where he started these Fraternités. In 1976 a community of nuns joined them.}

with children, lay people, and priests. Religious have sometimes tried to be affiliated with these communities. In the beginning we probably didn't see clearly what to do. Slowly, these communities got a structure and defined their direction. Quite a few, after a number of years, started to evangelize or to engage in specific apostolates, depending on the community and the type of location. Others preferred to welcome the poor while insisting on eucharistic adoration. Among other communities, this was the case for the *Communauté du Pain de Vie*, which I followed closely, since for a time from their foundation in 1978 to 1982, their main house was located in L'Aigle, about fifteen miles from La Trappe. We had frequent contacts with them, and I remained in a somewhat distant relationship with the founding couples.[4]

These communities draw their inspiration from the principles of the classic monastic life, but in general, their members do not recognize themselves as monastics *stricto sensu* even if they pronounce vows of obedience and poverty, and sometimes chastity. A life in community for people of both sexes, and for couples with children to bring up, inevitably raises some serious questions relating to the traditional concept of religious life, even if the communities themselves are commendable and exemplary. Nevertheless, in certain communities, like those of the Community of the Beatitudes, the members who devote their celibacy to the Lord wear a monastic type habit and call themselves monks or nuns, even though they live among lay people.

My purpose in this book is not to give a complete listing of these communities or to describe them in detail,[5] so I will refrain

---

4. {After many years of internal dispute and numerous departures of their members, the *Communauté* was dissolved on April 9, 2015, by a decree from Bishop Boulanger of Bayeux-Lisieux}.

5. A recent book published on the subject is Pascal Pingault, *Renouveau de l'Église: les communautés nouvelles* (Paris: Fayard, 1989). {For more information on new ecclesial movements, consult the document prepared by the Pontifical Council for Laicity, http://www.laici.va/content/laici/en/sezioni/associazioni.html.}

from any further discussion of them. But there remained one question: faced with this new blossoming, this "sign of the times" as it was called: how did we position ourselves? Very simply indeed! I mean that while we did not doubt the relevance of our own experience, we did not look down on the others with an air of superiority. Throughout the life of the Church, we have seen the foundation of communities that distanced themselves more or less from their predecessors in response to new needs. History shows that these communities have not eliminated the previous ones. They didn't replace the oldest ones either, but they satisfied and complemented legitimate and still current aspirations, just as younger adults do not eliminate their seniors.

These communities can lead us to wonder if we provide an appropriate answer to the present situation of the life in the Church. From our side, we did ask them some questions. The Bishops' Conference of 1982 in Lourdes asked us to reflect on these groups of Christians who got together almost everywhere to pray by placing themselves under the moving influence of the Spirit. We were also asked to reflect on the life communities that stemmed more or less directly from these groups. A statement was expected from the religious superiors present in that conference. As one of them, I had to speak on behalf of the others. We had prepared together what we would have to say. After indicating five points on which we were in complete agreement, I made a number of observations. Some concerned the workings of these mixed communities. The role of the person in charge was not always well defined. Neither was the situation of the religious who had joined them. Other observations concerned the way these communities conceived of themselves, even while they were using the terminology of traditional religious life:

> "We marvel," I said, "at the spirit of faith of these communities and their total sharing of property, which is one element of the religious life. But that life also entails a parameter that is constant in the tradition, celibacy for the kingdom. It is inherent in religious life. It is not sufficient for couples to

live jointly in a radical, Gospel-like simplicity in order to call themselves religious in the literal sense. Moreover, we think that a certain withdrawal from the world is a characteristic of the call to monastic life. It is not sufficient to adopt some monastic usages and customs."

Clearly, one should not focus solely on definitions—it's not the habit that makes the monk! But if the same expressions are used to refer to totally different realities, they risk losing all significance. We needed to define them better to avoid confusing them. If necessary distinctions remain, that will enable everyone to recognize the originality of the new foundations, in particular the ability to offer couples the possibility of living a deeper engagement following in the footsteps of Jesus Christ in a life community that goes beyond the household, while respecting and valuing it in a sharing of property and in a poverty that supposes a real evangelical self-denial. After all, isn't that how the first Christian community wanted to live, gathered around the apostles in Jerusalem, after the death and resurrection of Christ (Acts 2:44-45; 4:32-35)?

The bishop in charge of the final report on this matter, Mgr. Marcus, included our questions in the document. Probably it went higher up. In December 1982, Pope John Paul II welcomed the bishops of the Midi region in their visit *ad limina*.[6] The Holy Father invited each one of them to make an effort in discernment, and he provided this clarification about groups that were issued from the Renewal: "That the religious men and women who join them should not in any way loosen the ties they have with their Institution, nor the obedience towards their legitimate superior. Let's see to it that our words retain the significance they have in the language of the Church. The vocabulary of the religious life

---

6. {Visit *ad limina*: the discipline concerning visits *ad limina* is found in the Decree of the Consistorial Congregation, issued by order of Pius X (Dec. 31, 1909) for every bishop to render to the pope an account of the state of his diocese once every five years.}

does not always correspond to these new types of groups that are still looking for their canonical identity."[7]

I was already a member of the Committee of Major Superiors when John Paul II came to Lisieux during his visit to France in 1980. The permanent committee had an appointment with him in the sacristy of Carmel, on his way back from his praying in the cell where Saint Thérèse died. The people in his entourage came into this small sacristy through a narrow door one after another. Our president was waiting for everybody to be in place before starting the remarks he had prepared. Since it was taking so much time, and because of the narrowness of the passageway, the pope's secretary handed him the response that he was supposed to give us. The Holy Father started with it right away. The schedule was tight. We could do nothing but keep our peace! But John Paul II invited us to pray the Our Father together holding hands. I grabbed the Pope's hand, thereby short-cutting Cardinal Etchegaray, who was standing back. A good sport, he quipped, "Go on, today it's your turn!" Notwithstanding the setbacks, the encounter was more satisfactory than the one that took place in the great rooms of the Elysée Palace a few days later. We were packed like sardines: I only saw the white cap of the Pope and the bald head of President Giscard d'Estaing[8] passing a few feet from the place where I was stuck!

What should we think of the future of the communities that are set up almost everywhere? They certainly show the vitality of the church. To the extent that they develop one aspect that was not taken into account by the traditional orders, they will probably survive and will be recognized by historians as marking an

---

7. Ecclesia Catholica, Conférence épiscopale française, *Mission sans frontières: 25 ans de solidarité missionaire, la pastorale de la santé, mission en monde ouvrier . . . Lourdes 1982, Assemblée plénière de l'Episcopat français* (Paris: Centurion, 1982), 188; speech of John Paul II, *Documentation Catholique*, no. 1844 (Jan. 16, 1983), 73.

8. {Valéry Giscard d'Estaing (1926–): French politician, the third president of the Fifth Republic (1974–1981).}

important milestone in the long journey of the church. Orders or institutions are born, grow, and die, like any other organism, but their life expectancies can vary wildly. Some have a longevity that overcomes any trials. Others have not survived the hardships of time; many did not survive the French Revolution.

We could define this evolution of the religious life in the church the same way some imagine the evolutionary process of the world. According to certain theories—because in the matter nothing is plainly certain—the evolution of certain species takes the form of plant-like clumps, of which only certain branches have a future. At the birth of each clump, at determined periods of time, an innovative element appears. All the species in the clump might develop that element until some hit a dead end. The particular element that in the beginning was an advantage keeps growing until it becomes a handicap that prevents it from surviving. Others, on the contrary, remain more flexible, less specialized, and smaller, and are better able to adapt to changing circumstances and continue the evolution; they might be at the origin of a new clump carrying a better performing element. In the present proliferation of new communities, which are those with a fertile future, destined to advance this evolution? Only history will tell.

All the orders, even the oldest ones, started out as fragile cuttings! To tell the truth, Cîteaux was part of an older tradition; it began more as a reform than as a new creation, even though at its inception it was called the New Monastery. That was in 1098!

A certain Robert entered the monastery of Moutier-la-Celle, close to Troyes, when he was only fifteen years old. He became prior and a year later was elected abbot of the monastery of Saint-Michel-de-Tonnerre. After many adventures he found himself leading a few hermits in the forest of Collan. The whole group settled in Molesme, in the diocese of Langres, in 1075, this time establishing a coenobitic community. This did not mean the end of Robert's wanderings. On March 21, 1098, at the age of seventy, he left again with twenty-one of his monks to rediscover the purity of the Rule of Saint Benedict, because his monastery, based upon the model of Cluny, had become wealthy. A Cistercian chronicler noted, exaggerating somewhat, that "as temporal wealth entered Molesme, the spiritual wealth left."[9]

Robert's men stopped in a large forest about fifteen miles from Dijon on lands named Cîteaux.[10] They wore the black habit of the Benedictines, but a short time later they choose to use raw wool, undyed, as a sign of simplicity. Thereafter they became known as the White Monks. Soon Pope Urban II ordered Robert to return to his previous abbey, where the monks, confronted with difficulties, had asked for his return.

Robert's successor was Saint Alberic, who hurried to protect Cîteaux from any claims by placing it under the direct jurisdiction of the Holy See. The location of the monastery had not been well chosen, for there was a lack of water. Robert had probably only envisioned cabins for hermits. Alberic moved it somewhat further south and designed it to be more suitable for a coenobitic lifestyle. They quickly built the first church, which was consecrated in 1106 under the patronage of Mary, like all those that would be established in the Order. The early years were hard because of the austerity of their lifestyle. In addition, the famines of 1109 and 1112, as reported by the chroniclers,[11] didn't make it easier. Alberic died in sadness because he hadn't been able to attract new recruits to carry on the journey. Stephen Harding succeeded him in 1109.

9. {"Exordium Parvum," in *Narrative and Legislative Texts from Early Cîteaux*, ed. Chrysogonus Waddell (*Cîteaux: Commentarii cistercienses*, 1999), 416–40 at 419; "Exordium Cistercii," in *Narrative and Legislative Texts*, 399–404 at 399–400; Conrad of Eberbach, *The Great Beginning of Cîteaux. A Narrative of the Beginning of the Cistercian Order: The* Exordium Magnum *of Conrad of Eberbach*, trans. Benedicta Ward and Paul Savage, ed. E. Rozanne Elder, foreword by Brian Patrick McGuire, Cistercian Fathers Series 72 (Collegeville, MN: Cistercian Publications, 2012), 71–75.}

10. Local custom tells us that the name *Cîteaux* came from the many bulrushes growing in the adjacent swamps, called *cistels* in the local dialect.

11. Conrad of Eberbach, *The Great Beginning*, 105.

In the spring of 1112 or 1113 someone came knocking at the door—a young man of twenty-two, accompanied by thirty men from illustrious families, asking to enter. The one who would become Saint Bernard had convinced close relatives and friends, knights like himself, to renounce the world. Already for two or three years they had been leading a life of prayer and reflection together. Their entry into the monastery was the beginning of the extraordinary development that the Order would know under his influence. Almost from the moment of his entry, they began to spread out—they founded La Ferté in 1113, then Pontigny the following year, and in June 1115 Clairvaux and Morimond.

The young Bernard, barely twenty-five years old, was placed at the helm of the group founding Clairvaux, which was in large part comprised of those with whom he had entered two or three years earlier, in particular his four brothers, one uncle, and two cousins. The novices were coming in droves, and since the buildings at Clairvaux were cramped, they needed new foundations: Trois Fontaines in 1118, Fontenay in 1119, Foigny in 1121, Igny in 1128. Then the foundations multiplied at an average of two a year, and Bernard started to be known. He participated in regional councils, including the Council of Langres in 1125. Around 1127 at the request of the Bishop of Sens he wrote a long letter, *Tractatus de moribus et officio episcoporum*,[12] in which he gave a portrait of the ideal bishop. His correspondence multiplied, and he was called upon to resolve conflicts.

Up to this point, Bernard's activities had remained locally confined, but the schism of 1130 propelled him into the center of the history of the Church. Two popes were elected, Innocent II and Anacletus II. To which one should he rally? How could he recognize the real one? The merits of life should decide, it was believed, rather than legal regularity. The monastic circles chose Innocent II, who had been elected by the more rigorist prelates,

12. {The *Tractatus* has been translated into English by Pauline Matarasso and Martha G. Newman in *On Baptism and the Office of Bishops*, CF 67 (Kalamazoo, MI: Cistercian Publications, 2004), 37–82).}

the "saner part," and Bernard rallied to his cause. He put his talents of persuasion and his writing skills at the service of Innocent. He went with the pope on his trips, traveling to Rome three times, on a mission of persuasion to Mainz in the Rhineland, and then to Bamberg in Bavaria. He became Innocent's man, and he could write to him, "People say that you are not the pope, but that I am; people with pending matters come to me in droves from everywhere."[13] Clairvaux had become the branch office of Rome.

Bernard became more and more involved in settling Church matters and even political matters. He had to intervene between kings and barons, between knights, and between rival cities to bring peace. Only his words and intervention could stop the pogroms carrying out massacres of the Jews. When it became necessary to go to protect the Christians guarding the holy sites in Palestine, the pope called on Bernard to preach the crusade. He came back to Cîteaux to hide from the world, but when he died at Clairvaux forty years later, the whole western Church mourned him. Pope Eugenius III, who died just six weeks before Bernard, was one of Bernard's former novices at Clairvaux, his spiritual son, to whom he had just written a letter of advice titled *On Consideration.*[14]

Who was this man of fire who has been called the conscience of his century? He was foremost a monk, deeply linked to his community at Clairvaux, which he taught and directed. So as not to be separated from them, he stubbornly refused the dioceses to which he had been elected bishop.[15] He meditated and com-

---

13. {Bernard of Clairvaux, *The Letters of St. Bernard of Clairvaux*, trans. Bruno Scott James (London: Burns and Oates, 1953). The letters that Bernard wrote on behalf of others are too numerous to list here, but see especially nos. 285, 287, 288, 289, 291, and 292, in which he mentions the volume of correspondence with friends seeking his help in dealing with the Holy See.}

14. {Bernard of Clairvaux, *Five Books on Consideration: Advice to a Pope,* trans. John D. Anderson and Elizabeth T. Kennan, CF 37 (Kalamazoo, MI: Cistercian Publications, 1976).}

15. {Reims and Langres, both in 1138.}

mented on the Bible, and he led his men on the roads of spiritual experience that he lived and radiated. It was because of this experience that he had so much authority outside his monastery. He was called upon as a prophet, as a man of God. And it was a disaster for him when, for example, the crusade turned out to be a failure. Was he no longer a prophet? Was his word no longer God's word? A man of God, there lies his secret, the profound reason for his authority. That did not prevent him from being wrong sometimes, from reacting too humanly. Historians have a duty to deepen our knowledge about what Bernard was as a man of action. But Saint Bernard is also of interest to us because he was a saint and a spiritual master. It was in that capacity that he had a profound influence on our Order, and for that reason we consider him our Father Saint Bernard. His influence far exceeded monastic circles; he was later proclaimed a Doctor of the Church.

While Bernard was still alive his writings were intended to be disseminated everywhere. He knew this and saw to it. He left behind many sermons for the liturgical holidays and many spiritual treatises. One of the best known is *On Loving God*, which begins, "You want me to tell you why and in what measure God is to be loved. I reply, the reason for loving God is God himself, and the measure is to love without measure."[16] His eighty-six sermons on the Canticle of Canticles are a goldmine of teachings on the spiritual journey. I cannot resist quoting a passage from one of them:

> I love because I love; I love that I may love. Love is a great reality . . . . Love is the only one of the motions of the soul, of its senses and affections, in which the creature can respond to its Creator, even if not as an equal, and repay his favor in some similar way. For example, if God is angry with me, am I to be angry in return? No, indeed, but I shall

16. Bernard of Clairvaux, *On Loving God* 1.1, trans.by Robert Walton, analytical commentary by Emero Stiegman, CF 13B (Kalamazoo, MI: Cistercian Publications, 1995), 3–4.

tremble with fear and ask pardon. So also, if he accuses me, I shall not accuse him in return, but rather justify him. Nor, if he judges me, shall I judge him, but I shall adore him; and in saving me he does not ask to be saved by me; nor does he who sets all men free need to be set free by me. If he commands, I must obey, and not demand his service or obedience. Now you see how different love is, for when God loves, he desires nothing but to be loved, since he loves us for no other reason than to be loved, for he knows that those who love him are blessed in their very love.[17]

Paradoxically, in 1140 when Count Rotrou III of Perche wanted to settle a community of monks close to a shrine that he had built on the grounds of La Trappe in 1122, he did not call on Cistercians, but on Benedictines of the congregation of Savigny in Normandy, a couple of decades older than the Cistercians. The eleventh century had seen a flurry of new communities issued from a movement with eremitic tendencies, marked by austerity and destitution. Cîteaux was not the only New Monastery, even if, as history would confirm, it was the offspring with a promising future. Proof? In 1147 the whole congregation of Savigny packed up and went to the new Cistercian Order, epitomized by the abbot of Clairvaux. This is how La Trappe, created seven years earlier, became Cistercian and never ceased to be.

The foundation of the monastery was connected to a tragedy, the shipwreck of a royal vessel, the *White Ship*, which was bringing the grandchildren of William the Conqueror from France to England. The wreck occurred on November 25, 1120, and was caused by the negligence of a drunken crew, for the return to England was a festive occasion after some battles in Normandy. William Adelin, the legitimate son of England's King Henry I, and his half-sister Mathilde perished in the wreck. The king was inconsolable, as was Count Rotrou III, who had married Mathilde

---

17. {Bernard of Clairvaux, *On the Song of Songs*, 83.2–4, trans. Kilian Walsh and Irene Edmonds, 4 vols., CF 4, 7, 31, 40 (Kalamazoo, MI: Cistercian Publications, 1979–1983), 4:180–87 at 184.}

in 1102, upon his return from the First Crusade. In memory of this drowning he built a shrine in the middle of the ponds on one of his properties in 1122. The shrine was said to have the shape of an overturned ship's hull. Eighteen years later he brought the monks there; the laying of the first stone occurred on December 2, 1140.

Like other abbeys, La Trappe had prosperous periods and dark times. During the Hundred Years War (1337–1453), robberies and lootings severely tested the life of the community, and the monks had to take shelter for a year in a nearby castle. The buildings were torched by looters in 1376. But later a more formidable curse hit La Trappe along with other abbeys, the practice of *in commendam*. According to this practice the responsibility of the abbey was no longer in the hands of an abbot elected by the community but was given instead to a beneficiary appointed by the king, who thereby had at his disposal a way to reward his faithful servants. In this way in 1532 Cardinal Jean du Bellay became abbot of La Trappe. For 130 years, the governance of the community was in the hands of strangers, all of whom, of course, had less concern for the monks' spiritual well being than for their own financial interests. In the middle of the seventeenth century, La Trappe was one of the most dysfunctional houses of the kingdom. Its reformer would say, "iniquity ruled there in full force."

This reformer was one of those abbots appointed *in commendam*, an abbot from the court, a nephew of Richelieu, who converted slowly upon realizing how precarious and vain a whole life was when faced with eternity. Armand-Jean Le Bouthillier de Rancé was born January 9, 1626. His father, secretary of Marie de Médici for a year, would be a State Counselor, enjoying a nice career with the support of Cardinal Richelieu.[18] His mother was

18. {Armand Jean du Plessis, duke of Richelieu (1585–1642), is commonly referred to as Cardinal Richelieu. He became bishop in 1607 at the age of 22 and was a staunch defender of the Church. He became very influential in the court of King Louis XIII, becoming Louis's chief minister and fought to centralize power in the king and away from the nobles. He was a strong supporter of the arts and founded the Academie Française.}

the daughter of a "Maître des Requêtes" and chief advisor to the cardinal. Armand-Jean was the second of the boys but the fifth of seven children, and he was first destined for a career in the military. However, the health of his brother Denys, already the recipient of five benefices under the *in commendam* system, including La Trappe, was raising some concerns, and he died at seventeen years of age. A year earlier, Armand-Jean had received five abbeys or priories *in commendam* from his brother and had received the tonsure; he was not yet ten years old.

The death of his mother two years later, when he was still barely a teenager, afflicted him painfully. In 1657, the death of the Duchess of Montbazon completely overwhelmed him. Well read, with a subtlety that rivaled Bossuet's,[19] he had been a royal court abbot, a priest, and honest, perhaps, but mainly concerned with hunting and pleasure. The duchess, who was beautiful and stylish, probably helped Rancé to assert himself in high society. After some days of hunting he returned to her palace to find that after a brief illness, she had died.[20] Death struck again three years later, when Duke Gaston d'Orléans expired in the arms of Rancé, his chaplain. During the embalming of the body Rancé spoke with a priest of the vanity and the frailty of these earthly things.

In 1662, retired from social life since the death of the Duchess of Montbazon and relieved of the chaplaincy of Gaston d'Orléans, Rancé decided to sell everything except the abbey of La Trappe, where he settled down, but without yet becoming a monk. At the time only six monks remained in the monastery, spending most of their time playing bocce ball in the large dining room and holding the passersby for ransom to improve their daily fare. He ordered them to leave or to convert. As reinforcements,

19. {Jacques-Bénigne Lignel Bossuet (1612–1704): French bishop and theologian, renowned for his sermons. He was considered by many to be one of the most brilliant orators of all time and a masterful French stylist. Court preacher to Louis XIV, Bossuet was a strong advocate of political absolutism and the divine right of kings.}

20. {On the basis of recent scholarship on Rancé, some aspects of Dom Dubois's narrative have been amended.}

he brought in a few monks from Perseigne, an abbey open to the reforms that had been implemented in certain monasteries of the Order since the beginning of the century, now known as the Strict Observance.[21]

In 1663, perceiving that he needed to give a good example, Rancé decided to start a year of formation in the province's novitiate located in Perseigne: he became a monk. Back in his own monastery, he received the blessing transforming him into a regular—non-commendatory—abbot. From that time forward, the practice of *in commendam* ceased to corrupt La Trappe. Rancé was at the time thirty-eight years old and would live another thirty-six years in penance and prayer.

In his first years as an abbot, Rancé was preoccupied with recruitment and the deepening of La Trappe's observance. When twelve deaths took place between 1674 and 1676, critics blamed the excessively austere character that he had introduced into monastic observance. Nevertheless, he did not relax this austerity. His book *Relations*,[22] which he wrote from 1678 on about the edifying death of monks, was like a justification of the life at La Trappe.

21. {Clairvaux initiated reforms at the beginning of the 17th century and was soon joined by other houses of the Order, even though Cîteaux itself opposed the changes. Conflict between the two parties, which came to be known as observances, became so severe that in 1662 the Holy See stepped in and ordered the two sides to negotiate. At this point Abbot de Rancé emerged as the leader of the reform party, known as the Strict Observance. In 1683 the Strict Observance was granted the right to hold its own abbatial elections and to incorporate full houses into the reform if a majority of the members requested it. See for a fuller discussion Louis Lekai, *The White Monks: A History of the Cistercian Order* (Okauchee, WI: Cistercian Monastery of Our Lady of Spring Bank, 1953), 93–104.}

22. {Armand-Jean Le Bouthillier de Rancé, *Vie et mort des moines de La Trappe* (Paris: Mercure de France, 2012). See also *Everyday Life at La Trappe under Armand-Jean de Rancé: A Translation, with Introduction and Notes, of André Félibien des Avaux's* Description De L'abbaye De La Trappe *(1689)*, trans. David N. Bell, CS 274 (Collegeville, MN: Cistercian Publications, 2018).}

With regard to monastic observance, Rancé was stricter than anybody else, even within the Strict Observance. He reintroduced abstinence from meat and also forbade fish and eggs. Silence was absolute, and the monks had no communication or familiarity among themselves; their only mutual consolation, it was said, came from the view and presence of the others. Manual labor was compulsory for three hours a day, and studies were forbidden. Leaving the monastery for health reasons or to visit family members was not permitted, and all contact with family or friends was strictly monitored. In the infirmary the regime was somewhat relaxed, but still severe, and reliance on medications was not recommended.

Nevertheless Rancé did not easily allow extraordinary mortifications; he discouraged excesses of physical penance other than those provided for in the Rule. He knew that what counted beyond the exterior penances was humiliation and compunction, as well as obedience, the abandonment of all earthly goods, and brotherly charity. Sanctity did not consist in anything other than "a regard for and a continuous devotion to God." In his work *Treatise on the Holiness and the Duties of the Monastic Life,* Rancé defined a religious as someone "who having renounced with a solemn vow the world and all that is sensible and perishable, only lives for God and is only occupied with eternal things." [23]

What must be considered in Rancé beyond his teachings is his concrete attitude towards the monks. He always had a passionate concern for those who were in his care. A real affection united him with each one of them, even if he sometimes treated them harshly, and even if he knew how to humble them when it was necessary. The warm and understanding attitude of the abbot compensated for the austerity of La Trappe, perhaps explaining the atmosphere of joy and serenity of the community that visitors noticed, notwithstanding the everyday austerity. Why would so many people have entered La Trappe if not because the personality of Rancé attracted

---

23. {Armand-Jean Le Bouthillier de Rancé, *A Treatise on the Sanctity and on the Duties of the Monastic State* (Dublin: R. Grace, 1830).}

them? He spent many hours receiving his brothers and counseling them. He could adapt to each one of them, humbling the strong and often saving the weak. Since interactions among the brothers were forbidden, that of a brother with his superior was even more important. The silence between the brothers did not prevent brotherly charity, which is the cement of the coenobitic life. "It is the virtue that the saintly abbot most often recommended to his children," said a monk who was one of his biographers.

The La Trappe archives hold more than half of Rancé's two thousand letters. Until 1993 they were practically unusable except by specialists, because they were mixed up, hard to decipher, and especially difficult to interpret because of the lack of certain information. It was necessary to transcribe them, classify them, find the name of the recipient, and disentangle the questions they raised. In 1966 a professor of seventeenth-century French literature at Oxford, Alban John Krailsheimer, came to La Trappe for the first time. Chateaubriand's *Life* of Rancé did not convince him, and he wanted to write a biography with documents coming directly from the source. On his first visit he quickly understood that he would not be able to do anything without consulting all the letters. Professor Krailsheimer came each year to comb through the letters of Rancé in the archives. He also searched for materials in the French National Library and other large libraries. It was an exhausting task, but it did not discourage this man who in 1942 had been a lieutenant in the British counter-espionage service in World War II. He quickly became a friend of the abbey.

The culmination of Prof. Krailsheimer's work was the publication in 1993 of the correspondence of Rancé in four volumes, well received by literary critics.[24] It revealed a more human, warm, and straightforward abbot and reformer, the face of a man strangely

---

24. A. J. Krailsheimer, *Abbé de Rancé: Correspondence* (Paris: Cerf-Citeaux, 1993). {See also Armand-Jean Le Bouthillier de Rancé and A. J. Krailsheimer, *The letters of Armand-Jean de Rancé, abbot and reformer of La Trappe / presented by A. J. Krailsheimer*, CS 81 (Kalamazoo, MI: Cistercian Publications, 1984). For his biography of Rancé, see A. J. Krailsheimer, *Armand-Jean de Rancé: His Influence in the Cloister and in the World* (Oxford: Oxford University Press, 1974).}

free, notwithstanding the criticism of those he disturbed with his ideas.

Unlike the writings of Saint Bernard, the works on spirituality by Rancé no longer have a substantial influence on today's religious concepts. One can regret it or not. But Rancé's success and his influence were without a doubt felt in his community of La Trappe. Thanks to his inspiration, his influence remained powerful throughout the eighteenth century, playing an important role at crucial times in the Order's life and thereby saving it from the fury of the French Revolution. It gave birth to the Cistercian Order of the Strict Observance, and for that history is indebted to him.

On February 7, 1790, the community of La Trappe lost its abbot, Dom Olivier, who died at forty-six, just before the suppression of all religious orders by the decree of February 13, 1790, undertaken by the new Revolutionary Constituent Assembly. The community could not therefore proceed with the election of Dom Olivier's successor. First, financial reasons interfered. At the instigation of Bishop Talleyrand,[25] the National Assembly started to take measures against the religious orders, to put at the service of the nation their immense wealth, which exceeded their needs. But quickly this concern escalated to the level of conscience. At that time there was no separation of church and state. The vows were recognized civilly, so the National Assembly considered itself authorized to suspend them and even to forbid them in the future, and that is exactly what it did, calling on monastics to leave their communities. Those who didn't want to completely leave their community life were grouped together in specialized houses, with all the orders combined.

---

25. {Charles Maurice de Talleyrand-Périgord (1754–1838): although he became a priest at a young age, his main interests were politics and diplomacy. As a bishop he represented the Church in the États Généraux (the political assembly) before the Revolution. He assumed diplomatic duties during the French Revolution, then continued them for Napoleon, Louis XVIII, and Louis-Philippe before playing an essential role for France in creating the Treaty of Vienna in 1815.}

Overall, one historian noted that only exceptionally did one encounter among the clergy or the religious orders either the extreme desire to be faithful or the extreme impatience to desert. "Neither fervor nor denial dominated here . . . . I believe that for men weakness was stronger than stability . . . . monks welcomed trial, but not too much."[26] The nuns, on the contrary, showed an almost unanimous faithfulness. The situation became more dramatic once persecution increased from 1792 on. Many were put to death. The Order would count quite a few martyrs.

The majority of the La Trappe community under the authority of the prior wanted to remain in one group in their monastery. The novice master, Dom Augustin de Lestrange, was quite insightful in 1790 about the future turn of events. He was of the opinion that the community would have to take refuge abroad to continue its religious life. His opinion was not shared in the beginning, because nobody believed the threat to be serious, the more so because La Trappe had a good reputation in the region. It could as an exception, they believed, continue its existence. To this end it seemed important that all be unanimous instead of divided.

On the other hand, Dom Augustin had a strong temperament that frightened some. He realized that Rancé had not been able to follow to the letter the prescriptions of the Rule on certain points. Dom Augustin wanted to perfect Rancé's reform in that way, and this desire frightened others. Finally he obtained permission to take necessary steps to find a refuge in Switzerland and then to go there with volunteers. Twenty relatively young professed, with an average age of thirty-seven, and three novices left La Trappe on May 10, 1791, and reached La Valsainte on June 1. Later ten more brothers joined them there.

---

26. Pierre de La Gorce, *Histoire religieuse de la Révolution française*, 5 vols. (Paris: Plon-Nourrit et Cie, 1924–1925), 172–74.

Slowly the monks remaining at La Trappe had to face the reality that it was no longer possible to stay there. Several departures took place between 1791 and 1792, and the last twenty-eight occupants of La Trappe, with the prior, were expelled on June 3, 1792. Only on November 1, 1815, twenty-three years later, did a group of monks headed by Dom Augustin resume monastic life at La Trappe. In the meantime, the monastery had been destroyed, with only the outbuildings remaining. The toll of the Revolution had been heavy; four monks, including the prior, died as martyrs. Pope John Paul II later beatified the prior together with other priests who died in Rochefort on the two infamous pontoons that were supposed to take them to exile but turned into a deadly prison for many of them.

The exiled brothers did not live peacefully in Switzerland during these dark years. The advancing republican armies forced them to go on the road again in what became an extraordinary odyssey between 1798 and 1803, before a new dispersion. But the group did not include only the monks who came from La Trappe. La Valsainte, where they first settled in Switzerland, had witnessed an influx of vocations, mostly monastics running away from persecution in France. Daughter houses spread to Spain, Flanders, England, and Italy. Additionally, nuns had settled not far from Valsainte. Dom Augustin took them under his wing in 1796.

About two hundred fifty people, men, women, and children, were taken care of before in 1798 they marched off towards the east on foot or by boat to Vienna when they were able to use the Danube. But they then had to push on to Russia, where they spent two very harsh winters. In 1800 the tsar in turn expelled all of them, so they came back to Switzerland, some by way of the North Sea, some through Poland or Germany. Dom Augustin attracted the wrath of Napoleon when he publicly sided with the imprisoned Pope Pius VII, and the Trappists were—again—banned from the Empire.

In 1811, Dom Augustin, with a price on his head, traveled to North America. That was the start of the North American odyssey for the Cistercians. After Napoleon's defeat in 1815 Dom Augustin came back to France and repurchased La Trappe. From 1795 on, he considered himself generally responsible for the monasteries that owed their foundation directly or indirectly to the small group of Trappists who had left in 1791. In this way La Trappe, located in the village of Soligny, became the head of numerous congregations and took the title of *Grande Trappe*, giving its name to the totality. In France today, with the exception of the monasteries in Lérins and in Sénanque, all Cistercians are *Trappist*s, and their monasteries are called *trappes*.

But harmony was not complete between Dom Augustin and the bishop of Sées, the diocese in which La Trappe was located. So the abbot and most of the community withdrew to the Abbey of Bellefontaine in the Choletais region. After Dom Augustin's death in 1827, the monks took the road back to Soligny. They built a monastery, which sixty years later became too small and decrepit, giving way to the present buildings. The new church was consecrated with great fanfare on August 30, 1895.

In the turmoil of the nineteenth century, the Trappists divided into three congregations, of which two followed the regulations of Rancé and the third one the old usages of the Rule. In 1892 Pope Leo XIII unified the three into one order, which revived the medieval usages of Cîteaux but adapted them to modern times. The only remaining thing was to buy what was left of the monastery of Cîteaux itself, close to Dijon, where the adventure had started, and to breathe life back in to it, an event that occurred in 1898.

Monks from twenty-three monasteries and nine countries were sent to repopulate Cîteaux between 1892 and 1902. While Dom Robert Lescand was prior, from September 16, 1899, to October 25, 1923, there were forty-nine clothings, twenty-two temporary vows, ten solemn professions, seven ordinations to the priesthood, and fifteen deaths. Brother Guy, who was born in 1898 and entered in 1920, remained the living memory of that period until his death in April 1995. Originally from the Ardennes, he had survived the Spanish flu, which had devastated his home town, which during World War I was only about fifteen miles away from the front lines. He also suffered from food shortages and the presence of the Germans. Everywhere he had had to be satisfied with very little; life then was like that of the strictest Trappists.

"What was the hardest for you, Brother Guy?" I asked him one day in 1993.

"For me, nothing was harsher than what I had experienced during my youth," he answered.

I visited him in his room in the infirmary, where he was making wicker baskets, as he had taught Brother Pascal, whose memory I recalled and who had in his letters talked about Brother Guy's instruction.

The presence of elders in a community is precious, as observed a member of the new communities I mentioned in the beginning of this chapter. While visiting us one day, this visitor remained speechless as he watched an old handicapped brother who was continually praying, since he was not able to do anything else. The look on this brother's face deeply struck the visitor.

"What we are missing," he said, "is tradition. Our community is too young. We are an average of thirty-five years old. We are not grounded in a sufficiently rich soil. We have not been engendered. We are missing elders."

But the elders also need the young. If not, the chain would stop. Brother Guy confided to me, "I remained a monk with the grace of God, but I saw a century fly by, and I spent three quarters of it in a monastery. The changes have been unimaginable. Luckily I am good natured. My grandmother told my grandfather: 'Ah, you, when you are dead you will still be laughing.' I am made of the same wicker. If a monk spends his day in reflecting on what else he could be doing, he is not at peace. But I would not like to be in a nursing home. When the young brothers are present, there is life, there is hope."

I went to visit a nun in the monastery of Chambarand who was 102 years old. She was then the oldest one in our Order, our abbot general told us. I didn't dare knock at the door of her room in the infirmary, because I heard that she was on the phone. The communication went on for a long time, and I waited outside wondering what she was saying. When she finished I asked her, "Who were you talking to?" She answered me, "With my spiritual director, who is a young man ninety-six years of age." She was talking about Brother Guy.

"We are exceptions," Brother Guy said. "I saw all the monks now in Cîteaux enter the monastery. The cemetery was almost empty, and now it is almost full. I am a bump in the road."

The brother infirmarian of Cîteaux, Father Henri, had buried forty-six monks and had kissed each one of them on the forehead before throwing in the first scoop of dirt. When he walked among the white crosses, he was not visiting the dead but the living. He remembered each one of them and their stories, which still made him smile.

CHAPTER THIRTEEN

NEVERTHELESS, THERE IS A WORLD OUT THERE!

His name was Brother François. Since 1965 he had been in charge of welcoming young people to La Trappe in a building located a few steps away from the monastery. In 1980 two educators came to visit him. They were taking care of jobless North African and Turkish youngsters in a poor neighborhood in a city in Eure-et-Loire.

"Our location is really a disenfranchised urban area,"[1] they explained to him. "These young people are not well received, but we have to admit that they destroy the bushes and tear up the small trees and the mail boxes. When you see their family circle—. We first thought of bringing them to Bagnoles-de-l'Orne this summer, and we just came back from visiting the buildings. It is too risky—too nice and too new. Could they be allowed to come and camp here in the abbey for two weeks?"

"Of course, but there are probably two or three leaders, as in any group of thugs. I want their names."

"Mohamed and Abdouramane in particular, fourteen and thirteen years old."

---

1. {The exact term in French is "zone à urbaniser par priorité," a ZUP.}

"Very good! I'll take the risk and invite them both for two days to prepare the camp. Tell them that you have a project and that they will need to take care of everything. They can write to me to start. They can call me François and talk to me like a longtime friend."

The letter showed that the youngsters would probably not care to observe the monastic peace: "François, will we be allowed to build a tree house? We will come by bicycle—do you have woods where we can set up our tents?" The letter showed above all that the authors could barely read or write and that the educators probably had to work hard to dictate that letter to them. A later exchange of tape recordings between Brother François and the two boys enabled them to communicate better. The camp was a success, notwithstanding the price paid by the trees in resin and broken limbs. Three days later a tape with Moroccan and Turkish music arrived, along with a message that explained the Punchinello doll in the package: "François, this is for you, and it is me, Abdouramane who made it just for you. You, François, love us. Going home, Didier cried. We all tell you thank you, and we will come back to see you." They came back indeed, with a copy of the photo album of the camp. The hoodlums had become normal children again, with their hearts of gold, their projects, and their teenage dignity. Why is there so much violence and hate in the ghettos of our society?

The building used to receive groups of young people was an old sheepfold. Until 1960 there were still sheep in it, and cub scouts would camp where the hay was stacked. Once we got rid of the sheep we outfitted it very roughly. It then served as a more usual welcome place that nicely complemented the camp grounds. It had a small kitchen for guests. Three hundred youngsters visited in 1965, mostly from the region around Paris. On Wednesdays during the school year, we welcomed students from a medico-technical institute with epileptic youngsters. We called them the "Wednesday Club," because they arrived around 3 p.m. and left after finishing a good meal that we prepared for them. The most able-bodied ones would complete a few tasks. Brother

François was assigned to the Sheepfold to better welcome them. It was necessary for them to meet with a brother, to feel acknowledged and loved in their dignity as handicapped brothers.

But the safety conditions of the place were far from up to par. There was only one faucet for running water, only two run-down bathrooms in the building across the way, a home-made wood-burning stove that drafted dangerously when its pipe was hot, and a wall that threatened to collapse at any time. We realized that in the nineteenth century some load-bearing beams had been removed to provide space as a shed for a locomotive used for a small train connecting the monastery to the nearby village. A notary friend who was interested in Brother François's initiatives with the youth sounded the alarm, and a visit of the local safety agency sealed the deal.

The inspector asked, "Is this where you welcome the groups?"

"Right here, madam. I never go looking for visitors. They come, and nothing discourages them. We don't do any advertising."

"The amenities are very basic."

"Maybe you could write me a note stating that it is no longer possible for us to welcome those who often have no other vacation. I'll show them the note, because I never have the courage to turn them down."

"Absolutely not! It is good for them to come to the abbey, but nothing here is within the norms of either safety or hygiene. You need concrete floors, you have to change the tables, paint the interior of the closets—"

"Yes, I see. Will you provide financing?"

Of course, there was no budget approved for this project. We had to either stop all our welcoming in the Sheepfold or at our own expense undertake a total overhaul of the building to bring it up to code. In September 1985 Brother François went away for a couple of days of solitude close to a monastery of Trappistine nuns in the Morbihan. The business council of the abbey had just informed him that we were not able to launch such a massive undertaking, because we didn't have the necessary funds. He had reservations booked for the following six months. What to do? Cancel everything? He could not resign himself to do it. The heart has its own reasons. He left with sadness to spend a week of nightly prayers to learn more, he said, about Jesus' night. A great adventure started then for him and for the abbey. He decided, staying in an outbuilding of the nuns' monastery, to remain awake all night, go to sleep at 8:45 a.m., and wake up again at 4 p.m. The mother abbess notified him that the following Wednesday they were welcoming a group of severely handicapped patients, who might very well be loud.

"That won't bother you?"

"On the contrary, it's a grace from God to pray close to the handicapped," said Brother François.

Hearing the noise and the shouting when the handicapped arrived, Brother François understood that they were severely mentally handicapped. He decided to go greet them at the end of their meal. He carried close to his chest in a special case, called a *custodium*, a consecrated host, the real presence of Christ. "Let's go together," he told the Lord. There were introductions and a sharing of desserts and coffee. At the end, the people in charge gave a sign to the handicapped that it was time to go to sleep. A young woman, twenty-five years old, got up and went to François, threw her arms around him and kissed him. Everyone was astonished. She had never let anyone hug her and had never kissed anyone or allowed herself to be kissed. That was a revelation for Brother François—the young woman had recognized the presence of Jesus that he was carrying.

"During the following night," he explained, "I thought about the Sheepfold that we were supposed to close. We could not do this, but we didn't have sufficient funds to complete the work necessary to continue welcoming groups. Our notary friend had mentioned creating a foundation that would allow a better separation of responsibilities and enable us to collect gifts and subsidies. I didn't know anything about it and had not paid any attention to it. But why not, if that could resolve the situation? I told Christ, the Good Shepherd, he who had welcomed the young handicapped woman, 'OK, Lord as far as this foundation goes, you will be its honorary president, and since I don't have the first dime, you will also be its treasurer. You will find the money. You're the only one who can touch hearts.' "

When Brother François came back to the monastery, he came rushing to my office and explained his idea to me.

"It won't cost the monastery anything," he added when he saw my skeptical silence.

They were already three: the president, the treasurer, and he, the witness. He had roughly estimated the cost at $100,000, not realizing that we would probably need three or four times as much. I finally let him try, because I too wanted us to continue this outreach.

"For the last thirty years thousands of young people have come to the monastery. Many of them became fathers of families," he told me. "I will talk to them about this Sheepfold that we want to save."

The heart was not the only thing. You also needed both feet on the ground. Brother François had that. He had been brought up in a village in Brittany, "in wooden clogs behind half a dozen cows."[2] He was the thirteenth of fourteen children; his name was Yvon. Once he finished elementary school, his only degree, carrying with him as his only religious baggage what he called a "faith based on tradition," at age sixteen he joined the ship-boy school in Loctudy. He traveled the world for seven years on the *Richelieu* and the *Jean Bart*, but still he was missing a "faith based on conviction."

In Toulon on August 23, 1955, a brushfire broke out close to a Carmelite monastery. Petty Officer First Class Yvon rushed and got there before the fire fighters. For him the most famous Carmel was not in Lisieux but in Toulon, and he often wondered what kind of life went on there. The fire spread, thick smoke billowing behind the large wall of the convent. Isn't this an opportunity

---

2. Brother Francois had previously told his story to Gilbert Ganne, *Ceux qui ont tout quitté* (Paris: Plon, 1977), 117–24.

to climb over it? "What luck!" he thought. No hesitation. "I will finally know what these old maids do hidden in their convent." Standing up on the wall, he jumped and found himself in front of three Carmelites. He especially noticed a very pretty one who looked about twenty years old. Their eyes met, and he was shaken up. "I knew then what a pure look was," he said. "That was my road to Damascus. Such a beautiful woman, who could have been married—at that very moment, I believed that God existed and that it was worth giving yourself up for him, as she did."

Not only had the nineteen-year-old sailor literally jumped over a wall, but he had spiritually hit another wall. He had to give his answer. Years before he had been attracted by God and the idea of giving himself up for him had crossed his mind, but that would be for later on—maybe when he retired! In the meantime, he focused his life on marriage, convinced that he was meant to have a wife and children. When he was already engaged, he discovered La Trappe. God's call was getting clearer. He talked about it to his fiancée and told her one day that he wanted to leave the navy and enter La Trappe. She generously agreed to step aside and give him his freedom, although not without some suffering. He "shook up" God, you might say, hoping that he would make his will clearer: "I don't know if you are calling me to enter La Trappe," he said in his prayers, "but if you haven't done so yet, please hurry up, because I am going there." He became Brother François.

The jovial mindset of the new monk, prone to jokes, led him one day to accuse himself of having trapped a bat in a brother's locker, held by a cord tied to its foot. All the novices burst out laughing when they saw it. He quickly understood that the monastery was inhabited by men and not by angels, and that those always more or less kept their own qualities and faults. He deduced from this fact that contemplation was not limited to monks but was open to all, although monks might be in a privileged position.

His welcoming of the youngsters to the dormitory with hay, which had remained a delight for them for twenty years, could only continue if we complied with the norms of security and hygiene. To get to that point, we needed to set up a foundation that would take care of the undertaking and select in addition to the honorary president an earthly president. Paul Wargny, a high-school chaplain in Paris who had taken advantage of our Sheep-fold for his students, accepted our proposal that he be president. Our notary friend drafted the documents, and five days later the project saw the light. On October 20, 1985, we received the first gift of $5,000. An architect from Versailles, M. Tayeau, designed the plans for the restoration for no reimbursement, and another architect from L'Aigle, M. Masson, supervised the work. Many construction companies charged us discounted prices, while others made gifts, sometimes in kind, like a hundred gallons of paint and a ton and a half of cement. Brother François kept for himself the honor and pleasure of driving the excavator for the foundation, and the Apprentice Orphans of Auteuil installed all the bathroom fittings. The Ministry of Sports and Youth granted a subsidy, and the Christian Office for the Handicapped in par-ticular encouraged us by sending a substantial check of $10,000 in full payment for the foundation!

"The day we received that large amount," said Brother Fran-çois, "I also received a gift of $5 from an unknown donor. They both had the same weight of love. The $5 was the widow's mite. I wept with joy. Nothing could have been realized without the support of the seven hundred donors, often of small means, but very motivated, who joined the foundation."

The costs kept increasing, but the money never dried up, and the foundation was never at risk. By May 23, 1987, the day of the official opening, when all the authorities were present, includ-ing the county chairman, the congressman, the senator, and the mayor, the last invoice had been paid. The joy of all the mentally and physically handicapped people erased all our previous con-cerns, but so did the joy of the young people full of health who visited the Sheepfold and the camp grounds, sometimes for only one day. By 1990, six thousand young people had already visited our facilities. The Sheepfold is a successful business, which stays booked sometimes as far as a year in advance, and more often than not we need to turn guests back with a heavy heart because we are running out of space.

One of the monks who had known Brother François for more than thirty years and who couldn't be told tales, told him when he saw the donations coming in, "It is strange that a little guy like you was able to get millions."

And another: "You do everything backwards; nothing should have worked out, and look, it is a success. I can't understand this."

"But I had nothing to do with all this. I am a 'nothing in Everything.' God chose himself a nobody, as he usually does, and his secret for making it work out is that he surrounds that nobody with competent people. When you know me, you have to acknowledge: it is only that, François. But this gives courage to dare to undertake deeds without being paralyzed by thinking that such things are reserved for the powerful and perfect people of this world. You need to make the distinction between a deed for God, where our will prevails, and a deed of God, where the invisible is in charge of the essence."

The welcome at the abbey is not limited to the Sheepfold. We also have a guesthouse, like any other monastery, where the atmosphere is totally different, for the adults wanting to immerse themselves in permanent silence or in a more intense solitude. The term *guesthouse* can be misleading. It is not an inn where you spend the night, as in a hotel, but a place where you can spend a couple of days to meditate, reflect, or pray—or at least where you can try to communicate with an inner presence and in any event be face to face with transcendence.

"I never felt so alone in my life," said a student, who wanted to have the experience. "You are alone with yourself and with an almost palpable absolute."

Meals are taken in silence, and the guests try to avoid disturbing the monastic peace in any way. They participate in the community's Divine Offices, and they may ask if it is possible to meet with a monk to help them in their spiritual journey. Some have the impression of diving all of a sudden into a brand new universe. The anonymity of everyone who desires it is respected. The surrounding climate is not conducive to asking indiscreet questions about people's social backgrounds or private lives. Some retreatants spend a week with us without speaking more than a few words.

There is no required daily rate, but each guest pays what he or she can or wants. Overall, we break even as long as we don't consider any salary for the brothers who work in the guesthouse or any of the maintenance costs. Some communities would accept a financial deficit, even though their facilities are not devoid of all comfort, simply to enable everyone, even the poorest guests, to take advantage of this spiritual service. According to Pope Paul VI,[3] it is an essential service rendered to the Church. One can certainly wonder whether the service of listening or giving a space for dialogue to Christian people or to people involved in worldly responsibilities should constitute an employment worthy of a living wage. In this way the monks would be compensated by those who are benefiting from their competence rather than by the manual labor of other brothers, and they would probably be more available. An African bishop observed to the monks in his diocese, "Instead of spending all your time raising chickens, help the people to pray! That would be more useful."

To tell the truth, would the Africans be ready to pay them enough to exempt them from raising the chickens? That would probably bring on a conceptual change that might be detrimental. We would have to train personnel in spiritual listening and support, and that would probably lead our guesthouses to be

---

3. When he talked to the abbots gathered in their general chapter in May 1977, the pope told them, "without renouncing the silence, the prayer, and the sacrifice in your life, you can, you must, accommodate contacts for those seeking an environment of retreat, a spiritual pause: priests, religious, lay people, adults, and youngsters. The hospitality that you offer them generously is an essential service that you render to the Church today and that is happily sought after."

reserved for people who could afford it. Moreover, should we consider our spiritual welcome as an ordinary source of income? Some communities might perhaps consider it, but perhaps not all of them. The solitude and silence required by the contemplative life limit the type of welcome we can give, even if that welcome is essential, and material work remains an element that we cannot neglect. Our Constitutions refer to "the opportunity of sharing in the divine work of creation and restoration, and of following in the footsteps of Jesus Christ. This hard and redeeming work is a means of providing a livelihood for the brothers and for other people, especially the poor. It expresses solidarity with all workers. Moreover, work is an occasion for a fruitful asceticism that fosters personal development and maturity. It promotes health of mind and body and contributes greatly to the unity of the whole community" (Const 26). "Pray and work!" *Ora et Labora*, as the Benedictine motto reads.

Today's retreatants are no longer as homogeneous as they were forty years ago. Most of them then were Catholics, seeking to deepen their faith in a favorable environment. Of course, such people still make up the majority of our guests. We also welcome, often without knowing it, people who are searching, doubting, or unaware of where they are, or who do not know what to think of Christianity or of religion in general, and sometimes do not think anything at all about them. They may have encountered family or professional problems, or they may be torn or totally lost, and the practice of faith does not concern them anymore. Sometimes we need to acknowledge that the environment of contemplation that we need to maintain is not always what is needed for those whom life has profoundly wounded. We are not equipped to help them effectively, as other more professional centers are.

I think that the people who visit us also bring something to us, so that communication is not a one-way street, even if it is limited because of our claustration. Sometimes the human qualities present in our guests are so deep that the guest masters, feeling enriched, can in turn have our whole community benefit from it. We have to take seriously those who take us seriously, even if this manifests itself as criticism. Sometimes our guests hold a variety of responsibilities in the world, and especially in the church of France. I have invited quite a few to speak to our community about their concerns. This practice enables us to remain abreast of what is going on around us, sometimes first hand. When at the end of the year we look back at those who spoke to us, we can see that the list is long and varied, and those who don't know us very well are surprised when they learn about this. First among these guests are the bishops who come to spend a couple of days of reflection among us or to participate in organized retreats for the priests of their diocese. When he was our neighbor, Mgr. Gaillot was our guest quite a few times.[4]

Our Divine Offices are often an opportunity for people who have distanced themselves from the Christian faith to come back or to meditate on its value. They generally appreciate the sobriety and beauty of these services. But what is real prayer? There are thousands of forms of prayer, and only God can see into the depths of our hearts. At Cîteaux the church is accessible from the outside at all hours of the day. Father Placide was our sacristan for thirty-six years. He said with humor that "it must be that I was made for that function, since before me there was a waltz of sacristans." He told the story about one day when he saw a couple entering the empty church. As he was lining up the chairs, they knelt down in front of the tabernacle. The man took some pictures of the stained glass and the architecture and then came back and sat next to his wife. They both read from a psalter. For half an hour they prayed without paying attention to the sacristan who was cleaning up.

---

4. {Jacques Gaillot (1935–): a French priest who became bishop of Evreux in 1982. His many controversial positions on social and political issues earned him first the rebuke and then the censure of the French Bishops' Conference. In 1995 Pope John Paul II demoted him because of his repeated extreme stands contrary to the Church's doctrines. His removal from the diocese of Évreux created quite a stir in the Church in France.}

Another day, Father Placide was using the vacuum cleaner when he saw a young woman sitting down with her flute and a score in a corner that he hadn't cleaned yet. "She will understand," he thought, "that I am coming with the vacuum." Since she was not moving, he stopped the vacuum and spoke a couple of words to her. She answered in German. They started conversing in German, a language he had learned while he was a prisoner of war. The young woman stood up and went to a side chapel along the nave where there was a kneeler and a chair close to the tabernacle. She put down the score, sat down, and continued to play the flute.

These were very simple stories of prayer that led Father Placide to say that one of the great graces in his life had been to watch other people in prayer. He often walked through the church between the hours of community celebrations of the Divine Office. He noticed other monks who took advantage of a free moment to pray in a corner in a silent and hidden encounter with God. "I never saw a miracle, but I have seen brothers pray, and for me that is one," he said. "I have never seen a canonized saint, but all these prayers delved into the essence of sainthood."

The conditions of welcome changed in the 1950s, especially after Vatican Council II. Although monasteries had never ceased to welcome those who wanted to spend a few days of reflection in the guesthouse, our churches then were generally not open to the public during the celebrations, and the monastic welcome was limited to men. Our mothers, sisters, and women friends were not allowed to participate in our celebrations in our churches, not even in vows and ordinations. I already mentioned that La Trappe only opened its doors more widely after May 1976. It was one of the last three abbeys in France to do so. Most other monasteries had made that decision a decade earlier.

The change required some modification of our practices of separation from the outside world. The principle was not modified, but the way it was implemented changed. At that time, it became the superior's responsibility to determine which premises would be accessible to all and which ones would be accessible only to the monks, and even these limitations could be modified in particular cases. All this change gave our monasteries a more welcoming and less closed-in aspect.

In addition, the resulting influx of tourists required adaptations at the level of the first welcome in a zone that we call the porter's area. Often it was no longer the area of the porter's lodge, where a brother sat ready to open the door for anyone who had the right to enter. A larger space needed to be created to meet a first expectation. We offered an audio-visual presentation about a monk's life. There might also be an exhibit, a religious bookstore, or a shop with souvenirs or items produced by the monks or the nuns, all open to passersby to acquaint them with the activities of the monastery. The economic aspect of these monastery shops is real and normal, but that is not all, for there is also a certain welcome that takes place there.

To be complete, let us add that some monasteries, especially those for men, have some rooms for welcoming homeless people under certain conditions. La Trappe has set up three rooms with bathrooms for that purpose in a building facing the monastery. They are governed by a set of rules: usually people can spend only one day and one night a month there. We are one of the three places in the county that welcome the most homeless people. We remain in contact with Catholic Help. Of course, it is hard to avoid all professional beggars who are doing their "Tour de France" of all the French monasteries. It is hard to avoid any and all scams, but we console ourselves by saying that after all you don't get punished for trying to do a good deed even if it is a small one. The monastery has neither the ability nor the mission to wipe out all the misery in the world.

The guesthouses and the porter's lodge are privileged places for our contacts with the outside world, the vestibule where monks and worldly guests meet, as are the work and economic activities. They insert us into a certain geopolitical landscape, one could say, and they are an opportunity for us to interact with people on the outside. We also need to add our good relations with our neighbors and friends. In short, we do not live in total isolation, as some might think.

The economy of a monastery may sometimes look like a mystery, but there is nothing obscure or inappropriate about it. Traditionally, the income necessary for us to live came first and foremost from our labor. Agriculture and cattle raising were the two main sources of subsistence because of our monasteries' isolated and rural nature. Back then we had enough bodies to work in the fields, but we had also quite a few mouths to feed; those facts led to the rational development of farms that were well managed and sometimes envied. Agriculture meant large investments in material, and the size of our communities enabled us to achieve this more easily than small farmers. Nevertheless, we had our own constraints because of the monastic life. Prayer and spiritual activities took a substantial part of our day and allowed us generally only about five hours of work a day, except for some who worked longer hours and did not participate in the mid-morning prayer. Our expenses were less in certain areas, like vacations, entertainment, and other things of that type. Nevertheless, we did have special items in our budget, like the formation of the younger brothers, alms, and the welcome center, which was not always cost effective if you considered the expenses it incurred. We were, of course, subject to various taxes on the income from our sales and on our payroll benefits. The buildings, which were generally large, brought with them expenses for maintenance, repairs, and costly improvements. All this led us to look for ways to make our labor profitable. So for years now, monasteries have had small agro-food businesses that enable us to sell our processed products.

In France many monasteries in the nineteenth century created dairies of various sizes producing cheese, taking advantage of the know-how of the monks of Port Salut, who developed the famous cheese that bears the name of their monastery, although it is no longer produced by them. Some, like Cîteaux or Timadeuc, only processed what their own stable produced. Others, like

Tamié and Mont-des-Cats, collected the milk from the neighboring farms, while still others got their supply from cooperatives or regional dairies. La Trappe started with fresh products like yogurts, whipped cream, cream cheese, and caramelized milk-based desserts with the brand name of *Regal* and *Douceur* of La Trappe. There were other types of processing or production: cookies, chocolate, candies, fruit jelly, jams, syrup, and even liquor. The Belgian monasteries are famous for their unequaled Trappist beer! Other things that had nothing in common with agriculture were sometimes produced by the monasteries, mostly for religious use, such as host bread, candles, or religious images.

It was clear that from an economic point of view we were dependent on the evolution of the world surrounding us. We did not escape the various agricultural crises of the last fifty years. We have, like other farms, left some of our land uncultivated because of milk quotas, and we have sustained losses because of international crises. Agriculture is a decreasing part of our necessary income. For a number of monasteries, it is a money-losing proposition, but we accept paying the price to protect our environment for the sake of our monastic life. Sometimes we find ourselves at a crossroads. That is why at La Trappe we had to stop our dairy farming in 1987.

That decision became a media event, against our own will. When the brother in charge of our farm was taking part in a meeting of farmers, he was talking freely with his neighbor, without suspecting him to be a journalist. The latter hastened to communicate our news to the *Agence France-Presse*, which published it. We were overwhelmed with requests for interviews and news reports. We decided to ignore all the requests coming from television channels. But the reporters from *Antenne 2* (now *France 2*) tried to force their way in by filming over the wall of the abbey and interviewing our neighbors. When we became aware of this activity, I agreed that one of the brothers would meet with them, thinking that we were in a better position than our friendly neighbors to provide good explanations. The event was announced on the 8 p.m. nightly news one evening in August, resulting in about two thousand people showing up at the auction of our cows, not all of whom were buyers, although our cows were beautiful. Our herd of Normandy cows was famous. It was very sought after, and we had to give it up, not because of a lack of technical know-how or quality. To reach a satisfactory productivity one needs certain qualifications and good intuition.

The brother in charge of our farming certainly possessed all these qualities, and his competence was well recognized. Not only had he been awarded the Order of Agricultural Merit, but he was also for a time a member of the board of directors of a neighboring artificial insemination center. He was sometimes called to be a member of a jury. Once he was asked to be an arbitrator in Argentina, but we declined that invitation. Now that he had reached sixty-five years of age, it was getting difficult to find him a worthy successor. More often than not, our young people come from the city rather than from the farming world, because the rural section of our population has decreased, even though it remains essential to the survival of our nation.

But especially, the hours of work in the stable conflicted with the proper balance of our monastic day. We like to spend the first hours of the day in prayer and *lectio divina*, meditation on the holy Scriptures, and the reading of spiritual authors. Our work day rarely starts before 8 a.m., and that is way too late for the first milking. Years ago, there was no problem, because we had lay brothers, who left for work early in the morning while the choir monks went to prayers. But now the evolution of the community made it difficult for us to continue on that path. Moreover, European Union milk quotas[5] caused difficulty for us and damaged the profitability of our enterprise, so we had a change of heart. We didn't abandon raising cattle, but we limited ourselves to

5. {From 1984 until 2015 the European Union (EU) applied a quota on milk production with the goal of preventing an overproduction resulting from milk price supports. This price support was subject to objection, as it distorted global trade. In the 1990s, the World Trade Organization urged the EU to abolish its system of price support for the dairy industry.}

fattening the cows for their meat, giving up raising milk cows and the production of milk. By not requesting governmental compensation for closing down our dairy, we succeeded in keeping the freed-up quotas in our county, thereby helping some young farmers in the region.

But we had to compensate for our loss of income by developing other activities in our workshops. First, we continued the production of fresh milk products from milk we now purchased. We thought we could grow that sector, like the production of fruit paste, and start the making of religious artifacts. Manufacturing was a good idea, but to what end if the sales were lacking? Questions about marketing monastic products were getting more and more pressing. The old wholesalers were now in competition with co-ops working with supermarkets, and our handmade products, even if they were of well-recognized quality, did not enable us to get low production costs. That was a handicap. It was also not appropriate for monks to travel all over the country to drum up business for their products with retailers.

The best place to sell our products is still at the entrance to our monastery. The public visiting us is motivated differently there than when shopping at a supermarket. It is ready to accept a higher price for quality products and to help the monks by buying those items. It has also become more and more necessary for the monasteries to help each other. It may be insufficient to sell solely in the monastery shop, especially if the monastery is located away from the main roads and does not receive many visitors. Also, a wider range of products and better-filled shelves increase the gross revenue and enable us to cover our overhead better. Cooperating with other monasteries also offers work to the monks, because it requires us to communicate with them, receive their packages, label them correctly—we now have bar codes—stock them on the shelves, clean the premises, insure a presence at the cash register, and keep the accounts.

In short, a store needs to be managed, and that takes time. This work is remunerated with the normal commercial margin taken on the merchandise and is added to the income derived from the workshops, but they only make money if the products are in fact sold. If we had outside workers to run the store instead of our monks, as some suggest, that would provide the workers with a living wage, perhaps, but it would not bring any income to the monasteries, because the profit margin is almost nothing. We need to check the prices closely, even if they cannot be as low as the merchandise sold in the supermarkets. Our stores contribute to our survival at the same time as they offer a welcome to the tourists who come by.

This evolution was not unique to La Trappe. For a dozen years before us, other monasteries had done the same thing and had even shown us the way. At La Trappe, in addition to our own products, we market products from a good twenty other monasteries. Like other monasteries, we have also opened a bookstore selling religious books and books of local interest. This is a real service to those who visit us, as well as for the religious publishing industry in France. It adds a spiritual influence beyond our food products, even though the profitability of a bookstore is lower than that of a gift shop. Some discouraged us from adding books, saying that people did not read any more, but experience has proved them wrong. The Bible section is a privileged one.

For a number of years now, lay people have gotten organized to help the monasteries, especially the more isolated and destitute ones, those of the Carmelites and the Poor Clares, in organizing their work and marketing their products. They created an association to aid the work of the monasteries (ATC) and a limited liability company called Monastic Artisans, which gives legal support to stores opened in six large cities in France—Paris, Lyon, Marseille, Lille, Toulouse, and Rennes—where certain monastic products are sold. Some of those stores have started selling by mail order.

The quality of the monastic products is well recognized, as I said before. Isn't that why some of the advertising emphasizes the religious aspect? Some producers are attempting to suggest a monastic reference in their names and logos, but that risks confusing the consumer and trivializing the products that have a real monastic origin. Our cheese makers were the first to worry about this. It is true that a consumer who sees a fat monk on a Camembert cheese box might imagine that it does not really come from a monastery. We have a sense of humor, but no desire to be ridiculous by portraying ourselves like this—but sometimes we need to react through legal proceedings. That is why we filed for a trademark showing the monastic origin of our products and set up an association to promote our mark, *Monastic,* and protect it. It is represented by a logo affixed to the packaging. This association, which includes most monastic communities in France, was soon extended to all of Europe. It is also a support group for all of us for questions related to the economic realities of our monasteries, as well as for ethical, legal, administrative, financial, tax, and commercial questions.

Questions like these are becoming more and more complex, so we sometimes have to call on experts. For a long time, the treasurers and accountants of our communities have regularly met to review questions and share concerns. They share their financial reports, and all take the opportunity to look at their neighbors' numbers to detect any inconsistency before it grows and produces unintended consequences. The individual cheese makers also organized in order to know each other better, to cooperate, and to keep from inadvertently competing with each other. We do not hesitate to send our monks and nuns in charge of material responsibilities to attend seminars or continuing education sessions.

Some of my cousins teased me sometimes by saying that I was the only CEO in the family. In a sense I was, since the abbot has the ultimate responsibility for the whole monastery; nothing important could be undertaken without my consent, approval, or decision. This meant that I had to acquire some formation in economics, be able to read balance sheets, and follow experts' discussions. But my role was first and foremost spiritual, and I was always very diligently assisted with the temporal administration and did not micromanage. Other monks were more qualified than I was on many subjects. In that sense I ignored quite a few aspects of the enterprise for which I was responsible—a strange CEO! But our commercial enterprise was not the most important thing, even if it touched on a variety of sectors—they remained commensurate with the lifeblood of our community. Actually, we had about ten monks paid for by these activities. This was what we called for tax purposes "the maintenance value" of the community generated by its labor. To this we can add the social security payments to our elders after they turn sixty or sixty-five years old, and some gifts, offered at Mass or by those welcomed to the guesthouse.

Everything has been getting more complicated, as I mentioned. The accounting and everything else have required more thorough analysis, and we are subject to stricter and stricter controls. But on the other hand, these complications bring an element of security. In the past, before World War II, the economy of a monastery was managed by a single man, sometimes even the abbot himself, who was not surrounded by real advisers. Some were careless or of limited competence, and they brought their communities to bankruptcy or fell victim to swindlers. Actually, we act in concert with others, in committees with rather strict controls, by involving the whole community so that the risk of slipping is limited. The Order also exercises a certain supervision and subjects certain extraordinary expenses to prior approval, when for example we need to borrow money or to lower the value of the assets. Sometimes we have to turn to the Holy See when these expenses exceed certain levels.

Our monasteries may look like big enterprises, handling large sums of money and not giving the testimony of poverty that is expected of them. The size of our communities and the grandeur of the buildings that we have inherited naturally bring with them a certain volume of business that is not representative of real wealth. Nevertheless, we are no longer in the time when we needed to worry about the brothers coming into the refectory and not finding much to put on their plates. We are not the poorest in the region, and we are not deliberately looking to be so. The result may be a shortcoming in our testimony of poverty, yes, and this result may worry us, but only up to a certain point. Our essential role, in fact, is to lead a contemplative life while meeting our own needs. Our role is not, as in certain other religious families, to share the conditions of the poorest. Some monastics offer this testimony in the orders that we call *mendicant*, the sons and daughters of Saint Francis and Saint Dominic. Their begging no longer takes the form it did in earlier years, which at least for the Franciscans looked very much like that of homeless people, with added piety.

The same thing is also the case for more recent communities, like the Little Brothers of Jesus of Father de Foucauld,[6] who settle in very poor neighborhoods. These religious and other lay people perceptively realize "the preferential option for the poor" desired by the Church in faithfulness to the Gospel. But the charisms and the goals pursued differ among the orders or religious institutions. Our Benedictine tradition is based upon a community life in solitude, organized around prayer and ensuring "the humble and noble service of the Divine Majesty."[7] This tradition supposes a certain material security, time, and relative autonomy.

This does not contradict the fact that living simply is a characteristic of the religious and monastic life that we cannot brush aside by distinguishing between, for example, personal poverty and community poverty. A real poverty does exist—nobody denies that—at the level of each person in the use that he or she makes of the goods of the monastery. That person does not

6. {The Little Brothers of Jesus is a congregation founded in 1933, whose mission is to be among the people and in the heart of the masses, to be with God. It is inspired by the life and writings of Blessed Charles de Foucauld. The founders included Louis Massignon, a scholar of Islam and a contemporary of Foucauld. Officially recognized by the Holy See in 1968, the congregation now has over 250 brothers and priests with members living in small communities (http:www.jesuscaritas.info/jcd/node/18).}

7. Vatican II, *Perfectae Caritatis*, n. 2, taken from our Constitutions. {http://www.vatican.va/archive/hist_councils/ii_vatican_council/documents/vat-ii_decree_19651028_perfectae-caritatis_en.html.}

choose what to use but merely receives it from the community
through the brothers or sisters in charge. Sometimes one needs
to ask permission or report about what one has spent or used.
In my monastic youth one had to show to the whole community entering the refectory any object that he had broken. That
meant that we did not own that object and that we were not
supposed to use it as if we owned it. As the Rule put it, "All
things should be the common possession of all, as it is written,
so that no one presumes to call anything his own" (RB 33.6). In
that sense, monks should not get attached to their things. They
need to live with a free heart. They are not looking for the best,
and they know how to act economically. Luxury is not allowed;
neither is the superfluous.

This practice necessarily has a communal dimension. We do
not live surrounded by valuable furniture. Our Constitutions are
clear about this: "The brothers' lifestyle is to be plain and frugal.
Everything in the household of God should be appropriate to
monastic life and avoid excess so that its very simplicity can be
instructive for all. This is to be clearly apparent in buildings and
their furnishings, in food and clothing and even in the celebration
of the liturgy" (Const 27). Personal poverty is part of a community framework that is also poor. The twelfth-century founders
of Cîteaux were the sons of a spiritual movement rooted in the
traditions of the Desert Fathers, which insisted on poverty. They
faced a traditional monasticism, probably more settled within the
feudal system. They wanted to be "poor with the poor Christ."
An account from that time says about them that "they preferred
being busy with heavenly exercises to being involved in temporal
affairs. Soon, in their love for virtue, they started to meditate on
the fertility of poverty that is grounded in manly characteristics
[*qui trempe des caractères virils*]."[8]

---

8. Petit Exorde, XV, 9. Exorde de Cîteaux.I.3–4 (*de paupertate fœcunda vi-*
rorum). {*Exordium Parvum, XV*, in *Narrative and Legislative Texts from Early*
Cîteaux, ed. Chrysogonus Waddell (*Cîteaux: Commentarii cistercienses*, 1999),
434–35; *Exordium Cistercii, I*, in Waddell, *Narrative and Legislative Texts*, 400.}

But is this sufficient? In a society like ours, we must wonder how we should live real poverty at the level of our communal institutions. In truth, what do you call poverty? There is a poverty that we need to fight, because it is a wrong. Should we share it as a community with those who suffer from it, to show our support and our solidarity? Maybe. But, as I said before, this is not our primary monastic vocation, even if our work "demonstrates our solidarity with all workers" (Const C.26). There is, on the other hand, a poverty that we need to embrace: the evangelical poverty that requires that we give priority to others before ourselves, that we don't look first for profit, but "seek first his kingdom and righteousness" (Matt 6:33), so that we can help free of charge and promote the values of solidarity, loyalty, and honesty.

"How can we explain the religious search for what is priceless in an economy subjected to the law of the market?" wondered Cardinal Etchegaray.[9] "There is no place for a gratuitous act in a mercantile society; evangelical poverty seems to be a luxury or a mockery."[10] In that sense, of course, our monasteries have to be poor and set the example of a certain style of behavior that forbids any breach of economic, social, or tax laws. They also have to act in solidarity by participating in charitable actions by giving alms and gifts.

It is not easy to show ourselves as being deliberately generous. The best service is not always to blindly send a check to whoever asks us. The rules developed by Secours Catholique should inspire us, but we are not always able to implement them, and sometimes we prefer to bring our financial contribution to Secours Catholique itself and direct the person in need who contacted us to that service.

9. {Roger Etchegaray (1922–) was the French archbishop of Marseilles from 1970 to 1985. Pope John Paul II elevated him to cardinal in 1979. He held different prominent positions in the Holy See, e.g., president of the Pontifical Council *Cor Unum* (1984–1995) and president of the Pontifical Council for Justice and Peace (1984–1998).}

10. Communication at the October 1994 Synod in Rome, *Osservatore Romano*, weekly edition in French, 22 (1994).

Sometimes people are not aware of the procedures or not capable of taking action to obtain the legal or social help to which they are entitled. The greatest charity is to help that person do that.

A father abbot had given instruction to a community settled in the Third World in the midst of misery more widespread and more striking than anything in our region. "Help," he said, "must be normally temporary and should not lock people up in dependency or make them incapable of meeting their own needs. Help the poor to take charge of each other's needs and collectively." He added, "This should not make us give up, but force us to set the record straight: A monastery is not a lucrative institution or an aid to development, as it is also not a charitable center or health care provider. In the Church there is another charism that needs to be put forward. To acknowledge our incapacity to meet the needs of the very poor when we have honestly and generously done what is in our power is also to recognize and acknowledge the sin of our human community, which has created such inequalities among humans."[11]

Nevertheless, is the size of our buildings, of our means of production, even for certain monasteries their capital, contrary to this poverty that we need to embrace? This question is raised for each of our communities, while the answers may not be evident in each case or in the details.

In any case, the real poverty is insecurity. Our contemporaries bear the brunt with regard to employment, except for government employees. It affects the young people at the end of their training when they reach what is called the job market. It becomes dramatic for the unemployed who reach the end of their benefits. At that level our own insecurity takes a particular form that is not less real. Of course, we monks do not run the risk of unemployment or being cast out from society. But we do not control the flux of our personnel, and that fact can be very trying and lead to a real situation of insecurity, at least for our managers.

---

11. Denis Huerre, "Moines et pauvreté aujourd'hui," *Collectanea cisterciensia* 46 (1984): 186–96.

Employers hire in accordance with recognized needs; personnel managers choose the people who have the necessary abilities. Of course, they do not always find what they look for and are limited by certain social constraints, especially if they try to eliminate some positions. But abbots and abbesses do not hire novices in accordance with the community's economic needs. In the monastic life, there are only volunteers: "If you want, says Christ" (Matt 19:21). If superiors exercise careful discernment among those who enter, their criteria are totally different from those that human resource managers use.

Monastic criteria are essentially spiritual and psychological, as, referring to the Rule of Saint Benedict, our Constitutions indicate when they call for discerning "whether the novice has grown spiritually through his participation in monastic life. If he truly seeks God, is zealous for the Work of God, obedience and humiliations and is suited to living correctly, in solitude and silence, the community relationships that constitute Cistercian life in the Order" (Const 51). The community might find itself with three lumberjacks but lack electricians or vice versa. We must do with what we have and those we don't have!

Most of our communities suffer from a lack of vocations, a lack that adds to their difficulty. Sometimes it becomes difficult to find work that fits each member and to fill the variety of positions or responsibilities that good management would require. Certain brothers in charge tell me sometimes, "I am the only one who can do this or that; this is not prudent. We need to have another brother who is informed and trained. He needs to assist me so that he will be able to take over later." Yes—but I do not have these other "spare parts" at our disposal. There lies our real insecurity, and we need to rely on our confidence in Divine Providence. "Therefore do not be anxious about tomorrow, for tomorrow will take care of itself. Let the day's own trouble be sufficient for the day" (Matt 6:34).

Chapter Fourteen

God's Violin

At twenty-year-old young man entered Cîteaux, the mother house of our Order, on January 8, 1967, while I was novice master at Mont-des-Cats. Twenty-six years later, during the few months I was the superior *ad nutum* of Cîteaux, under circumstances I already described, I appointed him prior, and later he was elected abbot. Through the hierarchic relations among monasteries he then became the "father immediate," as we call it, of La Trappe, where I was then the abbot. His story, which he has allowed me to tell, accurately reflects in a vivid manner what I felt myself.

On that January 8 the weather was horrible. Olivier Quenardel was driving to Cîteaux, about fifteen miles from Dijon, passing through woods and fields covered by icy snow. His parents and a friend who was a priest went with him. The road was dangerous and the sky very low. "I was happy for that horrible weather," his father told him later. "Because I was driving I had to pay attention to the road and hold on to the steering wheel. The icy roads prevented me from thinking. It was providential, because I was devastated."

Olivier's parents had given him a sophisticated education and hadn't envisioned the asceticism and penance of the monastic life for him. They consented to it when he told them of his choice, but the pain remained acute at the time of that departure. The choice of almost all monks and nuns imposes a trial on their parents, as I mentioned earlier, but perhaps this was better than other less honorable trials.

Upon his return from the war and the prisoner-of-war camps, Olivier's father found his large farm, five hundred acres of rich soil in the Soissons and Laon area, totally stripped by the Germans, who had transformed it into an air base. "I don't know how my parents did it from then on," said Olivier, "but they gave my two brothers, my sister, and me a taste for simple joys and a profound family life in which we were happy. It was no longer the easy life that my father had known and that my mother had also known in her family before her marriage, but we were singing the whole time. Through the faith that they passed on to me and that they lived intensely, they were my first prophets."

The grandfather on Olivier's mother's side had founded a large company that sold religious objects, Saudinas-Ritouret, which occupied the building in Paris where later the publishing company Robert Laffont would locate, 6 Place St. Sulpice, before its transfer in 1993 to 24 Avenue Marceau. Having a law degree, his grandfather was a presiding judge at the Commercial Court of Paris and worked with his sons in the company. Olivier used to go up to the upper floor, at the corner of the square where pigeons swirled about, to greet his grandfather and the employees. "We took these trips twice a year with my parents. We would go to Saint Sulpice Church in Paris, close to the large fountain."

Olivier went to a boarding school in Reims run by the Jesuits. When he was about fifteen years old, when he hadn't yet made any decisions, his father said, "What you're missing are the failures. Everything is going too well for you. Failure is an important part of the life of a man. You need to fail somewhere to really win. If I had not experienced failure, what would my life have been? I would not really have had an inner life. It would not have stretched very far."

Of all that his father told him, these words probably made the most lasting impression on Olivier, but he took them in at that moment without paying too much attention to them. His father was a tough but also contemplative farmer, who would walk around his fields twice a day simply to watch a beet grow, or a wheat shoot or a sunflower. He taught his children to admire creation. One day, he told them that to ensure their educations he would sell Arx-en-Ciel, Oracle, and Rose d'Avril, his three race horses, which he kept as the sole memory of his pre-war equestrian competitions. Walking by these empty stalls, the young Olivier pondered his father's acts in giving up the horses that he loved for the sake of his family's well-being.

Now he had to endure more sorrow for the plans he had had for his son when he drove him to Cîteaux, knowing that once Olivier was behind these walls he wouldn't see him but once a year for three days, with very limited mail exchanges. This would go on until his last breath. An atmosphere of both prayer and endurance pervaded the car on the icy roads in this gray, cold weather.

"How is he going to live like that all his life?" wondered his mother and father.

"How will I be able to live like that forever?" the son also wondered silently. He didn't know how he would be able to stay in the same place without ever going out. He felt it with apprehension. Two years later, at the end of his novitiate, his anxiety disappeared completely while listening to a reading at Mass: It is a matter of confidence in God. Nothing else, he told himself. It is a test of confidence.

Ten years passed. In February, when Olivier, who had by now taken his perpetual vows, saw the first snowdrop coming back under the brambles close to the creek in the monastery park, he thought: "That's it! We're good until November. The flowers will come up in succession." He would sometimes be able to leave his work table in the reading room to read and meditate among the colors and the scents. He would walk under the white and then pink chestnut trees, and in the cemetery the tulips would follow daffodils and precede carnations. From the first petals of spring on to the fleur-de-lis and the cuckoo, to the anemones and to the violets, the plants followed each other. The largest tulip tree in the park, with an enormous trunk, planted there before the Revolution, raised its branches where in June small flowers grew, with red hearts and green rims that looked like tulips. He remembered Psalm 96: "Let the field exult, and everything in it! Then shall the trees of the wood sing for joy!" (Ps 96:12). Other psalms invite all creatures to marvel at God and to thank him: "Frost and cold, bless the Lord. Everything growing from the earth, bless the Lord. . . . Praise and exalt him above all forever," as the Canticle of Daniel says (Sg Three 51-77). In it Daniel invites all creation to join in the praise of God, and in so doing becomes "the priest of the creation."

Brother Olivier came back over and over to the nature that he loved. Around 1976 he was meditating while walking in the park. He rethought his whole life in one image, or rather one symbol, that enlightened him better than other events that had already brought him the light.

Music occupied a central place in his existence. He had learned to play the violin, and before his departure for the monastery he had looked a last time at his instrument and bow, telling himself that he would never touch them again. Since then he had sometimes thought about it, measured the sacrifice, and consented to give himself totally to God. While walking in the park, his thoughts led him first to Moses and then to Saint Peter—nothing surprising for a monk.

"All of a sudden I knew where I stood," he told me later:

> Moses was keeping the herds in the Sinai desert when he saw the bush that was burning without being consumed. What was the connection with my story? Moses walked around and abandoned his herd to see what was going on. There he got his call: "Moses! Moses! Put off your shoes from your feet, for this place on which you are standing is holy ground" [Exod 3:5]. Hearing this mysterious voice, he left his animals to become the shepherd of the people of Israel. He left his staff to be the pastor who would meet with the pharaoh. A similar event took place in the New Testa-

ment. This time it was Peter who was involved. He was throwing his nets in the Sea of Tiberias with his brother Andrew when Jesus called them. A little later he called James and John, who were arranging their nets in another boat with their father. Jesus told them, "I'll make of you fishers of men" [Matt 4:19; Mark 1:17]. And the four of them followed him to throw another net to the world.

What I had perceived about myself and about God's views of me now took on a new light. The violin that I had left was like Peter's nets and Moses' staff. I had left that violin that I had learned to play when I was nine and that I loved in order to become another violin for the virtuoso that is Jesus Christ. It was necessary that at the same time Jesus' heart become my violin. The heart of Jesus is the ineffable instrument of God, and all the harmonies of the world pass through him.

Words of a mystic? Reflections of a Christian? A search to place oneself within the Church and today's world? Overly complicated symbols, or inevitable symbols necessary to communicate something of an inner experience? Whatever it was, between the huge chestnuts in the park and the small cloisters of the monastic scribes of the fifteenth century, Brother Olivier was now seized by this idea. God's violin? Why not! He felt a swell of emotions, an overwhelming joy, and he burst into tears. He knew that his life would be turned upside down by this light of love. He had just touched upon a truth that transforms a person. From now on, he had to become God's musical instrument, and because the violin was one of the most difficult instruments to play, it would require the greatest of efforts. To achieve this, he had no choice but to dive more deeply into his monastic life and unite himself with the heart of God.

Grasping the significance of this symbol, he kept walking in the peacefulness of the trails and the lawns surrounded by the woods of Burgundy. Only moments before he had been thinking with nostalgia about his violin, and all of a sudden he understood with profound certainty that the violin was alive and that he was that violin!

His baptismal name—Olivier—now led him to another reflection. The olive tree is the wood of Israel. What can you do with wood if you don't cut it down first? He understood that for the Lord to continue his work, it would first be necessary to cut down the very young olive tree that he was. It had to become dead wood. This wood needed to die. That was the condition for the transformation to take place. If he held on to the ground with all his roots and refused to be felled, he could not serve. If he dreamed of growing up to the sky and being someone or something important, how could he lie down on the ground and be cut in pieces, molded into shape? He would never become a musical instrument in the divine hands. This olive tree, which had to accept being cut down to be transformed into a violin, is the image of the Easter mystery, with the entombment and the resurrection. And while walking in the park among the other trees, Olivier felt that he needed to be the trunk and the branches cut in the prime of life by the Lord. That was the price that had to be paid in order for his inner life to be fulfilled, a life that the Holy Spirit would be able to transform into the life of the risen Christ.

All of a sudden he realized that olive wood was never used to manufacture violins. You could not extract a Stradivarius from that wood. The great violin makers used wood from the fir tree and the maple tree. Is God not able to do better than these great violin makers? He disregards the common recipes and deliberately chooses the worst woods or the worst instruments to make music. The wood he prefers is that which nobody else wants. There would be no miracle if he were not playing perfectly with instruments that others had rejected. There lay the virtuosity of love. Crate wood is sufficient for him. From an ugly violin he can extract beautiful notes that fill angels with wonder.

"I also noticed," continued Brother Olivier, "that the violinist lays his head on the violin while playing. It is the only place where he can do it. That passage of Luke's gospel came to mind in which Christ says, 'The Son of man has nowhere to lay his head' (Luke 9:58)."

The monk becomes a live violin on which Christ can lay down his head. The whole Gospel came into the mind of Olivier, who discovered it as if for the first time, in all its entire freshness and power. Soon he revisited the Bible's majestic Song of Songs, in which the bride says of her bridegroom, "His left hand is under my head, and his right hand shall embrace me" (Song 2:6).

"In fact," Brother Olivier continued, "the left hand of the violinist, which supports the instrument, is placed as if under the head, since the violinist has become one with his violin. The right hand wraps around it with the bow. In this movement the violin and the bow form a cross!"

Bedazzled by the unending spate of symbols, the monk discovered in the fingers' play on the strings the personal relationship with God, the vibration of the soul and of prayer. The horsehair of the bow represented in this image all the events passing by, the noisy ones and the silent ones, the fast ones and the slow ones, the heavy ones and the light ones, the expected ones and the feared ones. Happy or sad, they all ended up one way or the other singing the glory of God, while the violinist forming the cross with his bow was a man sheltered within the hands of God.

His pots and pans—he was then working in the kitchen—were the set for his opera. The ovens were like an orchestra, and the walls were like those of a large concert hall. Secretly, he produced magical sounds. Events could come from within or from outside. There was nothing to fear; they were a philharmonic choir bending over an invisible score. Could the silence of the *trappe* be listening to the sound of God's music and to the beating of God's heart?

Brother Olivier would only leave his kitchen and the shadows in obedience to his superiors and his brothers. Withdrawal is part of the life of a monk, whose modesty prevents him from opening up to the world. He lives a hidden life. Monks don't open up to each other very much either, and then only in authorized circumstances. While a priest has a ministry that could be described as a daytime ministry, which leads him to show himself and to speak, the monk's ministry is mainly a nighttime one that leads him to hide and keep silence. The priest has to be seen and heard and be approachable, but the monk remains on the night's side. His ministry is accomplished in the shadows and in secret. The important moments of his life are not seen. He acts without being seen. The Church relies on the monk as on a spring of water beneath the ground or on a live violin playing in the silence of an abbey.

The superior sent Olivier to the Catholic Institute of Paris in the Latin Quarter to study for a master's degree in liturgy. Passing by his grandfather's old building, he was overwhelmed by the flow of memories linked to that place. Events go by, every being is overcome by time, and we are passersby. His university thesis was devoted to one of the most amazing spiritual writers of the Middle Ages, Saint Gertrude of Helfta. Also called Gertrude the Great, she was one of the first women in the Church to have left writings, which were so revolutionary that some have seen her as a precursor of Protestantism, for example in her way of speaking about the mercy of God and his abundance of free gifts.

Brother Olivier was ordained a deacon and then a priest, after which some would call him Father Olivier. He was named guest master and then made responsible for the formation of the young monks after their first vows, and then liturgist, all the while remaining cantor. During that time, he meditated a lot on the significance of this new function. Cantor? For him, this meant first and foremost standing in front of God, who sees a person giving him thanks and inviting all creation to praise him.

"A monk's day is often monotonous, and he does not always believe that he is successful," added Father Olivier. "But the trials or joys, the disappointments, come back to the same thing if all is in God's hands and if he is the virtuoso holding the violin. The monk plays heaven's music, and he has only one cry: 'My soul proclaims the greatness of the Lord' (Luke 1:46)."

You might wonder if that monk was not telling himself a beautiful story to give himself strength. Was he not living an illusion? Wasn't it a way to get over life's disappointments and to believe that there was still something to celebrate even when there was nothing left but absurdity? What would a psychoanalyst or psychiatrist say? To believe that you are God's violin, is that really humble and, more important, really serious?

"Yes, I am comforting myself, it is true," he confirmed. "So what? I concur with those who could criticize me. When I was going through that experience, I was the cook in the monastery; often I encountered representatives or food delivery people, and we would sometimes exchange a few words. One day, one of them, who was not very devout, told me, 'Brother Olivier, something bothers me. It seems that Christians have to be comforted all the time. How is that possible?' I answered him, 'You are absolutely right. Christians are people who need to be comforted. You get it. Let me tell you what I think. A person who has not in his life gone through the experience of crying out and of distress, of being in tears or anxious, or who has never had the need to be comforted, is a person who has not yet reached his full stature. Every person will have to be comforted. It is at the root of the spiritual experience.' The message of the Beatitudes pronounced by Christ on the mountain (Matt 5:1-12) indicates it clearly: 'Blessed are those who mourn, for they shall be comforted.' "

Father Olivier added: "Have you heard the scream of the violin? The gift of tears is a precious gift, and the saints, the important mystics, and the Church Fathers have all talked about it or have known it. Our Western world has trouble expressing compassion and empathy. It makes people look like wimps, so unfortunately they harden their hearts. Tears are part of the nobility and the grandeur of a human being. They are linked by nature to the Easter mystery, of which they are the first phase. But how do we reach the second phase, the one of resurrection, if we don't go through the first one? The access to freedom for the children of God is a Paschal journey and a narrow road.

"The small child who cries and experiences the comfort of his mother or father goes through a divine experience. In their arms the child in a certain sense finds God's comfort. God usually acts through other people. The child doesn't know, but his cry encounters God's comfort, and the child then has an experience that is at once exalted and humble. Later he will have to renew this experience more seriously in the course of more profound experiences, not without similarity to Christ's scream on the cross, the great and last scream before the resurrection. In growing to adulthood, the child will come to understand what the experience of the scream means. This cry that he has shouted out since his birth changes and over the years acquires a new gravitas and another tone, up to and including the silent screams that remain inside. Once more, that comfort should follow the scream. The child whom nobody comforts becomes disturbed and cannot find reference points later. All psychologists will tell you: crying and comfort are fundamental."

These strong convictions of Father Olivier were encouraging. They didn't mean that every person must have experienced distress up to the point of being tempted to commit suicide in order to reach maturity. In fact, temperament profoundly influences our perception of things and the way they affect us. I mentioned this before. But sooner or later, all of us, whatever our temperament, have to experience our own weakness—we cannot save ourselves. God does not take pleasure in manifesting his strength by humiliating us. Fundamentally a human being is powerless when faced with what God offers—to share one's life and to "be perfect, as your heavenly father is perfect," as Jesus says (Matt 5:48).

God has to get involved, and he requests from us a minimal collaboration whereby we realize that we are powerless and that we need to let go and abandon ourselves to God. It is all for our good and honor that God asks us for our collaboration. We need to transform the desire for conquest, quite ineffective in the case of sainthood, into receptiveness to the gift. Sainthood is not acquired, it is received; but to receive it, we have to be empty handed, empty of merits, as Saint Thérèse of Lisieux said, so that God himself can be our justice.[1] She was only recapturing the teachings of Saint Paul.

---

1. See her "Act of Oblation to Merciful Love—Prayer 6": "In the evening of this life, I shall appear before you with empty hands, for I do not ask you, Lord, to count my works. All our justice is stained in your eyes. I wish, then,

We know this intellectually, but sometimes we need to experience it psychologically and concretely. And that is where we again face our trials, such as a weakness that we cannot get rid of, a duty or function of which we are deprived, a distress, a discouragement, a feeling of exclusion or of abandonment. But we are not made to remain downtrodden. "Our misery," says Saint Bernard, "calls upon mercy,"[2] which means God's gift of comfort, as Father Olivier reminded us: "Blessed be the God and Father of all mercies. The God of all comfort, Saint Paul cries out, who comforts us in all our sadness so that through the comfort that we receive from him we can comfort others in all their affliction."

Like others, Father Olivier did encounter the temptation to go and announce this understanding to his contemporaries, to all those who suffered so much without feeling the comfort of God. He thought about the society that surrounded him, that knocked at his door, that he felt was present from the moment he woke up in the middle of the night. Should he not go and meet it and cry Jesus Christ out to it? The desert is arid and burning, and one may feel useless there. He thought that he might be more useful outside than inside the walls of a monastery where nothing ever seemed to happen. He imagined that he could do so much good somewhere else. When a person comes to maturity, it is common to want to do something of great significance. There comes a time when a

---

to be clothed in your own Justice and to receive from your Love the eternal possession of Yourself." See Conrad De Meester, *Les Mains Vides: Le Message de Thérèse de Lisieux, Foi Vivante* 146 (Paris: Les Éditions du Cerf, 1972). {For an English edition, see Saint Thérèse of Lisieux, *The Prayers of Saint Thérèse of Lisieux: The Act of Oblation*, introduction by Guy Gaucher, trans. Aletheia Kane (Washington, DC: Institute of Carmelite Studies, 1997), no. 6, 53–55 at 54.}

2. {Bernard of Clairvaux, *The Steps of Humility and Pride*, trans. M. Ambrose Conway, CF 13A (Collegeville, MN: Cistercian Publications, 1973), 3.6–12, pp. 34–41. For similar thoughts, see *On the Song of Songs* 10.10 and 83.1, trans. Kilian Walsh and Irene Edmonds, 4 vols., CF 4, 7, 31, 40 (Kalamazoo, MI: Cistercian Publications, 1979–1983), 1:61–68 at 68; 4:180–87 at 180–81.}

person wants to take on other responsibilities and arrive at the summit of his talents. But these ideas are often only temptations.

The monk represents Christ on the cross. Jesus seems as if he looks away from the world, but nevertheless he carries within himself the whole world. He draws it nearer and guides it to the Father. The monk perceives the universe in himself and offers it to God with all its troubles and pleas. The Sirens can sing to him as they did to Jesus on the Cross, "Let him come down from the cross and we will believe in him!" (Matt 27:42). The temptation might be terribly strong to free himself from the nails and to go back into the world so that the whole world would believe. It is nevertheless there that the monk is called to stand; there is where he will serve the world, with Jesus on the cross. He will only triumph over death after having gone through it like Jesus. Let him not tear himself from the cross by himself!

That is also what Brother Aelred, a young novice in the community, concluded. He declared himself "the novice of all novices" because at twenty-four years of age he was then the youngest in the community. "If I had to count the times that I had already wanted to leave—" he acknowledged. "Some days I felt like I was at the top of my game; on others I was about to cry with the urge to let everything go. Saint Bernard talked about the trials that every man encountered. The novice mostly considers leaving on difficult days."

It was not easy for Aelred to leave everything to follow Christ to Cîteaux. With his family in Burgundy, he had enjoyed everything a young man could dream of, including a swimming pool in his own backyard. He loved to dance, to go to parties, and to participate in rock-and-roll competitions. Something of a socialite, he enjoyed the society parties, and he followed the latest fashions. Recognizing that he had always had an attraction to religious matters, even though no one in his family practiced any religion, at nineteen years of age, he went to the abbey for an extended visit. Five years later he entered.

"Some come in smiling and enthusiastic, almost singing," Brother Aelred noted, "not concerned with the idea of a new way of life. They say: 'Ah, with you, my God, my place for eternity!' I didn't feel anything like this at the conscious level, and I wasn't far from walking in backwards."

But he knew, he believed with a pure faith, a naked faith, that his place was here and nowhere else. In the ninth grade he had gone through some intense moments of religious questioning and had started to pray every day, to become interested in the liturgy. Later he had become the master of ceremonies at the cathedral of Dijon. In 1991, having started to study medicine, he was on the list of nurses who could be deployed during the Gulf War against Iraq, in case the situation got worse. The day before his entry into the monastery he was still sitting on the edge of the swimming pool at his parents' home. His mother didn't want him to tell her the day of his departure because it was too painful to face. When she came home one evening, she realized that he was not there anymore. His gregarious temperament made it difficult for him to leave all his contacts and friends. Illness made his entry even more complicated. Two hours after having crossed the doorstep of the monastery, he was in the infirmary with a fever of one hundred and four. Quite a stripping away!

"I wondered if you would survive the first week," the novice master told him later. "But if you survived it would probably be for a long time."

"You need time to absorb this radical life change," Brother Aelred answered. "We all like our little comforts, our habits. But here they have to disappear; I noticed that right away. I also quickly became aware that the monastic life reveals us the way we are. Every character trait appears. Nothing is hidden. The conditions are there to be completely stripped. Where does it end?"

At becoming a monk.

You may see the results after many decades of this interior effort, if you persevere in it. In a monastery it is not possible to play a double game, to push yourself forward. Masks drop over time. You have your back against the wall.

"You can't pretend anymore," Brother Aelred confirmed, "not in front of the other monks and not in front of God. Eventually you can trick men but not God, and therefore we are not tempted to trick the former either, because we risk deceiving ourselves and feeling worse about ourselves."

"Our lives are printed on our faces," Brother Michel, another novice, observed to Aelred. "You have changed physically since you entered. Sometimes I passed you in the guesthouse before you entered, and now you have a different face, a different demeanor. You radiate joy."

Brother Michel had become a novice at forty-five years of age. "It is interesting to live the same experience with a difference of one generation," he noted. He had worked in the restaurant business from the age of fourteen. At twenty-five he got married and became a chef in a twenty-four-hour-a-day restaurant at the Halles in Rungis. He was also hired in a great restaurant in Orly, where two shifts of eight hours each took turns. Then came the cabarets in Paris. From 4 p.m. to 3 a.m. you could find him at the Don Camillo, Rue des Saint Pères, where Thierry Le Luron[3] was performing.

"It was funny," he said. "I got my paycheck at the same time he did. That was where stars like Enrico Macias, Serge Lama, Michel Lebb, and Jean Roucas were discovered and became famous. For a young chef the job was interesting. I also worked at the Alcazar, where the shows' artists wore fewer clothes!"

There he earned in a week what he had made in a month in Orly. This world of the night was special, and he realized that he could fall into many different bad habits. Nevertheless, something always held him back at the last moment from falling into the abyss that he walked alongside. Monks also belong to a world of the night, but in the opposite way.

After five years of marriage he got divorced. "At the time, you don't realize the deepest aspects of a separation," he observed, "but you are scarred for life. You think it will pass like everything

---

3. {Thierry Le Luron (1952–1986), a French comic and successful impersonator of political figures.}

else, but you only feel the repercussions little by little. We did not have children."

For ten years he traveled the world, starting with a bike ride from Paris to Dakar with a friend. The Sahara Desert marked him forever. Two years later he took the Trans-Siberian train in Moscow and traveled alone to China just before the massacre of thousands of students in Tiananmen Square in Beijing in 1989. He ended his life as a globe trotter with a one-month American stay with a family in New Jersey. This mini world tour had the one fortunate consequence of developing in him a universal love that had previously been hidden. He then opened a restaurant with his brother about ten miles from Cîteaux. Some days they earned up to $2,000. Nevertheless, around that time he realized that he was on the road to ruin. To run the restaurant and pay back the loans, he kept the bar open all night and took no rest. Depression was lurking. He wanted to avoid turning to alcohol for support or giving in to other forms of debauchery. He decided to sell his part in the business and chose the Trappist life after some time. His brother, who had a family, did not accept Michel's entering Cîteaux. He waited three years before visiting his brother and conversing with him for a few minutes two weeks before his brother's temporary vows, which I received in April 1993, when I was superior at Cîteaux.

"The walks in the park are important for many monks," said the novice. "It is an opportunity to admire a violet at the foot of a tree or to listen to a bird singing. Many times I have seen a blue heron or wild geese take off when I got near, or a superb blue jay or a squirrel, who are all God's smiles in my life. They are part of my prayer. Monastic life is in harmony with a return to nature. Over time the sight of the intense blue color of a kingfisher hidden close to the river or the flight of an insect appears more and more marvelous to me. I am so happy to be a monk! For work I am in charge of maintaining the park, something of a landscape gardener. When I took my initial vows I did not think even for a second that it could be for anything other than forever."

Brother Bernard, who had entered the community of Caux a few years earlier at the age of twenty-six, drew meditation from the company of the animals that he would never have imagined when he entered the monastery. It was a revelation for him about who he was and who we are in the Christian vision of the universe. While his reflection started with the seventy cows of his herd, it quickly dove into the mysteries of faith. The milking parlor was for him a place of spiritual struggle. Every day he was apprehensive before starting his work, first because there were many strong, heavy animals there, and also because he was alone away from the monastery. He had previously earned a degree in forestry, which qualified him to be hired at the National Forests Office. He worked three years as a civil servant, and he had a job for life. But in the milking parlor he slipped on his boots and apron and put himself in God's hands, just as he did for the offices in the church. To work up his courage, he sang loudly amidst the noise of the machines and the water jets.

> "How will I make this whole herd obey me?" he wondered. "Experience shows you don't achieve anything with force and violence. I have to be gentle so that the animals will also be gentle and the milking will proceed quietly. I draw general principles from this that also apply to other situations. The cows react instinctively, without being able to control their instincts like human beings. If I am irritated, in a bad mood, or even have bad thoughts, the cows will feel it and express it by being nervous. If I get a hoof kick or a tail blow I might be tempted to hit the cow with a stick. Usually that creates havoc, and you lose all control. I try to control myself and admit that the cow is not vicious when she strikes me. The violence of an animal is different from human violence. Vice is unique to freedom. Technical resources are not sufficient to master nature—an internal attitude is necessary. If I truly orient myself towards God in my ordinary daily existence, I can then have great power over creation, and that conforms to God's desire."

In 1985, when Father Olivier was ordained to the temporary diaconate, he evoked in his first homily his passion for the violin, which he had not forgotten. It was the feast of the Sacred Heart of Jesus, the third Friday after Pentecost. The story started on the evening of the seventh day of creation. The Father said to his Son, through whom everything was done:

"Adam, my child, sing me a song."

This one meditated and came closer to his Father to whisper in his ear, "Abba, Father, I give you my heart."

God was so happy that a big tear rolled down his cheek and fell into Adam's heart. This tear of joy and love, in the language of this tale, was the Holy Spirit. God began again:

"Adam, my child, sing me that song again. I like it very much."

To make his song even more beautiful, Adam had the idea of inviting all creatures to sing along with him. He meditated and went to each tree in Paradise to pick some wood, along with some fibers from the olive tree, to make a musical instrument, which looked like a violin. He gave the name *Church* to his instrument, but then he thought of a more beautiful name yet, *Myriam* or *Mary*. With the horsehair of his bow he made his incomparable song vibrate, and he traveled the whole world for centuries, not having any place other than the violin to lay his head. He courted all the creatures by teaching them his song: "Abba, Father, I give you my heart."

All the creatures formed a procession, men, animals, and all the plants, in a miracle that transformed the whole creation. Each one of them sang the song in its own language. But at the moment of crossing the threshold of the year 2000, Adam met five crazy old women, mentioned in the gospel (Matt 25), who opposed the wise virgins. They were the mothers of the five continents, and they insulted Adam and all his procession when it came by. They spat in his face and hurled insults at him, which are today's words *arms race, drugs, hunger, hostage takings, rape, murder*, and *war*. They took Adam, and they crucified him on his violin, and then they shared his clothes, and they pierced his heart with a spear. They drank the water and the blood that ran from his side, but in the depths of his heart they heard a voice that still whispered to them, "Abba, Father, I give you my heart."

It is by his dying and rising again that he becomes the king of glory and the king of the world. Dom Olivier commented on this allegory: "All this expressed my deepest thoughts on man, on the Christian, and on salvation. It is something that only can be understood in the Holy Spirit, but that gives enthusiasm to the faith! My spiritual journey occurred through meditation on the Beatitudes and the desire to live by them. They marked me deeply. I believe that the itinerary of the one seeking God ends with a bare prayer that can sometimes be summarized in simple words like these: 'I give you my heart.' I got them from my mother. Understand that if you can!"

One day from Dom Olivier's place in the church someone stole his book by Saint Gertrude of Helfta, whose spirituality had accompanied him since his novitiate. He inquired discreetly around him trying to find the book. When it didn't show up, he had a grin that should worry the fearless: "I prayed to Saint Gertrude that she would keep the culprit forever in her grip."

CHAPTER FIFTEEN

BEGINNINGS WITHOUT END

For more clarity and lightness of style, I have only used the masculine in this book, as if there were only monks. Everything I have said about the monastic life could also be said using the feminine gender, except for the discussions of the priesthood. In fact, if France today has sixteen monasteries for Trappist monks, there are no fewer than fourteen monasteries of Cistercian nuns.[1] Worldwide the proportion is slightly different; there are ninety-three monasteries of monks and sixty-five monasteries of Cistercian nuns. We live the same values and the same observances on both sides. Far from ignoring one another, we form a single order with very close legal connections among the monasteries of monks and nuns.

This is our uniqueness in the Church. In other orders or congregations there are also male and female branches, but in general these female branches constitute separate legal entities, as a "second order." This is not the case in our Order, which is really one and unites monasteries of the two branches with only one abbot general, elected by both the abbesses and the abbots.

1. {In 2019 the Order in France has twelve monasteries of nuns and fifteen monasteries of monks. Around the world, the Order counts 1,840 monks in 102 monasteries and 1,618 nuns in 76 monasteries. For more details, see www.OCSO.org/currentstatistics.}

The internal structure of the Order has nevertheless changed over the centuries, thereby adapting to the condition of men and women in society and in the Church. In the Middle Ages the nuns' monasteries were linked to a nearby monks' monastery. Nevertheless, the abbesses did not participate at the highest levels of the Order, including the general chapter, which was only attended by the abbots. Since the thirteenth century this chapter has made decisions affecting both nuns and monks. This situation could not last at a time when the role of women has rightfully been affirmed as equal to that of men, excepting only the priesthood and the priestly authority linked to it. Three times—in 1958, 1964, and 1968—the abbot general, Dom Gabriel Sortais, took the initiative of holding a meeting of abbesses so that they could express their desires before the general chapter ratified them, so giving them the force of law. When the Order asked for abbesses to be allowed to participate in the regular chapters of the monks and deliberate with them, the Holy See preferred, on July 15, 1970, that they hold their own meeting to establish their rules. At first this decision created some consternation within the Order, for would that not push us toward separation? In fact, the experience led some years later to a happy solution that respected both the unity of the Order and the specificity of both men and women.

Always holding two distinct assemblies could certainly have risked increasing the divide between the two communities, or, alternatively, having one community always follow the other without having its voice heard or taking up its share of responsibilities. The meeting of all of us in a single chapter could have led, because of the simple inequality in the number of votes, to the monks' having an overwhelming influence. Moreover, are the needs of one group always the same as those of the other group? Do we necessarily have to adopt common solutions that apply equally to both groups?

The solution we adopted in 1987 is that in accordance with canon law, we hold two general chapters, each one with supreme authority in the Order, but allowed to hold common debates.

When important monastic directions or the principal observances or structures of the Order are concerned, the decisions are inter-dependent: the decisions of one group need the approval of the other group to be enforceable. The common discussion enables everyone to hear each other's opinions and to form common convictions. The separation of the votes enables everyone to realize what each side really wishes for itself. In less important matters, only consultation with the other party is required, while each party retains sufficient authority to adopt resolutions at that level. Moreover, abbots and abbesses elect one abbot general, who presides over the chapters of both abbots and abbesses. There too the votes are not combined; the person elected needs to receive the majority of the votes on both sides (Const 77–79).

The result is a quasi-equality in the face of power, but without either confusion or complete separation. Isn't this an original formula for reconciling the roles of men and women in arrange-ments that could inspire other church structures, or even social and political ones?

Another particularity of our Order may be of interest in that regard: the way we reconcile local and central authority. Each monastery is independent. Saint Benedict wrote his Rule for a monastery, not for a congregation. Under the influence of Char-lemagne, monasteries created certain links among themselves according to certain affinities. Why? In fact the Rule remained generic, and, moreover, monks had to adapt to varying condi-tions of the times and locations in which they lived. They had to add to the requirements of the Rule the customs and regula-tions that governed their daily routine. It is understandable that those who had similar intentions or common interests found it advantageous to become closer. In that way they adopted the same regulations by getting common governmental structures. Through these regulations and customs—later we called them constitutions—monasteries gathered in congregations or orders. These orders then distinguished themselves from others, al-though they all followed the same rule of Saint Benedict. Cîteaux formulated its own usages and customs that met the needs of its particular project.[2]

What happens when autonomous monasteries join together and form a congregation or an order? One could say that each abbot or abbess shares with others his or her own authority. He or she gives up a certain autonomy to benefit from the assistance of the others. The authority of the whole results from the delegation of each other's power. But in sharing that authority no one really loses it fundamentally; that is why within a single order the monasteries remain essentially autonomous. If the Cistercian general chapter exercises an authority that we could call supreme, it results from the fact that the abbots and abbesses unite their supreme authority. All the abbots and abbesses gathered in a general chapter only exercise the supreme authority of each one of them. In that sense, there is no superior general on top of the pyramid with an independent and supreme authority.

Of course, we do have an abbot general. I have talked about it often. But he only presides over the general chapter and ensures that all the monasteries observe the chapter's decisions between the sessions. The abbot general also exercises certain powers well defined by these chapters. He himself is submitted to the authority of that chapter, although he enjoys an uncontested moral authority from the mere fact that he visits all the communities, provides common links among them, and assists the superiors who ask for his advice. The real supreme authority of the Order is collective.

Isn't that what is being slowly realized to a certain degree in the construction of the European Union? Each nation remains sovereign and autonomous but also exercises some of its power

---

2. {Dom Dubois is being too modest here. Modern scholarship considers the Cistercians to be the first modern religious order because of the structure governing the relationships between monasteries put in place by the primitive documents, especially the *Charter of Charity*. See Gert Melville, *The World of Medieval Monasticism: Its History and Forms of Life*, trans. James D. Mixson, CS 263 (Collegeville, MN: Cistercian Publications, 2016), 146–57.}

in common with the other member states. The power of the central organism is collective in nature (which does not mean that it acts according to a unanimity rule); it is only supreme because it combines the supreme authority of each nation. Instead of talking about "surrender of sovereignty" shouldn't we be talking about "sharing of authority"? We have been practicing that at our reduced scale for about nine centuries. One specialist in political science studied the evolution of the structures adopted by monastics to search for the success of their institutions. From that analysis it may be easy to draw some lessons that—maybe—the present architects of the European Union might benefit from hearing.[3]

Cistercian monasteries are spread all over the world. Though our houses in Europe and in North America have experienced a certain aging since World War II, they were in on the beginnings of a rather spectacular development in Africa, Asia, and Latin America. The size of the communities is getting smaller, but the number of monasteries keeps increasing. Between 1971 and 1995, thirty foundations of nuns or monks were made. Of those, only four were created in Europe or the United Sates. To a certain extent, one could say that after having been European and even French for a long time, the Order, like the whole Church, is becoming decentralized toward what we used to call the third world, even if vocations are as hard to find there as here.

This decentralization is not only geographic, but also cultural. Isn't it significant that the participants in the 1990 general chapter chose as abbot general the abbot of an Argentinian monastery founded in 1958, the Order's first foundation in South America? The abbot general in 1958 was a Frenchman who had serious doubts about the new foundation, which appeared to him to be contrary to the Argentinian temperament and culture. His

3. Léo Moulin, *Le Monde vivant des Religieux* (Paris: Calmann-Levy, 1964), Preamble, 24: "The world of the monastics contains a wealth of teachings, of setbacks, of lucky and unlucky trials, of ingenious solutions full of wisdom and of adventurous attempts, that deserve our full attention."

Argentinian successor thirty-five years later went to that predecessor's grave in the cemetery at Tre Fontane in Rome and mischievously knocked three times on the tomb, straining to hear an answer to the question, "Do you hear me? Do you remember? Do you still believe that it is impossible for a South American to become a Trappist?"

Life is full of surprises. Let's say that the Holy Spirit is alive and well and active within the Church. Our Order has developed its international dimension over the last fifty years, and the general chapter gathers superiors from many different cultures and languages. Three main languages are represented: French, English, and Spanish, meaning that at our meetings monks and nuns must provide a system of more or less simultaneous translation. Other languages are also present, though, such as Japanese, Portuguese, Dutch, Italian, German, and Javanese. African or Madagascan songs sometimes take place during chapter liturgies, with a beat that sometimes surprises our Western expectations. This diversity is a cause for enrichment but sometimes also a cause of problems, making communication among us hard to establish.

Sometimes superiors come together in smaller circles combining nuns and monks organized by nationalities or languages. We call these meetings regional conferences (Const 81). They allow more thorough and immediately beneficial exchanges, providing mutual assistance among monasteries. But the legal structure linking the monasteries is not a grouping by provinces. It is the relation by foundation: the monastery that founds keeps a legal link with the house that it founded. It continues to be its mother beyond the boundaries and the oceans that may separate it from its daughter. The abbot becomes what we call the father immediate of his daughter house. At least every two years the father immediate carries out a canonical or "regular" visitation. The Constitutions define the purpose of this regular visitation as "to strengthen and supplement the pastoral action of the local abbot, to correct it where necessary, and to motivate the brothers to lead the Cistercian life with a renewed spiritual fervor" (Const 75.2).

The system is different for the monasteries of nuns, who are attached not to their founding mother house but, if possible, to a nearby monastery of monks where the father abbot exercises the functions of father immediate. There are no "mothers immediate." This practice is an anomaly of the Order, intentionally maintained to keep a legal link between the male and the female parts of the Order and to avoid the nuns'—who are not priests—having to call on an ecclesiastical authority outside the Order.

As abbot of La Trappe, I found myself father immediate of four other houses, one of which was a monastery of nuns in the diocese of Périgueux. I considered my role as not simply a legal one, but even from that point of view everything went much more smoothly if there was a friendly relationship between me and the communities. I tried to develop that kind of friendship with the superiors of these houses. I can acknowledge now that I developed a very sincere friendship with the abbess of Echourgnac from 1978 until her sudden death following a massive heart attack in January 1995. That friendship was of mutual help to us in our duties, as was beneficial to both our communities.

The relationship uniting the mother house to her daughter houses goes largely beyond the individuals who are the superiors, especially when the distance between the two houses is limited and when they have opportunities to help each other and to have meetings at different levels. For that reason the medieval legal document organizing the relationship between the monasteries is called the *Charter of Charity*.[4]

As a father immediate I had to travel to visit other communities. Additionally, I was sometimes sent by the abbot general or as part of mutual assistance among abbots or to facilitate exchanges among regions. In that capacity I was able to travel outside France and to stop—sometimes for only a few days—in Algeria, Madagascar, Benin, Chile, Argentina, Brazil, the United States, Canada, and Israel, in addition to many countries of the

---

4. {For more information on the *Charter of Charity*, see http://www.ocso.org/resources/foundational-text/charter-of-charity. For the several versions of the *Charter of Charity*, see Chrysogonus Waddell, *Narrative and Legislative Texts from Early Cîteaux: Latin text in Dual Edition with English Translation and Notes* (Cîteaux: *Cîteaux–Commentarii Cistercienses*, 1999), 135–91.}

European Union. It is probably not over yet.[5] My brother-in-law talked about a first-class funeral when he learned that I was entering La Trappe, and look at me now! What struck me the most in these trips was the closeness I felt in every respect with the brothers and sisters of communities from cultures other than mine. Beyond the distance that created diversity of customs, languages, and ways of feeling and celebrating, I felt the affinity and the warmth that was implied by a common monastic culture. I was also surprised to realize how the literature of our twelfth-century Fathers, when it was highlighted as it was in South America, could transcend the cultural barriers and give us a common language.

I would like to broaden our overview. The Cistercian-Trappists are not the only monks in France. Cîteaux grafted itself onto the old Benedictine tree trunk as a particular reform. But this trunk kept growing authentically Benedictine branches; in the nineteenth century, Dom Guéranger and Dom Muard founded the monasteries of Solesmes and La Pierre-qui-Vire, which were at the origin of prosperous congregations. Other monasteries are linked to an Italian reform of the fourteenth century, like Bec-Hellouin, or are more recent independent foundations. Lérins, Sénanque, Boulaur, and Castagniers are Cistercian abbeys that are not linked to La Trappe.[6]

Next in the Benedictine tradition, we encounter the Carthusians, founded by Saint Bruno in the eleventh century. They live in solitude in small houses within the monastery and gather at certain times of the day or the week. Their separation from

5. {The book was written in 1995; Dom Dubois died in 2011.}

6. {As Dom Dubois mentioned earlier in the book, the reform in the Cistercian order led by Abbot de Rancé in the 17th century led to the movement called Trappists, later Cistercians of the Strict Observance. The monasteries that did not follow the reform of La Trappe became known as Cistercians of the Common Observance. The growth of the Cistercian Order of the Common Observance was especially strong in Germany, Poland, and Austria.}

the world is stricter than ours. They do not offer hospitality to retreatants desiring to spend some days in prayer with them. In France, there are four Carthusian foundations for men and two for women. There is also a more recent congregation linked to their spirituality, and one called "of Bethlehem," composed of communities of men and communities of women, which I mentioned in a previous chapter.[7] Certain Christians live as hermits, more often than not in isolated places, but sometimes also deep in the city. At the time of the Crusades, the Carmelite Order developed out of the Palestinian tradition and thrived. Its female branch owed a lot to the reform of Saint Teresa of Avila in the sixteenth century. That reform reached France in the beginning of the seventeenth century and survived the French Revolution as well as it could, but the influence of Saint Thérèse of Lisieux, after her death in 1897 at twenty-three, contributed to the growth of the Carmelites in France.[8]

Monks and cloistered nuns can be found everywhere in the world. But we need to give special credit to the monasticism of the Eastern Churches, because from the beginning it had a great influence on monastic life in the West, and we can recognize it as our foremost inspiration. Over time it took different forms, with that of Mount Athos particularly well known. That monasticism continued to live a spirituality that we can identify as ours. It owed a lot to the first monks of the deserts of Egypt in the fourth and fifth centuries as well as to the Greek fathers. These ancient sources were the soil in which the Rule of Saint Benedict grew, and we still like to refer to them. In that sense monks could be a

7. See above, chap. 12, p. 282.

8. In 1995, of 312 women's monasteries in France, 112 were Carmelites, with about 1,770 Carmelites among the 6,300 cloistered nuns in France. See *L'Église Catholique en France 1995*, publication of the secretariat of the bishops' conference of France, 352. {In 2016 there were only about 950 Carmelite nuns among 69 Carmelite monasteries in France. See http://www.service-des-moniales.cef.fr/ordres-monastiques/carmelites/.}

link between the sister churches of the East and the West, as John
Paul II expressly invited them to be.[9]

But we didn't wait for him to tell us that. I remember that in
March 1968, while the Iron Curtain was still impenetrable, we invited Archimandrite Plato of the monastery of the Holy Trinity of
Saint Sergius Lavra of Zagorsk, close to Moscow, to Mont-des-Cats.
He came accompanied by one of his monks and an interpreter. We
had organized a trip for them to a few monasteries in France; it
was a real discovery for everyone; the archimandrite reported on
his trip in an article in the *Journal de Patriarcat de Moscou*. The next
summer three Greek monks paid us a similar visit. Our abbot,
Dom André Louf, became heavily involved in the organization of
such meetings between Western and Eastern monks. He wasn't
authorized to travel to Russia, but at different times between 1969
and 1972 a few French monks were allowed to go on pilgrimage
to Mount Athos and to Romania. Our Father Daniel spent three
months in monasteries in Moldavia. From that time on he let his
hair grow, like the Eastern monks. Without any doubt these encounters left deep marks in the hearts of those who were lucky
enough to experience them. Father Païssius, a hermit of Athos,
requested of his superior, "When monks come from the West,
bring them to me. We will understand each other immediately."

But what are monks good for? People ask that question often.
They understand easily that Christians serve in the underpriv-
ileged world, for example, in the name of their ideal of love,
or that they participate in assistance agencies like the various

---

9. In his letter in *Orientale Lumen*, 25. We need to understand each other
better, said the Pope, and for that we need to meet one another: "In this
regard, I hope that monasteries will make a particular effort, precisely because of the unique role played by monastic life within the Churches and
because of the many unifying aspects of the monastic experience, and therefore of spiritual awareness, in the East and in the West." {http://w2.vatican
.va/content/john-paul-ii/en/apost_letters/1995/documents/hf_jp-ii_apl
_19950502_orientale-lumen.html.}

Catholic charities, or in organizations that strive to promote peace or access to culture for all. In past centuries many religious institutions were created to answer the needs that our society was not able to address. In the seventeenth century, when John-Baptiste de la Salle was confronted with the problem of poverty among children in the countryside, he created the Brothers of Christian Schools specifically to provide free and quality education for the lower classes. Others later followed his example.

The beginning of the seventeenth century saw Vincent de Paul, chaplain to the royal galleys, tirelessly take on the poverty of the farmers and organize for that purpose the Daughters of Charity, now also known as the Sisters of Charity of Saint Vincent de Paul. Popular imagery remembers them with their large white winged coifs helping wounded soldiers on the battlefields of World War I, or treating patients in the Hôtel Dieu.[10] They are still active, even if their habit has been simplified, and everywhere in the world, as in the past, they attend to the relief of all the miseries of our time.

Such religious institutions—and the list would be too long to detail here—are very useful; nobody can deny this, except some sectarian souls.[11] How many of the initiatives undertaken in the eighteenth and nineteenth century in the two most sensitive sectors of education and care for the sick led to the creation of communities of nuns! Certainly society has progressively taken charge of satisfying the basic needs of its people. It is no longer

---

10. {The Hôtel-Dieu ("hostel of God"), founded by Saint Landry in AD 651, was originally a hospital for the poor and needy. The most famous ones still in existence are those in Paris and Beaune (founded in 1443).}

11. Eighty-three different institutions—besides monasteries—report to the Conference of Major Superiors in France. The congregations of religious in the apostolic life in France number 355, spread over 6,750 communities, of which two-thirds are in urban areas. In 1993 there were about 1,650 monks and more than 13,000 apostolic religious or missionaries, while there were about 56,000 apostolic nuns. See *L'Église catholique en France 1995*, publication of the secretariat of the Conference of French bishops, 346–51.

necessary to become a religious to be an educator or a nurse; nevertheless, there is plenty of room for everyone in the vast field of relief of human misery. A religious motivation is a powerful way to entice human devotion and engagement in tasks that sometimes no one wants to assume because they are not gratifying. This we can understand, but monks—what are they good for behind their walls?

It is not everything to be a humanitarian, even when it is inspired by Christian charity. We can understand that some prefer to commit themselves to tasks that are directly apostolic: to be a parish priest, for example, or a theologian, or a missionary, to find oneself in the middle of diverse human situations and to proclaim there the message of Jesus Christ. A few men and women hear and know that message and let themselves be transformed and saved by it and join the church, that part of humanity that welcomes the word of love that God proclaimed to the world in Jesus Christ and that answers him by invoking him with the word *Father* and praising him while assuming a brotherly life of sharing and mutual assistance. The world needs to exert itself to perceive that it is saved in Jesus Christ and to open itself to this salvation. That men and women are becoming committed to such prospects while serving the mission of the church may be incomprehensible to someone who doesn't have faith, but it is justified from a Christian point of view. You can easily understand the role of the Jesuits and the missionary White Fathers and other similar institutions.[12] It is harder to understand it when you consider monks, who withdraw in solitude.

One could obviously answer that contemplative monks belong to the domain of the gratuitous, the useless, and that our society really needs to re-evaluate their value. But they live what is prescribed by apostolic action, welcoming God's words of love and

12. The distinction that I make between institutions with charitable purposes and those devoted to apostolic purposes should not be cast in stone, since both are often practiced simultaneously. That is why I have not made subdivisions in the numbers cited in the previous note.

man's response in praise and fraternal life. "For the aim and object of apostolic works," says Vatican Council II, "is that all who are made sons of God by faith and baptism should come together to praise God in the midst of his church, to take part in the (eucharistic) sacrifice, and to eat the Lord's supper."[13] There lies the essential being of the Church, its finality. And it is precisely at that level that the monks are situated. They only do that, I could say, by leading what is called a contemplative life. Their whole existence takes place at the level of the deep being of the church, by praising God in liturgical prayer, but also in their personal prayer and in paying attention to God. Isn't that sufficient on its own without having to wonder what it is good for? It may be good and necessary that the essential task of the church be experienced more exclusively by some, while others, occupied by the urgency of missionary needs, have less time to devote to this essential task and run the risk of no longer paying enough attention to it. Through its monks, the Church expresses its essence.

Calling to mind Eastern Christianity, Pope John Paul II observed, "monasticism was not seen merely as a separate condition, proper to a precise category of Christians, but rather as a reference point for all the baptized, according to the gifts offered to each by the Lord; it was presented as a symbolic synthesis of Christianity." We could state this also of Western Christianity: "The monastery is the prophetic place," John Paul II continued, "where creation becomes praise of God, and the precept of concretely lived charity becomes the ideal of human coexistence. Within it the human being seeks God without limitation or impediment, becoming a reference point for all people, bearing them in his heart and helping them to seek God."[14]

So what are monks good for? They live, very simply. But they live what constitutes the essence of the Christian life. I can

13. SC 10.
14. Apostolic Letter, *Orientale Lumen*, 9.

nevertheless hear the objection: can you live that essence while neglecting the rest? Nobody has the right to ignore his brother in need, that is true. Not everyone can do everything; a certain specialization is inevitable. The way chosen by monks has its value, but they know that they live in solidarity with everyone, according to the formula that has been around since the fifth century: "separated from all, united to all."[15]

I already mentioned our hospitality and our sharing with those who are in need. Nevertheless, in the context of this chapter, I would like to emphasize that we first exercise our solidarity through prayer. That solidarity also operates at a deeper level, but a more mysterious one, as a consequence of a phenomenon that you could visualize as "communicating vessels" and that in Christianity we refer to with a Latin expression, *communio sanctorum*, which we can translate as "communion of saints" or "communication of holy matters." Contemplation fosters action, while action prevents contemplation from closing in on itself. Living the essence of the mystery of the church, as I mentioned before, monks and nuns can be said to be at the heart of the church.

The great Pope Pius XI declared Thérèse of Lisieux, a monastic, "patroness of the missions" even though she never left her cloister in Lisieux. Using the image of blood that comes from the heart to irrigate all the parts of the body, she so defines her place in the Church: "*I understood it was Love alone that made the Church's members act, that if Love ever became extinct, the apostles would no longer preach the Gospel and the martyrs would refuse to shed their blood. . . . In the heart of the Church, my Mother, I shall be Love.*"[16] Saint Bernard, in accordance with the physiological concepts of

15. {Pope Francis in his address to the general chapter of the OCSO on September 23, 2017, quoting Evagrius Ponticus.}

16. Thérèse of Lisieux, Manuscript B, 3v, Archives of the Carmel of Lisieux, as translated by Washington Province of Discalced Carmelite Friars, Inc. {Saint Thérèse of Lisieux, *Story of a Soul: The Autobiography of Saint Thérèse of Lisieux*, MS B, fol. 3ᵛᵒ, trans. John Clarke, 3rd ed. (Washington, DC: ICS Publications, 1996), 194.}

his time, compared the prayer and the life of the monks to the nourishing saps generated in the organs of the stomach, which transported life to all parts of the body.[17] In modern terms, one can analyze the relation between action and contemplation by referring to that between the nuclear forces of fission and fusion. Without the power of fusion that holds them together in an organic whole, the multiplication of cells would lead to dispersion and explosion. It would be like a cancerous growth. But if there were only the power of fusion, the cells could not multiply. The whole would deny itself any development.[18]

The monastic mission goes to the boundaries of the church, outside itself; it is the net thrown into sea, the fission power; it is necessary to reach the fish where they are located but not to become dispersed in high seas and diluted—instead to bring the fish back to the boat, to unify them in a brotherly community joined together by the fusion power of mercy. The comparison with the net is not totally adequate, of course, because the point is not to catch anyone in a trap or to get him out of his or her vital element. To be part of the church is to find one's real place, one's deepest self-fulfillment.

This self-fulfillment is beyond but not less than a certain human well-being. Christians cannot remain insensitive before the injustices, exclusions, disparities, and shortages of all kinds that affect all too many human beings. They profess, of course,

17. {Bernard of Clairvaux, *The Parables and the Sentences* 3.118, trans. Michael Casey and Francis R. Swietek, intro. John R. Sommerfeldt, ed. Maureen M. O'Brien, CF 55 (Kalamazoo, MI: Cistercian Publications, 2000), 396.}

18. B. Besret, *Confiteor* (Paris: Éditions Albin Michel, 1991), 111–12. I am far from agreeing with all the points of view expressed in this book, but certain general ideas are interesting. Action and contemplation, Besret says, "call on each other to cross pollinate mutually. The outside is not the opposite of the inside. It is the flipside. The more the inside opens up to the transcendence, the better the outside can develop in the dimension of the world without running the risk of becoming wasted and exhausted" (117).

that the world is not an end in itself, since—and this itself is
the object of the Christian faith—it is called to transcend itself
in the higher place that is the world of the resurrection. In this
fertilized soil of today's world, the world of the beyond is elabo-
rated, because, as Pope Paul VI stated in *Gaudium et Spes*, promulgated during Vatican Council II, "we will again find—freed of
stain, burnished and transfigured—the values of human dignity,
brotherhood, and freedom, and indeed all the good fruits of our
nature and enterprise, which we have cultivated on earth according to the commandment of the Lord and in his Spirit."[19] It is
therefore normal that Christians become invested in this activity.
But the role of monks is to remind everyone where the world
should go. After having called to mind active members as well as
the contemplatives, the Council goes on: "He frees all . . . so that
by putting aside love of self and bringing all earthly resources
into the service of human life they can devote themselves to that
future when humanity itself will become an offering accepted by
God."[20] Isn't it good to position ourselves in relation to others
within one and the same spiritual quest?

I have tried to show where monks are positioned within
the church with respect to the needs of the world. My answer
may seem very theoretical and timeless, but I couldn't avoid
it. I would nevertheless like to clarify it for the present and the
future. Does monastic life still have meaning in this twenty-first
century? Is today's youth still interested in it?

If modernity is characterized by a strongly secularized mentality, full of rationalism, relativism, and a simplistic pragmatism
that is not favorable to the spiritual experience, we nevertheless
witness a return to the religious, as we say: "The 21st century

19. *Gaudium et Spes*, 3.39.3 {(www.vatican.va/archive/hist_councils/ii_
vatican_council/documents/vat-ii_cons_19651207_gaudium-et-spes_en.
html).}

20. *Gaudium et Spes*, 3.38.

will be religious or it will not survive." André Malraux,[21] who is presumed to have expressed this aphorism, may also be wrong. Some will prefer to say *spiritual* rather than *religious*. "Religious" is an ambiguous notion, and the search for the religious can lead to an introverted, closed-up sect, more inclined to syncretism and sentimentalism than to an open mindedness toward the Christian faith. Nevertheless, these words translate, perhaps awkwardly, a real quest pursued by many men and women, the one for a special relationship with the Transcendent.

Maybe Christianity too often appears with a moralizing face. I myself experienced that fact one day when welcoming a woman at La Trappe who was aspiring to a life of intimacy with God but didn't think it was possible to satisfy this aspiration without embracing some kind of esoteric doctrine. The call of the youth to John Paul II during his visit to France in 1980 was also significant. They had to answer a preliminary questionnaire for their wishes to be taken into account. Overall it can be summarized in three questions they put to the pope. The first one was, "Talk to us first about Jesus Christ, of this God crazy for love. This is what looks to us to be most important for today's youth and for the world. Don't talk to us first about morality and about prohibitions that block the hearts of many. Talk to us about this God who is madly in love, and morality will logically follow by itself."[22]

21. {André Malraux (1901–1976) was a French writer whose travels to Asia led to many celebrated books, like *La Voie Royale* (1930) and *La Condition Humaine* (1933), earning him the literary Prix Goncourt in 1933. In 1935 he joined the Republican Forces in the Spanish Civil War to fight against the Franco regime. When World War II was declared he joined General de Gaulle in London to continue resistance against the Germans. After the war he joined the de Gaulle government as Minister of Culture and worked to make culture accessible to all by erecting new libraries and "Maisons de la Culture" (cultural centers) all over France.}

22. For John Paul's responses to the young people, see *Dialogue de Jean-Paul II avec les jeunes réunis en parc des princes*, Paris, France, Sunday, June 1, 1980 (*w2.vatican.va/content/john-paul-ii/fr/speeches/1980/june/documents/hf_jp-ii_spe_19800601_veglia-giovani.html*).

Morality is necessary, and Pope John Paul II did well to recall it when faced with the "culture of death" that he denounced in his encyclical *Evangelium Vitae*.[23] What is our foundation for adhering to this morality but our desire to follow Christ, to live with him in a personal love relation? Christianity is mystical before it is a morality. If you forget this, you expose yourself to bitter disappointments. Paul VI recognized this, stating, "Today's youth is not looking for teachers, but for witnesses."[24] Probably many Christians only see in religion the aspect of duty, the moralizing aspect of good behavior that they need to observe, without realizing that they are called to a personal intimacy with Jesus and in him, with the Father: "My Father and your Father, my God and your God," Jesus said on the morning of his resurrection (John 20:17). Jesus gives us his Father, and by living the very life of the risen Christ, the believer enters, so to speak, into the dialogue of the Son with his Father in the Holy Spirit. He becomes a stakeholder. This goes beyond the level of morality; it is a spiritual and mystical adventure that arouses amazement.

Each Christian should have that burst of desire, characteristic of Christianity, which is being open to the Holy Spirit. In the eleventh century, Symeon the New Theologian, a monk of the East, prayed, "Come, Holy Spirit, for you are yourself the desire that is within me."[25] It is up to the Holy Spirit to make us live the true life of the risen Christ and to enable us to call God by the name

23. *Evangelium Vitae* 21–24 (w2.vatican.va/content/john-paul-ii/en /encyclicals/documents/hf_jp-ii_enc_25031995_evangelium-vitae.html).

24. {Paul VI made this point at the Pontifical Council of Laity (1974), as was reported by Mgr. Papin, bishop of Nancy and Toul (Pope Paul VI, *Address to the Members of the Consilium de Laicis* [2 October 1974], AAS 66 (1974): 568 (w2.vatican.va/content/paul-vi/fr/audiences/1974/documents/hf_p -vi_aud_19741002.html). See also *Evangelii Nuntiandi*, 15 (w2.vatican.va /content/paul-vi/en/apost_exhortations/documents/hf_p-vi_exh _19751208_evangelii-nuntiandi.html).}

25. {Symeon the New Theologian, *Divine Eros: Hymns of Saint Symeon the New Theologian*, trans. Daniel K. Griggs (Crestwood, NY: St. Vladimir's Seminary Press, 2010), no. 21, pp. 141–57.}

of Father. If Christians were more conscious of this, they would not have to "sit down with God," to run to India to a guru, or to spend time in a French Tibetan center. [26]

A stay in a monastery might help to raise this consciousness. By its lifestyle, the monastic life probably better demonstrates that to be a Christian does not simply mean respecting a moral code of good behavior but instead entering into this personal relationship with the living God that I just described and for which Tradition uses the image of nuptials—the one Saint Bernard prefers—or that of filiation towards God the Father. Many come to our guesthouses to participate in our prayers and find in the monastic experience something of the divine order. This discovery may even shine forth in certain attitudes and on certain faces.

Mgr. Coffy urged the superiors of the nuns who had invited him to their general assembly in 1975, "May you reveal the meaning of prayer for today's people and help Christians to discover that meaning . . . . While keeping your autonomy, your requirements, and your community life, may your monasteries become places of prayer for people looking for God!" Lay Christians sometimes ask more of us; they would like to be associated with our way of life and thinking while remaining of course engaged in their lay communities. The Benedictines have already welcomed what they call *oblates*, people who gravitate

---

26. A convention was held in Bangalore, India, in 1973 on the subject of Christian monasticism confronting the Asian religions. Mgr. D'Souza, then bishop of Benares and secretary of the Bishops' Conference of India, shared the bitter experience he had had when teaching in a Catholic school. His office was often filled with boys whom he tried to help. He was following thirteen of them more particularly: "One day," he confided, "I learned that these boys, who shared with me their most intimate problems, were visiting a Hindu guru to 'sit down with God,' as they said. They were coming to me for all their moral problems—they knew that I was celebrating Mass each morning, and nevertheless, when they wanted to 'sit down with God,' they went to the Hindu guru." That was, he acknowledged, one of the more painful experiences of his life. For them he was not the sign of the God living in him.

around a certain community while observing a rule inspired by Saint Benedict that has been adapted to their situation. They are bound by a certain commitment, an oblate promise. These Christians are assisted by monks in their spiritual journey. They meet at regular intervals in the monastery to which they are attached. A national secretariat exists that facilitates relations among the oblates of different monasteries.[27]

More and more in the Church lay people collaborate with religious not only in their apostolate but also in their way of thinking and living, in what we call a particular "school of spirituality." Some are of the belief that the "Cistercian school" could also animate the spiritual life of lay people while enriching their own experience. Saint Bernard did talk to monks, that is obvious, but he was recognized as a Doctor of the Church because his teaching had a more universal value that could sustain the spiritual search of our contemporaries. The same is true of other important witnesses from our history and from our own time, like Saint Thérèse of Lisieux, who in fact was very like Bernard. Ultimately, all the saints say the same thing, which is fortunate, because they don't really add anything to the Gospel. But through their own way of presenting it, through their personal experience, they seek to make us understand and live the Gospel better. There are spiritual fathers who take us by the hand and give birth to us in the Gospel. Bernard didn't invent anything that he hadn't drawn from Tradition, but he said it in an original and personal fashion with his own accent. He was gifted at finding well-turned formulas that can still instruct us.

---

27. {Dom Dubois's book originally included this statement: "The Trappists don't have such an organization. Nevertheless, the times may very well lead to that." Actually many Cistercian monasteries have or have had oblates, though they are now generally identified as Lay Cistercians. Dom Brendan Freeman, OCSO, reports that the term *oblates* is today somewhat old-fashioned, but "Most monasteries now offer some sort of live-in experience, especially for someone thinking about a vocation." We are grateful to Dom Brendan for his assistance on this point.}

A group of Christians gets together monthly in an ancient barn at Clairvaux to pray and be trained in the spirituality of Saint Bernard. They have formed an association, and some of them want to go further and take part at the end of the week from time to time in meetings at the Abbey of Cîteaux led by a monk of that community. Other experiences of this kind or under other terms are taking place with other monastic communities in the USA and Argentina.[28]

But are young people today still attracted by our life style? Yes, certainly, and this fact sometimes amazes those who discover us and think we are the last specimens of a dying breed! It is true that the dissolution of many households and the drastic reduction in the number of large families do not favor the blooming of religious or priestly vocations—on top of an ever-present materialism, aggressive advertising that pushes unbridled consumption, a lack of reference to values in the public debate, and the disappearance of Christian culture in our education. Our times undeniably suffer from what is called a vocation crisis, more in the apostolic and missionary orders than with us monastics; this fact means that fewer young people decide to embrace the monastic life, but they nonetheless exist without appearing out of sync or behind the times. You need a well-balanced temperament to fit harmoniously into an ever-present community in which, paradoxically, you live a certain solitude through silence and commit to a spiritual journey that is the monastic life. There is a lot of human frailty nowadays among the youth, more maybe

28. {Over the last twenty-five years many Cistercian monasteries all over the world have seen groups of Lay Cistercians being organized around their monastic communities. There are now about seventy such communities in the world with about 1,300 lay Cistercians. In 2007 at the OCSO general chapter, the Order recognized the Lay Cistercians as part of the Cistercian Charism. Dom Armand Veilleux, former abbot of Scourmont in Belgium, is the liaison between the Lay Cistercians and the Order. For more information, see www.ocso.org/who-we-are/our-lay-associates/.}

than at any other time. But, fundamentally, why would today's young people not be as capable as their elders of committing to the monastic life?

It is up to us elders to welcome them, to help them, to form them, because a novice is not formed in 1995 as he was fifty years ago.[29] The generations born in the '50s and '60s needed to find meaning in their lives, which had been lacking until then. They were thirsty for future direction, for solidarity, for real relationships, and that thirst could have been an opening to a deepening of monastic values, but perhaps ran the risk of giving into haste or of favoring warm and connected relationships too much. That danger may have surprised some elders who remembered their own novitiate, in which their relationship with the brothers was marked by silence. The situation of those who were twenty years old around 1990 was also different. They had often perceived their call while in the midst of a world almost estranged from faith. Some had to discover that God existed. Even if they were living in a Christian environment, they had often acquired little religious knowledge, and when they arrived at the monastery, they needed to deepen their understanding of the basic elements of the faith, as well as to learn how to connect with their inner self. Time punctuated by the liturgy, by work, and by other elements of the monastic day—the monastic lifestyle—became an ally enabling a person's maturing on every level. But nothing was self-evident for them, and the need to question their identity became more and more crucial.

But new generations coming up today realize that they cannot do everything they want anymore; unemployment, various forms of exclusion, and AIDS remind them of that fact daily, sometimes in dramatic fashion. Maybe a slow return to more stable values is taking place. The success of John Paul II's books may be a

29. I am referring in this paragraph to the conferences of P. Sylvain, Canadian monk of Oka, and of Sister Marie-Pascale, French nun of Chambarand, presented during the 1993 general chapter in Spain near Santiago de Compostela. I complement their thoughts with my own observations.

testimony to the search for certainties, which is not a bad thing, for sure! Within this context, young people who commit to the monastic life bear witness to a reality that may surprise their friends. But they may be confronted with their own insecurity and have to take root in faithfulness to Christ, in love.

The quest for God remains fundamentally the same, regardless of different social circumstances; the rules of the spiritual life are the same throughout the history of the salvation of God's people, from Abraham to the apostles. Moreover, deep down, do people change that much? Certain sayings of the Desert Fathers dating from the fifth and sixth centuries are marked by a delicate anthropological wisdom that is still confirmed by modern analysis. By helping young people in their journey, I feel that I can call on my own experience, even if each one is unique and marked by his or her own personal history, which is often very different from what my generation and I knew. All of us have to ask ourselves the questions, "Who am I?" "What am I looking for?"[30]

After all, more generally, monastic communities cannot ignore their environment, which is not only economic, as I mentioned in another chapter, but also cultural. We may wonder, for example, if we can correctly in the long run evaluate the impact on our lifestyle of the new technologies, like data processing and various communication techniques. Will the revolution that people predict have an impact comparable to that of the invention of printing on our way of reading and educating ourselves? Besides the Bible, Saint Bernard had only a few manuscripts of the fathers of the church to inspire his own thoughts. We have at our disposal large libraries, and any simple subject of study leads to impressive bibliographies! With all this, have we gained in the understanding of the mystery of God? What will it be in the future with the information highway? Already, we notice that some young people with a more technical than literary formation

---

30. Consider the question Jesus asked the two disciples when he turned and saw them following him: "What do you seek?" (John 1:38).

have difficulty becoming absorbed in the ancient authors and practicing *lectio divina,* which we see as a part of monastic culture.

Faced with these contemporary challenges, we remain full of hope. As Jean-Yves Baziou wrote, "In the Bible, we note, the cultural mutations, the times of transition and conflict appear as privileged moments for God's revelation, which break up the images that we have of him, of men, and of the Church. We discover them larger and newer than what we imagined them to be. Cultural novelty is an opportunity for spiritual progress."[31]

In 1995, the Cistercian Order was getting ready to celebrate its ninth century, in 1998. Christian France would then in 1996 have celebrated, probably with the pope, the fifteenth centennial of Clovis's baptism [said to be his own conversion to the faith]. A year later the church celebrated the sixteenth centennial of the death of Saint Martin, one of France's great bishops and the founder of monasticism in Gaul.[32] What does the ninth centennial of Cîteaux represent in this prestigious company? Remembering the past lays the foundation for our identity and enables us to know who we are. It should also help us to grasp what we are called for, because we need to turn to the future. We certainly need to continue in the right direction. The point is not to remain fixated on our past.

Jean Vanier,[33] who launched an important movement dedicated to welcoming mentally handicapped individuals in small

31. Jean-Yves Baziou, "Traverser la désillusion," *Christus* 158 (January 1993): 14.

32. He founded Ligugé, where there is still a community of Benedictine monks. But the flame lit by this dynamic bishop of Tours remains very much alive. {Ligugé is the oldest monastery in the Western world (dating from the 4th century) and still a leading practitioner of Gregorian chant.}

33. {Jean Vanier (1928–2019) was a Canadian humanitarian who in 1964 founded the communities called "L'Arche." Spread over thirty-seven countries, these communities house people with developmental disabilities, living together with those who assist them. For more information, see www .jean-vanier.org/en.}

communities by helping them live and flourish, observed that a community is never founded once and for all:

> Communities must be continuously attuned to the Holy Spirit and welcome new challenges. They need to be constantly re-founded. The foundation myth [meaning the inner experience or the real event that marked the beginning of the community, which is formulated in the origin story][34] remains, but the manner in which it is incarnated will change. That is where the presence of wise re-founders is necessary. They are capable of moving forward while maintaining and going deeper into that founding myth, while trimming and cutting down what may have seemed essential in the first years but in reality was not.[35]

Isn't that exactly what Vatican II asked of religious institutions in talking about an "adapted renovation"? If we want to preserve and carry on the intuition of the founders in a religious order like ours, is it not also necessary to re-verify that intuition for each period of history? The question that I ask myself at the end of this book, after looking back on the journey undertaken by our Order over the last fifty years, is really this: have we been and will we still be wise re-founders, faithful to the intuition of the beginning as well as to the Spirit that propels us forward?

Our generation became heavily involved in a profound revival, an *aggiornamento*, immediately following the decisions of Vatican Council II. What will be the task of those whom we have formed and who will take up the torch tomorrow? It is hard to predict, although certain facts enable us to imagine some characteristics. The most evident will be shrinking communities, with a large number of elders. Within fifteen years the number of brothers and sisters over seventy will be lower than today. The age pyramid shows us that. Will an influx of younger people compensate for this reduction? That is the "king's secret."

34. {Dom Dubois's insertion.}

35. Jean Vanier, "Le Mythe fondateur et l'évolution des communautés," *Vie Consacrée* (1994): 72–80.

In any event, there will be no lack of difficulty, even if only the unsuitability of premises initially built for larger groups. That may very well not be the most important. No community, in fact, has the promise of immortality. How many abbeys, even some of the more illustrious ones, are only ruins, like Cluny, or transformed into a prison, like Clairvaux, the abbey of our Father Saint Bernard![36] But the monastic life will still be present in the church, knowing that the Holy Spirit continuously breathes new life into her. Our successors will see further than we do, like those apostles shown on the stained glass of the Cathedral of Chartres, perched on the shoulders of the prophets, enabling them to see what their predecessors were unable to see. The future is in front of us, with the human uncertainty that every change generates, but also with the certainty that the Spirit cannot be extinguished or hidden. In the spiritual order, to which the monastic life pertains, we are going continuously, in the famous words of Gregory of Nyssa in the fourth century, "from beginnings to beginnings through beginnings that never end."[37]

36. {A number of Cistercian abbeys, like Hautecombe and Melleray, which lacked enough brothers, were taken over by new communities, like the Communautés du Chemin Neuf. That community also sent four of their members to the Monastery of the Atlas in Tibhirine, Algeria, in April 2018 to replace the brothers who had been murdered in 1996. See above, chap. 5, p. 95, n. 3.}

37. {Gregory of Nyssa, *Homilies on the Song of Songs*, trans. Richard A. Norris (Atlanta: Society of Biblical Literature, 2012), no. 8, 256–75 at 258–61.}

Bibliography

Abba Isaiah of Scetis. *Ascetic Discourses*. Translated by John Chryssavgis and Pachomios (Robert) Penkett. Cistercian Studies Series 150. Kalamazoo, MI: Cistercian Publications, 2002.

Aelred of Rievaulx. *For Your Own People: Aelred of Rievaulx's Pastoral Prayer*. Critical edition, introduction, and annotations by Marsha Dutton. Translated by Mark DelCogliano. Cistercian Fathers Series 73. Kalamazoo, MI: Cistercian Publications, 2008.

Alain (Emile-Auguste Chartier). *Alain on Happiness*. Translated by Robert D. and Jane E. Cottrell. New York: Frederick Ungar Publishing Co., 1973.

The Ancient Usages of the Cistercian Order = Ecclesiastica Officia. Translated by Martinus Cawley. Lafayette, OR: Guadalupe Translations, 1998.

Aubry, Lucien. "À la recherche du vrai portrait de l'abbé de Rancé." Abbaye de La Trappe.

Augustine. *Letters*. Translated by Sister Wilfrid Parsons. The Fathers of the Church: A New Translation 32. Washington, DC: The Catholic University of America Press, 1951–1956.

Bamberger, Dom John Eudes. "L'homme par la communauté: La dynamique de la communication." *Supplément à la vie spirituelle* (Sept. 1969): 414–27.

Baziou, Jean-Yves. "Traverser la disillusion." *Christus* 157 (January 1993): 8–17.

Beauchamp, Paul. *Psaumes nuit et jour*. Paris: Seuil, 1980.

Beauvoir, Simone de. *Memoirs of a Dutiful Daughter*. Translated by James Kirkup. Cleveland and New York: The World Publishing Co., 1959.

Bell, David N., trans. *Everyday Life at La Trappe under Armand-Jean de Rancé: A Translation, with Introduction and Notes, of André Félibien des Avaux's* Description De L'abbaye De La Trappe *(1689)*. Cistercian Studies Series 274. Collegeville, MN: Cistercian Publications, 2018.

Benedict of Nursia. *The Rule of St. Benedict in English.* Edited by Timothy Fry. Collegeville, MN: Liturgical Press, 1981. http://www.osb.org/rb /text/toc.html#toc.

Bernard of Clairvaux. *Five Books on Consideration: Advice to a Pope.* Translated by John D. Anderson and Elizabeth T. Kennan. Cistercian Fathers Series 37. Kalamazoo, MI: Cistercian Publications, 1976.

———. *The Letters of St. Bernard of Clairvaux.* Translated by Bruno Scott James. London: Burns and Oates, 1953.

———. *On Loving God.* Translated by Robert Walton. Analytical Commentary by Emero Stiegman. Cistercian Fathers Series 13B. Kalamazoo, MI: Cistercian Publications, 1995.

———. "On the Office of Bishops." In *On Baptism and the Office of Bishops.* Translated by Pauline Matarasso and M. G. Newman. Cistercian Fathers Series 67. Kalamazoo, MI: Cistercian Publications, 2004. 37–82.

———. *On the Song of Songs.* Translated by Kilian Walsh and Irene Edmonds. 4 vols. Cistercian Fathers Series 4, 7, 31, 40. Kalamazoo, MI: Cistercian Publications, 1979–1983.

———. *The Parables and the Sentences.* Translated by Michael Casey and Francis R. Swietek. Introduction by John R. Sommerfeldt. Edited by Maureen M. O'Brien. Cistercian Fathers Series 55. Kalamazoo, MI: Cistercian Publications, 2000.

———. "Sermon 1 on the Psalm 'He Who Dwells.'" In *Sermons on Conversion: On Conversion, a Sermon to Clerics and Lenten Sermons on the Psalm "He Who Dwells."* Translated with an introduction by Marie-Bernard Saïd. Cistercian Fathers Series 25. Kalamazoo, MI: Cistercian Publications, 1981. 119–28.

———. *The Steps of Humility and Pride.* Translated by M. Ambrose Conway. Cistercian Fathers Series 13A. Collegeville, MN: Cistercian Publications, 1973.

Besret, Bernard. *Confiteor.* Paris: Albin Michel, 1991.

———. *De Commencement en commencement. Itinéraire d'une deviance. Entretiens avec M.-Th. Maltèse et E. Milcent.* Paris: Seuil, 1976.

———. *Libération de l'homme.* Paris: DDB, 1969.

Bloy, Leon. *Oeuvres de Léon Bloy.* Edited by Joseph Bollery and Jacques Petit. 15 vols. Paris: Mercure de France, 1964.

Bourgoint, Jean. *Le Retour de l'enfant terrible: Lettres 1923–1966.* Collected by Jean Hugo and Jean Mouton. Paris: Desclée De Brouwer, 1975.

Chabanis, Christian. *La Mort, un Terme ou un Commencement.* Paris: Éditions Fayard, 1982.

"Charter of Charity." In *Narrative and Legislative Texts from Early Cîteaux: Latin text in Dual Edition with English Translation and Notes*. Edited by Fr. Chrysogonus Waddell. *Cîteaux: Cîteaux–Commentarii cisterciensis,* 1999. 442–50. http://www.ocso.org/resources/foundational-text/charter-of-charity.

Chautard, Dom Jean-Baptiste. *Soul of the Apostolate.* Translated by a monk of Our Lady of Gethsemani. Charlotte, NC: TAN Books, 2012.

Claudel, Paul. "Ma conversion." In *Oeuvres en prose.* Paris: Gallimard, 1965. 1008–14.

Commission Francophone Cistercienne. *La Nuit et le Jour.* Paris: Éditions Desclée/Cerf, 1973.

Congar, Yves. *The Meaning of Tradition.* New York: Hawthorn Books, 1964.

Conrad of Eberbach. *The Great Beginning of Cîteaux, A Narrative of the Beginning of the Cistercian Order: The* Exordium Magnum *of Conrad of Eberbach.* Translated by Benedicta Ward and Paul Savage. Edited by E. Rozanne Elder. Foreword by Brian Patrick McGuire. Cistercian Fathers Series 72. Collegeville, MN: Cistercian Publications, 2012.

Constitutions of the Order of Cistercians of the Strict Observance. http://www.ocso.org/resources/law/constitutions-and-statutes/.

Cordier, Bernard. *Dans le silence des étoiles: Pilote de ligne devenu moine à Cîteaux.* Éditions Parole et silence. Paris: Les Plans-sur-Bex, 2002.

Damian, Peter. *Letters.* Translated by Owen J. Blum and Irven Resnick. Fathers of the Church. 7 vols. Washington, DC: Catholic University of America Press, 1989.

Defois, Gérard; Ecclesia Catholica, Conférence épiscopale française. *Mission sans frontières: 25 ans de solidarité missionnaire: la pastorale de la santé: mission en monde ouvrier: Assemblée plénière de l'épiscopat français (Lourdes, Hautes-Pyrénées 1982).* Paris: Centurion, 1982.

Desfonds, Odette. *Rivales de Dieu.* Paris: Éditions Albin Michel, 1993.

Dimier, Anselm. *La Sombre Trappe: Les légendes et la vérité.* Saint Wandrille: Ed. Fontenelle, 1946.

Domergue, Marcel. "Le Dieu des commencements." *Croire Aujourd'hui* (1988): 29–74.

Epelbaum, Didier. *Alois Brunner: The Inflexible Hate.* Preface by Serge Klarsfeld. Paris: Callmann-Levy, 1990.

Etchegaray, Roger. "Communication at the October 1994 Synod in Rome." *Osservatore Romano.* Weekly edition in French. November 22, 1994.

"Exordium Cistercii." In *Narrative and Legislative Texts from Early Cîteaux*. Edited by Chrysogonus Waddell. *Cîteaux: Commentarii cistercienses*, 1999. 399–404. https://www.ocso.org/resources/foundational-text/exordium-cistercii/.

"Exordium Parvum." In *Narrative and Legislative Texts from Early Cîteaux*. Edited by Chrysogonus Waddell. *Cîteaux: Commentarii cistercienses*, 1999. 416–40. https://www.ocso.org/resources/foundational-text/exordium-parvum/.

Fackenheim, Emil Ludwig. *To Mend the World: Foundations of Post-Holocaust Jewish Thought*. Bloomington and Indianapolis: Indiana University Press, 1994.

Fénelon, François de la Mothe-. *Meditations on the Heart of God*. Translated by Robert J. Edmonson. Brewster, MA: Paraclete Press, 1997.

Francis, Pope. Address to the General Chapter of the OCSO. September 23, 2017.

———. *Laudato Si'*. w2.vatican.va/content/francesco/en/encyclicals/documents/papa-francesco_20150524_enciclica-laudato-si.html.

———. *Missa pro ecclesia* with the Cardinal Electors, Sistine Chapel, Thursday, March 14, 2013. w2.vatican.va/content/francesco/en/homilies/2013/documents/papa-francesco_20130314_omelia-cardinali.html.

Francis de Sales. *Consoling Thoughts on Trials of an Interior Life*. Compiled by Père Huguet. Charlotte, NC: TAN Books, 2013.

Ganne, Gilbert. *Ceux qui ont tout quitté*. Paris: Plon, 1977.

Gertrud the Great of Helfta. *The Herald of God's Loving-Kindness*. Vol. 4. Translated by Alexandra Barratt. Cistercian Fathers Series 85. Collegeville, MN: Cistercian Publications, 2018.

Gregory of Nyssa. *Homilies on the Song of Songs*. Translated by Richard A. Norris. Atlanta: Society of Biblical Literature, 2012.

———. *The Life of Moses*. Translated by Abraham J. Malherbe and Everett Ferguson. Preface by John Meyendorf. New York, Ramsey, and Toronto: Paulist Press, 1978.

Gregory the Great. *Dialogues*. Translated by Odo John Zimmerman. Fathers of the Church: A New Translation 39. Washington, DC: The Catholic University of America Press, 1959.

Heidegger, Martin. *Being and Time: A Translation of* Sein und Zeit. Translated by Joan Stambaugh. Albany: State University of New York Press, 1966.

————. *Introduction to Metaphysics.* 2nd edition. Revised and Expanded. Translated by Gregory Fried and Richard Polt. New Haven: Yale University Press, 2014.

Historical Memoirs of the Duc de Saint-Simon, vol. 1, 1691–1709. Edited and translated by Lucy Norton. London: Hamish Hamilton, 1967.

Huerre, Denis. "Moines et pauvreté aujourd'hui." *Collectanea cisterciensia* 46 (1984): 186–96.

Hugo, Victor. "La Conscience." In *La Légende des siècles*. Paris: Éditions Garnier Frères, 1974. 1st series.

————. *Les Misérables.* Translated by Julie Rose. Modern Library Edition. New York: Random House, 2008.

Irenaeus of Lyons. *Against the Heresies.* Translated by Dominic J. Unger. 3 vols. New York: The Newman Press, 1992–2012.

John Paul II, Pope. *Dialogue de Jean-Paul II avec les jeunes réunis en parc des princes.* Paris. Sunday, June 1, 1980. w2.vatican.va/content/john-paul-ii /fr/speeches/1980/june/documents/hf_jp-ii_spe_19800601_veglia -giovani.html.

————. *Evangelium Vitae.* http://w2.vatican.va/content/john-paul-ii/en /encyclicals/documents/hf_jp-ii_enc_25031995_evangelium-vitae .html.

————. *Orientale Lumen.* http://w2.vatican.va/content/john-paul-ii/en /apost_letters/1995/documents/hf_jp-ii_apl_19950502_orientale -lumen.html.

————. *We Remember, a Reflection on the Shoah.* Letter dated March 12, 1998. http://www.vatican.va/roman_curia/pontifical_councils /chrstuni/documents/rc_pc_chrstuni_doc_16031998_shoah_en .html.

Kipling, Rudyard. "If: A Father's Advice to His Son." https://www.poetry foundation.org/poems/46473/if---.

Kittel, Gerhard, and Gerhard Friedrich. *Theological Dictionary of the New Testament.* 10 vols. Grand Rapids, MI: William B. Eerdmans Publishing Co., 1977.

Krailsheimer, Alban J. *Abbé de Rancé: Correspondence.* Paris: Cerf-Cîteaux, 1993.

————. *Armand-Jean de Rancé: His Influence in the Cloister and in the World.* Oxford: Oxford University Press, 1974.

La Gorce, Pierre de. *Histoire religieuse de la Révolution française.* 5 vols. Paris: Plon-Nourrit et Cie, 1924–1925.

Laplace, Jean. *Le Prêtre à la recherche de lui-même*. Chire-En-Montreuil: Éditions du Chalet, 1969.

Le Bail, Anselme. *L'Ordre de Citeaux: La Trappe*. Paris: Éditions Letouzey et Ané, 1947.

Lekai, Louis. *The White Monks: A History of the Cistercian Order*. Okauchee, WI: Cistercian Monastery of Our Lady of Spring Bank, 1953.

Les Cisterciens trappistes: L'âme cistercienne. Une des conférences de D.R.A.C. donnée le 28 janvier 1931. Dompierre-sur-Besbre: Abbaye de Sept-Fons, 1937.

The Life of the Jura Fathers. Translated by Tim Vivian, Kim Vivian, and Jeffrey Burton Russell. Cistercian Studies Series 178. Kalamazoo, MI: Cistercian Publications, 1999.

The Lives of the Desert Fathers: The Historia Monachorum in Aegypto. Translated by Norman Russell. Introduction by Benedicta Ward. Cistercian Studies Series 34. Kalamazoo, MI: Cistercian Publications, 1981.

Martelet, Bernard. *La petite soeur de l'unité: bienheureuse Marie Gabriella 1914–1939*. Paris: Médiaspaul, 1984.

Martimort, Aimé Georges. "Le rôle de Paul VI dans la réforme liturgique." In *Le rôle de G.B. Montini—Paul VI dans la réforme liturgique. Journée d'Études Louvain-la-Neuve, 17 Octobre 1984*. Brescia: Pubblicazioni dell'Istituto Paolo VI, 1987.

Melville, Gert. *The World of Medieval Monasticism: Its History and Forms of Life*. Translated by James D. Mixson. Cistercian Studies Series 263. Collegeville, MN: Cistercian Publications, 2016.

Merton, Thomas. *The Seven Storey Mountain*. New York: Mariner Books, 1998.

Montcheuil, Yves de. *Problèmes de vie spirituelle*. Paris: Les Éditions L'Epi, 1947.

Moulin, Léo. *Le Monde vivant des Religieux*. Paris: Calmann-Levy, 1964.

O.C.S.O. *Declaration on Cistercian Life*. https://www.ocso.org/history/historical-texts/declaration-on-cistercian-life/.

———. *Decree of Unification*. https://www.ocso.org/resources/law/decree-on-unification/.

———. *Statute on Oblates*. http://users.skynet.be/scourmont/script/contemp/stat_oblat-eng.htm.

———. *Statute on Unity and Pluralism*. http://www.ocso.org/resources/law/statute-on-unity-and-pluralism/.

Pascal, Blaise. *The Provincial Letters, Pensées, and Scientific Treatises*. Translated by Thomas M'Crie, W. F. Trotter, and Richard Scofield. Great

Books of the Western World 33. Chicago, London, and Toronto: Encyclopaedia Britannica, Inc., 1952. 169–352.

Paul VI, Pope. *Address to the Members of the Consilium de Laicis* [2 October 1974]. AAS 66 (1974). w2.vatican.va/content/paul-vi/fr/audiences /1974/documents/hf_p-vi_aud_19741002.html.

———. *Evangelii Nuntiandi.* w2.vatican.va/content/paul-vi/en/apost _exhortations/documents/hf_p-vi_exh_19751208_evangelii -nuntiandi.html.

Péguy, Charles. *Le Porche du mystère de la deuxième vertu.* Oeuvres poétiques complètes. Paris: Gallimard, 2014. 629–773.

Pingault, Pascal. *Renouveau de l'Eglise: les communautés nouvelles.* Paris: Fayard, 1989.

Pius X, Pope. *Gravissimo Officii Munere.* http://w2.vatican.va/content/pius -x/en/encyclicals/documents/hf_p-x_enc_10081906_gravissimo -officii-munere.html.

Rancé, Armand-Jean Le Bouthillier de. *A Treatise on the Sanctity and on the Duties of the Monastic State.* Dublin: R. Grace, 1830.

Rancé, Armand-Jean Le Bouthillier de, and A. J. Krailsheimer. *The Letters of Armand-Jean de Rancé, Abbot and Reformer of La Trappe: Presented by A. J. Krailsheimer.* Cistercian Studies Series 81. Kalamazoo, MI: Cistercian Publications, 1984.

Rondet, Michel. "Dieu a-t-il sur chacun de nous une volonté particulière?" *Christus* 144 (1989): 392–99.

Rouet, Albert. "Moins de prêtres, plus de prêtres heureux, plus de prêtres." *Prêtres diocesains* (January 1995): 8–16.

Sacrosanctum Concilium. http://www.vatican.va/archive/hist_councils /ii_vatican_council/documents/vat-ii_const_19631204_sacrosanctum -concilium_en.html.

Saint-Exupéry, Antoine de. *Letter to a Hostage.* Translated by Cheryl Witchell. Babelcube, 2016.

———. *Lettre à un otage.* In *Oeuvres complètes.* 2 vols. Paris: Gallimard, 1994–99. 88–104.

Strack, Hermann Leberecht, and Paul Billerbeck. *Kommentar zum Neuen Testament aus Talmud und Midrasch.* 2 vols. Munich: Beck, 1922.

Sulivan, Jean. *Le plus petit abime.* Paris: Gallimard, 1965.

Symeon the New Theologian. *Divine Eros: Hymns of Saint Symeon the New Theologian.* Translated by Daniel K. Griggs. Crestwood, NY: St. Vladimir's Seminary Press, 2010.

Thérèse of Lisieux. *Collected Letters of Saint Thérèse of Lisieux*. Edited by Abbé André Combes. Translated by F. J. Sheed. New York: Sheed and Ward, 1949.

———. *The Prayers of Saint Thérèse of Lisieux: The Act of Oblation*. Introduction by Guy Gaucher. Translated by Aletheia Kane. Washington, DC: Institute of Carmelite Studies, 1997.

———. *Story of a Soul: The Autobiography of Saint Thérèse of Lisieux*. MS B, fol. 3vo. Translated by John Clarke. 3rd ed. Washington, DC: ICS Publications, 1996.

Vanier, Jean. "Le Mythe fondateur et l'évolution des communautés." *Vie Consacrée* (1994): 72–80.

Vatican II. *Gaudium et Spes*. http://www.vatican.va/archive/hist_councils /ii_vatican_council/documents/vat-ii_cons_19651207_gaudium -et-spes_en.html.

———. *Nostra Aetate*. http://www.vatican.va/archive/hist_councils/ii _vatican_council/documents/vat-ii_decl_19651028_nostra-aetate _en.html.

———. *Perfectae Caritatis*. http://www.vatican.va/archive/hist_councils /ii_vatican_council/documents/vat-ii_decree_19651028_perfectae -caritatis_en.html.

Veilleux, Armand. "The Witness of the Tibhirine Martyrs." *Spiritus: A Journal of Christian Spirituality* 1, no. 2 (2001): 205–16.

Zola, Émile. *Germinal*. Translated by Roger Pearson. London: Penguin, 2004.

INDEX